TOMMY DORSEY

TOMMY DORSEY

Livin' in a Great Big Way

A Biography

PETER J. LEVINSON

Da Capo Press
A Member of the Perseus Books Group

Designed by Trish Wilkinson
Set in 11-point Goudy by the Perseus Books Group

Library of Congress Cataloging-in-Publication Data

Levinson, Peter J.
    Tommy Dorsey, livin' in a great big way : a biography / Peter J. Levinson. — 1st Da Capo Press ed.
        p.   cm.
    Includes index.
    ISBN-13: 978-0-306-81111-1 (hardcover : alk. paper)
    ISBN-10: 0-306-81111-1 (hardcover)
    1. Dorsey, Tommy, 1905–1956. 2. Jazz musicians—United States—Biography. I. Title.
ML422.D67L48 2005
781.65'092—dc22   2005022430

First Da Capo Press edition 2005

Published by Da Capo Press
A Member of the Perseus Books Group
http://www.dacapopress.com

Da Capo Press books are available at special discounts for bulk purchases in the U.S. by corporations, institutions, and other organizations. For more information, please contact the Special Markets Department at the Perseus Books Group, 11 Cambridge Center, Cambridge, MA 02142, or call (800) 255-1514 or (617) 252-5298, or email special.markets@perseusbooks.com.

1 2 3 4 5 6 7 8 9—09 08 07 06 05

Contents

The two most important people in my life
have been my mother and Tommy Dorsey.
—FRANK SINATRA

Acknowledgments

IN THE SPRING of 2002, when I began researching the life story of Tommy Dorsey, I knew it couldn't be written after merely conducting a series of interviews and examining a plethora of previously published material. I realized it would be mandatory to go to the source—the former coal-mining towns of Pennsylvania, for this was where Tommy Dorsey and his brother, Jimmy, began their remarkable musical journeys.

In June of that year, I flew from Los Angeles to Philadelphia and the next day drove to Pottstown, Pennsylvania, ostensibly to attend the fiftieth reunion of my Hill School graduating class. But more important, Pottsville was 110 miles northeast. That's where the real story was.

Over the next few days, I conducted extremely illuminating interviews with retired Lucent Technologies supervisor Curt Williams, turned (Panther) *Valley Gazette* feature writer, who had only recently completed a series on the fervent interest in dance bands in the area during the late 1920s through the mid-1950s. It was prearranged that I would meet Williams and Richie Lisella, former bus driver and band boy for Tommy Dorsey, at Lisella's apartment in neighboring Coaldale. From these interviews, I gained a sense of how much music meant to the people of this region as well as the determination and strength of character that were so much a part of Tommy Dorsey. The best was yet to come.

The next day I interviewed Connie and Bill Motko, cousins of Tommy and Jimmy Dorsey. When I first approached Connie on the telephone, she said, "Why would you want to talk with us? We're just ordinary people." The Motkos were anything but ordinary—warm, gracious, hospitable, and very informative. I now knew what the Dorsey family was all about and exactly how its rich music heritage emanated from the first Tom Dorsey, the coal miner turned demanding music teacher who gave his sons the training and discipline that served as the foundation of what became two glorious careers.

It was Tom Dorsey III, Tommy Dorsey's son, who grew up with the nickname Skipper, who thought I should first see Connie and Bill. He was absolutely right. This was the first of several ways that Tom and his wife, Barbara, proved to be extremely helpful and accommodating.

Within the first two months of my research, I received a telephone call from Joe Scocco. Joe had read my two previous books and had learned I was researching a book on Tommy Dorsey. Joe is the nephew of the late Lee Castle, a longtime musical associate of the Dorseys. In addition, Joe is a trombonist who once played in the Tommy Dorsey "ghost" band. Over the next three years, Joe was of the utmost importance in helping me with every aspect of my book. He frankly knew more about Tommy Dorsey personally and professionally than anyone else I encountered.

It was through the suggestion of another trombonist, Billy VerPlanck, who had been with Tommy's last band, that I met Frank Riordan. This extremely insightful, humorous, and engaging former engineer had known the Dorsey brothers from his boyhood, although he was much younger. Frank grew up Lansford, Pennsylvania, where he was a student of Tom Dorsey. He was always available to assist me with his wonderful memory and his ability to put Tommy Dorsey's behavior into perspective.

I would be lax if I also didn't thank Rudy and Stacey Behlmer. Rudy, the noted film historian, knew considerable about Tommy Dorsey's several film appearances, but in addition, he exhibited a passionate interest in his entire career. Stacey, in her endeavors at the Academy of Motion Pictures Library, was very generous in introducing me to various background materials that concerned Dorsey's professional life.

I must also thank Tommy Dorsey's widow, the late Janie New Dorsey, for making herself available for lengthy interviews and for her assistance in providing important photographs. At first, I found New difficult, as others sometimes did, but as time went on, she lowered her defenses and was extremely candid about her life with "The Sentimental Gentleman of Swing." While pursuing my research on the Dorsey project, I discovered what a precarious position New was placed in after Tommy's death in having to fend for herself and her two children.

Pat Dorsey Hooker, Skipper's sister, the older of Tommy Dorsey's two children by his first wife, the former Mildred "Toots" Kraft, was completely open and revealing about her father's deficiencies as a father. Sadly, she passed away only a few weeks after the death of Janie New Dorsey.

Unfortunately, Steve and Susan Dorsey, the children of Janie New and Tommy Dorsey, chose not to make themselves available for interviews. Unlike their mother, it seems apparent that furthering the importance of their father's music is of small consequence to them.

I want to single out Peter Guralnick for his tremendous help in explaining how Elvis Presley came to the attention of Tommy Dorsey, which resulted in Presley's making his national debut with six guest shots on the CBS-TV variety program *Stage Show*, hosted by the Dorseys. The author of the definitive two-volume Presley biography, Guralnick also provided considerable important information surrounding Elvis's appearances on *Stage Show*.

I also want to emphasize the help as well as the recollections of such prominent ex-Dorsey musicians as Louis Bellson, Buddy DeFranco, Doc Severinsen, and Buddy Morrow, as well as arranger Bill Finnegan, singer Jo Stafford, Dorsey's last personal manager, Tino Barzie; and Charles Wick, a former Dorsey employee, and the head of the U.S. Information Agency (USIA) under Ronald Reagan. These individuals enabled me to gain an understanding of the complicated nature of Tommy Dorsey's personality.

There were so many others that contributed valuable and significant assistance. For example, former Dorsey pianist, Doug Talbert gave me access to printed material in addition to his incredible recall of events that transpired during the time he spent working for Tommy Dorsey. Walter C. Scott provided some rare important photographs. Saxophonist Bennie Wallace helped me gain access to Greenwich, Connecticut, Police Chief Peter Robbins, who contributed the complete death report on Tommy Dorsey. Writer and jazz historian Richard Sudhalter succinctly sized up the nature of Frank Sinatra's complicated personal relationship with Tommy Dorsey.

Fortunately, through the truly astounding memories of Roc Hillman, Kay Weber, and Bobby Byrne, I was able to reconstruct what took place on the road with the Dorsey Brothers Orchestra of 1934 and 1935. Rock and Kay were also eyewitnesses to the fateful breakup of the Dorseys at the Glen Island Casino on Memorial Day of 1935.

Additional thank yous must also extend to Dan Morgenstern, Betty Rose, Jess Rand, Mike Lanin, Essie Davis, the late E. C. Holland, Sandy Gillian, Burt Korall, Malcolm Rockwell, John Tumpak, Jay Corre, Kirk Silsbee, Campbell Burnap, Ross Firestone, Joe Pardee, Karl Stark, Chauncey Welsch, Ann King, Louise Baranger, Ray Hoffman, Arnold Jay Smith, Jon Burlingame,

Dennis Oppenheim, Jack Siefert, Graham Pass, Paquito D'Rivera, Barry Feldman, Chip Deffaa, Audree Kenton, the late Milt Bernhart, Nathan Sedlander, Dan Lewis, Frank Alkyer, Jon Krampner for providing extensive research on Tommy Dorsey's unusual court trial, and again Dale Olson for many important favors.

Ed O'Brien must be thanked for his attempts to be sure I was given certain details about Frank Sinatra's years with Tommy Dorsey and for supplying certain tapes as well. Thanks also go to Rob Fentress, another keen Sinatra observer, for his constant help and for supplying a very important tape of Sinatra's appearance at the twentieth-anniversary celebration of Tommy Dorsey and His Orchestra.

I cannot fathom what would have happened had I not had the use of William Ruhlmann's June 10, 1994, *Goldmine* magazine article, "Living in a Great Big Way in Swingtime." This article helped provide me with the title of my book, but it also served as a road map for the twists and turns so much a part of Tommy Dorsey's career. Conversely, Julia Suh from Senator Barbara Boxer's office was kind enough to provide access to Tommy Dorsey's FBI file. Unfortunately, most of what could have been important information was blacked out in that file.

This is not to negate the importance of my old friend Mort Goode's informative and humorous liner notes for *The Complete Tommy Dorsey*. It's a shame I can't tell him this in person, as he passed away a few years ago.

I want to also thank my editor, John Radziewicz, for seeing the worth of this project and his keen viewpoint on just what made Tommy Dorsey so special. I also wish to thank Anita Coolidge, the diligent work of Julie Compton in providing the transcripts of all the interviews, and my assistant, Linda Laucella, for her generous and invaluable contributions in many ways. And, as ever, my love and gratitude for the special assistance of my wife, Grace Diekhaus. I sincerely regret if I have overlooked the names of any others who were of help to me in writing this book.

Those interviewed for *Tommy Dorsey: Livin' in a Great Big Way, A Biography* were Berle Adams, Van Alexander, Trigger Alpert, Johnny Amarosa, Miles Anderson, Ray Anthony, Diane Atkins, Jean Bach, Jim Bacon, Bob Bain, Jimmy Baker, Danny Banks, Larry Barnett, Eileen Barton, Tino Barzie, Marle Becker, Rudy Behlmer, Louis Bellson, Noni Bernardi, Dr. Stephen Botek, Yvonne King Burch, the late Joe Bushkin, Bobby Byrne, Joe Cabot, Daryl "Flea" Campbell, Paul Canada, Smitty Carbone, Roger Carroll, Pat Chartrand, Buddy Childers, Gene Cipriano, Paul Cohen, Donna Fox Conkling, Frank Cooper, Jackie Cooper, Sid Cooper, Jay Corre, Marietta Cox,

Chick Crumpacker, Tom Cullen, Mike Dann, Michael Dante, Max David-son, Danny Davis, Buddy DeFranco, Karl DeKarske, Jeannie Thomas Den-nis, Morris Diamond, Janie New Dorsey, Tom and Barbara Dorsey, Steve Duncan, Milt Ebbins, the late Harvey Estrin, Vince Falcone, Gregg Field, Bill Finegan, Jamie Finegan, Craig Forchetti, David French, John Frosk, Al Gallodoro, Vince Giordano, Candace March Gould, Urbie Green, the late Chris Griffin, Charlie Grion, Peter Guralnick, Earle Hagen, Connie Haines, George Hamid, Jr., Neal Hefti, Skitch Henderson, Max Herman, Roc Hill-man, the late E. C. Holland, the late Pat Hooker, John Huddleston, Wayne Hutchinson, Dick Katz, John Kenley, Irv Kluger, Kay Kozlowski, Frances Langford, Charlie LaRue, Doug Laurence, Jack Lawrence, Marilyn Faith Leonard, Frankie Lester, Dan Lewis, the late Sal Libero, Art Linkletter, Steve Lipkins, Joe Lipman, the late Richie Lisella, Jack Lisella, Hugo Loewenstern, James Maher, Peter Marshall, Dick Martin, the late Billy May, Bob Merrill, Frank Military, Bill Miller, Jackie Mills, the late Artie Mogull, George Monte, Jack Morgan, the late Shirley Morgan, Buddy Morrow, the late Abe Most, Gussie Most, Connie and Bill Motko, Spud Murphy, Marty Napoleon, Clint Negley, Stretch Norton, Ed O'Brien, Larry O'Brien, Sol Parker, Don Pistilli, Seymour Red Press, Jesse Rand, Uan Rasey, Bill Ray-mond, Boomie Richman, Howie Richmond, Dr. Frank Riordan, Lynn Roberts, Les Robinson, Betty Rose, Johnny Rotella, Jerry Roy, Lindsay Sat-terwhite, Sol Schlinger, Harry Schooler, Walter C. Scott, Peggy Schwartz, Joe Scocco, John Setar, Doc Severinsen, Artie Sharpiro, Ed Shaughnessy, Dave Sheetz, Nancy Sinatra, Paul Smith, Pat Stacy, Jo Stafford, Leonard Stern, Herb Steward, Gil Stratton, Chuck Suber, Valey "Tak" Takvorian, Doug Talbert, George Thompson, Leonardo Timor, Renee Touzet, Michael Trantalange, Danny Trimboli, Danny Vanelli, Billy VerPlanck, Bea Wain, Bill Watrous, Kay Weber, Charles Wick, Audrey Wilder, Jimmy Wilkins, Curt Williams, Zeke Zarchy, and Tony Zoppi.

1

Music, Music, Music

> I'll do anything to keep my boys out of the mines.
>
> —"Pop" Dorsey

Tommy Dorsey, like so many accomplished men, was highly complex. Those who knew him well agreed. Buddy Morrow, trombonist, Tommy Dorsey and His Orchestra 1937–1938 and leader of the Tommy Dorsey Orchestra, 1979 to the present, remarked, "You take Jackie Gleason and his excesses, Frank Sinatra and his excesses, Buddy Rich and his excesses—put them all together, you'll find Tommy Dorsey."

"If you found him all good or all bad, then you really didn't know him. Within the space of a few seconds, he could turn from one to the other," said Sid Cooper, lead alto saxophonist and arranger, Tommy Dorsey and His Orchestra, 1944–1946 and 1947–1949.

"I think he was the toughest man I ever met in my entire life. He was fearless. He was like a breed apart, man," said Billy VerPlanck, trombonist, Tommy Dorsey and His Orchestra, 1956.

Toughness didn't come by accident if you grew up Irish in the hard-living anthracite mining towns in eastern Pennsylvania shortly after the turn of the twentieth century. By 1900 coal was the primary source of energy in the United States. There was no natural gas; oil didn't come in until the 1920s.

Anthracite coal had been discovered around 1805 in the Panther Valley of the Allegheny Mountains, seventy miles southwest of Scranton. As a result of this natural resource, local laborers, as well as immigrant Welsh,

Irish, Italians, and Slovaks came from across the Atlantic Ocean to work in the mines.

The first railroad in America may have been the Gravity Railroad, established to move coal from Summit Hill, Pennsylvania, to Mauch Chunk, Pennsylvania (now called Jim Thorpe in honor of the famous Native American athlete who is buried there). The coal was put onto canal boats on the Lehigh River and then sent down to Philadelphia. The railroad was referred to as "the switchback" because mules hauled the empty coal cars up to the top of Mount Pisgah and the cars were sent back to Summit Hill by gravity.

From the "Mammoth Vein" down thirteen hundred feet was the richest vein of anthracite in the world, located within a thirty-mile sector from Pottsville slanting upward toward Scranton. From the early nineteenth century until about 1950, many of the mine owners, who were Welsh and English, lived in Pottsville, the closest city of any pronounced wealth in the area.

Novelist John O'Hara chronicled the mores of this elite element in his hometown of Pottsville, which he referred to as Gibbsville, in works such as his breakthrough novel *An Appointment in Samarra*, all the way through his continuing studies of the town's upper-class WASPs, culminating in *Ten North Frederick*. (His own family was part of this elite group. Not surprisingly, Tommy Dorsey's band was one of O'Hara's favorites.) O'Hara mentioned touring dance bands in some of his novels. There was even a subplot in *Ten North Frederick* that involved a big-band musician.

The owners' wealth did not trickle down to the workers. The 1970 Paramount film *The Molly Maguires* (starring Sean Connery and Richard Harris), partially shot in Jim Thorpe, depicted the hopelessness of the Irish who had fled the potato famine in the Ould Sod and settled in the Panther Valley to work in the anthracite coal fields. The Molly Maguires made up a secret organization composed of dissident miners that murdered many of the money-hungry Welshmen who had left the coal mines in Wales to immigrate to eastern Pennsylvania in order to manage the thriving coal industry. These Welshmen had no interest in improving safety conditions for the miners. The slogan of the times was "The Welsh pray on their knees and prey on everyone else." This ongoing hatred toward the mine owners would linger among the Irish and their descendants, who, along with other minorities, were fundamentally treated as serfs while performing the arduous, backbreaking work of mining coal for their prosperous employers.

Tommy Dorsey knew about the coal miners' hardships from his father, Thomas Francis Dorsey, a warm and dignified man, who had worked in the mines for over twenty years before becoming a musician, music teacher, and band director. Tommy's toughness was at the core of his disciplined work ethic, as were his uncompromising efforts to achieve musical perfection, characteristics he also learned from his father.

Pop Dorsey, as he was known, was born in Mount Carmel, Pennsylvania, in 1872. He married the former Theresa ("Tess") Langton in 1901, and their first child, James Francis Dorsey, was born on February 29, 1904 (a leap year), in Shenandoah, forty-five miles southwest of Scranton. Three other children followed. Thomas Francis Dorsey, Jr., came next on November 19, 1905, in Mahanoy (pronounced Ma-noy) Plain, a small coal patch of a town, nicknamed "The Foot," just outside Shenandoah, in the Dorsey family home located at 331 Center Street, directly across from the church where he would be baptized. Tess would brag that on that Sunday morning, "When he was born, the church bells were ringing." Mary was born in 1907, and Edward, in 1911. Edward lived only to the age of three; one day while his mother was washing clothes in their home, he fell into a tub of lye and was scalded to death. The town legend was that Edward was singing "Yankee Doodle Dandy" as a doctor tried in vain to treat his wounds. In the years following, the family never spoke of the tragedy.

Tess's father and all of her six brothers were self-taught musicians. Tom Dorsey, on his own, had become musically adept, first on the drums and then on cornet. His parents would fuss over his constant practicing of scales and chords on his cornet rather than playing Irish jigs and reels. Tess acknowledged the fact that her mother was at first opposed to her marrying a man who made his living by playing cornet in a band, but she persisted.

Years later, Tommy Dorsey proudly repeated the family story he had learned: "Dad got hold of a horn [cornet] one day after coming up from a mine and decided to play it. After feeding his mule, he took the horn out to a shanty and sat down to play by the light of a kerosene lamp. He got so good at it that he quit the mines for a while and traveled around with a circus band. His closest friend was a young magician named Harry Houdini, who made good!"

After Tom and Tess got married, Tom settled down to coal mining. But Tom never gave up music. "During the coal strike of 1902, while he was living at Green Ridge near Mount Carmel he took a coal miner band up to Williamsport, Pennsylvania, pitched a tent on the river bank and gave concerts."

In September 1903, Tom and Tess gathered up their household possessions at Green Ridge and moved back over the hill to the Brownsville section of

Shenandoah. They made the move at the urging of Professor Wild, a music store owner and instructor, presumably because the professor convinced Tom Dorsey that he had a future in music. Tom obtained a job as a loader/boss at Packer #4 Colliery (the place where coal was sized and cleaned for sale) and also became a member of Riley's Orchestra, a popular local dance band.

Working at the colliery meant frequent strikes and layoffs as a result of reduced coal consumption during the warm weather of the late spring and summer months. This ultimately led to the Dorsey family's move to Mahanoy Plane, where Tom continued to teach music, which he had begun doing in 1902, for fifty cents a lesson (at the same time, George Gershwin was paying one dollar for piano lessons—New York prices!) and played in lodge bands. In those days, every small town, lodge, and church had its own brass band. He often found himself coaching as many as five bands at a time. Over a period of years, he was the band director of some sixty-eight brass bands.

Having worked in the mines since his boyhood, Tom Dorsey knew that due to frequent strikes employment opportunities were at best erratic. More important, he abhorred the dangerous conditions that miners endured working hundreds of feet underground. John L. Lewis founded the United Mine Workers in 1928 and finally succeeded in obtaining higher wages and better working conditions for its members.

Tom fully realized that the mines were a dead end for both him and his sons. He saw music as their only salvation. Several people who knew him at the time well remember his saying, "I'll do anything to keep my boys out of the mines!"

Years later, Jimmy would relate the story that his mother had told him and Tommy: "Mom claimed that Dad would kneel down by the crib and study our lips. He had a theory that people with thin lips make good horn players."

Tommy and Jimmy didn't have much choice about starting to play music. Tommy explained, "Dad bought us some instruments and ordered: Learn how to play them!" At five, Tommy began playing the alto horn, which was the bell-type horn used in brass bands, then switched over to a double-bell euphonium. At the age of six, he took up the cornet. But he had problems with the instrument, and at ten, he started on the saxophone. At twelve, he began playing the trombone. It's generally believed that his early experience playing the alto horn, the double-bell euphonium, and then the cornet developed Tommy's ability to play high notes, which later became a particular keynote of his trombone playing. Eventually, he and Jimmy could play all the brass and woodwind instruments, just as their father had. Tommy said he learned to play the tenor sax, "but very badly."

Jimmy had started playing the slide cornet when he was only six years old. Within a few years, he was sitting in with Riley's Orchestra, though his feet didn't reach the floor. At ten, he soloed during a local appearance with John Philip Sousa's famous band, which was making a local appearance at the town pavilion. Two years later, when the Sousa band returned, Jimmy duplicated the triple tonguing solo of Sousa's famous cornetist, Herbert L. Clarke, on "Carnival of Venice." Clarke was so flabbergasted that he reportedly said it was discouraging to find a twelve-year-old who could play it as well as he could.

Jimmy switched from the slide cornet to the alto sax. He soon learned to play the tenor saxophone, the soprano saxophone, the baritone saxophone, and later piano and violin. Proudly, Tom would hustle photos of his gifted son for ten cents a piece at his band concerts.

Tom also bought Jimmy a clarinet. The fingering on the old Albert System (the earlier method by which clarinetists learned to play) is close to that of the alto saxophone, so Jimmy had little trouble learning the clarinet. Jimmy never had a lesson on the instrument, but he left his first clarinet on a train ride between Shenandoah and Mount Carmel, and his father informed him he wasn't about to buy him another one.

By 1915, Tom Dorsey left the mines, where he had been making $10.20 a week. He began teaching other youngsters in Shenandoah, in addition to his sons, even though he was blind in one eye, the result of a bout of scarlet fever as a child, and had been deaf in one ear since infancy. Despite these physical handicaps, he was always quick to detect a wrong note played by one of his pupils.

That fact was revealed by Dr. Frank Riordan, Jr., the eminent retired chemical engineer, who, according to Mom Dorsey, was also a distant relative. Frank was one of Tom's students, who had a weekly Friday night clarinet lesson at 7 P.M. Pop Dorsey's fee had increased to one dollar a lesson.

Dr. Riordan continued, "Do you remember the picture *The Fabulous Dorseys* [United Artists, 1947]? Well, the guy who played Pop Dorsey, Arthur Shields, looked a great deal like him." (Shields was the brother of the well-known Irish character actor, Barry Fitzgerald.)

Riordan explained the strong family resemblance between "Mr. Dorsey" (or "The Professor" as he was also sometimes referred to, with decided respect) and his oldest sons. "If Jimmy put on glasses, he would look like Tommy. They all looked a lot alike." Tommy began wearing glasses at a young age like his father.

But while Jimmy practiced nonstop, Tommy enjoyed playing baseball, and his love of the sport would last all of his life. Mr. Dorsey forbade both of his sons to play football, fearing that they would break their hands or injure their mouths.

Wearing glasses and playing a musical instrument, Tommy often found himself the subject of ridicule from kids in the town. He had to learn to stand up for himself. He built up a strong physique from playing baseball and various jobs as a laborer and soon was able to handle himself in any kind of a fight. He had an explosive Irish temper, and he became absolutely fearless—a trait that would remain with him the rest of his life.

Because of his size and the erect way he carried himself, exuding determination and an authoritative air, many townspeople assumed that Tommy was older than Jimmy. Except when it came to music, Jimmy was gentle, quiet, and easygoing; in that way he was more like his father.

Almost from the beginning, the two brothers referred to each other as "The Brother" or "Brother." Tess constantly referred to her husband as "The Father." Not only the Irish, but also Slovaks, another one of the many minorities that flocked to the Panther Valley mines, often used such terms when referring to their siblings or the head of the family in everyday conversation. The Dorsey brothers also had their own nicknames for each other: Jimmy was "Lad" and Tommy was "Mac."

A strong family loyalty was instilled in them, and they were taught to always speak of each other with respect. But from the beginning, the relationship between the Dorsey brothers was volatile. It didn't take much to start a fistfight between them, and anyone who tried to intervene was in danger of being attacked by both of them. Their rivalry was to become part of their fame, and it lasted as long as they lived.

Tommy may have initially been jealous of his older brother. The former bandleader Artie Shaw believed, "Since Tommy came along after Jimmy, he was the one who had to prove his worth." Even in knee pants, they fought over who played the cornet—their father's instrument—better. Perhaps hoping to stem this rivalry, Tom switched Jimmy to playing saxophone and Tommy to playing trombone.

Speaking of the differences, Tommy once observed, "It was a combination of things, but never money, which most people fought about. For instance, we had different ideas on how to run things, and we had different styles, too. I leaned more to brass, Jimmy to the sax section."

Their mother, Tess, who spoke with a pronounced brogue and was always extremely candid and often profane in her language, contended, "Jimmy's always been the shy one, like his father. Tommy was always a great one for pushin', and Jimmy for takin' his own sweet time. There was always this bickerin' between them. They both always got where they were going, but they had to do it in their own way." In fact, Tess may have favored her first-born.

According to Connie Motko, the Dorsey brothers' cousin, "No matter what Tommy did, Jimmy was always Aunt Tess's favorite." She recalled a childhood incident when Tommy teased Jimmy about his being often stung by bees. "How come you always get bitten by the bees, and I don't?" he chided. Jimmy replied, "Because I'm much sweeter than you, Tommy!"

Neither son imitated Tess's brogue, but her outspoken manner and use of profanity echoed in Tommy's own way of speaking. Academics meant little to either of the young Dorseys. Tommy dropped out in the seventh grade, while Jimmy remained in school until the second year of high school. Music had already become the defining factor in both of their young lives.

Their father at first insisted on two hours of practice from his sons on a daily basis. In time, he increased it to four hours. It was either that or a whipping. The first time that Tommy was given a piece of music by his father to sight-read, he did it extremely well. Tom Dorsey then asked him to read it backward!

There is an amusing incident in *The Fabulous Dorseys* in which Mom Dorsey sternly orders the brothers to remove their shoes, thus preventing them from going outdoors to play baseball instead of practicing. Tom Dorsey proudly told Frank Riordan that *he* was the one who actually took his sons' shoes away from them.

"Another thing he told me," Riordan added, "and a lot of people didn't believe this story—but Mr. Dorsey was not a liar—was that one day he locked Tommy in the boys' bedroom to ensure that he would continue practicing. He unlocked the door and looked in. Tommy was playing 'Flight of the Bumblebee,' lying on his bed with his head on the pillow. He'd taken a couple of rubber bands and wrapped them around the bottom of the slide of his trombone and put his foot in between the rubber bands and the end of the tubing. And there he was, using his foot to move the slide, reading a magazine and playing the piece!'"

Many believed that Tom Dorsey pushed his sons too hard in his mission to eventually turn them into highly qualified professional musicians. Even Tess was known to occasionally raise her voice in protest. But whenever she'd ask her husband to go easier on the boys, saying "Ah, Tom, they're but lads!" her husband would shout, "Damn it, Tess, I want them to be something, to go somewhere. They got me to teach 'em. I didn't have nobody!" Tommy's competitive temperament internalized this perfectionism, and it never loosened its grip.

During the summertime, the young Dorseys cooled off at places like the Jigger Dam in the Kahley Run ravine just north of Shenandoah (now the site of the Sandy Beach Recreation Area) or picked huckleberries on a mountain north of their homes. These were brief respites from their many intense hours of practicing.

Their sister, Mary, also exhibited a musical bent in the early years of her childhood. Therefore, her father paid for music lessons for her to develop her talent. He also said, "She could whistle like a bird." Soon, she learned to play the E-flat ballet horn (a combination of French horn and trombone) rather well and then the piano and saxophone. Her father also often praised her ability as a singer. The four Dorsey musicians often practiced together, sometimes as a saxophone quartet. But Mary's interest in music faded as she began to grow up.

Frank Riordan believes that of his musically inclined children Pop Dorsey favored Jimmy's talent, perhaps because of his proficiency on several instruments. However, when asked what the ideal orchestra would be like, Tom said, "Ninety-nine trombones like Tommy and a piano!"

The brothers played together in parades and concerts as members of the Elmore Band in Shenandoah under their father's direction. Soon they became local celebrities. Along with their sister and father, they found frequent work at church, civic, and fraternal functions as well as at other local concerts. One night, a highly touted touring brass band composed of black musicians made an appearance in town, but it was Tommy's euphonium playing as a soloist that stole the show.

Still, it was hard work for children. Tess pitied Jimmy when he left the house dragging his trumpet case on the way to a gig. "Every time he worked he'd bring his five dollars, or whatever he earned, home. Five dollars was a lot of money in those days. I remember him saying to Father, when he was only nine years old, 'Pop, I'm tired of playing for *this* and he'd clap his hands.' 'It's *this*'—and he'd rub his fingers together to mean money—'that counts.'"

The brothers were compelled by Tom and Tess to take nonmusical jobs in order to supplement the family income. Finances were a frequent issue in the household. At ten, Tommy opened a store in the family parlor selling taffy which his mother had made. The price was a penny a piece, but there were few customers. At thirteen, he expanded his horizons by selling canned goods, groceries, and sugar. Tess remembered him even buying an elaborate brass scale. "That cost seventy whole dollars! I kept tellin' him he didn't need it, but he had made up his mind, and get it he did."

Tommy also earned a few dollars as a delivery boy at a butcher shop. Meanwhile, in the summer of 1919, despite their father's determination that his boys would never go to work in the mines, Jimmy got a job as a blacksmith's helper, separating slate from coal at a local colliery. He skipped the celebration of his leap year birthday in February 1920, for fear word would get around that he was only sixteen. Pennsylvania law prohibited children under eighteen from working in the mines, and when eventually Jimmy's true age was discovered, he lost his job.

In January 1920, the Dorsey family moved from Shenandoah, twenty miles east to Lansford, another mining town. Stephen John Botek, a local grocer, cook, and amateur clarinetist, offered Tom Dorsey the leadership of the Lansford Municipal Band, of which he was a member. This meant Tom could count on a weekly pay check. He also became a music teacher there and soon built up a clientele in the town that included Botek and often traveled by trolley to nearby Tamaqua to give additional lessons.

His sons were becoming young men, but Tom didn't relax his hold on them. One day the town band, with Tommy and Jimmy as members, was parading through town; the Dorsey boys were looking at the pretty girls on the sidewalk and were kidding around when, to their complete surprise, Pop Dorsey sneaked behind them, slapped them on the back of their heads, and proceeded to reprimand them in public.

Lansford High School was conveniently located just around the corner from their row home at 227 East Abbott Street. The Dorsey home, "a half of a double" (half of two houses built together), was a typical coal miner's home. It had two floors. Upstairs there were three bedrooms and a bathroom, and there was a small attic. Downstairs there was a small kitchen, a dining room, and a living room, and below that a basement. The house sloped to a backyard, where the family once raised tomatoes and beans. When Tommy and Jimmy started going out on the road, the house would be a frequent stopover point for them and their fellow musicians. Mom Dorsey would be waiting for them with her famous pot pies.

In Lansford, the Dorsey brothers' advanced musical training would begin. Their frequent local gigs further honed their music skills. Tom Dorsey told Frank Riordan, "They learned a lot when they left here, but I gave them the foundation."

Valley Gazette feature writer Curt Williams recently explained, "Here in coal country, there has always existed a sort of 'battle of ownership' between the communities of Shenandoah and Lansford, both claiming it was 'they' who had the most influence on the Dorseys becoming stars." Today, there are two plaques in downtown Shenandoah commemorating their importance: The first was installed in 1979 outside the public library and the other in 1991 at the intersection of Main and Centre Streets. Jimmy is buried in the Annunciation BVM Cemetery in Shenandoah Heights.

Driving northeast through the towns of Barnesville, Tamaqua, Coaldale, and Lansford on Routes 54, 309, and 209 in 2002 felt like I was entering a time warp. In Lansford the architecture is much the same, particularly the similarities in the look of the houses and commercial buildings. There are many churches (Catholic, Greek Orthodox, Russian Orthodox, English Congregational, Baptist, Lutheran, and Presbyterian, among others) and corner bars, which total thirty-six. There is a malaise that permeates the atmosphere of the town.

Today, the wealth is gone from coal-mining country; only the poverty remains. One ballroom still stands: Lakeside, where Jimmy once played with his band, and where five thousand people used to dance nightly. Between the 1920s and the early 1950s, oil completely replaced coal as the main source of fuel in the nation and caused a catastrophic change in the town's employment picture. Lansford shrank from a population of about 10,000 residents in the late 1920s to 4,230 by 2000.

When one walks down the streets of the old mining towns, the limited prospects of the people who lived there are almost palpable. For most of them the options were constricted even when coal mining was booming and the population was still growing.

"In explaining this area, you have to realize that for many years for most young men growing up here there was only the mines. For young women it meant going to work at the Kiddies Clothes or the Eagle Brothers shirt factory," noted WBAI New York radio host Marle Becker, who grew up in Mahanoy City, and whose coal miner father died of black lung disease like many men in those years. Becker reports, "My mother told me the Dorsey brothers had holes in their shoes and were poor as church mice."

Becker continued, "As a young man I knew I was homosexual, and that made it a big challenge for me living there. I loved music, and I worked at the box office at the theater that John Kenley ran immediately adjacent to the Lakewood Ballroom, which was owned by the Guinans in Barnesville. Going out dancing was the only outlet for the people. It was the television of its day, so business at Lakewood and Lakeside [the other ballroom only twenty-one hundred feet away], playing name bands, was always good.

"I saw Tommy and Jimmy Dorsey perform with their orchestra around 1955 at Lakewood. Seeing them leading the band, playing their wonderful music, gave me the inspiration to leave. I realized that in order to continue to pursue their interest in music they had to get out of that town. As a result of seeing them perform, I moved to Washington and eventually to New York to start my career."

The psychiatrist Stephen Thomas Botek (the son of Stephen John Botek), who practices in New York, as well as in Lansford on weekends, explained the importance of music in immigrants' lives. "When I was six years old, my father said to me, 'Which instrument do you want to play?' Each ethnic group had its own music, and the sons were expected to perpetuate its musical heritage."

Those people, they worked their butts off during the week, but on Sunday after church they would go places. If there was a band playing, you went to see a band on a Sunday night. Those good, hardworking immigrants like my dad and the coal miners liked to drink. But they also liked music. They wanted to integrate and move up. A good musician could move into different circles. I swear you could walk down the street in Lansford—you'd hear somebody rehearsing, singing, playing trombone, clarinet—that little town was unbelievable.

Music was the ticket up; for the Dorseys, it would be their ticket out.

Tommy and Jimmy Dorsey played their first professional gig in 1919 with the Syncopators at the Flagstaff Pavilion in the neighboring town of Mauch Chunk. Jimmy was still playing cornet, as well as alto saxophone, switching from one side of his mouth to the other so as not to interfere with

the embouchure (a position and use of the lips, tongue, and teeth in playing a wind instrument) he had developed while Tommy was still experimenting with his trombone style. Stints playing in the Tamaqua P.C. Band
and Abby Morgan's Band and with the Scranton Serenaders followed.

They continued working with their father's band at Gorman's Hall in
Lansford playing waltzes, plain and fancy quadrilles, square dances, and two-
steps. One night after a concert, Tom came home with a strange, quiet look
on his face and remarked to Tess, "It's a proud day when I can't be playin'
with my own sons any more. They're getting too fast for me."

Tess had already told her sons that if they stayed together they would be
unbeatable. This was also probably Tom Dorsey's feeling. The brothers continued to relish the thought of working together. By 1910 they had their first
chance to colead a dance band. They called it Dorsey's Novelty Six—The
Jazz Band of Them All. The band's lineup included their father on cornet
and trumpet. It was a co-op band, with each member being an equal partner.
The band was later renamed Dorseys' Wild Canaries by the woman owner of
an amusement park, the West Side Park in Berwyn, Pennsylvania.

Among various gigs, the band played for dances after the basketball
games at Liberty Hall in Lansford. Jimmy remembered fondly, "We learned
a lot of tricks from those early local Pennsylvania tours that served us in
good stead years later." On the road, the members of the band often slept
on pool tables in pool halls they frequented. There simply wasn't enough
money left over for lodgings.

After Tom Dorsey departed, Zugg Reichelderfer of Reading joined the
band on banjo. Besides Tommy and Jimmy, the other members were Vollmer
"Soccer" Miller of Coaldale, who replaced Tom on trumpet; Jim Crossan of
Nesquehoning on violin and tenor sax; his sister Katherine "Kay" Crossan
on piano (who was later replaced by Mickey Carey of Girardville), and Don
Neyer of Hazelton on drums. The band's repertoire consisted of various
dance tunes, like "The Turkey Trot" and waltzes.

Improvisation, an integral element of the new musical phenomenon
called jazz, had already seeped into the solos played by musicians in other
dance bands touring the area. The most influential of these bands was
probably the white Original Dixieland Jazz Band, which had made its debut
at Reisenweber's Restaurant in New York in 1917, bringing an awareness
of jazz to New York. (Dixieland is now frequently used to describe early
New Orleans jazz as played by white musicians.) The band had appeared
in Scranton at the Armory and made a profound impression on many
young musicians.

The Wild Canaries ventured forth from the Panther Valley for the first time in 1921 to headline a sixteen-week engagement at Carling's Amusement Park in Baltimore for $285 a week. Jimmy complained, "When we got set up for the job, the man told us we couldn't play any of the published tunes, so all we played was the blues—blues fast, blues slow, blues in E-flat, and blues in B-flat." Apparently, during the engagement, fifteen-year-old Tommy would fall asleep on the bandstand each night around 11 P.M. When he was awakened he would say it was time the dancers went home anyway.

Dance halls such as this one, where young people met, would presage the ballrooms. Dancing was the means of communication between the sexes. (Ballrooms later would become the pickup bars of the Swing Era.)

What was perhaps most noteworthy about this booking was that it marked one of the first times a jazz-flavored dance band had been heard on radio, the new communication device that had become the rage of the nation. Why, the Wild Canaries could even be heard for fifty or sixty miles, and in both Maryland and Pennsylvania! A decade later radio would become the prime ingredient in building dance bands through live "remote" broadcasts.

While working at Carling's Park, the Wild Canaries were seen by violinist Bill Lustig, leader of the Scranton Sirens, the most popular dance band in eastern Pennsylvania. After the Canaries returned to Lansford, their popularity waned. Other territory bands were more accomplished and had developed a greater following. Pay for dance dates dwindled to seven dollars for bands, and the Wild Canaries finally broke up.

Late in 1921, Jimmy Dorsey accepted an offer from the Sirens at a salary of ninety dollars a week. For the first time, the brothers weren't working together on a steady basis. But the separation was short-lived. Trombonist Russ Morgan, who would later lead his own successful dance band ("Music in The Morgan Manner," now led by his son Jack) and who wrote such hit songs as "You're Nobody 'Til Somebody Loves You," "Somebody Else Is Taking My Place," and "So Tired," received an offer from Paul Specht, the leader of what was then the number three band in the country. He decided to leave the Sirens, and Jimmy suggested Tommy as his replacement. For his audition, Tommy played, "When You and I Were Young, Maggie." Morgan related, "The kid brother played eight bars when Lustig stopped him cold. 'You're hired,' he snapped."

Becoming members, at seventeen and fifteen, of this well-established territory band, playing "head arrangements" (arrangements worked out in rehearsal and memorized by the musicians), gave the Dorseys an entrée into the upper strata of touring bands as well as exposure in important locations.

For the next several years, they lived the life of road musicians, their careers closely intertwined.

Russ Morgan and Tommy Dorsey had actually worked together previously at various times as members of a regional band. Morgan, nicknamed "The Old Coal Miner" (which he indeed had been briefly and which later became his label as a bandleader), told his old friend, the veteran saxophonist Clint Neagley, that more than once when he and Tommy returned on the early morning "milk run" train from dance dates they would run into trouble. They were dressed in tuxedos, their bowties askew, and Tommy was resplendent in the de rigueur 1920s fashion, a raccoon coat; already clothes were important to him. As various miners came aboard the train on their way to work, they would begin mocking the appearance of the two musicians. Before long, Tommy would take the bait and start a fight. Russ often found himself drawn in.

Pennsylvania's vast expanse was then a haven for dance bands. The nine-member Scranton Sirens band was so much in demand that it also toured southern New York state and New Jersey. John O'Hara remembered seeing posters with the banner "The Sirens Are Coming! The Sirens Are Coming!" Most of the band's traveling was done over dirt roads in a big open Packard. It was perhaps the first band to travel by car.

Trumpeter Phil Napoleon, who led the Dixieland band The Original Memphis Five, saw the Sirens on tour and recalled Jimmy as being "a terrific trumpet player. So was Tommy." In 1927 Tommy would record with The Original Memphis Five on trombone.

The Sirens' solid dance beat, laid down by drummer Joe Settler, made it a particular favorite of the Slavic, Polish, and Irish who lived in the greater Scranton vicinity and loved to dance. The repertoire included such contemporary fare as "The Johnson Rag," "Blue and Broken Hearted," "Do You Ever Think of Me?" "I'm Just Wild About Harry," and "Beebie," the latter a showcase for Jimmy on alto saxophone.

The first known recording to feature the Dorseys was the Scranton Sirens' "Three O'Clock in the Morning" backed with "Fate." It was recorded in New York on the OKeh label, in the spring of 1923, but never released. Jimmy and fellow alto saxophonist Sid Trucker imitated the sound of a Hawaiian guitar on this latter number.

The Sirens had been brought to New York by the Remick Music Company's song plugger, Sammy Collins, who had seen the band in Scranton the previous fall. The Sirens contract was the biggest contract given to an out-of-town band. The Sirens were featured in the show "Dancing Carnival" at the St. Nicholas Arena on West Sixty-sixth Street, known later by boxing fans as the venue, which was the stepping stone to Madison Square Garden. The reputation of the Sirens quickly spread. Such important band-leaders as Paul Whiteman, Vincent Lopez, and Ted Lewis came to see them perform. Within a few years they would employ the Dorseys.

Following the "Dancing Carnival" appearance and recording dates, the Scranton Sirens headed for Atlantic City, a city the Dorseys would visit many times in the next three decades, particularly while leading their own bands. Working there at the Beaux Arts Cabaret that summer, Tommy and Jimmy met jazz violinist Joe Venuti and guitarist Eddie Lang, who would become close friends.

Tommy and Jimmy Dorsey were now becoming accepted as jazz musicians with a future. Their tenure with the Scranton Sirens had been of decided significance. It was now time to move out of the cocoon of eastern Pennsylvania and its immediate area. Detroit, the Motor City, which was becoming a scene of burgeoning musical importance, beckoned.

Trumpeter "Fuzzy" Farrar left the Sirens in 1923 to travel to Detroit to join the Jean Goldkette Orchestra as lead trumpeter. He managed to get Goldkette to hire Russ Morgan and pianist Irving "Itzy" Riskin, also from the Sirens. The French-born Goldkette, who had been a concert pianist, real estate speculator, and band booker, led one of the first dance bands to incorporate the new spirit of "hot music." Though not a jazz musician, he became an important organizer and agent for many bands during the 1920s, including McKinney's Cotton Pickers and the Orange Blossoms, which later became the Casa Loma Orchestra.

Hot music was introduced to Chicago in the spring of 1923, when Joe "King" Oliver's Creole Jazz Band—featuring his protégé, fellow cornetist Louis Daniel "Satchelmouth," "Satchmo," "Pops" Armstrong; clarinetist Johnny Dodds; and his brother, drummer "Baby" Dodds—debuted at the Lincoln Gardens. Oliver's brand of jazz was innovative, passionate, and zestful—considerably more stimulating than the music that had originated with the also New Orleans–based Original Dixieland Jazz Band.

Armstrong's playing was revolutionary. As acclaimed jazz writer Whitney Balliett described it, "Louis Armstrong was the first sunburst in jazz—the light a thousand young trumpeters reflected." In addition, "[Louis's] basic style—a lyrical hugging of the melody and a rich, fervent texture—was already unmistakable." Armstrong's instrumental and vocal artistry would soon change popular music, trumpet playing, and singing forever.

A zealous contingent of young white Chicagoans—The Austin High Gang, which included cornetist Jimmy McPartland; his banjoist brother, Dick; tenor saxophonist Lawrence "Bud" Freeman; clarinetist and tenor saxophonist Frank Teschmacher; and drummer Dave Tough, all of them Austin High School students and therefore under age—stood outside of the South Side on an almost nightly basis completely mesmerized by this amazing music.

Other Windy City jazz babies such as cornetist Muggsy Spanier, clarinetist Milton "Mezz" Mezzrow, pianist Joe Sullivan, banjoist and guitarist Eddie Condon, and drummer George Wettling similarly raved over the white New Orleans Rhythm Kings working at the Friars' Inn that featured the daring clarinetist Leon Rappolo, trombonist George Brunis, and drummer Ben Pollack. The advent of the Creole Jazz Band's engagement at the Lincoln Gardens along with, to a lesser degree, the debut of the New Orleans Rhythm Kings, led to an influx of young white jazz musicians intent on capturing the essence of hot music. These young disciples, and others, would help create the sound of what was to become known as Chicago-style jazz, the boisterous offshoot of New Orleans jazz, which substituted the tenor saxophone for the clarinet in the front line.

The most important white jazz musician to emerge from Chicago during this period, however, was cornetist Leon "Bix" Beiderbecke, a refugee from an upper-class Davenport, Iowa, family background. In 1918, at the age of fifteen, Bix had seen Louis Armstrong, then seventeen, perform on a Mississippi Riverboat visit to Davenport while Armstrong was a member of the Fate Marable Band. The image of the quiet and affable Beiderbecke was described well by trombonist Spiegel Willcox when he said, "He almost smiled with his eyes." The promise and the ultimate sadness of Beiderbecke's life had all the ingredients of an F. Scott Fitzgerald hero.

Bix first made a significant impression with The Wolverines, working around Chicago in roadhouses and on college dates in 1923 and 1924. His cornet tone, record producer George Avakian said, was "something that will never fade away as long as there is a record around; once heard it's a sound you'll never forget." Eddie Condon said, "Bix's sound came out like a girl saying 'yes.'" Composer Hoagy Carmichael once noted that Bix's notes "weren't blown—they were hit, like a mallet strikes a chime." (This led to the young Indianan being so inspired by his musical hero that he incorporated Bix's musical influence in the writing of his majestic popular song "Star Dust.")

This sound, and his fertile lyrical ideas and progressive harmonic sense (influenced by Debussy), earned him a formidable reputation with the young white Chicagoans, as well as with Louis Armstrong and other formidable black jazz musicians who worshipped his extraordinary talent. On hearing Bix play for the first time, the young Chicago-born clarinetist Benny Goodman remarked, "What planet did this guy come from?"

Naturally, the new music early on had come to nearby Detroit. Jimmy Dorsey was intent on following his Scranton Sirens bandmates to Detroit, where Jean Goldkette held forth. Jimmy joined the Jean Goldkette Orchestra on Fuzzy Farrar's recommendation. Finally, Jimmy got Tommy a job with the band, and in March 1924 Tommy joined Goldkette at his headquarters, the elaborate Graystone Ballroom in Detroit.

The jazz flavor of the Goldkette band was enhanced at one time or another in the next few years by the presence of clarinetists Don Murray and "Pee Wee" Russell, trombonist Bill Rank, slap-bass specialist Steve Brown, Joe Venuti, Eddie Lang, and the Dorseys, as well as Frank Trumbauer, who played the C-melody saxophone (a cross between a tenor and an alto), and his sidekick, Bix Beiderbecke.

Bill Challis, who, as a Wilkes-Barre teenager had first heard of the Dorseys' sterling musical reputation from Fuzzy Farrar, knew precisely how to showcase this bevy of Goldkette soloists in his driving arrangements.

Never one to bestow praise upon anything musically mediocre, Artie Shaw saw the Goldkette band perform as a young musician. Shaw was quoted as calling it "the first really great white big band . . . unbelievable, [it] swung like mad."

The contributions of these young and accomplished musicians, deeply inspired by what had recently taken place in the two major urban centers of Chicago and New York, hugely influenced the course of twentieth-century music. By the mid-1920s, jazz was providing the musical roar of the so-called Roaring '20s.

These talented musicians were now honing their individual talents further within the framework of large dance orchestras, playing structured arrangements that also provided ample solo opportunities for them. These developments were fateful. Over the next ten years they would usher in a brilliant musical era, one in which Tommy and Jimmy Dorsey would be at the forefront.

2

Bites of the "Apple"

Praise Allah! Wiggle, wiggle, wiggle,
Praise Allah! Wiggle and dance . . .

Everybody's doin' fine
All you folks that ain't in line
Come on out and rise and shine
BIG APPLE! (Have a bite . . .)

P LAYING WITH the Jean Goldkette band proved to be extremely rewarding for the Dorseys. As members of this formidable big band, made up of experienced professionals, Tommy and Jimmy were learning the essence of the new music on a nightly basis. On March 27, 1924, in Detroit, they recorded their first commercially available product with Goldkette for RCA Victor.

Before joining Goldkette in 1924, Tommy, on Jimmy's suggestion, worked around Detroit for several weeks. Detroit was a major distribution center for hard liquor, which was smuggled down from Canada (where prohibition didn't exist) and moved east and west from there to such major distribution centers as New York and Chicago. The notorious Purple Gang had the same hold on business in Detroit that Al Capone had in Chicago. As part of that, there were a large number of nightclubs and speakeasies in operation—and therefore considerable work for musicians.

Besides the musical and professional rewards for the Dorseys, there were also personal ones. Jimmy met Jane Porter, who was Miss Detroit of 1925, a petite and vivacious blond, at a Goldkette dance date. Their courtship lasted for three years before they finally married in 1927. Jimmy gave Jane the nickname of Beebie, based on the name of the tune which he had recorded for OKeh Records with the Scranton Sirens. Over the years he recorded it three more times.

Integrated bands were years away; however, clarinetist Milton "Mezz" Mezzrow became renowned for being one of the first of the young white jazzmen to be a partisan for the cause of black jazz musicians (as well as he was for his uncanny ability to make readily available a supply of choice marijuana). He met Tommy while playing in a pickup band opposite the highly regarded black orchestra McKinney's Cotton Pickers at a club date arranged by the Goldkette booking office. "The corny stocks [arrangements] and jumbled-up special arrangements we had to read that night must have seemed pretty cute to those colored [sic] boys, whose numbers were all fixed up by solid arrangers like Don Redman. . . . They came on with a steady rock beat that was really groovy." A rewarding musical experience like this one, witnessing a collection of exemplary black musicians, would have repercussions in an important musical decision of Tommy's some thirteen years later.

While becoming established in Detroit, Tommy played all kinds of gigs, mostly dance dates, at hotels, roadhouses, and private parties. He was becoming a striking young man—five feet ten inches tall with dark eyes, black hair, and an erect carriage that made him appear inches taller. With his slicked-back hair and formidable Dorsey family nose, his steel-framed glasses did not detract from his masculinity one iota. He was a "man's man" who exhibited a pronounced self-confidence, an appreciation for women, and a serious interest in drinking. He had a ready smile, a keen sense of humor, and a blunt way of expressing himself.

One night, while playing a dance date with a local band at a college fraternity house, Tommy met a five-foot-five young brunette named Mildred Kraft, whose nickname was Toots. Tommy was immediately attracted to her. They danced together and won a Charleston contest later that evening but were disqualified because Toots wasn't wearing any stockings! (Tommy later laughingly admitted that the best thing he did that night was to merely shuffle his hands on his knees while dancing the Charleston.)

Tommy and Toots were instantly attracted to each other and made the decision to get married two weeks later. But Toots was only seventeen and Tommy not yet nineteen, and Toots's stepmother, Frieda (her mother had died when Toots was only a baby), was adamant about her not marrying a traveling musician.

As a result, the young couple decided to elope. Tommy's best man was Bill Rank, a trombonist he was soon to team up with in the Goldkette band. Jimmy reportedly broke into tears during the wedding ceremony, lamenting the loss of his brother and roommate.

Toots's father immediately vowed to get their marriage annulled, but Toots closed off that possibility by telling him that the relationship had already been consummated. The newlyweds settled in Detroit, where Tommy soon began his steady job with Jean Goldkette.

Tommy's impulsive marriage was characteristic of his behavior. Once he made an important decision, nothing and no one could make him change his mind. This became a significant aspect of his personality and a cornerstone of his determined personality.

According to Bill Rank, "Jimmy was always the level-headed one. Tommy was always impulsive and aggressive. They used to fight like cats and dogs, but no one had better say anything about either one of them because down deep they loved each other."

Tommy had already begun to exhibit a violent streak that he didn't attempt to control. As Rank remembered, "One time in Hazelton, Pennsylvania, Tom and Jim got into it in a room at the Altamont Hotel. Jim had a new sax, gold-plated on the bell. Tommy picked it up and threw it on the floor and stomped on it. You can guess what happened after that."

After Tommy had been with the Goldkette band for just over six months, Bix Beiderbecke became a member of the band. Like his cohorts, Tommy marveled at Bix's blazing talent. After their shows, he often went out drinking with Bix. He couldn't help but notice the hold Bix's drinking had on him. As a musician, Bix was a poor sight reader, which caused problems for Goldkette and resulted in Bix's being fired a few months later. A first-rate orchestra leader could not allow a musician, even one as important as Beiderbecke, to display an inability to play any music part put in front of him. Bix's ongoing drinking was still another problem.

On January 26, 1925, Bix included Tommy in his first recording session under his own name, in Richmond, Indiana, for Gennett Records, the fledgling hot jazz label. One of the tunes Bix and his Rhythm Jugglers recorded that day was "Toddlin' Blues." Tommy soloed in a context closely akin to that of a tailgate trombonist (so called because New Orleans trombonists played outdoors on the tailgates of their wagons), not surprising, for at this juncture most jazz played by white musicians was merely following the New Orleans model. Still, his solo exhibited his credentials as a capable, if uninspired, jazz trombonist.

It was on this same recording session that Bix asked Tommy to provide a name for a song he had written on the spur of the moment on the record date. Tommy suggested, "Why not call it 'Davenport Blues' after your hometown?" "Davenport Blues" became one of the signature records of the Beiderbecke canon and was recorded by Tommy thirteen years later with his own band. Tommy later recalled how the gin he had bought as fuel for the session flowed so freely it made him forget the fact that other tunes had been recorded that day.

The jazz historian, writer, and cornetist Richard Sudhalter has said that Bix's contemporaries "regarded him as some sort of spiritual force, [an] avatar or something of jazz, yet beyond it. Otherworldly, it's that aspect of him that stayed with his colleagues most tenaciously after his death." Both Dorseys would deeply revere Beiderbecke for the rest of their careers.

In the meantime, Jimmy had returned to New York and had joined The California Ramblers, whose name was a misnomer as the band had nothing remotely to do with the state of California. The name had a certain ring to it that fit the Roaring '20s sensibility. Ed Kirkeby, the leader of the Ramblers, had originally seen the Dorsey brothers play at the St. Nicholas Arena, when they were members of the Scranton Sirens and recognized their talent.

Toots was then in the last stages of her pregnancy with their first child. Tommy figured that New York, with its many recording opportunities and Broadway musicals—not to mention nightclubs, dance halls, and speakeasies—was the ideal place for an ambitious young musician to find himself, and in addition, perhaps the right place to raise a family. For some time he had been anxious for the brothers to move to the "Big Apple" (or merely the "Apple," as most musicians referred to the new musical mecca), almost since turning professional. For the third time, Jimmy opened a door for him when Tommy was offered a permanent gig with the California Ramblers. The Dorsey brothers continued to enjoy working together in constantly challenging musical environments. Jimmy officially transferred from the Detroit American Federation of Musicians (AFM), Local 5, to the newly formed 802 Local in New York.

Living in Manhattan was an expensive proposition. This caused Tommy and Toots to rent a small home on City Island, not too far from the Rambler's Inn (home of The California Ramblers) on Pelham Bay. Tess Dorsey's visit to New York to meet her new daughter-in-law for the first time coincided with a visit from Bix Beiderbecke, who was making an exploratory excursion looking for work. Tess wound up cooking dinner for Tommy, Toots, Jimmy, Bix, and their new friend, cornetist Red Nichols on the night of March 15, 1925.

Nichols was a Beiderbecke disciple without much originality. In addition to Nichols, the Ramblers musical lineup included clarinetist and alto saxophonist Arnold Brillhart, Adrian Rollini on bass sax, and drummer Stan King. The band displayed spirited musicianship and a freewheeling jazz concept that made it a favorite of the college crowd. In addition to its popular records on various labels, once the Dorseys came along Ed Kirkeby put together various recording combinations within the band, such as the Varsity Eight and the University Six. These ensembles were forerunners of the small bands featured within big bands that became popular during the latter part of the 1930s.

At that time, Tommy wasn't a proficient sight reader. Arnold Brillhart recalled that Tommy used to say all the notes above the staff looked like telephone poles. Jimmy, more musically advanced, however, supplied fresh ideas for orchestrations, as in the case of the Ramblers' popular version of "Sweet Georgia Brown."

Bass saxophonist Spencer Clark, a member of The Ramblers, recalled, "Jimmy . . . made the bigger impression on my memory. His playing ability and thinking was far beyond any reed player of my knowledge, and I listened with a feeling and awe. . . . Tommy's forte was conversation—sharp, cutting, and very humorous. His playing at that time was acceptable. No one cared about straight playing and his jazz was as good as any other trombonist."

The Dorsey brothers were moving rapidly in the big-time music business. Jimmy would still take the lead, but Tommy's personality was increasingly making an impression of him as a take-charge kind of guy. This aspect would soon have an important effect in their chosen musical directions in the years just ahead.

April 11, 1925, marked the birth of Patricia ("Patsy" or "Pat") Marie Dorsey. It was then customary for young marrieds to start a family in their first years of marriage. Tommy was a proud parent but left the care of his newly arrived daughter to Toots. He felt secure in knowing that Toots had been blessed with obvious maternal instincts. Toots, in turn, believed Tommy would be a reliable financial provider for her and their family. One more child would follow four years later, a son, Thomas Francis Dorsey III.

The fact that Toots wasn't Catholic was a source of friction between her and her mother-in-law, Tess. One day Tess announced to Toots, after the birth of Tommy and Toots's second child, that the children were illegitimate since Toots and Tommy hadn't been married in the Catholic church! The pride Tess never ceased to show with regard to her sons, and her dedication to Catholicism, sometimes interfered with their marriages.

Pat Hooker, a widow after fifty-six years of marriage to the highly respected college professor and basketball coach Lester Hooker, with whom she had three children, remembered:

> Every time we went to Lansford, my grandmother [Tess] would drag us to church. The house always had priests running around . . . and she would give me rosaries. One time, when my mother announced that she was going to convert, my grandmother was very insulting to her and called her some uncomplimentary names. There was a big argument, and I remember my father saying, "Toots will become a Catholic over my dead body!" And she never did any more with it. Being Catholic didn't mean that much to Dad. He only went to church on Palm Sunday. He was not a churchgoer. (According to Frank Riordan, Tommy, in fact, delighted in telling humorous Catholic stories.)

On June 8, 1925, Tommy doubled from the California Ramblers by recording with the Roseland Orchestra, led by Sam Lanin, one of the seven musical Lanin brothers. Arnold Brillhart recalled an incident that took place with the ever-battling Dorseys on the Lanin bandstand during a break. Tommy and Jimmy got into a fistfight over some probably insignificant slight, whereupon Tommy once again stomped all over Jimmy's brand-new saxophone. "He made scrap metal of it," Brillhart said and added, "Jimmy grabbed his brother's trombone and just wrapped it around his knee, slide and all. Ruined it."

Among the other bandleaders Tommy worked for and recorded with were violinists Eddie Elkins and Joe Candullo, as well as pianists Vincent Lopez and Freddie Rich. During most of the winter of 1926, he was a sideman along with Eddie Lang and Joe Venuti in Roger Wolfe Kahn's Dance Orchestra, which played at the Biltmore Hotel in midtown Manhattan.

In the spring, at the suggestion of Bix (who had rejoined the Goldkette band), as well as Don Murray and Jimmy, Goldkette offered Tommy a chance to return to Detroit to work with one of his various bands. Tommy accepted the offer and joined the principal Goldkette band on tour at the Nuttings-on-the-Charles Ballroom in Somerset, Massachusetts. He respected Goldkette, and by returning to Detroit he would be guaranteed plenty of work. The Goldkette orchestra also made frequent personal appearances in the Chicago area. One night in December 1926, Tommy ventured into the Sunset Café to see Louis Armstrong, who had just returned from New York after a year with Fletcher Henderson's band. Armstrong was now featured with Carroll Dickerson's Orchestra in Chicago. The renowned jazz pianist Earl "Fatha" Hines, then with Dickerson's band, recalled, "Most of the clubs and hotels where the white bands played closed down between one and two o'clock. And they'd come down either to [catch] King Oliver at the Plantation or where we were. Benny Goodman used to come in with his clarinet in a sack. Tommy was there with either his trumpet (which he had been playing occasionally) or trombone because he hadn't decided which one he wanted to specialize on. His brother Jimmy would come with his alto and clarinet. Muggsy Spanier, Joe Sullivan, Jess Stacy, and I don't know how many different musicians came in to jam with us. . . . We all got a kick out of listening to each other, and we all tried to learn. We sat around waiting to see if these guys were actually going to come up with something new or different."

From sitting in with Louis, and then later seeing him play in New York's Harlem, Tommy gained a deep appreciation for Armstrong's true genius. In time, a lasting friendship took hold. In the late 1920s, Tommy's records, which featured his trumpet solos, would reflect Louis's unmistakable influence. Tommy's sound was intense and guttural and often displayed a wide vibrato—a far cry from the smooth legato sound of his trombone that would later become his trademark.

One night at the newly built Book-Cadillac Hotel in Detroit, a scion of the Fisher Body (the body builder for General Motors cars) family kept approaching the band to play "The Missouri Waltz" (much in the same manner as the fabled drunk who constantly wants to hear "Melancholy Baby" being played). Tommy told the young man to "fuck off." The manager of the hotel wanted Tommy fired immediately from the band for his insolence.

Cork O'Keefe, agent for the Goldkette Orchestra, interceded, but as a result of the incident Tommy was demoted to playing in second-level Goldkette bands.

After seven months in Detroit, Tommy returned to New York in late September and rejoined Sam Lanin. He went on to record numerous times with Lanin and during the spring worked a lengthy engagement in Atlantic City with Lanin's orchestra. Jimmy was also prominently featured on several of Lanin's record dates playing clarinet and alto sax.

The year of 1927 marked an important milestone in the careers of the Dorsey brothers. First Jimmy, then Tommy a few months later, joined Paul Whiteman, billed as the "King of Jazz." The rotund "Pops," as he was affectionately nicknamed, knew full well that his music didn't deserve such an accolade, but he also realized such hyperbole well fit the "Jazz Age."

Born in Denver in 1890, and originally a violinist, Whiteman led his first band, a dance orchestra in the Los Angeles area, in 1918. Two years later he moved to New York and formed a concert orchestra. Whiteman had infinite respect for jazz musicians and willingly hired such important practitioners as Bix, Frank Trumbauer, Joe Venuti, Eddie Lang, and later on trombone Jack Teagarden. The first four of these musicians had, of course, come from Jean Goldkette, who had finally been compelled to disband after trying unsuccessfully to establish himself as "The Paul Whiteman of the West."

Reportedly, at one time Whiteman seriously considered incorporating black musicians into his combined concert and dance orchestra of thirty pieces or so. His management, however, warned him of the grave consequences of doing so. But that didn't prevent him from hiring black arrangers such as Fletcher Henderson, whose distinctive charts would later be of major importance in Benny Goodman's success; Don Redman, one of the true pioneer arrangers of big-band jazz, who combined original harmonies and advanced sectional counterpoint; and W. C. Handy, composer of "St. Louis Blues," who had been dubbed the "Father of the Blues." And like Duke Ellington, Whiteman realized the importance of showcasing a cadre of first-rate soloists and fully realized how that could translate into significant commercial value for his orchestra. Whiteman was now about to lead the most musically outstanding orchestra of his long career.

Paul Whiteman was *big time*—*the* towering musical figure of the post–World War I era. His success had even extended to Europe, which he toured in concert. He had an incredible succession of hit records over a period of several years, during the 1920s, many of which were million sellers at a time when no one else's record sales reached anywhere close to that.

Among them were "The Japanese Sandman," "Whispering," "Hot Lips," "Three O'Clock in the Morning," "The Birth of the Blues," "Wang Wang Blues," "Ramona," "Valencia," and "Rhapsody in Blue."

Whiteman had commissioned George Gershwin to write the epic composition "Rhapsody in Blue" for a concert held at Aeolian Hall in New York on February 12, 1924. It elevated Gershwin to major prominence and suddenly gave a new cachet to jazz. Whiteman soon adapted the well-remembered refrain from "Rhapsody in Blue" as his theme song.

Whiteman enjoyed his fame and practiced living in a great big way. He wore expensive, custom-tailored clothes; loved the ladies; was a heavy drinker; and relished traveling with the band in his own railroad car. He was also a great businessman and had a thorough understanding of how to present commercial music. All of this made an indelible impression on Tommy Dorsey.

As a leader, Whiteman showed the Dorseys the same kindness and consideration he showed all his men. Just as he tried to help Bix with his drinking problem, sending him away for a cure (which didn't work), and on occasion bailed out Harry Lillis "Bing" Crosby (who along with Al Rinker and Harry Barris comprised The Rhythm Boys, the featured singing group with the band) after his drinking escapades landed him in jail.

Al Gallodoro, whom Jimmy Dorsey once called "the best saxophone player that ever lived," and who was the featured alto with Whiteman from 1936 to 1940, said of Whiteman, "If he ever insulted anybody, he'd make a laugh [out] of it. He would never hurt anyone. He was a hell of a good conductor and knew what he wanted . . . big arrangements and all. He was also intelligent. He had three and four arrangers (two of whom were Bill Challis and Ferde Grofé) so his numbers wouldn't sound the same."

Trombonist Buddy Morrow, who in 1938 left Dorsey to join the Whiteman Orchestra, said, "Of all the bandleaders I worked for, some of my best memories are with Paul Whiteman. Paul had the greatest players in the world. And when you were warming up, God help you if you had to play something difficult 'cause he'd be onto the next arrangement. He was one of the greatest frontmen I've ever known. His baton was about a yard long. If you got in the way of his downbeat, your head would come off!"

Pop and jazz musicians of this era were a hard-drinking lot. Morrow continued, "Whiteman would drink from Wednesday night after the show until the following Sunday, when the doctor would come and shore him up for the Chesterfield Show on Wednesday. If you didn't drink, you were an outcast."

On July 6, 1927, the Dorsey brothers were with the Whiteman band when it recorded "My Blue Heaven" on Victor. It, too, became another one of Whiteman's number one hits. Tommy was featured on other Whiteman records like "The Calinda (Boo-Joom, Boo-Joom, Boo)," "Just a Memory," "Shaking the Blues Away," "Among My Souvenirs" (another number one record), "Washboard Blues" (with Hoagy Carmichael singing and playing piano), and "Changes," which featured a memorable Beiderbecke solo.

While the Whiteman band was on a location date at the Indiana Theatre, in Indianapolis, Tommy and Jimmy recorded with Hoagy for Gennett. Whiteman heard Hoagy "noodling" his composition "Washboard Blues" in Bill Challis's Indianapolis hotel room, whereupon he had Bill arrange the song to include a solo by Bix for the band to record. Soon afterward, when Bix first left the band for health reasons, Whiteman used Tommy as his trumpet soloist playing two muted solos and an open-horn Armstrong-like cadenza on "It Won't Be Long Now."

It was in 1927, while working for Whiteman, that the Dorsey brothers' talents reached a new level and Tommy began to enjoy a greater respect for his own trumpet playing. Not surprisingly, Tommy would often regale his fellow Whiteman musicians with imitations of Armstrong's famous solos on cornet, and in a demonstration of his desire to become a respected jazz trombonist, in his solo on "Whiteman Stomp." Jimmy Dorsey played one of his most renowned alto saxophone solos on Whiteman's "Tiger Rag" recording of November 18, 1927.

Frank Riordan claims that Art Tatum, generally recognized as the dean of jazz pianists, copied Jimmy's solo in his interpretation of the tune. A few years later Jimmy recorded it again in London, playing both alto sax and clarinet. In the 1950s, his live clarinet solos on the tune became equally celebrated among musicians. Today, almost every Dixieland band playing "Tiger Rag" duplicates verbatim Jimmy's original clarinet solo.

A scene in Chicago related by Eddie Condon in his biography *We Called It Music* encapsulates the camaraderie that existed among this group of talented young musicians. He describes going with Bix after hours

> to a speakeasy around the corner at north State Street. It was a no-knock place, just walk in, with a lot of five- and ten-cent bums, Burnett's White Satin gin, and a cellar with cement walls and an upright piano. Some of the

other Whiteman boys followed us. Suddenly everybody was there and everybody was playing along with Bix. Some singers arrived but they kept quiet and listened. They were the Rhythm Boys—Al Rinker, Harry Barris, Bing Crosby—sharp-looking lads, slightly young.

We played until dawn; I bought a quart of milk off the wagon on my way home. The next night we were back again; Bud Freeman dropped in, the Dorsey brothers were there, Harry Gale and Ben Pollack played drums. At half past seven the following morning Bix was playing *In a Mist* and Joe Sullivan was sitting next to him, hypnotized. The room was getting crowded; customers were coming down to listen—the Whiteman players and their wives were enough to put the place on a paying basis. Tesch and McPartland showed up; George Wettling and young Gene Krupa helped out on drums. There was a lot of music, a lot of gin, and a lot of talk. It was noon before I got home. Without pre-arrangement, we all turned up again twelve hours later in the cellar.

Appreciating the importance of the time they spent with Whiteman, the Dorseys now figured it was time to return to New York. Their last appearance with Whiteman was on a November 25, 1927, recording session that produced "Mary, What Are You Waiting For?" with Crosby's solo vocal. The close friendship that Tommy and Jimmy had developed with Bing would be of great consequence in the years ahead.

That same year and early the following year, Tommy made two valuable and personally meaningful musical discoveries. While the Whiteman band was working at the Palais Royale at Forty-eighth Street and Broadway in New York (later the site of the famous Latin Quarter nightclub), Tommy, Jimmy, and other Whiteman musicians made frequent visits to the nearby Kentucky Club to listen to Duke Ellington and his so-called jungle music. Tommy sensed the unique and sophisticated quality of Ellington's music. Years later, he featured Ellington playing piano with the Dorsey band on an RCA Victor recording session, and he, in turn, recorded with the Ellington band.

His other major find occurred in the spring of 1928, when he met Weldon Leo "Jack" Teagarden, the laconic, "lazy-talking" trombonist. Tommy had first heard about Teagarden from Red Nichols and others after Jack had participated in several New York jam sessions. The musicians quickly grasped his extraordinary musical mettle. Many believed that Jack, with his jet-black patent-leather hair, dark eyes, and high cheekbones, was of Native

American descent; in reality he was of German stock. He had, however, gained his initial musical inspiration as a child in Vernon, Texas, listening to both Negro spirituals and Native American music.

After driving up from Texas in late 1927 as a member of the Doc Ross band, a territory band (that is, a dance orchestra, usually, whose work was confined to a specific region), Teagarden had arrived in New York jobless. After several weeks of scuffling, he found work at Roseland with the Scranton Sirens, who were working as the relief band for pianist Fletcher Henderson's orchestra, then the foremost black orchestra. Jack and Jimmy Harrison, the highly regarded Henderson trombonist, discovered that they had much in common musically; "Smack" Henderson himself was immediately awestruck by Teagarden's talent and took him up to Harlem to sit in with several bands.

Soon a legend surrounded "Big Tea," or the "Big Gate," as Jack was called. He exhibited perfect pitch, a sound that Artie Shaw called "the first new sound on trombone," and he could both play and sing the blues like no other white jazzman.

Tommy frequently walked into the Silver Slipper, the midtown Manhattan nightclub where Jack was working with the Tommy Gott Orchestra after finishing his nightly gig with the Scranton Sirens. Sitting alone in the back of the club, Tommy was riveted on Jack's playing. A friend of Jack's, guitarist Tony Colucci, noticed Tommy one night in this enthralled state and watched him sneak out of the club and teased him mercilessly about it.

Many musicians believe Tommy's musical taste and lip control stemmed directly from Jack Teagarden. Teagarden's astonishing ability to play jazz, however, was something Tommy realized he simply could never emulate. Still, he was never adverse to praising Teagarden's true greatness.

Previously, Tommy's principal inspiration had been Irving Milford "Miff" Mole, whom he'd met while playing for Sam Lanin at Roseland. Hailing from Roosevelt, Long Island, Mole had adapted his childhood violin technique to the trombone. In 1921 and for several years thereafter, Mole had been featured with Phil Napoleon and The Original Memphis Five before becoming in demand for a myriad of jobs and recording dates. With small groups (where he especially shined) as well as on big-band dates, Mole often worked as a team with Red Nichols. His fast, clean staccato approach to the instrument and his jazz sensibilities made him the most emulated trombone player of the time.

The late masterful guitarist Alvino Rey was then a radio and recording-studio musician in New York. Appraising the late 1920s Dorsey, in one of his last interviews before passing away in 2002, he said, "I think Tommy was very good then, but I think he was still in pursuit of developing a sound of his own."

According to one-time Dorsey guitarist Carmen Mastren, "Tommy contended that, 'I never played anything original in my life. Everything I play is Miff Mole.'" Mastren added, "When it came to jazz, all he could talk about was Miff Mole and Jack Teagarden."

In his 1977 autobiography, *The World of Earl Hines*, Earl Hines somewhat facetiously summed up Tommy's eventual destiny: "You take Tommy Dorsey. Miff Mole stopped him from playing hot trombone, and when he went to play trumpet, Louis Armstrong stopped him from playing that! So he went into the 'wood-shed' and came out with that 'tonation' using his horn as a voice, making a sound people loved right away."

In the 1920s, the growing popularity of the phonograph was of primary importance in spreading the gospel of jazz throughout America. Seventy-eights (records named for the number of revolutions they made per minute) became a staple of home entertainment. In 1927, some 140 million records were sold in the United States.

By 1928, the Dorseys were at the forefront of the New York recording scene, often as members of the orchestras of Nat Shilkret, Emmet Miller, Seger Ellis, Boyd Senter, Ben Selvin, and Victor Young, the latter the composer of such standards as "Sweet Sue," "When I Fall in Love," and "Street of Dreams," and later an important screen composer. They realized they could fare much better financially doing studio work than by working for Whiteman or any other bands. Besides that, Toots wanted Tommy to get off the road.

Strangely enough, it wasn't until March 23, 1928, that the Dorseys actually had the opportunity of recording with their old friends from Atlantic City, the dynamic duo of Joe Venuti and Eddie Lang, who had practically invented chamber jazz. This took place while they were all working for Boyd Senter. The group, that recorded on October 4, 1928, was billed as Joe Venuti and His New Yorkers.

The brothers had become so well established as "first-call" musicians that they were also often enlisted as contractors, responsible for booking individual members of an entire orchestra for recording dates; this meant sometimes hiring themselves for particularly difficult recordings. But their musical activity was about to take an even more lucrative turn: their expansion into radio. The immediate success in 1930 of this new medium at first caused a sudden slump in record sales. In time, listeners' ears became reoriented, and records again became popular.

The various network and independent radio stations that beamed out of New York required an abundance of music for their dramatic programs, along with comedy and variety shows, plus commercials. The wide assortment of white jazz musicians (black musicians needn't apply) and dance band musicians—at least those who could read any kind of music put before them and were personally reliable—were suddenly making great sums of money for both daytime and evening radio work.

The Dorseys' old friend and musical compatriot Itzy Riskin, who now worked with them on radio shows, said, "Tommy was always an idealist and played the way he wanted to. In the early days of radio, leaders geared their music to suit the sponsors, but not Tommy. Jimmy was even worse—he wouldn't budge an inch for anybody!"

The Dorsey brothers on a daily basis moved quickly from one radio show to another, sometimes on the same floor with a different orchestra, and sometimes to a different building. (Most of the networks were located on the west side of midtown Manhattan.) Tommy and Jimmy were averaging fifteen radio shows a week. Producers of the most important shows clamored for the musical services of "the brass section," namely trumpeters Manny Klein and Charlie Margulis and trombonist Tommy Dorsey.

Freddie Rich, a frequent employer of the Dorseys, was the leader of the first Columbia Broadcasting System staff orchestra, which included Tommy when it convened at the end of February 1931. This job required working a mere twelve hours per week but paid two hundred dollars—quite a generous retainer in the Depression era. (Commercials paid twenty-five dollars a session.) Tommy explained that his workday at CBS didn't start until 5 P.M., "after the record dates were finished."

Once again, Tommy was reunited with Joe Venuti, the colorful South Philadelphia native who grew up there with Eddie Lang (Salvator Massaro). Venuti had become the first important jazz violinist. They also worked together in various radio studio bands. A noted prankster, Venuti was the instigator of one of the most famous musician stories, wherein he hired thirty-seven tuba players in Hollywood and told them to meet at Sunset and Vine for a gig. From a nearby building, he looked down at the street corner and broke up with laughter watching all the musicians congregating. The musicians' union, however, socked it to him and made him pay for the consequences of his prank.

On one particular New Year's Eve radio broadcast, an anonymous bandleader unwisely angered Tommy and Venuti at rehearsal. Before anyone returned for the program, they sneaked back into the studio and inside the big stand-up set of chimes inserted a piece of paper, rolled up in the bottom of each pipe, so that, when released, the paper would expand and deaden the note completely. When the old year went out, the leader signaled for the chimes and got "tick-tick"; a little louder, "TICK"; a really hard blow, but no note—and finally the chimes player, realizing he'd been had and the bandleader having a change of mind, gave a full golf swing on the last note, which overturned the whole chimes set. It sounded as if they were taking the annual inventory at Hammacher Schlemmer!

Society gigs were still another important outlet for the best musicians. Benny Goodman, Artie Shaw, the Dorseys, et al. found considerable work with such musical outfits during the 1920s. The pay was good and the settings where they played were lavish. This latter fact wasn't lost on Tommy Dorsey. He yearned to be part of the high life with the swells. The important society bandleader Meyer Davis, for one, made frequent use of the Dorseys.

Sam Lanin and his brother Howard, Philadelphia natives, had their hometown social scene locked up and put together bands for important New York "400" events, attended by the most prominent socialites. Howard also led his own band on the *Campbell Soup Show* on WEAF, weeknights starting at 7 P.M., which included Tommy.

Lanin was booked for one of the most important society parties of the time: the 1930 coming-out party for the famous debutante and Woolworth heiress Barbara Hutton, which was held on Park Avenue at the Ritz Carlton Hotel in New York. The band was booked to start playing at 11 P.M. A few days before the date, Lanin asked Tommy to play with his band at the party, and he agreed.

On the night of the Hutton party, Lanin was dressed in white tie and tails while conducting the orchestra for the *Campbell Soup Show*, ready to dash off to a party in Montclair, New Jersey, where one of his other bands was playing, before the Hutton party. As soon as the show was over, he turned to Tommy, who was on the platform with the band talking to Manny Klein, and reminded him to be sure to arrive on time at the Ritz Carlton. Tommy replied breezily, "Take it easy. I'll be at the clambake on time!" Lanin, inflamed, asked, "What did you call that?" and Tommy replied, "You hoid me!" Lanin stalked out the door saying, "You Irish son of a bitch, don't you dare come down there!" This was not his first altercation with Tommy. One night during the course of a *Campbell Soup Show* Tommy was drunk and fell off the bandstand.

For versatile musicians, like the Dorseys, there was motion picture work in addition to records, radio, and dance dates. Silent films used pianists, organists, and occasionally full orchestras to play in theater orchestra pits to provide a musical background or "live" soundtrack.

With the release of the Al Jolson film musical *The Jazz Singer* on October 6, 1927, by Warner Brothers, which included only a few lines of dialogue, including Jolson's famous edict, "You ain't heard nothin' yet!" and his singing of six songs, films began to talk, and suddenly music was heard coming from the screen. Within a year, movie attendance had doubled to 95 million tickets sold per week.

Part of the early sound-movie craze was a series of one-reel "shorts" made at the Vitaphone and Paramount studios on Long Island. On one of these shows made in 1929, a mediocre musical-comedy singer named Alice Boulden is seen featured. Tommy is visible in the accompanying band. Another features Harry Reser and his Eskimos, whose radio show was sponsored by Clicquot Club Ginger Ale and had an Arctic motif. Once again, Tommy and his trombone can be seen in a panning shot. This time, however, like all the other "Eskimos" he is dressed in an authentic Native Alaskan parka with hood and boots. The Eskimos' girl singer receives a box of candy from an admirer brought by a Western Union representative. She opens the window of her igloo and then jubilantly breaks into song.

In one of several theater pit-band jobs, the brothers worked for Eugene Ormandy, later the highly respected conductor of the Philadelphia Orchestra. (Ormandy's first job in the United States had been conducting the Dorsey brothers' pit band for the Broadway musical revue *Earl Carrol's Vanities*.) The brothers' frequent colleague Arnold Brillhart once said, "Ormandy would start the downbeat for the overture when he left his apartment and finished it just in time for the music to begin."

Phil Napoleon, a member of the orchestra, which included the Dorseys, that Ormandy conducted for a stage show at the Capitol Theater, remembered, "One day we had just come from Plunkett's [a popular speakeasy]. The show was so boring that when Tommy took his horn apart and started shooting spit balls with the slide into the audience, five patrons grabbed him out of the pit and carried him out to the street while the crowd clapped like hell."

Despite this incident, the Dorsey brothers got along well with Ormandy. He was made the musical director of the newly formed Dorsey Brothers Concert Orchestra's two-sided recording of "Was It a Dream?" for OKeh in July 1928, and the next year he hired them again as sidemen for his Salon Orchestra recordings for OKeh.

At this point, Tommy's freewheeling ways, often fueled by alcohol, added to his growing reputation as a character. At the same time, his musical ability kept him constantly in demand. Although by now he was an alcoholic, he could still be counted on to deliver musically. Toots was worried about his drinking problem but said little about it. She knew better. Tommy didn't take criticism lightly.

He continued to be a big wage earner, and she believed her job was to keep the household going.

According to their cousin Connie Motko, the brothers were doing so well that they each sent home fifty dollars a week and continued to send money to their mother for several years in addition to taking care of their own immediate families.

Tommy's work in movies and musical theater continued to expand. He played an imposing solo on the title song on the soundtrack of *The Broadway Melody*, the popular 1929 MGM film musical. Next, Tommy worked in Billy Rose's Broadway musical version of Vincent Youmans's *Great Day!* which only lasted for thirty-six performances but introduced such important songs as "More Than You Know" (sung by Mayo Methot, who later became Mrs. Humphrey Bogart), "Without a Song," and the title song. The historic stock market crash took place on October 29, 1929, and caused the abrupt closing of *Great Day!*

The Dorseys continued to work together frequently through the fall of 1930 and 1931. Throughout the Great Depression, the country hungered for escapist entertainment, and music was an integral part of it. Top musicians, including Tommy and Jimmy, along with Benny Goodman, Jack Teagarden, Glenn Miller, and Gene Krupa, made up the orchestra that played in the pit at the Alvin Theater on Broadway, under the direction of Red Nichols for the George and Ira Gershwin musical *Girl Crazy*, on its opening night of October 14, 1930. Ethel Merman became a star that night when she introduced "I Got Rhythm."

Tommy estimated that from his various radio and recording sessions and pit-band jobs he was sometimes making as much as $750 a week. As fellow musician Artie Shaw pointed out, "This was at a time when a four course dinner at Delmonico's or Luchow's, two of the foremost restaurants in New York, cost three dollars."

Tommy was rapidly moving up in the world. He had bought a house and moved with Toots and Patsy to Merrick, Long Island. He had a shiny new Buick to drive himself into New York for his heavy work schedule. And his family was growing. On September 9, 1930, months shy of Tommy's twenty-fifth birthday, the Dorseys' second child, a son, Thomas Francis Dorsey III, was born.

Early on, Tommy saw the importance of dressing well and with a certain flair. To him this meant success and position, two things that were very important to him. He also wanted to have the best clothes and the best car, and he wanted to be seen dining at the best restaurants in New York. Money was no object.

For decades in New York, well-established upper-class professionals with the same religious or ethnic backgrounds had had their own clubhouses, for example, the Union League for WASPs, the New York Athletic Club for Catholics, and the City Athletic Club for Jews. The club for musicians in New York in the late 1920s and early 1930s was Plunkett's, a narrow speakeasy located at 205½ West Fifty-third Street, four doors west of Broadway, next to the Elks Club. It was listed in the telephone directory as the Trombone Club; some say that was because Tommy was the hangout's principal customer. There must be some truth to this because in order to be allowed in the password spoken through the peephole was "Tommy Dorsey sent me."

According to Jimmy Dorsey, "One time that I know of he owed eight hundred and fifty dollars to Jimmy Plunkett and the German bartender-philosopher, Gene O'Byrne." Neither Jimmy nor Gene could afford to be mad at Tommy; he owed them too much money.

Barreled beer arrived from Canada via bootleggers on a daily basis, sometimes in a florist's delivery truck, other times in a milk wagon, and once even in a hearse. Above the bar, which extended for ten feet, were a half dozen nondescript beer steins sitting on the shelves. A bulletin board on the wall adjacent to the front door was filled with notes announcing radio, recording, and other types of musical jobs. Contractors in trouble over cancellations by musicians knew exactly where to call to find last-minute replacements. Where else could a musician socialize with his best friends and obtain work as well?

The story goes that one afternoon Tommy Dorsey came into Plunkett's and instructed Jimmy Plunkett, "I'll have to drink in a hurry. I also need a shave. I have a radio program to do at Radio City in half an hour." Standing quietly down the bar was Tommy O'Connor, a former wrestler, who also hailed from Lansford. He had stopped in for a drink and overheard their conversation.

"You'll not have to stir from this place," said one Tommy to the other. "It so happens that I myself am now in the profession you intend to patronize. I am a barber."

O'Connor reached into his vest pocket and took out a straight razor and proceeded to shave Tommy using beer suds for lather and gin for aftershave.

All the Dorsey cohorts spent much of their leisure time there: Red Nichols, Phil Napoleon, the one-armed trumpeter Wingy Manone, clarinetists Pee Wee Russell and Benny Goodman, cornetist Jimmy McPartland, trombonist Glenn Miller, clarinetist and saxophonist Frank Trumbauer, drummer Gene Krupa, Bing Crosby, Jack Teagarden, fellow trombonist Jerry Colonna (later a comedian and sidekick of Bob Hope), pianists Eddy Duchin and Joe Sullivan, trumpeter Manny Klein, Stan King, Miff Mole, cornetist Muggsy Spanier, Eddie Condon, and vocalist Red McKenzie (who led the Mound City Blue Blowers and whose instrument was the kazoo, a tube of plated metal or plastic that amplified the human voice while also imparting a buzzing, rasping quality). Late in the afternoon one might find Bix Beiderbecke and Frank Teschmacher taking a nap (or sleeping off too much drink) in one of the booths in the back room after a difficult record date. The Chicagoans had immigrated en masse to New York in 1928 when the Chicago speakeasies had closed in droves. This was part of a reform movement against the hold Al Capone had maintained on the Windy City.

There was a large refrigerator at Plunkett's, the kind with a door you could open and walk into. Eddie Condon used to keep his entire wardrobe there. Before a Mound City Blue Blowers job he would use it as the star's dressing room.

Many instruments also found a home there, from Jimmy Dorsey's famous collection of gold saxophones, to Pee Wee Russell's crud-caked clarinet, to Bix's cornet in a corduroy sack, to pianist Arthur Schutt's gold-headed cane. Laundry, raccoon coats, and baggage belonging to the regulars were also stored in the refrigerator.

There was no class distinction practiced here. Plunkett's clientele was composed of radio and studio musicians as well as stars. But there were no black musicians among the regulars. They were rarely hired for recording and radio work. Black musicians knew the way it worked but could do little to change it.

During this period, the Cotton Club was thriving in Harlem. Black orchestras led by Duke Ellington and Cab Calloway were the main attractions; the clientele, however, was exclusively white. Segregation, even in music, both onstage and in the audience, prevailed. It was the system.

During a 1951 *Kraft Music Hall* radio show, hosted by Bing Crosby, Bing reminisced with Tommy about Plunkett's, referring to it as "the old lending library." Tommy recalled, "Some days we did so much reading there we came out blind," and Bing remarked, "We certainly soaked up a lot of knowledge."

Pat Dorsey Hooker laughingly recalled that during one of Bing's visits to their Merrick home, her father and Bing began brewing their own beer in the basement bathtub. "Daddy bought a brand new broom for him and Bing to stir up their concoction. I charged my girl friends a nickel a piece so that they could look at Bing from the outside of the basement windows." (Tommy made it a habit of developing and bottling his own homemade brew with his own bottling machine throughout Prohibition.)

The late trumpeter Chris Griffin was a contemporary of Tommy's. Griffin, a highly successful radio (and later television) as well as recording musician, discussed the reasons studio musicians drank so much during this period and how it was thought to be a natural part of the jazz life:

> We would get breaks from radio shows—two or three hours—so we had time to kill. There would be three or four who would go to the nearest bar, which might be Plunkett's. Another group would go to an empty room and play cards and maybe have a sandwich. There was a combination of time to kill and boredom; drinking was an easy thing to do and, of course, it was a stimulant. You got used to it and you could perform at ninety-five percent—I didn't say a hundred percent! If you drank, it gave you a badge of honor. My guess is that Tommy and Jimmy got into that same pattern.

In late June 1933, Tommy collapsed at Plunkett's and had to be carried out and taken to the hospital. He firmly believed his heavy drinking had brought on the attack of appendicitis.

Now, after his appendectomy, the discipline ingrained in him by Pop Dorsey came to his aid. After the operation he vowed to stop drinking entirely. He realized his drinking was beginning to hinder and could possibly destroy what was already a successful musical career. Making a lot of money was Tommy Dorsey's principal motivation throughout his career. He managed to keep his pledge not to drink for close to a decade. Jimmy, on the other hand, except for occasional periods of abstinence, continued as a prodigious drinker.

Plunkett's was the setting for more than a few Dorsey brothers' fights. The musicians got so used to them they paid little attention. Pianist Arthur Schutt was often involved in trying to keep peace between the brothers. Once, Tommy got into an argument with Jimmy at Plunkett's and then went over to the "work" apartment Jimmy shared with Benny Goodman and did his usual number by smashing all of Jimmy's saxophones on the radiator.

In one year, Tommy, sometimes billed as "Tom" Dorsey, recorded with some twenty-two different orchestras. As a sideman, Tommy had also already recorded an astounding total of over two thousand records. It was, therefore, inevitable that the Dorsey brothers would think about recording with their own band.

In 1928, they signed with OKeh Records for the first series of Dorsey Brothers Orchestra (DBO) recordings. The first two tunes were cut on Valentine's Day; "Mary Ann" featured Tommy on trumpet, backed with "Persian Rug." Their many friends in the vast pool of superb New York musicians made up the band's personnel. For a while, Jimmy Crossan, from the Wild Canaries days, played tenor saxophone. Bob Stephens, whom they had known in the Scranton Sirens days, was the recording director at OKeh and arranged the record deal.

By today's musical standards, these were rather typical 1920s-sounding dance-band records that featured exuberant playing with a pronounced joie de vivre. But in addition, they had a contagious spirit that sprang from real camaraderie and first-class musicianship. There were many eventful moments—"Breakaway" featured Tommy on both trombone and trumpet along with Jimmy on alto sax and clarinet. Tommy again played trombone and trumpet on their record of "'Round Evening" in which he made use of his idol, Jack Teagarden, who soloed on trombone. Bing Crosby sang memorably on "The Spell of the Blues" and "She's Funny That Way" (both of which were arranged by Glenn Miller) and "My Kinda Love," which became one of Bing's signature records of the period. These records revealed the continuing refinement of Bing's patented crooning style. "Melancholy Baby" found both the brothers contributing noteworthy solos on trumpet and clarinet, along with Adrian Rollini's extended solo on the difficult to play and cumbersome bass saxophone. Jimmy's nimble clarinet solos predominate on many of these recordings.

The band's precise musicianship paid off commercially. "Yale Blues" was their first (at number twenty) of some twenty-five Billboard Chart–making successes; "Dixie Down" came two months later, hitting the charts on September 18, 1928. Continuing to record sporadically, with three violins added in order to create a more romantic aura on "Cross Roads," and "She's Funny That Way," the DBO had its third chart hit in February 1929 with Smith Ballew's vocal on "Sally of My Dreams." Its biggest success was Bing Crosby's version of Cole Porter's highly risqué "Let's Do It," which reached number nine. "Ooh, That Kiss" was another chart entry in 1931.

These marked the first of almost two hundred recordings of the Dorsey Brothers Orchestra released over a seven-year period. During 1929 and 1930, sometimes the DBO was billed as the Travelers and scored a hit once again with its recording of "Fine and Dandy."

As a respite from all this recording activity, Jimmy finally was able to offer Beebie a honeymoon by accepting an offer from the old vaudevillian and clarinetist Ted Lewis to tour Europe in July 1930 in a band that also included Muggsy Spanier and trombonist George Brunis. (Eddie Condon once remarked, "Ted Lewis could make the clarinet talk. What it said was, 'Put it back in the case.'")

Within minutes of Jimmy and Beebie's return to New York on the ocean liner Île de France, when Tommy met them, the brothers started arguing anew. As usual, it could have been caused by almost anything.

Following their spate of hit recordings, the Dorseys' OKeh record of "Was It a Dream" was used as a demo record. Their band was considered for possible participation in the radio show of the American Oil Company (AMOCO) after a deal with Duke Ellington's orchestra was quashed at the last moment. (This situation marked one of the first commercial opportunities for a black orchestra on radio at the time.) And in a rare mixing of black and white performers, the Dorseys were signed, along with the jazz singer Ethel Waters, when the show debuted on October 23, 1933.

Five weeks later the sponsor spoke to Tommy, who conducted all the business for the DBO, about changing the style of its music for the show. Sponsors, then as now, knew little about what they really wanted and often displayed tone-deaf musical judgment.

"Tommy," he asked, "could you, for instance, make your music sound like George Olsen's?" (a "sweet" band of the time). Tommy quickly replied, "If you like George Olsen, why don't you get him!" The Dorseys abruptly lost the show.

Jimmy was by now almost immune to Tommy's outbursts, deferring to him on almost all business matters. Besides that, he would rather spend his off time drinking or playing golf with fellow musicians.

Artie Shaw remembered an incident in late 1930 at Plunkett's when trumpeter Bunny Berigan formally introduced him to the Dorseys, although he had worked on a radio show with Tommy shortly before that. Shaw was then under police jurisdiction and couldn't leave the New York area after he had an unfortunate automobile accident in which he had killed a man.

The late bandleader remembered that after exchanging pleasantries, "Tommy asked if I could cut [outplay] his brother, while standing right next to Jimmy. I told him, 'I don't think I can. I know I can.' Then Dick McDonough, the guitarist, and a few others talked to Tommy about me. He got curious about me."

Tommy subsequently called Artie about playing a date with the Dorsey Brothers Orchestra at a Yale fraternity party in New Haven, Connecticut, in the spring of 1931. (This may have been a residual booking from their having recorded the hit record "Yale Blues.") This was but one of the dates Tommy booked for the DBO out of an office in the Hammerstein Building.

Seventy-one years later Shaw vividly recalled that night, saying, "That date really made my career as a freelance musician in New York." He also remembered how good the band was and reeled off the names of several members of its all-star thirteen-piece lineup: "Bix, Bunny Berigan, and Charlie Margulis formed the three-man trumpet section; only Bix, of course, was playing cornet. Bud Freeman was in the saxophone section, Arthur Schutt played piano, and Stan King was on drums."

Shaw also had strikingly perceptive observations about the dynamic between the brothers. He continued:

Tommy and Jimmy took turns standing out in front of the band that night. When it was Tommy's turn, I played lead alto, 'cause that's what I did. Jimmy couldn't play lead alto. . . . He didn't like it that I'd cut him. Tommy had me get up and play a chorus, but I played about twelve choruses. Bix put his thumb and index finger around his nose and then touched his ear lobe indicating how much he liked what I'd played.

Jimmy didn't particularly like that, but Tommy was putting him on. He never missed a chance to put Jimmy on. Whatever it was, his motivation was to show Jimmy he was ahead of the ball. You could articulate it in any number of ways, but Tommy was intent on being the boss man. He was younger, but as he grew older he became the boss.

Shaw expressed his appraisal of the brothers' comparative musicianship. He minimized the influence Miff Mole had on Tommy's playing: "Tommy was his own influence! He could do something with a trombone that no one had ever done before. He made it into a singing instrument, but he worked at it. Before that it was a blatting instrument." Shaw pointed out that Tommy worked at developing his prowess as a trombonist, whereas "Jimmy reached his apogee in the mid to late 1920s. He was then the guy to listen to, and then it stopped. He played things like 'Beebie' and 'Oodles of Noodles' [the source tune for "Contrasts," later the theme song of Jimmy's orchestra], stuff like that, and he could play. He had this strange little sound on alto, which just fell by the wayside. Make no mistake about it, though, Tommy was the dominant brother."

In the early 1930s, the personnel of Tommy and Jimmy's orchestra included some of the most imposing new musical talents. One of them was trumpeter Bunny Berigan, whose open, expressive horn on tunes like "Mood Hollywood" is a constant delight. Bunny's playing on several of their records presaged his dominating presence later in that decade when, along with Harry James, he became the most acclaimed big-band trumpet soloist. This was in addition to the Dorseys' association with three of the best female jazz singers: Mildred Bailey, Lee Wiley, and the aforementioned Ethel Waters, along with the Boswell Sisters.

The approach to pop music material and to vocal group singing of the New Orleans–born Boswells was highly original. Their warmth and sense of swing was a true revelation. In 1931 they began recording under the supervision of Jack Kapp at Brunswick Records. Kapp had been the record producer for Al Jolson and now was Bing Crosby's producer. Connee, the leading light of the Boswell Sisters, speaking of working with various Dorsey bands, once said to record producer Michael Brooks, "They were just the greatest bunch of fellows to work with. Crazy, but all wonderful musicians who understood exactly what we were trying to do."

The musical rapport between the Dorseys and Boswell was evident on "Nothing Is Sweeter than You," in which Connee's humming and Tommy's muted trombone combine to carry the melody. On "It's the Girl" and "Put That Sun Back in the Sky," Jimmy's clarinet plays both counterpoint and in unison with the sisters. And then there is Bunny Berigan's solo on "Everybody Loves My Baby," Jimmy's alto on "Sleep Come On and Take Me," and the tribute Tommy paid to Jack Teagarden in his blues playing on "Hand Me Down My Walking Cane." These three gifted soloists combined with Dick McDonough on "Forty-second Street" (which also featured the Boswell Sisters' musical references to "Between the Devil and the Deep Blue Sea"), "Brother, Can You Spare a Dime?" and "Ten Cents a Dance." Connee also recorded on her own with the DBO on "Time on My Hands" and "Me Minus You," the latter with Tommy, Jimmy, and Bunny swinging hard behind her.

Tommy employed Bix Beiderbecke at a time when most bandleaders found him completely unreliable because of his raging alcoholism. He and Tommy worked as sidemen for Benny Goodman, who had put together a band for a Williams College prom in June 1931. Tommy had a recording date in New York, and Bix stayed behind with him when the Goodman band traveled up to Williamstown, Massachusetts. Tommy thought he and Bix could take a train to New Haven, figuring Williams was close to Yale, though actually it was 140 miles away. Instead, they wound up chartering a plane on Long Island to get to the date, flying to North Adams and then to Pittsfield, Massachusetts, before finding an airport to land at. Once they got there, Bix passed out on the bandstand. He died less than two months later.

That same year the Broadway musical *Everybody's Welcome* found Tommy in the pit band while Jimmy was the conductor. Although the production was mildly successful, running 139 performances, it included a ballad called "As Time Goes By," which would languish until drummer turned piano player (at least on-screen) Dooley Wilson sang it in the movie *Casablanca* eleven years later and made it a resounding and enduring hit.

The Dorseys had worked as the backup band for Bing Crosby's records and individually on his CBS radio shows. It was Tommy, then, who first called Bing the "Groaner," referring to him as the "Groaner from Tacoma" (Washington, where Crosby hailed from). The nickname stuck.

By 1933 Bing, who referred to the Dorseys as "genuine geniuses," was a superstar, having registered with tremendous impact on radio and records and in movies. He recorded again with the DBO on the tunes "I've Got the World on a String," "My Honey's Lovin' Arms," "Someone Stole Gabriel's Horn," and "Stay on the Right Side of the Road." Naturally, Bing got top

billing. He liked and admired both Tommy and Jimmy and was very familiar with the difference in their personalities.

By September 1931 305 banks had failed, and in October 522 more closed
their doors. The following year there were 12 million unemployed. Tommy
and Jimmy kept working throughout the Depression even though some of
their recording checks were sometimes slow in coming as record companies, like so many other businesses, were failing as well.

Eddie Condon, in the 1950s, reminisced about Tommy's generosity during
these years in his *New York Journal-American* column "Pro and Condon":

> Back in the early '30s, when things were about as tough for jazz musicians as
> they are for button-shoe manufacturers, Tommy was only a sideman working
> in various bands around New York. But whenever Tommy was eating, they
> ate, too. Many a week he would load up a bunch of hungry musicians in a
> couple of cars and haul us out there [to Merrick], and we'd play ball and
> drink beer and eat as though we hadn't eaten for a week, which in most cases
> was true. Those weekends made a lot of us feel that the weeks of looking for
> and never finding any work were actually worth it. Tommy was the greatest
> host I've ever known in my life.

In the winter of 1934, with much of America still immersed in desperate
financial straits, Tommy, confident of his own abilities as a musician and
bandleader, convinced Jimmy that they could succeed with their own orchestra. Their own, lucrative musical endeavors away from the DBO would have
to cease so they could concentrate on the Dorsey Brothers Orchestra.

Tommy figured that their band had already registered significantly on
records. With the repeal of Prohibition, nightclubs that hired dance orchestras would provide important opportunities. He and Jimmy had played
enough college dates so the college students certainly knew them, and these
institutions continued to have sizable budgets for prom dates. Beyond that,
plenty of ballrooms wanted to hire them, and their records were constantly
being programmed on the radio. Tommy figured the best was yet to come.

3

"I'll Never Say
'Never Again' Again"

Bruce Springstein is known as "The Boss"; to me
Tommy Dorsey was the real "Boss."

—KAY WEBER

FROM TIME to time previously, the Dorseys had briefly considered
trying seriously to succeed with their own orchestra. Now there were
two prime catalysts that encouraged the Dorseys to go out on their own. The
first was the partnership of Tommy Rockwell and Cork O'Keefe. The importance of the Rockwell-O'Keefe talent agency in establishing the Dorsey
Brothers Orchestra is often overlooked, as is the part other talent agencies
played in launching various big bands during the 1930s.

The other catalyst was Alton (Glenn) Miller, who had been with the
DBO from its inception. Besides a top booking office to book it on the road,
a new band also needed a first-rate library of arrangements, and Miller delivered them. Miller, then sporting a mustache, was the DBO's musical director and arranger, as well as one of its trombonists.

Rockwell had started in the music business as a Columbia Records salesman, succeeding Jack Kapp as the label's Chicago branch manager. He then
signed several artists to the label, including two such diverse personalities
as the notorious evangelist Aimee Semple McPherson and the blues immortal Mississippi John Hurt.

Rockwell met Louis Armstrong, who at the time was recording for OKeh Records, and signed him to Columbia, producing Louis's highly influential "Hot Five" and "Hot Seven" albums. This led to his becoming Louis's personal manager for two years, beginning in 1929.

He next moved over to Brunswick Records, where Jack Kapp was in charge. At Brunswick he produced records for the Boswell Sisters. When Brunswick was incorporated into the new American Decca Records, he produced, among others, Bing Crosby, the Mills Brothers (whom he discovered), the Casa Loma Orchestra, and the Dorsey Brothers Orchestra.

His partner, the agent Francis "Cork" O'Keefe, had started in the music business with Jean Goldkette's booking office. He was the agent for the Goldkette band when Tommy Dorsey was with Goldkette and had mediated the altercation at the Book-Cadillac Hotel in Detroit involving Tommy. In 1929 he signed the Casa Loma Band to a personal management contract. Within a year, under his direction, the band was on its way to stardom. Since Tommy Rockwell was the Casa Loma's record producer, it was only natural that the two would meet. They soon became fast friends and in 1933 decided to form a talent agency.

Rockwell-O'Keefe was an important entity almost from the outset. Rockwell parlayed his success as an A&R (artists and repertoire) man to become an agent, which gave him a certain cachet with the musicians he recorded. From this vantage point, he was able to evaluate the commercial value of various artists. He brought Bing Crosby, the Boswell Sisters, and the Mills Brothers with him to add to O'Keefe's representation of the Casa Lomans. Supersalesman Rockwell and the more reserved and deep-thinking O'Keefe, coming from opposite yet closely related aspects of the business, proved to be a winning combination.

In a short time their agency emerged as a serious rival to Jules Stein's firmly entrenched MCA (Music Corporation of America), which had branched out from booking bands in the Chicago area to setting its sights on signing nationally known orchestras. It now became Tom Rockwell's mission to firmly establish the Dorsey Brothers Orchestra.

The dour Miller, born March 1, 1904, in Clarinda, Iowa, but raised in Fort Morgan, Colorado, had briefly attended the University of Colorado and then begun working with territory bands. An invitation to join the Ben Pollack band in 1926 brought him to New York. From 1926 to 1934, he was a member of the bands of Paul Ash, Red Nichols, Benny Goodman, and Smith Ballew. Glenn had first become friendly with Tommy and Jimmy Dorsey while working with them as recording-studio and radio musicians.

Through this association, they developed considerable respect for Miller's writing ability. For much of the next decade, the careers of Tommy and Glenn would closely parallel one another.

At the outset Glenn made an economic decision that affected the size of the band. The Dorsey Brothers Orchestra would consist of only eleven musicians, including the coleaders. (For the most part, Tommy stood out in front of the band since Jimmy wasn't always diplomatic with the customers.) Its unusual instrumental lineup called for only four brass (one trumpet and three trombones, with Tommy sporadically doubling on trumpet), three reeds (which included Jimmy playing alto and clarinet and also occasionally dabbling on trumpet, cornet, and baritone saxophone), a four-piece rhythm section, and a girl and a boy singer.

In spite of these musical limitations, Miller was confident that he could write the proper voicings for such a small-sized big band. Ray McKinley, the band's splendid drummer, acknowledged, "The emphasis on the trombones was to give the band a Bing Crosby quality. The Dorseys had often played for Bing, and they felt that they could achieve some relationship importance if they pitched their sound like his." (In view of Rockwell's close association with Crosby, one wonders if this was perhaps not a suggestion of Rockwell's that the Dorseys and Miller bought into.) Tommy admitted, "We were trying to hit somewhere between Hal Kemp [a sweet band] and the Casa Loma Band."

The Dorsey Brothers Orchestra's musical approach, however, stands out in stark contrast to "the wall of brass," the trademark sound of the sixteen-member Casa Loma Orchestra. An offshoot of one of Jean Goldkette's bands, and originally titled the Orange Blossoms, in 1928 the band had been scheduled to play an engagement at the Casa Loma, a chateau outside Toronto built by its millionaire owner to house the visit of Edward Windsor, the celebrated prince of Wales. The gig never materialized, but the exotic name of the locale stuck and was adopted by the orchestra.

The driving arrangements of such instrumentals as "No Name Jive," "Casa Loma Stomp," "White Jazz," "Black Jazz," "Wild Goose Chase," and "Maniac's Ball," the latter written by the guitarist, Gene Gifford, helped make the Casa Loma the first important white jazz orchestra and a favorite of the college crowd. It was a co-op band consisting of formidable soloists—clarinetist Clarence Hutchenrider, trombonists Billy Rausch and Pee Wee Hunt, trumpeter Sonny Dunham, and drummer Tony Briglia (whom drummer Buddy Rich acknowledged as his first inspiration)—under the leadership of its lead alto saxophonist, the handsome and debonair Glen Gray

(Knoblaugh). The Casa Loma's strong esprit de corps was reflected in its exacting musicianship and elegant appearance on the bandstand.

Arranger Lyle "Spud" Murphy, who at ninety-seven, resembles a cross between such one-time Hollywood leading men as William Powell and John Gilbert, prides himself on his photographic memory. He recalls the night in early 1935 when he caught the Casa Loma band during its extended engagement at the Essex House in New York when Pinky Tomlin, one of the songwriters of "The Object of My Affection," asked him to arrange the tune so he could submit it to the band. The arrangement was accepted and later recorded. In the next two years Murphy contributed seventy-four charts to the Casa Loma band.

At the same time, Spud was also writing for Benny Goodman's newly organized band, which was about to make its debut as one of three orchestras on NBC's *Let's Dance* radio program. One night Goodman, for whom Spud was to write a total of 102 arrangements, came into the Essex House to see the Casa Loma band. "He really was there to see if I was writing the good stuff for the Casa Loma instead of for him," Murphy recalled with a gentle smile, "but the two bands were much different. The Casa Loma was a section orchestra—four trumpets [playing] against four trombones or all of them at once, whereas Goodman had a sectionless band with lots of solos."

Murphy preferred the Casa Loma band to the Dorsey Brothers Orchestra. The Casa Loma band "was a well oiled machine and the musicians were absolutely impeccable in their playing," he contends. "The Dorseys had a smaller band with more solos all the time, whereas the Casa Loma, it was mostly ensemble stuff." Nevertheless, Murphy agreed that at least at the outset, the Dorsey Brothers had a looseness that neither the Casa Loma band nor the Goodman band possessed. He believed praise was due Ray McKinley for the snap that the Dorsey Brothers Orchestra exhibited.

Glenn Miller was as much of a perfectionist as Tommy and Jimmy. In the role of putting together absolutely the right blend of musicians to play his arrangements, Glenn brought in almost half of the band's initial start-up personnel. They got there by a series of fortunate twists.

In late 1933, Miller had become the arranger and quasi leader of Smith Ballew's orchestra at the Cosmopolitan Hotel in Denver. The band was offered a location date at a nightclub on Long Island the following March. The musicians made the jaunt east in various cars. But for guitarist Roscoe "Roc" Hillman, alto saxophonist Skeets Herfurt, and trombonist Don Mattison, getting from Denver to New York was anything but easy, as the ninety-four-year-old Hillman recalled:

The three of us . . . drove east in a convertible through one of the worst snowstorms in years. In some localities there were rainstorms followed by snowstorms. Of course, there were no freeways in those days, but somehow we made the trip in a little over three days. By the time we got to New York the job had fallen through.

We checked into the Manhattan Towers Hotel, which Glenn got for us. I'll forever consider him my benefactor. A few nights later he asked us, "Are you fellas going to be around this evening?" He didn't even tell us [that] he was bringing Tommy Dorsey up to the apartment we had taken. We couldn't believe it. Tommy asked me to get out my guitar and play the song I had written, "Long May We Love." Don Mattison got out his trombone and played it with me. Then Tommy said, "Let me see that." He took Don's trombone and sight-read the lead sheet while I accompanied him on guitar. We played the song and, man, I was ten feet tall!

Tommy said he would talk with his management office of Rockwell-O'Keefe. He took the sheet music of "Long May We Love" to O'Keefe, and soon the Casa Loma band recorded it. Then he talked to Jimmy. They thought the time was right to start their own band. About a week or so later, Ray McKinley, and the three of us, plus the girl singer [with the Smith Ballew Band], Kay Weber, joined us in the Dorsey Brothers Orchestra. I think we got forty or fifty dollars a week, no more than that, when we started playing with the band. It was like a fairy tale to us. We knew of the Dorseys' importance. We used to sit in Skeets's basement in Denver and listen to their records.

Vocalist Kay Weber had made the same arduous trip with Glenn and his wife, Helen Miller, and pianist "Chummy" MacGregor. (Their journey was later the basis of a scene in the Universal film biography *The Glenn Miller Story*.) Shortly after their arrival in New York, Glenn and Helen took Kay out to Tommy's house in Merrick, where several other musicians had gathered to meet the Dorseys for the first time. "I accompanied myself on piano and sang for them that night," she recalled. This was her entrée to becoming the girl singer for the Dorseys.

What followed were weeks of intense rehearsals in a rehearsal room within the office suite of Rockwell-O'Keefe in Rockefeller Center, starting in the evening and often lasting all night. "Sandman," written by Bonnie Lake, sister of the late film and television star Ann Sothern (Harriet Lake), was selected as the band's theme song with Tommy and Jimmy naturally each taking solos.

They weren't naturally cooperating as leaders, however. Ray McKinley recalled, "The Dorseys were screaming at each other during the second rehearsal. Jimmy yelled, 'I suppose you think that means you're the boss,' and Tommy yelled right back, 'You know damn well I'm the boss because I can talk louder than you.'"

Tom Rockwell set up an audition for a job at Billy Rose's Music Hall, but instead Benny Goodman's band got it. A series of one-nighters in the Northeast was set for the late spring of 1934 to begin to get the band known by a young audience before a major New York area gig could be secured.

During the tour, the Dorsey Brothers Orchestra played at the Lakewood Ballroom, near Lansford, on June 14, 1934. The Dorseys were friends of the owner of Lakewood, Daniel Guinan. (Their heirs still own the property where the imposing ballroom once stood on the crest of a hill.) It was a night of triumph for Tommy and Jimmy.

Frank Riordan still remembers the exact date because that night one of the Guinans came up to the microphone to announce that Max Baer had just knocked out Primo Carnera to become the heavyweight champion of the world:

> I was standing right next to Pop Dorsey—real close to the bandstand. I saw Jimmy look up at Tommy and point to his saxophone and his clarinet and ask, "Which?" Tommy pointed to the sax and the band started to play the next tune. Jimmy stood up and walked out in front of the band holding his alto saxophone. He saw his father and bowed to him in recognition and then blew the hell out of the horn on his famous chorus from "Tiger Rag," which was often played at the end of a set. The houselights were turned down, and I can sort of remember that Jimmy wore a jeweled ring on his little finger of his left hand. The spotlight bounced off that jewel.

Glenn Miller's biographer, George T. Simon, then a student and would-be drummer attending Harvard, witnessed the infant Dorsey Brothers Orchestra at the Nuttings-on-the-Charles Ballroom a few weeks later. Simon recalled standing transfixed in front of the bandstand with several of his fellow college musicians, amazed at "the huge sound coming from just eleven men." To Simon and his friends, the band was much more swinging than Glen Gray and the Casa Loma Orchestra. Simon praised Glenn Miller's charts of "St. Louis Blues," "Dinah," "Honeysuckle Rose," and "Stop, Look and Listen," which made frequent use of riffs, rhythmic interludes, and fade-outs.

Casa Loma was still the bigger draw, however. At Amherst College, the crowd was made up of the overflow from another dance on campus, which featured the Casa Loma band. When the Dorsey Brothers wrapped up their break-in tour, appearing at the General Motors Auto Show in Brooklyn, Jean Goldkette fronted the band because the promoters insisted that "The Dorsey Brothers name doesn't mean anything."

Almost immediately, the comely and dignified Kay Weber registered equally with the coleaders and the audience with her superb ballad singing. Weber revealed in a recent interview that she was called on to dance with some of the unaccompanied men at college proms. They'd inquire, "Whose band is this? "The Dorsey Brothers. Isn't it wonderful?" she'd respond. The answer was usually "Never heard of them."

A boy singer to work alongside her had been hired but quickly fired. Perhaps on Bing's prodding, Tommy Rockwell suggested one of his other clients, Bob Crosby, Bing's brother, as his replacement. The younger Crosby had been singing with Anson Weeks's Orchestra in San Francisco.

Bob Crosby had a hard time in the band from the start. According to Weber:

> Tommy resented the suggestion that the vocalist chose him, and he took it out on Bob, who was a pretty scared kid at the time. He began needling him when the office insisted he sing on the next radio broadcast, which was our opening night at the Sands Point Bath Club.
>
> At the rehearsal that afternoon, Tommy kept calling off names of tunes and saying, "Can you sing this one and that one?" and Bob kept saying, "No" until finally George Thow [trumpeter Bunny Berigan's replacement], who was a Harvard graduate and never talked much, called out from the back of the band, "CAN YOU SING?!" It was cruel but it broke the tension, and even Tommy laughed. Bob was terribly embarrassed.

As a final humiliation, Roc Hillman remembers Tommy saying to Bob, just before the start of a subsequent recording session, "Why did I have to hire the *wrong* Crosby!"

Today, listening to the individual records recorded by the Crosby brothers with the Dorsey Brothers Orchestra, it's difficult at first to distinguish which Crosby brother is singing. Soon, however, one hears the difference.

There's no comparison in their technique: Bing is considerably looser, already well on his way to becoming a master interpreter of lyrics, and, from listening to Louis Armstrong, by the 1930s, he exhibited an unfailing sense of time.

Bob Crosby later claimed, "I was singing songs out of my range. Tommy wouldn't have anything made up for me, and I would sing stock arrangements or whatever I could find. I developed a vibrato it took me twenty years to overcome. I was unhappy."

Roc Hillman put it simply: "Bob was a sad character. He wasn't up to the standard of the other guys in the band. Tommy didn't hold back on his feelings toward him, which didn't affect the rest of the band too much."

According to Hillman:

The band turned out real good. Of course, we had the finest musicians. . . . We had formed a vocal trio—Don, Skeets, and myself. On the way to New York we sang to pass the time so we had some practice. Maybe that was one of the things that Glenn sold Tommy and Jimmy on. We became The Dorsey Brothers Trio. When we got up to sing, the bass fiddle dropped out. We didn't like that too much, so in time—just a few weeks—they moved me over to the guitar, which was my first instrument. I managed to take some lessons from George Van Eps, who was way ahead of all the other guitar players of the time. He changed the outlook on my playing.

In August 1934 the Dorsey brothers had switched on paper from Brunswick to Decca Records under Jack Kapp when he became recording director of the American branch of the label. Among the mixture of ballads, vocals, up-tempo tunes, and Dixieland jams recorded presumably during an all-day session that took place on August 23, 1934, was the double entendre novelty song "Annie's Cousin Fannie," which featured Tommy, Don Mattison, Skeets Herfurt, Kay Weber, and even Glenn Miller singing a chorus each. How such a song with several risqué lyrics (working off the word *fanny*) got played on the radio at this time is rather a mystery. The Hays Office was governing the censorship of sex and violence in Hollywood, and it was thought a similar code would soon prevail on radio.

During the same record date, the band cut some of its best records: "Milenberg Joys," "St. Louis Blues" (with George Thow's muted solos and Bob Crosby's vocal), and the two-sided hit "Honeysuckle Rose." On the latter, after a rather perfunctory saxophone chorus, there are solos by both brothers, George Thow, and Skeets Herfurt, and Bobby Van Eps on piano, as well as a zesty vocal by The Dorsey Trio. Once again, Glenn Miller's arranging touch is shown by the unusual way the trombones support Jimmy's solo and Glenn's effective use of dynamics in the ensemble passages. Late in September, a salute to Tommy's wife was recorded, which was entitled, "Okay Toots." During 1934 alone, the Dorseys' recorded output totaled almost sixty tracks.

But in the course of their recording there was one great song that got away. Kay Weber sang a beautiful ballad for which Miller had written both the words and the music. "I sang it at a recording session when it was called 'Gone With The Dawn.' When we finished a good take, Glenn told Jack Kapp and Tommy and Jimmy that they shouldn't release it. 'The lyric isn't good enough,' he protested. So it wasn't released. Years later, he collaborated with the celebrated lyricist of 'Star Dust,' Mitchell Parish, who wrote a brand-new lyric. It turned out to be the song that became a big hit for Glenn—his theme song, 'Moonlight Serenade.'"

These recordings were made in New York simultaneously with the key summer-long booking at the Sands Point Bath Club in Port Washington, Long Island, due to Jimmy's friendship with its president. The club had become well known two months earlier when the "Kingfish," the notorious Huey Long, then governor of Louisiana, was assaulted on the premises by a club member who disagreed with his populist political beliefs.

The band was such a hit with the swells on the North Shore that NBC requested that the club's board of governors allow the band to do remote broadcasts from there three nights a week. Approval, however, took almost a month, but *Billboard,* on September 8, 1934, conspicuously headlined, "NBC has set a wire at The Sands Point Club, where Tommy Dorsey and his orchestra are now playing, and Huey Long doesn't play anymore."

The band was resplendent in double-breasted blue blazers and white shoes, the perfect garb for this WASP venue. In the years ahead impressive-looking clothes would be an important visual aspect of any Tommy Dorsey band. Kay Weber, usually attired in evening gowns, remembers that the look of the Dorsey Brothers Orchestra was another of Tommy's decisions.

Remote broadcasts were extremely important in introducing dance bands and helping to build them into attractions. They became a staple of evening network radio.

On the night of the Dorsey Brothers Orchestra's first network broadcast there was a severe storm—thunder, lightning, wind, and rain—and then the lights went out. During the first set, the band valiantly played its arrangements by memory. Jimmy asked, "Mac, how are we going to do the broadcast without any lights?" Tommy, always prepared to handle almost any situation, disappeared and returned with enough candles to light all the musicians' music stands. He had taken them away from the waiters, who were trying to calm the screaming patrons. The candlelight and the Dorseys' music had a soothing effect, and the performance proceeded flawlessly.

Immediately afterward another important engagement began on September 19 at Ben Marden's Riviera, across the Hudson River from New York in Fort Lee, New Jersey. The *New York Times* advertisement hailed the appearance of the prominent song-and-dance-man Harry Richman "and introducing the Dorsey Brothers and their Orchestra with Bob Crosby, Bing's glorious-voiced young brother!" Another NBC feed on Thursday night emanated from there at 11:30 P.M. Ray McKinley created a minor furor by shooting rubber bands and bursting the girl dancers' bubbles onstage.

The two New York area engagements were the prelude to a highly coveted booking that began on October 18, 1934, which lasted until early 1935 at the Palais Royale, where the Dorseys had last played with Paul Whiteman. The band played for dancing preceding and following a musical revue that featured, among others, the tenor Morton Downey. Once again the band got valuable radio exposure on WEAF, by now NBC's Red Network station, at 7:15 P.M. and at 11:30 P.M. on WJZ, its Blue Network station.

The DBO was gaining stature fast. The band's musicians firmly believed it was headed for ultimate success.

Tommy was still on the wagon. He was a regular at certain bars where the bartenders would keep cases of sarsaparilla for him. "He would drink it all night," recalled Weber, "it was a drink like root beer."

One night at the Palais Royale, a scene occurred that would have countless variations over the years. Bobby Van Eps, George's brother and the band's pianist, became very angry with Tommy and, while the relief band was playing, told him, "I'm just tired of your nonsense, Tommy. I'm giving you my notice right now."

Kay Weber recalled, "Tommy leaped at him like a tiger. Bobby fell back against the backstage clothes rack where the chorus girls' costumes were hung and became tangled up in it. Tommy screamed that he was going to kill him and kept pummeling him. I was scared silly!" Nevertheless, Van Eps stayed with the band. "Tommy had a way of sweet-talking musicians who wanted to leave and often succeeded in getting them to change their mind," Weber noted. There were no changes in the personnel of the DBO in the last nine months of its existence.

Weber maintained a keen respect for Tommy based on his extraordinary musicianship and leadership. "There was also a side of him that could be very lovable," she opined. Yet Weber, too, felt the sting of Tommy's whiplash temperament:

> At the Palais Royale, I was singing "I'm Okay." There was an optional trombone solo. Tommy played it when he felt like playing it. One night he refused to look at me so as to cue me. We were on the air. Do I sing it or not?
>
> Well, I'm damned if I do, and I'm damned if I don't. I went up to the microphone and started singing. He decided he wanted to play it. Well, he came right up to the microphone and whispered these curse words while I was on the air singing. He was mad because I didn't "read him" correctly.
>
> I had to keep my focus because I started trembling. I walked over to him after the set was over and said, "Look, I never heard my father curse, and I'm not taking it from you. What you tried to do to me was really rotten, and I quit." Ray McKinley and the guys from Denver and just about all the guys said, "Ray Noble will take you right away." Then Tommy came over and did the sweet talk, "I'm sorry, Mac. I'll make a star of you if you'll forgive me"— the blah, blah, blah! Mac was the name he gave to anybody he liked.

Tommy set the musical direction for the DBO with some output from Jimmy. The brothers continued to have great faith in Glenn Miller's suggestions, in addition to his arrangements.

In November the band recorded the title song from Cole Porter's new Broadway musical, "Anything Goes" and "You're the Top," both of which featured Ray McKinley's vocals. The former was another Billboard Pop Chart hit; interestingly, the high-stepping tempo of the latter closely resembles the society beat of this and other Porter tunes which for years were the trademark of Lester Lanin's band. In another recording from the same score, "I Get A Kick Out of You" was an example of Kay Weber's perfect fit with Porter material.

Weber contrasted the brothers' leadership styles: "If Jimmy wasn't pleased with something he would very quietly needle somebody. Tommy would yell to high heaven. They were coleaders, but Tommy usually got his way. Tommy was the dynamic one of the duo. He had such charm and was so charismatic that when he walked into a room you *knew* he was there *absolutely*."

After a time Miller had become increasingly weary of the unceasing arguments between the Dorseys, making conducting his arrangements at rehearsals virtually impossible. Often, he had to serve as an intermediary between them during their frequent serious arguments. When Ray Noble invited Glenn to put together an orchestra to debut at the Rainbow Grill in New York, he readily accepted the offer.

On Glenn's departure, Joe Yukl took over his trombone chair. Yet Glenn continued to supply arrangements for the band. In the meantime, Bobby Van Eps, Herb Spencer, and others also contributed charts for the band.

Ray McKinley pointed out that some of their most exciting numbers were strictly "head arrangements. We'd make them up as we went along. . . . You know, somebody would come up with a riff, and somebody would add something else, and soon we'd have an arrangement all wrapped up."

In less than a year, and in spite of their volatile relationship, the Dorsey brothers had made significant progress with their orchestra both artistically and commercially. Revered *Variety* editor Abel Green included them in a front-page article entitled, "Rating the Dansapators," on the emergence of a "second generation of new b.o. [box office] orchestras": "The Dorseys have come to the attention in recent months strictly on a radio and disc rep." (At that time, powerful disk jockeys on radio in metropolitan areas, such as Martin Block in New York and Al Jarvis in Los Angeles, could single-handedly "make" a hit record for a big band.)

Like most bandleaders (Woody Herman was perhaps one of the few exceptions), Tommy didn't like being upstaged by another soloist, even at a recording session. But Tommy's jealousy went to another level. In the midst of the recording of the Dorseys' twelve-inch version of Duke Ellington's "Solitude," which featured Kay Weber's vocal, trumpeter Charlie Spivak's solo made a much greater impact than Tommy's solo. Spivak, who had replaced George Thow, told Frank Riordan that after a particularly good take that followed, Tommy made him record the next take in the hallway outside the recording studio, which therefore lessened the sound, much less the impact of his solo.

Strange as his own behavior often was, Tommy was highly conformist in certain respects and intolerant of idiosyncrasy. Skeets Herfurt was a musician whom Tommy often mocked. "He couldn't ridicule him for his playing or singing," pointed out Kay Weber. "Herfurt was, however, a nondrinker and a health nut whose behavior, therefore, ran counter to the thinking of most young musicians. Herfurt watched his weight, maintained a carefully planned diet, and lifted weights. He even insisted on sitting in a certain position on and off the bandstand so that his diet would take hold. Weber recalled that Herfurt's barbells would occasionally fall off his seat on the bus and roll down the aisle."

Weber commented further that Ray McKinley considered himself the intellectual in the band, even though he'd left high school at fifteen, and George Thow boasted a Harvard education. McKinley tried to represent the musicians' point of view when they had serious problems with Tommy. By early 1935 there was a growing resentment toward Tommy's actions.

After a plethora of recording activity in January and February 1935 that encompassed twenty-six tracks, a tour of Pennsylvania and New England preceded the band's first excursion into the Midwest. Weber recalled:

Tommy very rarely rode with the band on the bus. Jimmy rode with us, and some of the wives would ride with us, too. Tommy always had to get there faster. He always had to be number one. One day, around Altoona, Pennsylvania, while we were on our way to the Midwest, Tommy's car zipped by us at probably about eighty miles an hour and then pulled up in front of the bus, and the bus pulled to the side of the road. When the bus driver opened the door, Tommy strode onto the bus.

He was crying like a baby, absolutely bawling, when he came in and said, "Everybody in this band hates my guts!" Everybody was so embarrassed and so surprised! Ray McKinley was very articulate. He stood up and said, "Well, Tommy, nobody hates you, but we hate your behavior a lot of the time. When you organized this band, you led us to believe that you were picking people that were decent people as well as good musicians and we expect to be treated as such. You have treated us in a very bad way at times, and it's not that anybody hates you, but we don't like your behavior." Suddenly, Tommy stopped crying, and he was "I love you, Mac!" and all that kind of stuff. He was [suddenly] as happy as a clam. This happened when Jimmy was there. He didn't say a word.

No one in the band could dispute Tommy's talent as a trombonist, which, in fact, served as an inspiration. For the most part, they also looked up to his take-charge style of leadership. His constant pursuit of perfection, however, was sometimes grating. The charm and humor he displayed were often a welcome relief.

Always on the lookout for new talent, and quick to recognize musical prowess, Tommy could be both solicitous and charming in his pursuit of hiring a young musician. Speaking generally about Tommy's way of discovering young musicians, former trombonist Bobby Byrne observed, "He had an innate way of bringing talent together for his benefit. He had a great lyrical sense in his playing, and that was transformed into his business approach. Of course, it was Tommy and Jimmy who put me in the music business."

While playing a date in the spring of 1935 at the Fox Theater in Detroit, Tommy was invited by Clarence Byrn, the head of the music department at Cass Tech High School, to attend a performance of the student band led by his trombonist son, Bobby. The affable former musician, record producer, and recording executive, Bobby Byrne (who added an *e* to the family name, which had originally been O'Byrn), remembered, "We played five or six selections and then Tommy invited me to come backstage after the band's performance at the theater to say hello to 'The Brother,' as he referred to Jimmy. I had never heard of the Dorseys because I was too busy taking care of my high school duties. Then I heard them play, and of course, I was impressed. It was their final day at the theater. They were playing next northeast of Detroit, about forty miles away, at a place called Walled Lake. Tommy suggested, 'Why don't you come along, and you'll hear the band on a one-nighter.' I didn't even know what a one-nighter was."

Byrne sat in with the band. The young musician quickly grasped the power dynamics between the brothers: "Jimmy was in the band. . . . Tommy was the boss, and you'd better recognize it! He had an overpowering personality and a [particular] way of dealing with things. Tommy said to me, 'You sit here,' and it turned out to be his seat—actually his chair. There were notes on the page, and it was in the key I could play in. I played for about five or ten minutes, not extensive at all." (Roc Hillman, however, still remembers how taken the brothers, as well as the band, were with the teenager's playing.)

"At that point," Byrne recalled, "I thanked them, probably halfway through the evening and said good-bye, and that was that. And I never thought of a thing until about a month later, when an agent named Cork O'Keefe called me."

From Michigan the band crossed over to Toronto and then began a string of twenty one-nighters in a month starting in Erie, Pennsylvania, then back to Cleveland before heading east through Pennsylvania. To conclude this grueling tour, it was up to New Hampshire, Massachusetts, Connecticut, and down to Baltimore before returning to the Apple.

Before the tour was over, Bob Crosby, tired of Tommy's taunting, gave him his notice, even though his vocals on hit records like "Lost in a Fog," "I Believe in Miracles," "What a Difference a Day Made" (which reached number five on the Billboard Chart), and "Lullaby of Broadway" (a number-one record), had significantly contributed to the band's popularity.

Well aware of the untenable situation between Tommy and Bob Crosby, Tommy Rockwell had found a graceful exit for Crosby. A sterling group of musicians—trumpeter Yank Lawson, tenor saxophonist Eddie Miller, clarinetist and alto saxophonist Matty Matlock, bassist Bob Haggart, and drummer Ray Bauduc among them—had bolted from Ben Pollack's aggregation and were in search of a leader for their newly formed co-op band. Within several months of its formation, Bob Crosby and His Orchestra, featuring the Bobcats (the Dixieland group within the band), started to make an impression and went on to become one of the leading orchestras of the time. Here, in addition to his singing, Bob's talent as an emcee, first on display with the Dorsey brothers, was of decided importance in the success of his band.

On their trip home, the Dorseys played a date in Troy, New York, on April 29, 1935. The police there had hired a young man from neighboring Hoosick Falls named Bob Eberly (originally Eberle) to sing at intermission on the date. He came onstage wielding a four-string guitar, but it was his voice that scored a big hit. Already a winner of the "Allen's Amateur Hour" segment of Fred Allen's radio show, Eberly had continued working around the Troy area when the Dorseys discovered him.

Tommy asked the young singer to come on the band right away. Decades later Eberly related how deeply impressed he was from the start by Tommy's tremendous drive and energy. He grasped the underlying reasons for Tommy's side of the tension that existed between him and "The Brother" as perhaps few other did:

> He was doing everything—leading the band, making up the radio programs and all the things a leader does. He resented Jimmy for several reasons. For one thing, Jimmy was drinking quite a lot, and Tommy, even though he may have wanted to, didn't. That alone made him mad. But then Jimmy used to needle Tommy, too. He'd just sit there in the saxes, and when Tommy was

leading he'd make cracks like, "Smile, Mac!" and "You're the big star!" and that sort of thing. Tommy just kept working harder. I remember how he used to drive himself. He never had more than five hours sleep a night.

Tommy was asserting himself in ways apart from the deep personal and artistic differences with Jimmy. With his purchase of Tall Oaks, a 20½-acre estate in Bernardsville, New Jersey, in April 1935 for the sum of $32,000 Tommy was about to make a significant status statement. (A listing in the *New York Times* real estate section in December 2002 advertised a newly constructed colonial estate with eight acres in Bernardsville on the market for $5,499,000!) In essence, while America was mired in the Great Depression, Tommy Dorsey was telling the world, "I came from a working-class background, but I am an extremely successful musician. I am a self-made millionaire!"—this was at a time when being a millionaire was truly significant.

His new home was located right off Route 202, seven miles from Morristown, New Jersey, in the heart of the horse country. This area later was made famous by its renowned part-time resident Jacqueline Kennedy Onassis, who owned an estate in the vicinity; its irrepressible congresswoman Milicent Fenwick; and former New Jersey governor and U.S. secretary of the interior Christie Todd Whitman.

The Dorsey family moved into the house in late April, not long after Patsy's tenth birthday. Nine of its sixteen rooms were bedrooms. Throughout, Tall Oaks (later referred to as the Brick House) reflected the sense of taste and elegance that its proud owner brought to music.

There were seven fireplaces; a swimming pool was put in two years later, designed and built by the man who had been responsible for Bing Crosby's pool and whom Dorsey brought to New Jersey in order to duplicate it; tennis courts; and two apartments for staff (which numbered six people) over the garage. Several years later, a wall was built around the house and barbed wire installed atop the wall. An electric remote was installed at the gate, a device considerably ahead of its time, as was one of the first high-fidelity sound systems, which Dorsey had installed on the third floor.

It was here that Tommy Dorsey made one of his first innovations after buying the house. He had a large area on the top floor gutted and turned into a dormitory, complete with bunk beds and five showers, to accommodate the band and other guests on weekends. There was a wet bar as well.

The first-floor dining room had a huge block of anthracite located in a prominent place as a reminder not only to Tommy, but to everyone else, of where he had come from and how far he had gone from his humble origins. Justifiably, his new home became his pride and joy. It was his refuge for having fun and unwinding, and he often confided to friends that he never felt more relaxed than when he was just sitting on the spacious front porch of this mansion, hidden far back from the highway.

On its return to New York, The Dorsey Brothers Orchestra opened on May 15 at the Glen Island Casino in nearby New Rochelle, overlooking Long Island Sound, where the Casa Loma band had headlined the previous two summer seasons. This venue had long since become recognized as the most important location for bands in the East.

According to Kay Weber, their opening night brought out a group of their musician friends—including a triumvirate of trombonists: Jack Teagarden, Jack Jenney, and Jerry Colonna—with Tommy doing his utmost to impress them with his playing. Perhaps more important to Tommy, in the audience were such celebrities as the "Great Profile," John Barrymore, and his young lover, Elaine Barrie; Lennie Hayton with Lena Horne; pitcher "Red" Ruffing and the great first baseman Lou Gehrig from the New York Yankees, who was a friend of Roc Hillman; and Connee Boswell. Weber added that there was "Franklin D. Roosevelt, Jr.—I think he was in college then. I recall his white shoes were smudged." Mom and Pop Dorsey were there as well, beaming proudly over their sons' accomplishments. Weber recalls Tess saying to her, "My boys are getting so rich. Why Thomas has just bought me a new Lincoln Zipper [Zephyr]!"

It was obviously a smash opening night. A great summer loomed ahead. Perhaps this booking would provide the final link in establishing The Dorsey Brothers Orchestra as the leading band in the country.

In the meantime, Jack Kapp had set up a recording session for May 27. This marked Bob Eberly's first record, "You're All I Need." Another one of the band's fine recordings that day, which featured The Dorsey Brothers Trio, was the highly entertaining "I'll Never Say 'Never Again' Again." "Chasing Shadows," with Tommy's remarkable solo and Bob Eberly's vocal would become another number-one record.

Despite the success of this recording session, there was constant tension between Tommy and Jimmy. Roc Hillman recalled, "They often argued about tempo. Jimmy wanted a kind of a floating tempo; Tommy wanted the tempo very precise. It seemed to me and to others, too, that Tommy had a split personality. It didn't happen all too often. He controlled it, I would say. He could get very angry at people and then be charming in the next minute. The guys in the band liked Jimmy more. Tommy was a high strung perfectionist; Jimmy was non-aggressive, calmer, and laid back. Both of them had short fuses. It was just a matter of time." In fact, it was a matter of days.

May 30, over Memorial Day (then called Decoration Day) weekend of 1935, was the date Tommy and Jimmy Dorsey would refer to over the years as their Separation Day.

Roc Hillman recalled Jimmy showing up hungover for the matinee that day. About an hour into the set, Tommy called "I'll Never Say 'Never Again' Again" and kicked off the tempo. Hillman said, "Don, Skeets, and I were about to sing our vocal chorus. We were on our way up to the microphone when I heard Jimmy raise his voice a little and say something like, 'Hey Mac, that's a little fast, isn't it?' He had a kind of a snarl on his face. And then Tommy said, 'You want to take over? It's yours. Take it.' Jimmy just said, 'Yeah,' or words to that effect. Then Tommy picked up his horn and walked off the bandstand. We finished singing the tune." Hillman also recalled that Jimmy reluctantly stood up from his seat in the saxophone section and walked out in front to lead the band. He did so for the remainder of the set and for the sets that afternoon and evening.

Soon after the incident took place, Cork O'Keefe got an urgent telephone call from Michael DeZutter, the manager of the Glen Island Casino at the nearby Wykagyl Country Club where he was having dinner. He was told, "You better get over here." After the last set, he hurried over to Glen Island only to find Jimmy staring into space, smoking a cigarette.

"Where's Tommy?" O'Keefe asked.

"He's gone," Jimmy replied.

"Why?"

"You know how Mac is," said Jimmy. "It's the problem we've always had. I was playing baritone, the tempo was too fast for the cornets, so I told him, 'Mac, the tempo stinks!'"

The Dorsey Brothers Orchestra's contract with the Glen Island Casino extended through September 21. Moreover, the band's book was written to cofeature Tommy's trombone. O'Keefe hoped against hope for several days that Tommy would return. Jimmy came back the next night to front the band. Then, facing the reality of the situation, O'Keefe contacted three of Tommy's fellow trombonists: Wilbur Schwichtenberg (who later changed his name to Will Bradley), Jack Jenney, and Jerry Colonna, all of whom spent a few evenings after Tommy left sitting in with the band after they had finished work in various radio bands in New York. Colonna had also regaled the audience with his comedy vocals on "You're My Everything" and "Vesti la Giubba." It isn't clear whether it was their loyalty to Tommy, their reluctance to step in as permanent replacements, or perhaps the sense of being caught in the middle of this difficult situation, but all of them turned down the job.

O'Keefe's phone call to Bobby Byrne in Detroit came soon after the final confrontation between the Dorsey brothers. The sixteen-year-old musician was offered seventy-five dollars a week and happily agreed to join the band at the Glen Island Casino. His mother made immediate plans for them to drive east.

Byrne arrived with three trombones and a harp. Larry Clinton, then arranging for the Dorseys, observed, "He was the only trombone player who wasn't scared by Tommy's book." George T. Simon remarked, "His debut with the band was like that of a rookie pitcher tossing a no hitter his first time out in the majors." He took over Tommy's trombone parts with amazing confidence and played his solos for almost two months.

The band continued to be billed as The Dorsey Brothers Orchestra. Jimmy's name, however, suddenly appeared as the band's "director." This was a move to eventually build up to solo billing for him. It was also based on the assumption that the brothers' split was now permanent.

In late July, DeZutter, who was also Jimmy's drinking partner, demanded that Tommy return to finish the engagement or he would nullify the existing contract. This demand wasn't unjustified. After all, this was an engagement that was booked for the entire summer season. After a strategically planned trip to Walled Lake, Michigan, Tommy returned to New York and started hanging out nightly at the Onyx Club on Fifty-second Street, the successor to Plunkett's as the musicians' headquarters.

With great reluctance, he agreed to return to New Rochelle to play with the band on a nightly basis. He had little choice. If he refused, he would have faced an unwinnable lawsuit as a result of his actions. On his return, he told Bobby Byrne, "You sit over here off the stage and just listen."

His close friend and later longtime press agent, Jack Egan, recalled often driving up to the job in New Rochelle with Tommy. "He and Jimmy never talked to each other. . . . Tommy kept crucifying Jimmy, but no one else could say a word. It was all right for Tommy to say anything he wanted, but if you dared to agree with him or say, 'Yeah, what a rat,' you'd get hit over the head. You just had to sit and listen."

The Dorseys' Decca contract was also still in effect. In a session on August 1, the band recorded six tunes. Kay Weber and Bob Eberly's duet on "My Very Good Friend the Milkman" and Don Mattison and Skeets Herfurt's duet on Irving Berlin's "Top Hat, White Tie and Tails" were two highlights.

Tommy was finally released from his contract with the Glen Island Casino on August 30, yet he remained until September 21, playing only an hour a night. He made the one-hundred-mile round-trip commute from Bernardsville on a nightly basis. Jimmy assumed the role of the band's conductor until the end of the season. Many nights after the job Tommy would drive down to the Onyx, where Mike Riley and Ed Farley were the headliners, and jam with them for three or four hours for nothing.

Meanwhile, the various radio network and advertising executives were making plans for the 1935–1936 season. Kraft Cheese had signed Bing Crosby to replace Paul Whiteman as the host of its hit Thursday-night half-hour show on NBC. Cork O'Keefe had been planning to add The Dorsey Brothers Orchestra to the package, but he had to have Bing's approval. The remote broadcasts featuring the DBO didn't reach California in those days, and Bing hadn't seen the band in person. His previous recording association with the Dorseys had been with almost an entirely different band.

When O'Keefe initially suggested that Bing come east to record with the Dorseys, Bing said that in August he would be up in Saratoga, where the horses were running, and would gladly come down to the city. Tommy Dorsey told O'Keefe that he would be happy to record with Bing. "For you I'll do it," Tommy said, "and for Bing. But not for my no-good bastard brother!"

The recording session took place on August 14, a typical hot, muggy August day in New York. Bing heard the DBO play and liked what he heard. Their first tune together, "From the Top of Your Head to the Tip of Your Toes," featuring Bobby Byrne's first recorded solo, would reach the Billboard Pop chart in September.

Despite Bing's throat problems that day, he is heard singing in his usual jaunty fashion. But after completing the fifth song, without a word of warning, Bing and Jack Kapp got into a serious row over the arrangement on the next tune. The argument was recorded and has since surfaced as a bootleg tape. Interestingly enough, Tommy and Jimmy are heard laughing at what was taking place in front of them.

Bing left the studio but told O'Keefe he wanted to do his radio show with the brothers. As far as the feud between Tommy and Jimmy went, Bing's professionalism prevented him from taking sides. Completely impartial, he said he would gladly work with either Tommy or Jimmy. (Adding another dimension to this picture, it's Kay Weber's belief that Bing helped finance The Dorsey Brothers Orchestra.)

Another post–Separation Day gig found the brothers appearing as guest stars, along with Bing, on one of Paul Whiteman's last *Kraft Music Hall* shows. Whiteman diplomatically introduced Tommy as "The Master of the Trombone." After Tommy played "I'm Getting Sentimental over You," he introduced Jimmy as "The Master of the Saxophone," and Jimmy played "Oodles of Noodles."

O'Keefe tried one more time to orchestrate a reconciliation between the Dorsey brothers. He arranged a meeting in his office. Tommy agreed to attend but made it abundantly clear that he wasn't about to change his mind. True to his word, at the end of the meeting, after repeating that he wouldn't go back to work with Jimmy, he rose from his chair and headed for the door with these parting words for O'Keefe, "And you—what I won't do to you!" After he had left the office, Jimmy, who had been looking out the window during Tommy's outburst, looked tearfully at O'Keefe and asked, "What'll I do?"

"From now on, you're the boss," said the agent.

The highly respected composer and arranger Johnny Mandel, who also played trombone for Jimmy Dorsey years later and also arranged for Tommy Dorsey, says, "I don't think Jimmy would have ever have been a bandleader if Tommy hadn't walked out of The Dorsey Brothers Orchestra. Jimmy was a sideman in temperament. He was the total opposite of Tommy. Tommy gave orders; Jimmy didn't mind taking them."

Thus ended The Dorsey Brothers Orchestra. Jimmy was thirty-one years old, and Tommy was not yet thirty. It is significant that Tommy left the orchestra to Jimmy; Tommy saw no problem in starting another band. The Dorsey Brothers Orchestra under Jimmy Dorsey's leadership became known as Jimmy Dorsey and His Orchestra. Jimmy remained with Rockwell-O'Keefe and Decca Records.

Each of the brothers would ultimately benefit from their split. They knew that their separation was inevitable and over the years realized it turned out better for them both. They had learned considerably about what constitutes a successful dance orchestra. And "I'll Never Say 'Never Again' Again" would prove to be the byword of their unique and combative relationship.

4

"I'm Getting
Sentimental over You"

Tom was a great patron of excellence.
—JO STAFFORD

TOMMY DORSEY began his solo bandleader career with another display of calculation, opportunism, and ruthlessness worthy of a Wall Street takeover specialist. No sooner had he quit his old job than he stole another man's band, put him to work for him until he'd gotten all he needed out of him, and then fired him.

The split from Jimmy surprised no one. It had been an open secret among New York musicians that Tommy and Jimmy simply couldn't last much longer as coleaders. Tommy's departure wasn't the momentary impulse that it seemed to be. Weeks before Separation Day, Tommy had been meeting at the Onyx Club with Joe Haymes, a cousin of singer Dick Haymes, about the possibility of taking over Haymes's floundering dance band, then working at the McAlpin Hotel in New York's Herald Square.

On May 30, 1935, Paul Barry, the singing star of the popular *Your Hit Parade* radio show, was at the Glen Island Casino and saw Dorsey make his abrupt exit. Barry had been a friend of Tommy's dating back to the time when Tommy played in the band on the show under Lennie Hayton's direction. Barry said, "When he got off the stand Tommy got on the phone. I think he was talking to Arthur Michaud, who, though I'm not sure, was standing by ready to become Tommy's manager."

When Tommy encountered Barry, he asked him, "How about it, Paul, wanna go out to Detroit with me to sing with the band?" Barry replied, "What band?" And Dorsey told him he was going to pick up what had been Joe Haymes's orchestra, out at the New Casino at Walled Lake, Michigan.

Barry called his family from a pay phone and told them of his plans to go out to Michigan with Dorsey. That very night Barry left with Tommy in Tommy's car. The singer still recalled with amazement Tommy's road sense: "I was driving at one particular point and came to a fork in the road. He was sleeping, sensed it, sat up, and said, 'Go left!' and went right back to sleep. We were absolutely on the right road." (This was but one of several examples of Dorsey's uncanny ability to momentarily regain consciousness while seemingly fast asleep.)

Barry wasn't Tommy's first choice for a traveling companion. Weeks earlier, according to Spud Murphy, *he* had gotten a call from Tommy asking him to accompany him. Murphy described himself as having been "one of the woodwind guys—a reed player, same as Goodman and Artie Shaw and those people. We were all sort of a club. Tommy was a little on the outside, being a brass player, but Jimmy hung out with us."

Murphy told the story behind the car ride to Michigan that he had refused: "I have nothing against him as a trombonist, but I found Tommy a little bit strange once in a while in his dealings with people. That is true of lots of artists so you can't just say that he's the one, but he was one of them. I didn't write for him. The way it worked is that the only thing ever credited to me, I didn't do. He put out a record ('I've Got a Note') that says 'Arranged by Spud Murphy,' and that was not true. It was actually written by Noni Bernardi."

Murphy was also a close friend of Joe Haymes, who was well respected as an arranger but too unassuming to make it as a successful bandleader. This was not the first time that Haymes had put a band together only to have another leader take it over. "There were some takeovers that took place in those days, but not many quite like this one," Murphy acknowledged.

Murphy referred to Haymes, the self-absorbed, near-sighted pianist, as the "Little Giant"—"He was short in stature, but he was very up there in brains, especially in writing arrangements for tunes." Murphy remembered this telling incident seventy years later with decided assurance. He knew exactly what Tommy Dorsey was about and related the story with an underlying humor. It was readily apparent, however, that he abhorred the way Dorsey conducted himself in business matters.

When Dorsey told Murphy that he was going to be taking over Haymes's band in Walled Lake:

I told him, "If Haymes wants to do that, you go talk to him. If he wants to do it, I will not oppose it. But I will make a deal with you."

Dorsey asked, "What do you mean by that?" I said, "I'm not going to tell Joe which way to go because I don't want to be accused of any trickery by you." Then I said, "But I want you to retain him as [the] arranger for your band. As long as he's there, whether he writes anything or not, you pay him a hundred dollars a week 'cause you're getting his band. You could never organize a band like he does." He agreed to all that stuff as long as he used Haymes's band because it was Haymes's band. Dorsey didn't build it. It might be called the Tommy Dorsey Orchestra but he knew better. Then I said, "You don't fire him. If you fire him, the band goes or the music goes [all of Haymes's charts]—take your choice."

When I asked Spud how he could speak for Haymes, Murphy replied, "Because Haymes and I were very good friends. I worked for him all the time." He went on, "After Dorsey hung up I called Joe and told him I'd made the deal without his permission because [otherwise] he would probably have given everything away. Dorsey would have gone out there—I knew him and his clever tricks [from prior experience]—and he would have said, 'Joe, I came here to make a deal with you. Spud Murphy told me it was okay to do it.' After I told Joe what I'd done he said, 'Wow! Okay, I guess.'"

Murphy described the Haymes band as being more jazz-oriented than The Dorsey Brothers Orchestra and compared the strength of Haymes's writing to that of the long-admired big-band arranger Bill Holman. As composers and arrangers, Joe Haymes and Bill Holman knew precisely the instruments they were writing for. Murphy pointed out, "Everybody wanted to work with Joe." Trumpeter Pee Wee Erwin, a member of the band, called it "very definitely a musician's band—because money we didn't make."

Dorsey met with Haymes shortly after arriving in Walled Lake with Paul Barry. The reluctant bandleader called Murphy, his facilitating friend, in New York and told him that Dorsey wanted his band: "He offered me everything you told me he would."

Murphy asked, "Did he say anything about how long the agreement would last?" "No," said Haymes. Murphy added, "That's why I'm representing you 'cause he could say to you, 'I want you to be the arranger for the band,' and he shows up the first day, and he gives you two weeks' notice."

Dorsey now had a working band with a library of its own. It was amusingly billed as "Tommy Dorsey and His Boys—Stars of Stage and Radio." He brought his old friend Stan King out from New York to play drums, only to fire him over his heavy drinking. Haymes wrote new charts for the new Tommy Dorsey band. After six weeks of getting the band into the kind of musical shape he wanted with frequent afternoon rehearsals (for which he generously paid the musicians), Dorsey essentially said, "Joe, everything's great. Thanks a lot. Good-bye." Dorsey kept Haymes's library of arrangements and his entire band as well. The musicians liked playing the music and liked each other and looked ahead to working with a new leader. Murphy pointed out, "Dorsey knew how to charm people when he really wanted something, as he tried to do with Joe Haymes, and succeeded."

When asked if Dorsey's eventual success leading the nucleus of Haymes's band bothered Haymes, Murphy said, "No, he didn't care. He just said, 'I'll build another band.'" Sure enough, Haymes later started still another orchestra, for which Murphy wrote arrangements. In time it was taken over by Ray Noble, a high-principled leader—"Someone you could admire," said Murphy.

Haymes's stoicism may not have been as complete as Murphy's account suggests, that Haymes didn't feel ill used by Dorsey. Trumpeter Zeke Zarchy was a member of a later Haymes band and rode in Haymes's car on one-nighters. He disputes Murphy's statement: "I only heard him bad-mouth one person, and that was Tommy Dorsey, for taking his band out from under him."

Before turning thirty, Tommy Dorsey had what he wanted, a band that reflected *his* particular musical vision. How he had achieved it meant little or nothing to him.

In August, Tommy brought his newly revamped aggregation to New York. Realizing he couldn't start working with his band while the Glen Island Casino contract was still in force, reluctantly he went back to work in New Rochelle, where Jimmy was leading the DBO.

First, in this interim period, he signed with Arthur Michaud to become his personal manager after dispensing with the services of Joe Haymes's manager, Charlie Bush. More important, he signed a contract with MCA's Willard Alexander, to book the band. Alexander, a violinist and formerly a bandleader while attending the University of Pennsylvania, had recently sent his client Benny Goodman west on a trans-America tour. Finally, he signed onetime leader of the California Ramblers, Ed Kirkeby, to produce his records at RCA Victor, then the record industry's leading record company.

With his purchase of Tall Oaks, plus his several-week sojourn in Walled Lake, Tommy had overextended himself financially. It wasn't the first time, and it wouldn't be the last, but the advance from RCA bailed him out. Tommy wanted to be billed on his records as "Thomas," but the label insisted on using his more boyish nickname.

A succession of one-nighters in the East preceded the debut of Tommy Dorsey and His Orchestra for a four-week booking at the French Casino in New York that began September 1935. Years later, George T. Simon described in his book *The Big Bands* the musical outlook of the new twelve-piece band as representing "hotel swing with little distinction."

The entire Haymes saxophone and trumpet sections were intact along with the Little Giant's trombonist, bassist, guitarist, pianist, and his talented and versatile young arranger, Paul Weston. A magna cum laude Dartmouth graduate who had majored in economics, Weston (originally Wetstein) studied in New York after his graduation with Joseph Schillenger, a highly regarded music teacher. This gave him the credentials to begin writing arrangements for various dance orchestras.

In musical history, however, something of much greater significance was taking place during that same month in Los Angeles at the Palomar Ballroom. After a mostly indifferent reception during its cross-country jaunt, Benny Goodman and His Orchestra had opened on August 21 at the famous ballroom for two nights. On its opening night, the bespectacled, self-involved clarinetist and his band, which combined brilliant soloists Bunny Berigan and Gene Krupa and dynamic arrangements, created a sensation. The engagement was extended to seven weeks, and overnight a new trend in popular music was born. The first "youthquake" that was to define pop culture in America was suddenly at hand. Here the so-called Swing Era began.

Several factors combined to make Benny Goodman America's first pop-culture hero. There was his faithful fan base, made up of teenagers as well as a large contingent of University of Southern California students. This latter element had tuned in and danced the Lindy in their sorority and fraternity houses to NBC's *Let's Dance* radio show at 9:30 P.M. on Saturday nights as the Goodman band was hitting its stride playing Fletcher Henderson's arrangements of tunes like "Down South Camp Meetin'," "King Porter Stomp," and "Blue Skies." Goodman, at twenty-six, was also only a few years older than his college fans.

Significant record promotion didn't hurt either. Al Jarvis on his KFWB show, *The Make Believe Ballroom,* had heralded the arrival in Southern California that August of this musical Pied Piper and constantly played the Goodman band's current RCA record of "The Dixieland Band." But more important, the times were ripe for a radical change in popular music. The musical theme of the day was evolving from "Brother, Can You Spare a Dime?" to "Happy Days Are Here Again," the song closely associated with the administration of Franklin D. Roosevelt.

Upon being inaugurated president on March 4, 1933, Roosevelt had offered the American people a "New Deal," emphasizing, "The only thing we have to fear is fear itself—unreasoning, unjustified terror, which paralyzes needed effort to convert retreat into advance." The misery of the last few years had encompassed an unemployment rate of 25 percent, a failed stock market, soup kitchens, and Hoovervilles (shanty towns that desecrated even New York's Central Park), while people rode the rails and hitchhiked along the nation's highways in search of a fresh start. As *Ava's Man* author Rick Bragg wrote, "It was a time when a nation drowning in its poor never so resented them!"

The challenge seemed impossible; the performance was superhuman. During the first hundred days of the New Deal, more meaningful and far-reaching social legislation was put into motion by the Congress than at any time in the history of the republic. The nation's banks were closed, and Federal Deposit Insurance and Social Security were established. Under the direction of Harry Hopkins, Roosevelt's closest adviser, the Civilian Conservation Corps (CCC), Works Progress Administration (WPA), and National Recovery Administration (NRA) began to repair the decaying infrastructure of the cities, roads, and public works, putting thousands of people back to work. There was soon a feeling in the land that the new man in the White House cared about the plight of the common people.

By 1934 the economy had begun to improve. Over the next several years, there was an ever-growing feeling of optimism that pervaded the country. This, in turn, had a pronounced effect on the state of popular music. More than anything else, this new spirit provided the setting for the birth of the Swing Era. Swing music provided a respite America felt it deserved from its troubles. And for the one and only time in the country's history, jazz became *the* popular music of the land.

It was Jelly Roll Morton, the jazz pianist and composer, and Louis Armstrong who invented what became known as swing. Armstrong had sold over 100,000 records in 1931 with his big band. The following year Duke

Ellington wrote one of his many hit tunes, "It Don't Mean a Thing If It Ain't Got That Swing." But America was not ready to bestow idol status on African-American bandleaders, however great their musical talents or the popularity of their records. White "swing bands," such as the Casa Loma band and The Dorsey Brothers Orchestra didn't rankle whites' sensibilities or their consciences.

To their fervent young admirers, swing musicians suddenly, as a result of Goodman's success at the Palomar, became as celebrated as baseball players and movie stars. Personnel changes among the leading big bands were as closely observed as lineup changes on the New York Yankees.

Young people crowded ballrooms to dance and watch their favorite musicians play their now-familiar instrumental solos. The dance they were dancing, the Lindy Hop, had actually predated the 1927 Charles Lindbergh solo hop to Paris for which it was named. It most likely originated in Harlem when it became highly popular with the dancers at the famous Savoy Ballroom, the "Home of Happy Feet." The Lindy was essentially choreographed swing music.

After its triumph on the West Coast, the Goodman Band headed east, playing one-nighters en route to Chicago, where it opened on November 6, 1935, at the Congress Hotel. Here the term *swing band* was coined by none other than Gene Krupa. The handsome Krupa single-handedly became the first showman drummer, exhibiting blinding speed and power in his playing. His fast-growing popularity was a key component in Goodman's success. But it was not until sometime in 1936 that the press formally dubbed Benny Goodman the "King of Swing."

Lewis A. Erenberg, in his 1998 dissertation, "Swingin' the Dream" (University of Chicago Press), observed:

Part of swing's appeal lay in bringing the egalitarian urban jazz world to the middle and working classes. What counted was how one played. As a result, swing bands were profoundly cosmopolitan, including Italians, Irishmen, Poles, Jews, Catholics, and Protestants. It wasn't until pianist Teddy Wilson became a member of the Benny Goodman Trio in 1935, and the following year, when vibraphonist Lionel Hampton joined to form the Benny Goodman Quartet, that integration of white musical organizations began to take place. Goodman's urban Jewish roots and "Negroid" accent were a primary part of his appeal.

Each big band had a theme song that was its musical signature. Goodman had adapted Von Weber's "Invitation to the Dance," which became "Let's Dance" when his band debuted on the NBC radio program. This arrangement emphasized the jazz orientation of his band's presentation. While Goodman also wanted his music to be danceable, he fundamentally wanted his music to swing. Unlike Goodman, Dorsey was fundamentally interested in his band's music being danceable. He also knew he was a different kind of musician who lacked Goodman's ability as a jazz player. He had soloed on one of Goodman's first noteworthy records in 1930, "He's Not Worth Your Tears." They would continue to have an on-again–off-again musical relationship over a period of decades.

As his theme song, Dorsey decided on George Bassman and Ned Washington's ballad "I'm Getting Sentimental over You," which he had recorded with Jean Bowes and Bob Crosby and the Dorsey Brothers Orchestra in 1932 and 1934 and played on the *Kraft Music Hall* show hosted earlier in the summer of 1935, when Paul Whiteman introduced him as the "Master of the Trombone." He had even jammed on the tune during his nights at the Onyx. He realized how well his performance of the ballad registered in front of an audience.

The arrangement by Noni Bernardi was actually a miniconcerto that showcased Dorsey's uncanny ability to play facilely in the upper register with perfect control, building to a high C. Even more important, it showcased the exquisite and romantic quality of his tone.

Bernardi, a saxophonist, explained, "Tommy never mentioned one word about how he wanted it [arranged] or anything. What I did was the way *I* wanted to do it." The record of his treatment of "I'm Getting Sentimental over You" also includes eight bars of a flowery, Eddy Duchin–like piano solo by Paul Mitchell, playing on what sounds like a slightly out-of-tune instrument. Bernardi changed the context of Tommy's solo in order to more effectively highlight his playing. As he explained it, "I put the structure down, but Tommy Dorsey *made* the song."

This October 18, 1935, recording (a remake of the September recording in which Dorsey flubbed ten takes and gave up) features the exact arrangement that Dorsey would feature henceforth. This is what audiences wanted and expected. It became one of the most immediately recognizable and favorite theme songs of the Swing Era.

Tommy's new theme song proved to be the occasion of further bickering between the Dorsey brothers. Jack Egan recalled one night in the fall of 1935 when Jimmy came into the Onyx (soon to be known as the "Cradle of

Swing") after Tommy's radio remote. Jimmy, well on his way to intoxication, approached the table where Tommy was sitting with his band singer, Edythe Wright, and Egan, and Tommy asked his brother if he had heard the show. When Jimmy answered curtly, "Yeah," Tommy asked what he thought, and Jimmy began to criticize Tommy's theme song.

"By that time, Tommy had his hand on the sugar bowl," Egan recalled, "and I was scared to death he was gonna hit Jimmy with it. Jimmy just smiled and walked over to the bar. Of course, then they began arguing over the tempo."

It would take geographical separation to effect a truce. Jimmy would be en route to California. Cork O'Keefe had scored a coup by getting Bing Crosby to hire Jimmy's newly constituted orchestra, soon to be known as Jimmy Dorsey and His Orchestra, on the *Kraft Music Hall*, which was based in Hollywood. Kay Weber and Bob Eberly didn't appear on the show. The band's trip to the West Coast included a successful several-week engagement stopover in Houston.

Noni Bernardi recalled the way Tommy worked on the bandstand: "Tommy had the habit of leaving after we played a dance set for dinner and then for a show. He would come back ten or fifteen minutes before two o'clock, and then he played for five to ten minutes." Sammy Weiss, the drummer, had set an alarm clock for 2 A.M., when the band was supposed to stop playing. When the alarm clock went off, Tommy exploded. Despite Sammy's protests that it was two o'clock, Tommy insisted on playing as long as he felt like it.

Bernardi later worked for Bob Crosby, Benny Goodman, Jimmy Dorsey, and Lawrence Welk. He subsequently spent thirty-two years (eight terms) on the Los Angeles City Council. Of Jimmy, Bernardi said, "I can't say enough about him . . . I can say he wasn't anywhere near as intense as his brother. Off the bandstand Tommy was a real enjoyable person. He had the mansion in Bernardsville, and he always used to invite the musicians."

That fall, with the advent of the first Tommy Dorsey orchestra, a series of firings of musicians began. It also marked the start of a succession of raids of other bands for replacements. This imperious behavior became as much a trademark of Tommy's as his theme song. Once again, he knew what he wanted and sought out the musicians who could help him achieve the results he demanded.

In October, he heard a network remote broadcast of Bert Block's dance band from the Roadside Rest in Freeport, Long Island, and admired the orchestra's singing group, The Three Esquires. It comprised Jack Leonard, Block's male singer, whom Tommy had seen a year before at Ben Marden's Riviera when Block's orchestra preceded the DBO's engagement, along with the trumpeter and singer Joe Bauer and the trumpeter and singer Axel (whose actual first name was Odd) Stordahl, who was also a formidable arranger. Tommy made them a good offer they couldn't refuse, and they joined him early in December at the Mosque Theatre in Newark.

Fellow Irishman John Joseph (Jack) Leonard, a hardworking professional who described himself during his time with Dorsey as "never being a flamboyant performer, on the shy side and scared to death," was in awe of Tommy:

> I was only about nineteen when I joined Tommy. His greatness had already been established—not as a bandleader [yet] but as a respected instrumentalist. I was so young I thought everybody played like Tommy.
>
> When we first started recording, it was always first chorus, Tommy. He was so brilliant that I figured sometimes, "What the hell am I doing here?" I just thought I was out of my league until [we recorded] "For Sentimental Reasons," and then I began to loosen up. It took that period of time, but Tommy was patient with me. He never advised me, but his phrasing rubbed off on me. . . . I guess I was even subconsciously tying phrases together. I started taking a breath. Tommy could play a thirty-two-bar chorus without taking a breath. He used to tell the guys in the band how he did it. He said his embouchure was such that he would just let so much air out of a little hole in his mouth and be able to fill his lungs and sustain.

Tommy, in turn, developed a deep respect for Leonard's superb ballad singing. In the next four years he would be featured on some forty-two hit records with the Dorsey aggregation, twenty-four of which would reach the top ten on the Billboard Pop Chart, with four becoming number one. These were some of the most significant records that would help establish the Dorsey orchestra.

Axel Stordahl would become one of the behind-the-scenes operatives who had a pronounced effect on the fortunes of the Dorsey band (and later Frank Sinatra) over the next seven years. Never much of a trumpeter (he played fourth trumpet in the band), the pale, soft-spoken, and sensitive musician, of Norwegian descent, suffered from a rheumatic heart. As soon as he joined Dorsey, he began altering stock arrangements in the band's library. This ability, along with his highly developed harmonic sense, earned him Tommy's attention and the nickname "A." He would remain with the band until the fall of 1942. Stordahl's fervent interest in classical composers, especially Frederick Delius, influenced the beautiful ballad arrangements he began writing.

The band's first trumpeter, Andy Ferretti, came from the Haymes band. Ferretti's range, strong lip, and perfect intonation made him the ideal leader of the section. In starting a new band, however, Tommy could only afford to pay Ferretti fifty dollars a week. Yet he remained with the band almost three years.

It was third trumpeter, Sterling Bose, nicknamed Bozo, apparently for good reason, who played the hot solos. In the months ahead, he became the band's "character" and often the object of Tommy's wrath because of his use of alcohol and marijuana. One winter night, while en route to the Normandy Ballroom in Boston, ten miles from the destination during zero weather, Tommy yelled out, "Who's the hop man? You guys think you're playing better on that stuff, but you're not." Discovering Bose as the culprit, he proceeded to order him off the bus.

Tommy then announced that if Bose showed up for the next gig unfit to play, the whole band would be put on two weeks' notice, just like in the army when one soldier screws up and the entire outfit takes the blame. True to his word, he did just that the next night when Bose showed up drunk. Only after a few days, when Arthur Michaud came up from New York to mediate the situation, did Tommy change his mind.

Despite Tommy's problems with him, Bose's playing appealed directly to his musical sensibilities, especially when it came to Dixieland tunes, which had become an important element of the band's repertoire. When, a few months later, the trumpeter told Tommy he wanted to leave the band to join Ray Noble for an engagement at the Rainbow Room, however, Tommy may have felt real loss and not merely a threat to his need for control. But Tommy's differences tended to end up as a power struggle, which he had to win. In any case, Tommy insisted Bose give him a month's notice. Bose protested that would prevent him from accepting the Rainbow Room gig.

The next morning, after a one-nighter in Toledo, Bose had stayed up all night and was still drinking, building up his courage to confront Dorsey. He started verbally attacking him from the back of the bus. Dorsey strode back to Bose's seat, screaming, "If you want to quit this outfit, I'll show you how to leave!" grabbed him by the collar and the seat of his pants, and literally threw him off the bus and out of the band. Bose was stranded and had to wire his wife to get money for transportation to New York to join Ray Noble's band. This was not the last of such incidents.

Bassist Gene Traxler, who also came from Joe Haymes's band, estimated that 250 musicians came and went during the 1935–1940 period he was a member of the Dorsey band. "He used to fire guys one at a time or in small bunches," Traxler said. These constant turnovers would contribute to the ongoing legend of Tommy Dorsey.

Brockton, Massachusetts, native Max Kaminsky, who sat in one night for Bose in Boston and eventually got his job, genially remarked, "Working for Tommy Dorsey was like cooking on a hot stove that might explode at any moment—and always did. . . . His temperament was so volcanic and his rages so explosive that you could smell the fire and brimstone. No one was safe. . . . He took pleasure in the fight for the sheer love of fighting, and as mad as you could get at him, it was hard to stay mad because he got over it so quickly, with no trace of animosity."

Fundamentally, Dorsey was looking to offer the public a sweet-sounding dance band with a strong sense of melody. The section work in his orchestra had to be perfectly clean, and the vocalists had to come up to another high level of performance.

Kaminsky described the difference between Dorsey's approach to the trombone and that of Tommy's hero, Jack Teagarden: "When Tommy Dorsey played a melody it was a very straight melody and it had a silken quality to it. When Teagarden played the same song he could interpret it more deeply in the jazz idiom, but he still had that wonderful tone and taste."

Dorsey knew that he had to have the right kind of drummer to drive his brass section. In March 1936 he found him in his old friend the diminutive Dave Tough, originally from Chicago, who spent much of his off time reading and appreciating great art and literature (Cézanne and F. Scott Fitzgerald, who was also an acquaintance)—something rare indeed among musicians of that era. Over a period of two years, Tough's drinking problems led Dorsey to pay for his periodic stays in rehab.

Although lacking virtuosic technique, Tough was soon to make an important impact with the consummate musical taste and subtlety he displayed. Johnny Mandel noted, "Davey tuned his drums. He was like Jo Jones that way. He always knew what cymbals to use. He supported the band totally." Jazz critic and drummer Burt Korall said of Tough, "Like an extraordinary supporting actor, he adds to the overall performance without making you too conscious of his presence." The master vibraphonist Lionel Hampton called him "the most imaginative drummer we ever had in the business."

Whereas drummers like Krupa and Buddy Rich exhibited great power and flash in their approach, Tough became renowned for playing *for* the band with an unerring sense of swing. Rich acknowledged that Davey's "energy force was so strong that you'd think there was a four hundred pound guy sitting up there."

Tough's twenty-two-year career would span the early days of Chicago-style jazz; he was a member of the Dorsey, Norvo, Berigan, and Goodman swing bands, Artie Shaw's navy band, and later Woody Herman's First Herd, one of the first significant modern big bands. Many jazz critics consider Tough one of *the* most versatile and talented of all the big-band drummers.

Tenor saxophonist Bud Freeman, who had been a frequent musical associate of Dorsey's during the 1920s and early 1930s, joined Tommy's band a little over a month after his old friend Tough. Dorsey, knowing full well his own limitations as an improviser (he referred to his shortcomings as "Civil War Jazz"), revered Freeman's playing. He enjoyed letting him loose, often yelling out, "Take another one, Bud!" Yet Tommy often criticized his ensemble playing because, as Freeman admitted in his *Crazyology* autobiography, "When I say [I was] independent, I mean I wasn't playing with the rest of the musicians. I was always thinking about what I was going to do for my solo."

Dorsey's inflexibility often gained the upper hand. He could be utterly humorless and unforgiving about any deviation from his notions of perfection. One night, during the playing of the theme at a Duke University date, a new trombonist nervously thrust his slide out so far that it sailed into the footlights. The band roared with laughter. The trombonist looked up at Tommy in horror. Tommy was livid. The hapless musician was fired soon afterward.

Dorsey wasn't always all business. He also relished having fun on the bandstand. He delighted in spoofing the "wah-wah" sound of his old band mate Russ Morgan's orchestra by having Freeman reinstitute the English accent he had acquired while working in Great Britain in singing "Am I Dreamin'." He would then have Freeman do an instrumental takeoff on Freddy Martin's alto saxophone sound. After that, trumpeter Pee Wee Erwin imitated Clyde McCoy's corny muted trumpet sound.

But such flights of playfulness were overshadowed by Tommy's inability or unwillingness to control his temper. Occasionally someone would stand up to him. Sometimes that worked—temporarily. One night during a Commodore Hotel engagement, Dorsey became so angry at the band's performance that he walked off the bandstand and didn't return for a few days. Because of Freeman's closeness to Tommy, several musicians approached Freeman about contacting him and asking him to return. Freeman called, but during their phone conversation, he called Dorsey "a big fucking baby." There was complete silence on the other end. Dorsey wasn't used to being dealt with that way. He returned to the bandstand radiating smiles, acting as though nothing had happened.

Freeman also explained that Dorsey "would become angry, and we'd shout back and forth and he would [then] say 'You're fired!' At the end of the night, he'd call my hotel and say, 'Would you like to have a bite?' I'd join him. . . . At other times I'd quit and he'd say, 'Come on back!' As it turned out, I was fired three times and quit four [times] because I had to be one up on him. The day I left Tommy I went down to his dressing room to say good-bye. No one had done that before because whenever anyone had left it had always ended in a big fight."

As it turned out, Bud joined Benny Goodman. In retaliation, after several attempts, Tommy finally succeeded in inducing Hymie Schertzer, the peerless lead alto sax of the Goodman band, to leave Benny and join his band.

According to Chris Griffin, "Dorsey's approach was to come over to the New Yorker, where the Goodman band was playing, along with Jack Leonard, Axel Stordahl, and the rest of his entourage, and sit as close to Benny as he could get. Then he'd invite Ziggy [Elman] or Harry [James] or me to his table and say very loudly so Benny would be sure to hear him, 'Why don't you join a good band. What do you want to stay with this shitheel [one of his favorite expressions] for?'"

By early 1936 Tommy Dorsey and His Orchestra was starting to make an impression on the "alligators and their chicks" (swing lingo for jitterbug-dancing couples) on one-nighters. But the band's success primarily was the result of its hit records. The first was the instrumental "Take Me Back to My Boots and Saddles," which became number one on the Billboard Chart (the weekly arbiter of America's taste in popular music, with the standings based on the number of records sold) on December 1, 1935.

On that same date, its next record went on the chart: "The Music Goes Round and Round," which featured "Tommy Dorsey's Clambake Seven"

(Sterling Bose, trumpet; Tommy on trombone; Joe Dixon, clarinet; Sid Block, tenor saxophone; Dirk Jones, piano; William Schaeffer, guitar; Gene Traxler, bass; and Dave Tough, drums) along with a vocal by Edythe Wright. The Clambake Seven, a New Orleans–Chicago-style jazz group, represented Tommy's concept of jazz based on his own influences. The group would be featured on an almost nightly basis during a dance date. The record of "The Music Goes Round and Round" also went to number one. Tommy had first heard this memorable novelty tune during the many nights he spent at the Onyx, where it had been introduced by the duo of Mike Riley and Eddie Farley.

Tommy's use of the Clambake Seven on recordings and personal appearances wasn't an original idea. Benny Goodman had already begun featuring a trio consisting of himself, Teddy Wilson on piano, and Gene Krupa as an added attraction to his band.

On its second Manhattan location engagement in March 1936 at the popular dance spot the Blue Room of the Hotel Lincoln, George T. Simon, in a second review in *Metronome*, wrote, "Dorsey's settings of tempos and choice of tunes to suit the prevailing mood are rhythmically and psychologically excellent. The contrast of ensemble arrangements and frequent solo passages is pleasing while Dorsey's personality and screwy gags help out, too." Simon gave the band an A.

The third number-one record for Dorsey, "Alone," which had been introduced in the Marx Brothers' memorable comedy *A Night at the Opera*, featured trumpeter Cliff Weston supplying the vocal and was released in early 1936. Despite these hit records and its growing popularity, the Dorsey band was nevertheless limping along playing a difficult schedule, starting that winter, of five months of mostly one-nighters from Canada to Texas booked by MCA. This meant weeks of previously booked dates that were often three hundred and sometimes as much as five hundred miles apart. According to Max Kaminsky, there wasn't a week in 1936, the first full year of the band, in which Tommy wasn't ready to give up the band. His hair actually started to turn gray in April 1936.

The musicians often slept overnight curled up on stiff wooden seats in a frighteningly cold, dilapidated former school bus, or if they were lucky, they checked into third-rate hotels. On occasion they started a fire on the floor of the bus to keep warm. Tommy recalled, "We'd be freezing in the bus, crawling from one small town to the next, and we'd hear the Crosby program with Jimmy playing out there in that nice weather. For a while there I was tempted to kick myself but hard."

Yet there was decided camaraderie among the players, and the hardships that challenged them brought out Tommy's generosity and endurance. Jack Leonard well described this tour: "We paid our dues playing innumerable one-nighters in every city and hamlet, in ballrooms, tobacco warehouses—any place that had a roof." Gene Traxler added, "Tommy always made the long jumps bearable by stopping to play [base]ball [in warm weather]. . . . One of the most difficult things to get Tommy to do was stop the bus for a rest stop. He either had a reserve tank built in or he had no bladder at all."

When the bus couldn't climb steep hills or mountains, the band would get out, simultaneously curse the cold and the music business, and as a combined unit would push the bus uphill or shovel snow to extricate it from a snowbank. When the bus driver nodded out from fatigue, Tommy would take over the driving for hours and sometimes even a day. One day he stopped the bus in a coal town in the Allegheny Mountains, went into a general store, and emerged carrying ear muffs, mufflers, coats, and sweaters and personally helped his men put on their new outfits.

For the remainder of their lives the musicians on this first tour would never forget these trying common experiences, which helped them to develop drive, determination, and stamina and often formed the basis for lifetime friendships.

Dorsey often picked up the check for the entire band in restaurants following the gigs several nights in a row. He also had sandwiches sent to rabid teenage fans who would stay for five or six shows in movie theaters. Tommy may have started with a reign of terror, but now he was leading a band that had a distinct future.

For eight weeks in the summer of 1936 the Dorsey band was the Sunday-night replacement for Fred Waring and the Pennsylvanians, a popular dance orchestra that prominently featured its Glee Club. The program was sponsored by the Ford Motor Company and broadcast from the Texas Centennial in Dallas. For the first two weeks the band was working at the St. Anthony Hotel in San Antonio. The musicians had to travel each Sunday morning in a non-air-conditioned train to Dallas for the broadcast. Early in this engagement, several members of the band were severely injured in a taxi accident while en route to the train station for the trip to Dallas. Among them was clarinetist Joe Dixon.

Bobby Burns had joined Tommy as manager. The extremely capable Burns, during the course of a six-year stint, would become impervious to Tommy's yelling out from the side of his mouth in his rasping voice in the midst of a performance, *"Burns,"* when something displeased him. He showed his resourcefulness after the accident: "That was the day we had scheduled our arrangement of 'Finger Buster,' which featured Joe Dixon . . . When we got to Dallas, I found out that Isham Jones was playing there. I quickly borrowed the services of his clarinet player—Woody Herman."

On top of their weekly salary, at the end of the first month of the radio show, Tommy paid each of the musicians an additional eighty dollars. Dave Tough told him, "I don't mind the salary. It's just that I can't afford it." He had spent more than that in transporting himself and his drums to and from the rehearsals and the two train stations. Tommy got a good fee for the radio show, but it only served to pay himself back for what he had lost on the preceding road tour.

One night, just before a remote broadcast from the St. Anthony Hotel, the engineer noticed how nervous Tommy was and asked him, "Why are you so worried?" "Because," Tommy replied emphatically, "This is going to The Brother!" He assumed Jimmy would be listening in Southern California, and he wanted him to be favorably impressed.

One important musician who was listening to these broadcasts was Marcel Tabuteau, then the foremost oboist in the classical world, who had been brought to America by Leopold Stokowski to become first oboist in the Philadelphia Orchestra. Tabuteau was also teaching a chamber music class at the Curtis Institute, which included Julius Baker, later to become the preeminent flutist.

Baker told the renowned musicologist James Maher of Tabuteau's tremendous respect for Dorsey. Tabuteau became incensed because none of the students except Baker knew who "Tommeee Dorseeee" was. He felt that they were terribly indifferent to what was happening on the many radio remote broadcasts of Tommy Dorsey and His Orchestra. In addition to giving instructions to the class about Dorsey's amazing breath control and inflected style of phrasing, Tabuteau raved about Dorsey's sound production and breath support of long tones, along with his freedom in playing—the way he played with such feeling and expression. Tabuteau concluded by saying, "Let your feelings get into the music the way Tommy Dorsey's does."

Another admirer of Dorsey was the eighteen-year-old trumpeter Steve Lipkins, who played lead in the Dorsey band. Lipkins found Dorsey "fascinating. The trombone was an extension of his body. All his mechanics were just perfection: his breath control, his phrasing, his conceptions, his pitch. Everything about him was superb. [He was] probably the best trombone of that type for his day. As a leader he was a smart guy." Lipkins later worked for Jimmy Dorsey, who, he said, "was just as good an organizer and leader, but I don't think he had the flash . . . He had a different personality."

After several months on the band, Lipkins incurred Tommy's displeasure during an RCA Victor recording session in New York. Tommy blamed him for ruining several takes. A few days later, Tommy continued his rage on a dance date: "Don't you know what D.S. means?" (In musical terms, it's an abbreviation for *dal signo*, which means go to the top of the page and continue down.) Lipkins countered with, "Yeah! D.S. means Dorsey stinks." The band broke out in laughter, but two weeks later Lipkins was gone. "It was no disgrace to be fired from that band," Lipkins observed.

(Interestingly enough, from a letter provided by Viola Monte, the widow of Harry James's longtime manager, Frank "Pee Wee" Monte, dated October 15, 1936, I learned that James had been offered a job by Dorsey. Presumably, this was at the time when Dorsey was becoming disenchanted with Steve Lipkins. In the letter, the young trumpeter wrote, "Dear Mr. Dorsey," and went on to explain that he had earnestly discussed Tommy's offer with Ben Pollack, for whom he was then working, but that Pollack had offered him a raise to stay. If James had accepted Tommy's offer, he probably would never have joined the Benny Goodman band, where he gained his initial fame.)

The summer 1936 replacement radio job had important repercussions for the Dorsey band. Network radio comedians Jack Benny, Fred Allen, Eddie Cantor, and George Burns and Gracie Allen had become major figures through the popularity of their weekly half-hour shows. Many of them hired bands, and sometimes the bandleader acted as a buffoon for the star to poke fun at, as in the case of Phil Harris with Jack Benny.

The Brown & Williamson Tobacco Company took a serious look at comedian Jack Pearl, who had created a sensation with his Baron Munchausen character, whose "Vas you dere, Sharlie?" became a popular expression. Once again, a big band was considered, although it would only play one number on the weekly show. The growing popularity of Tommy's orchestra got him the job on NBC's *Jack Pearl Show*, which debuted on November 4, 1936. Ultimately, Pearl's Baron Munchausen character wasn't enough to sustain a national following, and the show didn't last.

Brown & Williamson thought the Dorsey band, however, was worth becoming the centerpiece of a new show. Dorsey's girl singer, the smart and sassy Edythe Wright, could sing ballads and up-tempo songs equally well. Wright knew one of the important executives at Brown & Williamson and brought the band to the company's attention. At first, there was talk of the Dorsey orchestra's sharing a variety show with a young comedian and pantomimest named Red Skelton. Tommy demurred, insisting, "No way am I going to split the billing with some hillbilly comic out of the Middle West!"

In the meantime, the Dorsey band kept touring. Bunny Berigan, who had replaced Max Kaminsky in the trumpet section in December 1936, had become a particular favorite of Tommy's through his bold and assertive trumpet solos. His drinking, however, could be a problem. After three months, he left to start his own band.

The thirty-minute-long *Tommy Dorsey Show*, sponsored by Raleigh and Kool cigarettes was launched on NBC on Friday nights from 9:30 to 10 P.M. during the summer of 1937, coming from Studio 8G in Rockefeller Center. A commercially sponsored (radio) program gave a band an enormous financial cushion, sometimes as much as $250,000 a year and a showcase for its recordings. Dorsey was officially introduced as "That Sentimental Gentleman of Swing—Tommy Dorsey, His Trombone and His Orchestra—with Edythe Wright and Jack Leonard." For Tommy Dorsey, the lean days were history.

Living in Brooklyn, Richie Lisella, originally from Summit Hill, Pennsylvania, read an item in a New York newspaper in December 1936 that said, "Tommy Dorsey and His Orchestra will be rehearsing in the afternoon at Radio City for its weekly appearance on the *Jack Pearl Show* on NBC." Lisella went up to the eighth floor in Rockefeller Center, took a seat in the audience in the studio, and watched Tommy and his charges run down various songs. Suddenly, Lisella heard the bandleader yell out, *"Burns."* Dorsey ordered Burns to call Ronnie Lampere, the band's bus driver, and to get rid of him. Dorsey further suggested to Burns, "See if you can find somebody in the audience who would be interested in driving the band to our date at Villanova College (outside Philadelphia)." Considering the times and the remaining high rate of unemployment, this wasn't an idle suggestion.

Burns approached Lisella and asked him if he could drive a bus. The two went down in the elevator to West Forty-ninth Street, whereupon Lisella said, "Yeah, I think I could drive that." He had previously driven a beer truck and figured it was very similar.

Lisella drove the Dorsey band bus to Villanova and then returned the band to New York. He never got a chance to talk to Dorsey, as Tommy drove in his own car. Burns then asked Richie if he would drive the band up to Connecticut for a few dates, which turned out to be almost a week of one-nighters.

Dorsey approved of Richie's work, as he had now become the band's regular bus driver. After almost three weeks, Dorsey finally spoke to him, "My mother was asking about you. She wanted to know how you were getting along." Lisella's cousin Tony was then dating Mary, Dorsey's sister. "Why didn't you tell me you were from Pennsylvania?" Tommy said.

For the next six months, Lisella drove the band bus throughout New England and as far south as North Carolina. Dorsey asked him to move into his home in Bernardsville. When the band was working in New York, the fast-driving Dorsey would make the forty-eight-mile journey with Richie to the city in his new Buick Roadmaster in an hour.

Reflecting on those years, Lisella remarked, "I still think of him. He was a very gutsy kind of guy who took care of everything and looked out for his musicians. He was always the boss and very much of a leader. I learned everything from him. From being with the band on the road I got to know songs. I found what makes a commercial song from watching Tommy and the band play." Years later, Lisella discovered the successful 1950s singing star Teresa Brewer and became her manager. It was he who found what became her megahit songs "'Til I Waltz Again with You" and "Richochet Romance."

Lisella recalled being with Dorsey in Texas, which was then a dry state. Male patrons would bring whiskey to dance dates and add Coca Cola in paper cups purchased at the dance hall counter: "The bandstands were very low and I had to constantly prevent those drunks from trying to jump on the bandstand while the band was performing. This caused many fights. I remember one week of one-nighters down there when there was at least one fight every night. Tommy wasn't afraid of anybody. I got into some of those fights myself." (Lisella was only five feet four and weighed 135 pounds.)

Appearing on the Raleigh-Kool radio show allowed Dorsey to try out a considerable amount of new material on a weekly basis before both a studio audience and a national listening audience. This meant working closely with his arrangers. Paul Weston contributed some ballad arrangements, but mostly he wrote arrangements for jazz tunes; Axel Stordahl and Dick Jones wrote the charts mainly for the ballads. Paul and Axel became close friends, an association that lasted to the end of their lives.

Although Weston had written arrangements for Joe Haymes's band, he was relatively inexperienced. Tommy recognized his talent, but he would carefully dissect his work from beginning to end, removing entire sections, rephrasing, and continually editing. Axel's first arrangement, "Gotta Go to Work Again," was reworked by Dorsey, who insisted that the introduction to the song should be played three times. The songs that worked best soon became RCA recordings, and the Raleigh-Kool show then showcased them.

Both Goodman and Dorsey were signed with RCA. In 1936 Benny had enjoyed five number-one records in a row. As a marketing ploy, the behemoth recording company paired the two bands on alternate sides of a record of "Star Dust"; Goodman's version was the more popular in air play.

Tommy turned out far more recordings than Goodman, most likely because he was paid $250 to $300 per record but received no royalties. Therefore, at each recording session, four or five records were cut, which helped finance the band. In those days hit singles were everything; a band would record an album only every few years.

The first *Tommy Dorsey Show* that debuted on NBC's Blue Network of stations opened with a swing arrangement of the haunting theme from Nicholas Rimsky-Korsakov's "Song of India," from his opera *Sadko*. The featured number, however, on the show was a new arrangement of Irving Berlin's "Marie," which was originally written as a waltz and had been the musical theme of the 1928 film *The Awakening*. These two significant tunes were recorded on January 29, 1937. "Marie" had made its radio debut, however, on the January 11 broadcast of the *Jack Pearl Show* and was repeated the following week due to its heavy audience response.

Tommy and Carmen Mastren contributed the initial outline for "Song of India," but Paul Weston and trombonist Red Bone also contributed various sections of the arrangement. Dave Tough's introduction on the tom-toms precedes the saxes and brass riffing against each other, utilizing the call-and-response device (thought to have been originated by Don Redman in the Fletcher Henderson band) so prevalent in swing arrangements, before Tommy's trombone states the theme. This leads right into Dorsey's piercing, pristine muted solo that immediately seizes the listener's attention. The sixteen-bar sax section chorus comes next. This is followed by Bunny Berigan, who comes in on the next chorus before Dorsey's solo takes the recording out.

One of the outstanding elements of the "Song of India" recording is the perfect intonation displayed by the saxophones and the exacting section work of the entire orchestra. Tommy had at last succeeded in putting together the kind of orchestra he'd always wanted. For Dorsey, a big band was everything; it combined three elements that were extremely important to him: power, precision, and discipline. His band was the embodiment of what a big band should sound like. In December the *DownBeat* Readers' Poll picked "Song of India," second only to Goodman's brilliant "Sing, Sing, Sing," as the best big-band arrangement of the year.

Equally exciting for other reasons is "Marie." Jack Leonard's hearty vocal tapers off before Berigan's stupendous solo—surely one of the most familiar trumpet solos in jazz history—in which he coyly and strategically plays with both the beat and the melody, starting with a clarion F to a high F, and then changing the key as well as the mood. But it's the exuberant, rhythmic vocal chorus by the band that ends with "Livin' in a great big way—*Mama*!" that sets up the tremendous impact of Berigan's trumpet chorus. (This device was radical for its time and not too far afield from early examples of rap.) Freeman and Dorsey followed that, contributing impressive solos before the out chorus.

"Marie" was not a group arrangement but a "borrowed" effort. Bobby Burns remembered that the band had been working at Levaggi's, a restaurant in Boston, "and was really dying. A local agent in Philadelphia named Harry Squires called and asked if we could come to Philadelphia to play Nixon's Grand Theatre. . . . I spoke to Mr. Levaggi, who was delighted to get rid of us." On the bill in Philadelphia that October was a black choral group, the dancer Peg Leg Bates, and Doc Wheeler's Sunset Royal Orchestra, all of whom preceded the Dorsey band, which closed the show.

Jack Leonard added:

The Sunset Royal Orchestra [was] a black band and man could they swing! We were there in a "Battle of the Bands." They were on stage. Axel, Tommy and I were standing in the wings watching and listening before we went on. Tommy said, "Boy, we got our work cut out for ourselves." Then they went into their arrangement of "Marie." Tommy turned to me and says, "I like that!" and Axel says, "Yeah." We all discussed it for a bit and what we'd do with it. . . . We really stole their arrangement.

The Sunset Royals had it in 4/4 time and what they did was play a whole lot of instrumental and then the whole band would sing "Marie" etc. We lifted that part of it, at least the idea, note for note. Then we refined it with

Tommy, I think, saying, "Hey Jack, you sing the lead and the guys will do a patter background." There was no lead in their arrangement, of course, just the whole band singing together. . . . When people ask me who did that arrangement, my answer is: You know, nobody did it. Axel had a hand in it. Paul Weston had a hand in it. Alto saxophonist Fred Stulce, I think, did the basic arrangement. Tommy, too, added a little bit.

Carmen Mastren contended that Freddie Stulce wrote the entire chart.

Dorsey never denied the story. In the June 1938 issue of *Metronome* he stated, "I traded them about eight of our arrangements for [that] one of theirs." Some say there was a fifty-dollar payment made to the Sunset Royal Orchestra as compensation. Those who knew how Dorsey conducted business dispute both of those explanations. This was only one of many musical innovations "lifted" from black musicians during this era.

As an example, Gerald Wilson, then a trumpeter in Jimmy Lunceford's band, wrote "Yard Dog Mazurka," which the Lunceford Orchestra recorded. Later, it became the basis of Stan Kenton's theme song, "Artistry in Rhythm."

On March 29, 1938, "Marie" became the most popular record in the country and stayed there for another week. "Song of India" reached number five that same week. The two-sided hit sold over 150,000 records at a time when a successful record sold 20,000 copies. By 1946 the sheet music and the record of "Marie" would each have sold 1 million copies.

It was these two recordings that fundamentally established Tommy Dorsey and His Orchestra as a major attraction. Even today, almost seventy years later, these recordings are often programmed on syndicated nostalgia radio shows as prime examples of swing music at its best.

Trying to strike gold again, Dorsey quickly adapted several other classical pieces and attempted to turn them into swing hits. He made use of various arrangers in the transformation process. Carmen Mastren worked on "Liebestraum," Dvorak's "Going Home" (which became "Rollin' Home"), "Oh, Promise Me," and "Melody in F"; Axel Stordahl wrote a chart based on Mendelssohn's "Spring Song," "Humoresque" was arranged by Paul Weston, and "The Blue Danube" and "Hymn to the Sun" were arranged by Red Bone.

The band soon wearied of having to deal with the overwhelming popularity of "Marie" by playing it several times a night. Dorsey, however, knew the importance of the song's arrangement. Not long afterward, Tommy dispatched Weston and Bobby Burns to go up to Harlem and buy the Sunset Royals' arrangement of "Who," but they were rebuffed by Doc Wheeler.

Weston and Freddie Stulce ultimately collaborated on the "Who" chart, once again having the band sing a countermelody, with lyrics this time specially written by Edythe Wright. This preceded the extended trumpet solo by Pee Wee Erwin, who had replaced Bunny Berigan.

The success of "Who" followed the band's second number-one hit of 1937, "Satan Takes a Holiday." After that, other prototypes of "Marie" recorded by the Dorsey band were "Yearning," "Sweet Sue," "Blue Moon," "How Am I to Know?" "Blue Skies," "Deep Night," and "East of the Sun."

With a weekly national radio show, a continuing series of hit records, and frequent New York location engagements, the band was a magnet for song pluggers. It was the song plugger's job to convince bandleaders to have arrangements written of their company's latest songs, which would then be played on the air and might therefore become hit records. Invariably, many of the song pluggers would show up at 2:30 A.M., just before the band's weekly rehearsal that followed the nightly job that ended at 2:00 A.M.

As with the payola of the 1950s, bandleaders were deluged with baseball tickets, bottles of expensive whiskey, and other "personal" gifts. On the other hand, Dorsey, exercising his "quo" part of the bargain, was sometimes vengeful toward a publisher who had double-crossed him, destroying arrangements of new songs or those already a part of the band's library.

Bobby Burns kept track as Tommy tried out new tunes, telling him to "keep it in" or "send it to the file." One night the band ran down a new tune called "Dancing with You," written by Michael Edwards, a family friend of Dorsey's from Coaldale, who had originally played in a band with Pop Dorsey. Tommy instructed Axel Stordahl to write a standard arrangement, following the usual practice of trombone in the first chorus, a vocal, eight bars, and out.

After a year of being played irregularly and getting little response, "Dancing with You" was sent to the file. Jack Robbins, the prominent music publisher, attended one of the late-night rehearsals and begged Tommy to allow him to get a new lyricist for the song. Bud Green, writer of "Alabamy Bound," "Sentimental Journey," and other hit tunes, was brought in to rework "Dancing with You." His new lyric worked under its new title, "Once in a While," won the 1937 American Society of Composers, Authors and Publishers (ASCAP) Prize and had the longest run as number one on *Your Hit Parade* of any song in the history of the radio program up to that time.

By 1938 the Dorsey band had no one particular musical image, with its combination of classical numbers; various novelty hits, like Larry Clinton's "The Dipsy Doodle"; the many sweet ballads sung by Jack Leonard and

Edythe Wright; the "covering" of the hits of other bands, often with "Mickey Mouse" (square or pedestrian) arrangements; Dixieland tunes delivered by both the band and the Clambake Seven; and the major hits "Song of India" and "Marie." That's exactly the way the leader wanted it. His music reflected the complete range of his diverse musical tastes, and his band's popularity was considerably more than that of a niche band among swing fans.

The summer of 1939 the band played the Hotel Pennsylvania Roof in New York City and basked in the adulation of the nightly capacity audiences. With this key booking, following up his great success on records, Tommy Dorsey had reached the top of his profession. All those invaluable years on the road that followed Pop Dorsey's incessant music lessons and constant admonishment had made it all happen.

Celebrities, then as now, wanted to be associated with what's hot in entertainment. Many of them came in to dance and watch the Dorsey band. From the film world came Merle Oberon, Reginald Gardiner, and Hedy Lamarr; from the tennis world, Don Budge and Gene Mako; and from baseball, Jimmy Foxx and Bill Dickey. Red Ruffing and Franklin D. Roosevelt, Jr., who had attended the opening of the Dorsey Brothers Orchestra at the Glen Island Casino, were in attendance once again. The Tommy Dorsey band was "in the groove." Tommy made sure he and the band dressed the part.

Lisella became both Bobby Burns's assistant and the band boy, responsible for setting up and tearing down the band's setup on the bandstand every night. He remained in that job the next five years, which coincided with the zenith of the Dorsey orchestra. Besides expressing his admiration and gratitude for everything he learned from Dorsey about the music business, Lisella recalled the stylish clothes Dorsey wore on and off the bandstand: "He always looked good; all the musicians tried to look as good as he did."

In his heyday it's been said that Tommy Dorsey had a wardrobe that consisted of sixty suits and sports jackets (most of them tailor-made), forty pairs of slacks, and forty pairs of shoes. He always wore matching neckties and socks with sets in every color imaginable, basic and otherwise. It served as another reminder that he had come from a poor family and had made good in a great big way.

In June 1937 he was photographed walking along the promenade of Atlantic City's famous Steel Pier with Edythe Wright, resplendent in white walking shorts—undoubtedly a trend-setting fashion statement for American males at the time. Tony Zoppi, former Dallas *Morning News* columnist and later the Riviera, Las Vegas, talent buyer, who referred to Dorsey as the "Vince Lombardi of the band business," recalled, "Believe it or not, I used to go to the Paramount Theatre in New York as much to see what he was wearing. My father was a tailor so that stuff meant something to me. He had the most beautiful dinner jackets and things like that."

Pat Hooker contended, "He would never allow himself to blow his nose on anything but a twenty-five-dollar handkerchief. And like Joan Crawford, he insisted there could be no wire hangers in his closet, insisting instead on having wood hangers so that his trousers would hang properly."

Jess Rand, the retired publicist and personal manager, began working in the music publishing business as a counter boy. One day he was in Leighton's, the Broadway and Forty-eighth Street clothing store then frequented by performers. Rand recalled, "Tommy was looking through bolts of material until he saw a tweed he particularly liked. He asked the salesman, 'How many colors do you have in this one? He wanted six of them." Not long after that, one of Dorsey's nicknames justifiably became "Tweed." Retired comedian and director Dick Martin called him the "Godfather of Clothes."

His onstage clothes always accented his broad shoulders, barrel chest, thin waist, and long torso. He wore slightly raised heels on his shoes—all of which contributed to his appearing much taller than he actually was. His distinctive look on the bandstand was specifically designed to distance himself from the image of a stern schoolmaster, which he indeed resembled.

He was almost psychotic about rumpled clothing. No one could figure out how he could possibly keep creases out of his sleeves, since his arms and shoulders were always in motion blowing the trombone and directing the band. Jack Egan had one explanation: "The first thing he did when he came off stage or the bandstand back was to go back to his dressing room to take off his trousers and jacket. He never sat around in them, only in a robe. It was one of the ways he stayed neat." His undershorts had a button with a little tag on it so it would attach itself to the shirt, and the shirt wouldn't wrinkle. His socks and undershorts contained his initials.

This penchant for neatness carried over to his entire musical image: his well-groomed musicians, who were clean-shaven, wore shined shoes, and dressed in immaculate, well pressed band uniforms, and who played the best arrangements clearly, and singers who sang with style and verve.

Jimmy Dorsey, in the meantime, was living the good life in Los Angeles. His weekly appearances on the *Kraft Music Hall* helped considerably to establish his band. He, of course, fully realized that Tommy's band had become more popular than his. There was little communication between the two of them at this juncture.

That summer of 1937, the Jimmy Dorsey band finished working for Bing Crosby on the *Kraft Music Hall* and was replaced by John Scott Trotter's orchestra. Jimmy's band had recorded a few hit records. "Is It True What They Say About Dixie?" became number one. But Jimmy realized he was already late in cashing in on the swing craze and yearned to get his band out on the road. Bob Eberly had become close to Jimmy and was on his way to becoming an outstanding ballad singer.

After a separation of almost two years, the long-standing feud between the brothers suddenly came to an end. In September, Joe Helbock, the owner of the Onyx, threw a lavish party to celebrate Jimmy's return to New York and invited members of both Dorsey orchestras, plus other bandleaders such as Artie Shaw, Joe Haymes, Lennie Hayton, and Wingy Manone. It was Helbock's last hurrah—the celebrated Fifty-second Street club soon went bankrupt.

Jimmy seethed underneath, but he could live with the success of "The Brother." They were now friends again.

Tommy's brisk record sales in 1937 also enabled RCA to make a financial killing as a result of the unconscionable record deal it had signed with Tommy. Later, RCA's recording director, Eli Oberstein, was fired and attempted to take Goodman and Dorsey with him to his new label, the United States Recording Corporation. This serious threat caused RCA to offer Dorsey a new contract guaranteeing him sixty thousand dollars a year.

By 1938, Tommy's considerable attributes as a musician, bandleader, and cunning businessman had all combined to make him an unqualified success. In that year, it's estimated, Tommy Dorsey and His Orchestra grossed $600,000. He opened an office in the Brill Building at Forty-ninth Street and Broadway under the name of TomDor Enterprises. The Brill Building was where Tin Pan Alley was then located.

In July 1938, at a time when the *DownBeat* and *Metronome* yearly polls were of vital importance, the Tommy Dorsey band came in second in the "swing" and "favorite" categories and third in the "sweet" division in the *Metronome* poll. Its high standing in all three classifications gave it a commanding lead in total popularity among all the orchestras. According to the magazine, it was the first time that any dance orchestra had garnered such a decisive lead in popularity.

On January 11, 1939, the first *Metronome* All Star Band, whose members were determined by the votes of readers of the magazine, convened for a recording session in New York under George T. Simon's supervision. Dorsey's longtime musical hero, Jack Teagarden, had been featured on "The Blues." On the second tune, "Blue Lou," Tommy was taken aback when Simon asked him to play a solo. "Nothing doing," he protested, "not when Jack's in the room." With great reluctance, he nevertheless played a pretty blues chorus while Teagarden improvised around it. The result was quite emotional.

Tommy's great popularity had transformed his usual self-confidence into cockiness. He enjoyed being a star bandleader, but he maintained a cordial relationship with his bandleader colleagues. His relationships with some of the musicians in the band became even more fractious. He was constantly aware of the fact that he had to maintain the high quality of his band's music or he might falter.

Dorsey's success now enabled him to willingly help out other bandleaders in financial trouble that year and in the next several years, among them Harry James, Artie Shaw, Will Hudson, Larry Clinton, and Glenn Miller. He genuinely enjoyed helping them, but at the same time it fed his need to be powerful and important.

First, he secured a spot for his established colleague Miller on the Raleigh cigarette commercial on his radio show. Miller had been busy working around New York. Earlier, Tommy had invited Glenn to live with the Dorsey family in Bernardsville before Glenn got married. Then he loaned Miller what his then publicist, the long-retired music publisher Howie Richmond, believes was five thousand dollars: "It was the godsend Glenn and his wife, Helen, needed at that point." This was at a time when Glenn's first band was scuffling. A few months later, watching the Miller band perform at the Glen Island Casino, Dorsey predicted, "That's gonna be the next [major] band."

Beneath this surface cordiality, however, was a fierce personal rivalry that dated back to Miller's time with the Dorsey Brothers Orchestra. Although Glenn soon paid back the loan in full, Dorsey, in his own inimitable fashion, saw the loan in a different light: He believed it entitled him to a piece of all the Miller band's future income.

It's often impossible to figure out Dorsey's thinking; however, it probably stemmed from his penchant for always having to have the edge on anyone he viewed as a competitor. Familiar with Tommy's predatory business behavior, Glenn walked away after firmly turning down his demand. Their once close relationship cooled.

For Dorsey, however, this was not the end of the matter. In early 1939, he decided to finance tenor saxophonist Bob Chester in a new band venture to get back at Miller. He hired arrangers who could duplicate Miller's newly patented romantic sound, which consisted of having his clarinetist, Willie Schwartz, supply the lead by playing an octave over the saxes. He also saw to it that Chester was signed to Bluebird, RCA's subsidiary label, in direct competition with Miller. All of this maneuvering, however, had absolutely no effect on Miller's continuing popularity.

Soon after the association with Miller ended, another musical star came onto the horizon of Dorsey's career. One afternoon Dorsey sat at a table at the Nola Studio in Manhattan listening while Bob Chester auditioned band singers. A twenty-three-year-old New York–area club-date and radio singer named Frank Sinatra walked into the studio for his audition. When it was his turn to sing, Sinatra was so awestruck by Dorsey's presence that he completely froze and was unable to sing. Somehow or other Sinatra got the job, however, as he sang with the Chester band on a subsequent New Yorker Hotel gig. Less than a year later, Sinatra would become the male singer for Dorsey's orchestra over a 2½-year period. This tenure would have a tremendous effect on both his musical direction and his way of living.

If Benny Goodman was "The King of Swing" and soon after Artie Shaw, who would make his breakthrough in 1938 with the beguiling "Begin the Beguine," was dubbed "The King of the Clarinet," then Tommy Dorsey would have to have his own label. Subsequently, he would become "The Sentimental Gentleman of Swing," a term obviously derived from the title of his theme song.

In early 1938, the seventeen-year-old trombonist Earle Hagen, later the composer of the musical scores for such television shows as *The Dick Van Dyke Show, Make Room for Daddy, The Andy Griffith Show,* and *I, Spy,* rejoined Dorsey from Benny Goodman. While the band was at the Commodore, Dorsey took a ten-day vacation to Bermuda and entrusted Hagen with the job of leading the band and playing his solos (shades of Bobby

Byrne). He wasn't permitted to work on the *Raleigh and Kool Radio Show*, however, because he wasn't yet a member of Local 802.

Will Bradley was brought in to substitute for Hagen on the radio show. On his return from Bermuda, Bradley said to Tommy, "You haven't been at the hotel for a couple of weeks." "That's right. I guess you noticed the difference," remarked Dorsey. "Yeah, I noticed the difference," replied Bradley, an ace needler. "Whoever that was who was playing for you was dead in tune. That's the first time I ever heard 'Sentimental over You' without the high note being sharp." (Many musicians noticed that Dorsey often played a half tone sharp, in order, he said, to create a richer, more brilliant sound. It was also more commercial.) Prickly as ever, Dorsey took out his sense of injury on Hagen. After Bradley's comment, Dorsey didn't speak to Hagen for a week.

According to Hagen, Tommy wasn't drinking when Hagen first joined the band, but soon, after seven years of sobriety, he began to waver. He started sipping an Italian digestive bitter called Fernet Blanca that contained 12 percent alcohol, and occasionally he would come on the bandstand stoned from taking it. One might surmise that the pressure of staying on top and the constant traveling were the principal causes of his drinking again. He would never fully control his desire for alcohol.

In March 1938 the Raleigh-Kool show moved to Wednesday nights on NBC's Red Network, right after being renewed for an additional twenty-six weeks. After the initial broadcast, the show was rebroadcast for Mountain and Pacific stations at 1 A.M. The various shows were done live from New York or from wherever the band was working.

As a gimmick to keep the momentum going, "The Amateur Swing Contest" became an important feature of the weekly show. A breathless NBC press department news release revealed that "Dr. Dorsey" ("He's the Doctor of Swing") had held auditions for 140 midwestern amateur swing stars in Chicago over a four-hour period. A ten-minute segment featured four young instrumentalists with the band. The winner, determined by an applause meter in the studio, won seventy-five dollars. Even young women auditioned, usually guitarists and pianists. The duality of Dorsey's keen ability to spot talent and his equally shrewd sense of what was commercial intertwined here.

The contest accomplished just what it was supposed to: It built ratings, especially with young people. But it also drew some genuine talent. Some of the winners became noteworthy professional musicians, such as the esteemed guitarist George Barnes, who, among his many musical affiliations, was featured with Tony Bennett. Clarinetist Buddy DeFranco won "The Amateur Swing Contest" on March 14, 1938, at the Earle Theater in Philadelphia; several years later he became a mainstay of the Dorsey band.

Still another winner was clarinetist John Setar, a student of Pop Dorsey from 1934 to 1937, while growing up in neighboring Nesquehoning, who also won the contest at the Earle Theater that year. Eighty-one-year-old Setar continues to be a working musician in Los Angeles and remembers Tom Dorsey as "a very gentle man and very kind. If I made a mistake, he'd say, 'Just take it over again.' There was no admonition there. He realized I was trying so he was nice about it. . . . Studying with Tom, he had me branch out into many different facets, including jazz. He naturally continued with my classical studies as well. He was the best of the three teachers I ever had."

It's Setar's recollection that by then Pop Dorsey charged five dollars a lesson, which took place in the living room of the Lansford house: "The lesson was supposed to be an hour, but sometimes it would be a lot longer. It would last as long as it was necessary. He was not a clock watcher."

Max Kaminsky by this time was a part of Artie Shaw's band. Shaw had made a significant impression with his jazz-flavored instrumentals. Kaminsky contended, "As beautifully as Tommy could play, he was never much of a swing man. . . . Tommy's band had a lot of great soloists and a lot of polish. It didn't have that exciting, infectious feeling of guys wanting to play." That comment could sum up the way many musicians felt about Tommy's music.

Kaminsky recalled that in 1937 both bands were booked for the Dartmouth Winter Carnival dance: "We blew Tommy off the stand. He was a man who was always mad about something, but that night he was so burned up that he grabbed his horn and stalked off the stand. Tommy wasn't one to take a losing game; he'd never trained himself to lose."

Shirley Morgan, Russ Morgan's widow, delighted in telling of another incident that took place when the Dorsey and Morgan orchestras shared the bill on a college date: "Before the dance, Tommy said to Russ that since he was the best trombone player in the world his (Tommy's) band should close the show. Russ said that was fine with him. As he was finishing his set, Morgan said, 'And now I bring you the greatest trombonist in the world,

Tommy Dorsey.' However, this was immediately after his band had played 'I'm Getting Sentimental over You,' 'Marie,' 'Song of India,' and some of Tommy's other hits. Tommy wouldn't speak to Russ for two years after that."

Much of the time, Tommy was on the road with his band. His main contact with Toots and his two children was by frequent long-distance telephone calls. Pat Hooker was very vocal in describing how little attention she received from her father. This was not much different than the way other bandleaders treated their families. Tom Dorsey III was then still a little boy. Tommy's life centered on the band.

Edythe Wright was his wife away from home. In addition, there were also his many clandestine liaisons. He enjoyed the company of musicians and performers in general. There was a comfort factor in hanging out with those who shared the same passion for performing and living an itinerant and loose lifestyle.

In May 1938, the band crossed the country for its first excursion to California with a four-week booking at the Palomar beginning on June 28. Tommy planned to spend some time with Bing Crosby. Bing always brought out the clown in Tommy. It was then that Tommy asked him if he would play drums in the Amateur Swing Contest, and Bing agreed. With that as a start, Tommy and his radio producer, Herb Sanford, convinced actor and singer Dick Powell, a former trumpeter, to play trumpet; comedian Ken Murray, a clarinetist in vaudeville, to play clarinet; and singer Shirley Ross (who had introduced "Thanks for the Memory" with Bob Hope in *The Big Broadcast of 1938*) to play piano. Finally, Jack Benny insisted on joining the group, playing violin in his own inimitable style.

Sanford recalled, "We pretended that the applause meter was so overwhelmed by the individual swinging performances that it ceased to function. We declared a five way tie. This led to the five contestants launching into an animated discussion of how they would handle the $75 dollars, including such matters as social security and agents' commissions."

The show closed with the five "contestants" joining in on a jam session playing "When You and I Were Young, Maggie," backed by Tommy and the band. It was terrible, but the audience loved it. Over the applause, Bing exclaimed, "Hey Tommy, you better tell that man from *Metronome* to take back the award."

While doubling between the Palomar and the Raleigh-Kool show, Tommy auditioned a new singing group called The Pied Pipers that Paul Weston and Axel Stordahl had brought to his attention after originally learning about them from the popular singing group the King Sisters. The Pied Pipers was composed of seven men and a woman and was led by John Huddleston. The lone woman, Jo Stafford, formerly of the three-member Stafford Sisters, had joined the group after it started at Long Beach Junior College. The Pipers made an impression on Tommy, but the connection wouldn't happen for several months.

As often happened when he wasn't pleased with either the overall sound of the band or individual members of a particular section, he fired the entire trumpet section. A new trumpet section joined the band after it returned to New York in August. It consisted of Charlie Spivak, who had been a member of the Dorsey Brothers Orchestra; Yank Lawson, who played the jazz chair, and whom, like Spivak, Tommy stole from his old nemesis Bob Crosby's band (which had just won the *DownBeat* poll); and Lee Castaldo, who had left Artie Shaw to join the Dorsey band. (By then Dorsey had achieved such a reputation for stealing musicians from other bands that he was dubbed Bruno Hauptmann, after the notorious kidnapper of the Lindbergh baby.)

Tommy recognized Castaldo's ability as an all-around trumpeter but noticed he had decided problems with intonation in his playing and an inability to play well in the upper register. The answer: Give him fifty dollars a week for board and spending money and dispatch him to Lansford to live and study with Pop Dorsey. The elder Dorsey straightened out Castaldo's musical problems in close to a year while he lived in Lanseford. Lee told now-retired trumpeter Eddie Bailey, "Pop Dorsey wouldn't even allow me to drink out of a Coca Cola bottle. He said it would ruin my embouchure."

On his return to the band, a close personal relationship ensued between Lee and Tommy, who thereafter treated him like an adopted son. Castaldo (later Castle) would later play with other important bands but would return to the Dorsey fold in the early 1950s and become an important member of that orchestra.

The new trumpet section participated in the four tunes that were recorded at RCA on August 16 and 22, 1938, the most noteworthy of which was tenor saxophonist Deane Kincaide's "Boogie Woogie" arrangement. Kincaide, another acquisition from Bob Crosby, had already shown his ability to write spectacular jazz arrangements for Dorsey like "Wabash Blues,"

"Panama," "Copenhagen," and later, "Hawaiian War Chant" and a two-sided version of "Milenberg Joys." "Boogie Woogie," however, was his pièce de résistance.

Pianist Howard "Pine Top" Smith carried the "Boogie Woogie" melody, but it was the rocking ensemble sound of the band that preceded Tommy's bluesy solo on the last chorus, one of the outstanding solos of his entire career, that made it such a hit. It also cashed in on the craze that derived from the revival of the Pine Top Smith composition that highlighted a percussive style of piano blues.

Playing in the Dorsey trombone section at this time was Moe Zudekoff, who, as Buddy Morrow, would eventually lead the Tommy Dorsey "ghost" band. Buddy claims that Kincaide knew the trombone as well as he did the tenor saxophone and actually wrote out Dorsey's epic solo. Strangely enough "Boogie Woogie" wasn't a major hit until 1942, when it was reissued, sold over a million copies, and became an essential of the Dorsey library from this moment on.

Looking back on that period, Morrow said further:

I was too young to appreciate Tommy as a leader. Artie Shaw [for whom he had worked earlier] had a deeper musical sense. Tommy had more drive and was more primitive. Benny [Goodman, for whom he later worked] was like the Picasso of the era—very few lines but very, very important. In Benny's own way, things floated like oil on water, just lovely. You looked at him, and you were allowed the privilege of living with him.

Dorsey knew what he wanted, and if something you were doing [musically] appealed to him, he didn't think two seconds whether he was going to steal it or not. I used to call him the "benevolent pirate." He also knew his audience, what kind of people are dancing, and who's not dancing—why aren't they dancing? I also learned self-discipline from him.

Morrow described asking Tommy for a raise:

While working for him, I discovered that Elmer Smithers, the third trombonist, was getting a hundred sixty-five a week, and I was being paid a hundred and twenty-five. When I told Dorsey that I wanted a raise, he said, "Let me think about it." If he didn't like what you did that night, he wouldn't sign the check. The next week he said, "Have you looked at the check? What do you think?" I said, "It's a ten dollar raise—not enough." He looked at me . . . about ready to kill.

When Paul Whiteman offered Morrow $375 a week for three days a week or less, Morrow says, "I went fast. I told Tommy, and he said, 'I wish you'd go with Benny Goodman or Shaw . . . a jazz player,' which was good advice 'cause I was still at a formative stage as far as jazz. I still didn't know what the hell it was, but I enjoyed [playing] it."

Morrow says that when he told Tommy he was leaving, Tommy said, "Some day this band will be yours. Or could be yours."

Morrow offered an interesting insight into Tommy's trademark long-phrasing and, indirectly, his musicianship. "Long phrases were not necessarily Tommy's interpretation of the tune; long phrases were a way to be safe. In trombone playing at the time, when you were up in the upper register and you weren't articulating, it was dangerous. So rather than take a breath in the upper register where you might miss, you would carry the phrase over." He concluded that Dorsey's practice of concentrating on playing long phrases was his way of protecting a pretty solo, afraid that he might miss the top note: "The long phrases lots of time didn't fit the lyrics of the song he was playing. That's my theory. I always wondered where the warmth and intensity in his playing came from. I realized with him it came from within. It looked like he was just using his arm, but believe me it was his whole body working."

At the end of the very good year of 1938, on December 28 The Pied Pipers began a five-week stint on the Raleigh-Kool show. The octet had driven from Los Angeles to New York in two cars for the coveted gig. On their first appearance, they sang the standard "All of Me" and the spiritual "Joshua Fit the Battle of Jericho" and got a favorable reception. After that they were stranded without any work and eventually had to return to Southern California.

In January 1939 Tommy Dorsey inaugurated his own monthly publication, *Bandstand*, "a newspaper for musical students and bands." It was his feeling that there was room for an alternative to *DownBeat* and *Metronome*. (An unfavorable *DownBeat* review may have inspired the idea.)

Jack Egan, an obvious choice because he knew so much about Tommy's operation, working as his publicist, was named the editor of *Bandstand*. According to Bernie Woods, then a *Variety* reporter, Tommy had wanted him to be the editor, but he turned it down. He explained, "I knew there was no way I could work for T.D. He was a martinet with people under him. I saw the way he treated Bobby Burns, his road manager, and I would never have put myself in a similar position."

Bandstand lasted only six issues. Of course, it was a promotional vehicle for the Dorsey band, with a thorough sprinkling of news such as the Clambake Seven's jamming for apes at the Philadelphia Zoo! It also contained bylined articles by members of the band and associated personnel (Jack Leonard, Freddie Stulce, clarinetist and alto saxophonist Johnny Mince, Paul Weston, Yank Lawson, Howard Smith, Axel Stordahl, Bobby Burns, Richie Lisella, Herb Sanford, et al.), all of whom described their jobs and how they functioned on the road. Other bandleaders like Benny Goodman, Artie Shaw, and Kay Kyser were given a forum to explain their music in bylined articles as well.

Despite its quality and interesting features—and a large circulation of 180,000—its $65,000 cost became prohibitive, and Dorsey's quixotic brainchild faded into history with the June issue. Nine years later Egan would become the New York editor of *DownBeat*.

On January 10, 1939, shortly before the debut of *Bandstand*, the Dorsey band closed at the Terrace Room of the Hotel New Yorker. Jimmy Dorsey's band was booked to open the next night. Jimmy was now doing well on the road and getting important hotel jobs.

Instead of playing until 2:00 A.M. on its closing night, Tommy had his band play "Auld Lang Syne" at midnight and then quickly segued into "Sandman," the theme of the Dorsey Brothers Orchestra, which Jimmy had continued using as his theme. Jimmy then made his entrance with his band playing his new theme song, "Contrasts."

The capacity-filled audience included the celebrated actor Robert Taylor, former heavyweight champion Max Baer, and bandleaders Larry Clinton and Glen Gray, along with most of the Casa Lomans. And, of course, Tom and Tess were there beaming approval from a ringside table. Tess broke into tears when her sons embraced and started reminiscing on the bandstand. Tom the elder was given a trumpet and played a solo with his sons. It marked the first time the three of them had played together since Lansford days. In *Metronome*, George Simon said, "There arose a feeling of sincerity and reality that'll seldom be equaled in the history of dancebandom."

This emotional performance caused Tommy to book Jimmy and his band for his next radio show. On January 18 the Tommy Dorsey band played "Marie" and then Jimmy's band, after opening with "Contrasts," played "Pagan Love Song." A short sketch followed with child actors portraying the brothers taking a music lesson in Lansford with their father, as Tommy and

Jimmy played cornet and peck horn, respectively, off mike. The two bands together concluded by playing Glenn Miller's original arrangement of "Honeysuckle Rose," a hit for the Dorsey Brothers Orchestra, an apt closer for a Dorsey radio reunion.

A few months later, trumpeter John Best recalled sitting with Tommy in a booth at the Hickory House on Fifty-second Street watching Jack Teagarden and his trumpeter brother, Charlie, playing alongside saxophonist Frank Trumbauer. Tommy spontaneously commented, "I wish my brother and I got along like Jack and Charlie do."

For Tommy Dorsey's band the hit records kept coming. Jack Leonard's vocal on "This Is It" became another *Billboard* Top Ten hit. Heading back to the Midwest, in Chicago the band recorded still another classical adaptation. This time it was Tchaikovsky's theme from "Romeo and Juliet," which became "Our Love," the band's next number-one hit.

Returning to New York, Dorsey opened at the Paramount Theater in April 1939 for a successful run, which preceded a return engagement at the Hotel Pennsylvania Roof. It was during this interval that the band recorded a two-sided arrangement on a ten-inch record of "Lonesome Road," written by twenty-two-year-old arranger Bill Finegan.

Finegan, his wife, Kay, and a Catholic priest named Daniel Lyons had attended a Dorsey performance at the New Yorker back in early January and sent a note to Tommy requesting him to have a drink with them. "That was a symbol of courtesy in those days," Finegan recalled. "Tommy came by the table. Since he was a Catholic, meeting the priest was the kicker. He talked for quite awhile, charming everybody. Any guy who worked for Dorsey— even if he hated him—will tell you that he was charmed by him."

When Finegan told him he had written a chart for his band, Tommy told him to bring it to the Monday-night rehearsal after the gig:

"I remember that Nelson Riddle, who was then a student of mine down in Rumson [New Jersey], watched me through this chart," Finegan says. "The Monday night I brought the chart in I sat there listening to the arrangements written by Dorsey's own guys. My confidence was going down by degrees. They sounded so great. I said to myself, "Jesus I've got a hell of a nerve coming here."

Finally he said, "Where's the kid with the arrangement?" I came up and passed out my parts. I had written a part for Tommy. He started playing everything in sight . . . the cues, he's playing the saxophone part. I stopped him saying, "No, no, that's cueing, you don't play that."

Finegan, in retrospect, is surprised that Dorsey said nothing about his interruption. "When he was involved in music, man, he was one hundred percent concentration," Finegan remembered:

> We got through it, and it was not an easy chart to read. It showed that my main inspiration was Sy Oliver's charts for Jimmie Lunceford.
>
> Unbeknownst to me, there were two factions in the band. One of the leaders of the group, who wanted to update the band's music, was the tenor saxophonist, Babe Russin. Yank Lawson was the leader of the Dixieland faction. He and Babe got into an argument. Tommy was staying out of it. We polished things up. It was Tommy's idea to make a two-sided record of "Lonesome Road" 'cause it ran that long."

After the rehearsal ended at 5:00 A.M., Tommy told Finegan he had four guys on salary and couldn't afford another arranger: "I'm going to do something for you. I don't know what, but there's a place for you somewhere. . . . You're going to be hearing from me. Don't worry about that." About a week later, just before midnight, Finegan got a call from Glenn Miller, who said, "I heard something you wrote for Dorsey. I'd like you to write something for my band."

Finegan says that "Lonesome Road" was a "showoff chart," and he did the same chart for Miller with "Blue Skies," sending it to him in Boston, where he was playing at the Raymore Ballroom. A few nights later, Finegan heard it played on a radio remote from there. Miller then called to say, "Write me another one." Finegan would go on to enjoy a lucrative four-year association with Miller that included writing such standout arrangements as "Song of the Volga Boatmen," "Sunrise Serenade," "A Nightingale Sang in Berkeley Square," and the classic hit record of "Little Brown Jug."

His relationship with Tommy Dorsey was over for the time being but not forever.

Writing "Lonesome Road" for Dorsey had an importance beyond the immediate collaboration with Miller that it led to. Though a man of pronounced reticence, Finegan declared proudly, "I like to think that [recording] my arrangement led to Tommy's wanting to incorporate [Jimmie] Lunceford's kind of music into his band, and that's what caused him to hire Sy Oliver in the first place."

During the late 1930s, the black orchestras led by Duke Ellington, Count Basie, and Jimmie Lunceford were revered for their unapproachable jazz credentials and showmanship. James Melvin "Jimmie" Lunceford for too long has been given short shrift by the jazz critical establishment as compared to the huzzahs long given Ellington and Basie. Yet no less an expert than George T. Simon referred to Lunceford's aggregation, as "without a doubt the most exciting big band of all time."

Although he played alto saxophone and other reed instruments, Lunceford led his band with a baton. He could boast of a corps of first-rate soloists that included Willie Smith on alto, Joe Thomas on tenor, Trummy Young on trombone, and Jimmy Crawford on drums. His immaculately dressed, showmanly, precise, and constantly swinging orchestra consistently outdrew Basie's and Ellington's.

Central to Lunceford's success was the extraordinary self-taught writing talent of Melvin James "Sy" Oliver. While playing trumpet for the Lunceford orchestra starting in 1933, he developed an original and distinctive two-beat style based on swinging effects, staccato phrases with a sense of humor, and a brilliant sense of continuity and climax. Oliver's splendiferous arrangements of "Dream of You," "Four or Five Times," "Swanee River," "My Blue Heaven," "Organ Grinder's Swing," "For Dancers Only" (Lunceford's theme), "Margie," "Sweet Sue," "Belgian Stomp," "By the River St. Marie," "'Taint Watcha Do," "Cheatin' on Me," "Ain't She Sweet," and others were so popular that Lunceford sometimes had three records on the *Billboard* Pop Chart simultaneously.

The *DownBeat* poll had named the Dorsey band the number-one "sweet band" that year. A sweet band was a more conventional dance orchestra as opposed to a swing band, which was, therefore, more of a jazz orchestra. This was exactly what Tommy had wanted. Sweet bands made money.

Johnny Mandel offered, "Dorsey had begun to feel bored by his own band. He saw that the country was swing crazy. The audiences were changing. The war was coming on. Glenn Miller's band, for what it was, was playing more up-tempo and more rousing numbers."

The record producer and talent scout John Hammond, who had helped put together the great Benny Goodman band of the 1930s and discovered the Count Basie band, among his many finds, bluntly referred to the Dorsey orchestra as being "about the dullest big band on the market." He chided Dorsey "for letting me and the rest of the public down with inferior musicianship and a basic lack of sincerity." Hammond favored the jazz orchestras of Goodman and Basie, yet surprisingly he had little regard for the Ellington band. He blanched at the seeming lack of interest in jazz that Dorsey was presenting.

Tommy's interest in Lunceford's music turned serious within a few weeks. Buddy Morrow remembers him addressing the band one night: "'Guys, your rehearsal tonight is to go see Jimmie Lunceford at the Famous Door.' We went over to Fifty-second Street and listened. Tommy knew all about Sy Oliver, but he wanted everybody to see and get a sense of what his approach was."

Herb Sanford remembered Tommy's running through a new swing arrangement with the band and telling them, "Look, make it sound like Lunceford. He was thinking about those Sy Oliver arrangements."

Finally, early in the summer of '39, Paul Weston and Axel Stordahl arranged for Dorsey to met with Oliver. He met him in his hotel room in the Brighton Beach section of Brooklyn. While Dorsey was shaving, he asked Oliver, "How much is it gonna' cost me to get you to come with my band?" "Five thousand a year more than Lunceford's paying me," said Oliver smartly. Dorsey smiled and barked out, "You've got a deal!" As George T. Simon related in *The Big Bands*, a close and enduring personal relationship based on complete mutual respect developed almost immediately between the two of them.

Sy (given the nickname because he once studied psychology) said, "When I moved from the Lunceford band to Tommy Dorsey, I didn't change my writing approach. He made the transition. The band that Dorsey had when I joined him was Dixieland-oriented, and my sort of attack was foreign to most of the fellows he had. We both knew that to be the case, but he wanted a swing band, so he changed personnel until he got the guys that could *do* it."

The late arranger and composer Buddy Baker pointed out that Oliver could also write quite effectively in four-four time: "It was the way he voiced things. Since he was a trumpet player, he wrote the brass in a register that he knew sounded good. He created that rocking feeling by having the various sections play rhythm while playing the melody. For example, he would have the trombones playing a pattern that really laid down a beat. Then he would have the saxophones going against that."

Oliver's first chart, recorded by the Dorsey band on July 20, 1939, was his re-creation of one of his first Lunceford hits, appropriately titled, "Stomp It Off." When the record was released in November, the reviewer "Barrelhouse Dan" in *DownBeat* noted, "'Stomp' finds Tommy's big band getting into the spirit of things as it hasn't on records for months." He went on to praise the solos by saxophonist Johnny Mince, as well as those of Yank Lawson and Babe Russin.

The aforementioned Gerald Wilson, who replaced Oliver in the Lunceford Orchestra as trumpeter and arranger and who would eventually create his own formidable reputation as an arranger and bandleader, said, "When Sy joined Dorsey, Sy became the number-one writer in the world. And it was good to see because jazz was one of the first integration things. I always say this: I want to thank Tommy Dorsey for hiring Sy Oliver because had he not hired Sy, I would not have had that job with Lunceford. I met my destiny that day. And after Sy came to Dorsey, Dorsey's band became a hard-core jazz band." Like Benny Goodman's hiring of Teddy Wilson and Lionel Hampton, Dorsey's motivation for hiring Sy Oliver was less about making a racial breakthrough and more about what was fundamentally good for the band.

Right after the change in Dorsey's musical outlook came a change that wasn't planned. Edythe Wright, the tall, statuesque, green-eyed, wavy-haired redhead, and Tommy had been lovers since she joined the band in September 1935. Toots had long suspected Tommy's involvement with Wright, and in August 1939, when she discovered that he had bought mink coats for both her and Wright, her suspicions were confirmed. Toots insisted that Wright leave the band. Anita Boyer, who later sang with the orchestras of Artie Shaw and Jerry Wald, was Wright's replacement a month later. However, for several months Wright continued to travel with Tommy on the road as his companion, even though she realized Tommy would never divorce Toots.

Dorsey reveled in his hard-earned stardom. Being a star meant more than dressing like one. He became a man about town, frequenting places like El Morocco with the chichi crowd, where he was welcomed. And having worked with enough comedians and possessing his own quick wit, he also enjoyed spending time at Lindy's, where the comedians congregated. Suddenly more than a famous musician and bandleader, he was now an important show business personality.

Glenn Miller's longtime bassist, Trigger Alpert, noticed that with his becoming a star Dorsey became even more regimental in his leadership. "But it was a good way to run a band," Alpert said. (His own boss, Miller, had a universal reputation among those who knew him for being a martinet.)

Riding the crest of its popularity, on September 8, 1939, the Dorsey band flew round-trip to Toronto on a chartered American Airlines Flagship to play the Canadian National Exhibition. It was the first time a big band had flown to an engagement. During the exhibition, a determined twenty-three-year-old songwriter named Ruth Lowe left a demo record for Tommy with Bobby Burns at the stage door. She had written a song that had been recorded by a singer and a studio orchestra arranged and conducted by

Percy Faith, who in the 1950s would become an important recording star. Guitarist Carmen Mastren listened to the song and saw great potential in it, but it took six months before it was first recorded by the Dorsey band. In the meantime, Tommy, thinking little of the song's potential, had given it to Glenn Miller, whose recording was unsuccessful. The song was entitled "I'll Never Smile Again."

With Sy Oliver's becoming part of the Dorsey band, it became a magnet for jazz musicians who noticed the difference Oliver's presence made. One of these was trumpeter Zeke Zarchy. In his continual quest for the perfect trumpet section, Tommy had pursued Zeke Zarchy during his stint with Joe Haymes's 1936 band. That year Zarchy had substituted several nights during Dorsey's Lincoln Hotel engagement before joining Benny Goodman and then Artie Shaw and Bob Crosby. He finally joined Dorsey to play lead trumpet during the band's engagement at the College Inn of the Palmer House in Chicago in the fall of 1939.

Zarchy observed, "When Sy came on the band, a lot of the personnel had changed considerably since the day when I used to sub. And the addition of a lead alto like Hymie Schertzer [back for the second time] gave the saxophone section a completely different sound." The two instruments that determined the sound of a band were the lead trumpet and the lead alto.

Zarchy remembered a three-week period when Lee Castaldo was out of the band undergoing dental work. Sy took over Castaldo's chair and sat next to Zarchy. "It was like I had died and gone to heaven. He wrote an arrangement that had a high F for me. God, I loved his solo playing. His solos were very sparse. He didn't play a lot of notes. I, of course, grew up with that driving four-four to the bar of the Northern American Negro."

Zarchy made an interesting general observation about the several months he spent with Dorsey: "I noticed that anybody who played in that band automatically got free lessons on their instruments. In other words, by the time they left Tommy Dorsey's band they were better players because of the standard that he set. . . . I felt I improved because the standard of his playing raised everybody else's. Whenever you played in that band, you automatically realized what he was doing to get that sound of his was his breath control. So it brought to mind: I should use more breath control in my own playing."

Another musician who would come into his own while playing with Dorsey was drummer Buddy Rich. He also came to the band during the Palmer House engagement, replacing Cliff Leeman. Rich had first created a considerable reputation for himself when he debuted with the Artie Shaw band in January 1939 after having worked briefly for Bunny Berigan. Bobby Burns tried to induce Rich to join Dorsey several months later, but Rich wasn't interested. "It's strictly a dance band. It's like a society band, no jazz in it," he told Burns.

Months later, when he learned that Sy Oliver was coming to work for Dorsey, Rich was suddenly intrigued. In mid-November, just before Shaw abruptly walked off the bandstand at the Hotel Pennsylvania, labeling the jitterbugs as "morons," and headed for Mexico, he told Rich, "Buddy, you're a wonderful drummer, but are you playing for yourself or for the band?" When Rich replied that he was playing to satisfy himself, Shaw suggested, "Perhaps you'd be better off working for somebody else." Rich got the message and soon headed for Chicago to become Tommy Dorsey's drummer at the reported extraordinary salary of $750 a week.

Rich displayed his considerable attitude with the Dorsey band, too. Zeke Zarchy remembered that when Buddy arrived in the midst of the Palmer House engagement, guitarist Carmen Mastren led the band on the first set. Buddy therefore chose not to play the drums. "He thought it was beneath him. He would either write a letter on his snare drum, eat something from the hotel kitchen, or read a magazine," Zarchy recalled.

But for the first few months after he joined the band, Rich was well on his way to becoming its center of attention as he swung the band relentlessly, relishing the opportunity to play the ever-increasing number of Sy Oliver charts. One of these, "Quiet Please," which Oliver wrote specifically for Rich on a flight to Chicago the night before Rich joined the Dorsey band, never failed to elicit a big response from the fans. On hearing various "live" recordings from this period, one can readily sense Rich's exhilaration in playing with this brassy, swinging aggregation, constantly shouting out his encouragement.

Years later he said, "I was able to take the band and give it a totally different attitude. Even the ballad tempo had some kind of beat behind it. Instead of a bland ballad thing, there was something going on behind it. And I thought that was important."

Male singers with bands were expected to be versatile—able to handle love songs and up-tempo material equally well. Jack Leonard, a superb ballad singer, was now firmly established as the nation's favorite male band singer. He was not, however, much of a jazz singer.

Another seismic change was about to take place in the Dorsey band. In a late 1970s radio interview, Leonard related that one night in the early fall of 1939 Jack was driving down to Bernardsville with Tommy after work at the Hotel Pennsylvania Roof. He asked Tommy if he had heard the Harry James band's record of "All or Nothing at All." "No," replied Dorsey. Jack went on to elaborate on the virtues of James's singer, Frank Sinatra, who delivered the vocal.

While working at the Palmer House in November 1939, Jack and Tommy had an argument over the way Tommy was treating some of the musicians. Leonard felt Tommy was being more difficult than ever. Despite rumors that he wanted to go out on his own, Leonard had no such intentions, but he had had enough of Dorsey. Everyone thought somehow Jack would return, but he didn't. On his departure, Allan DeWitt was hired to take his place, but within a few weeks, Dorsey had decided he didn't much care for DeWitt's singing and let him go. DeWitt went on to sing with Bob Chester.

Jimmy Hilliard, a friend of Dorsey's who was then the music supervisor at CBS in Chicago and later an executive at Warner Brothers Records, in the 1960s and 1970s, listened to Dorsey complain about his problems with Leonard over dinner. "Have you heard the skinny kid who's singing with Harry James?" Hilliard asked Tommy. "He's nothing to look at, but he's got a sound!"

Hilliard went on to regale Dorsey with a tale of having seen Sinatra with the James band at the Panther Room of the Palmer House a few months before. "My back was to the bandstand," he recalled, "but when the kid started taking a chorus I had to turn around. I couldn't resist going back the next night to hear him again. He's got something besides problems with acne. Harry can't be paying him much, maybe you can take him away."

Dorsey sent Bobby Burns to attend the annual Christmas party given by Mayor Ed Kelly, which the James band was playing while doubling from the Chicago Theater. After the James band's performance, Burns slipped Sinatra a note asking him to meet with Dorsey the next afternoon in his suite in the Palmer House. "I couldn't believe it when Frank showed it to me. The note was written on a torn off piece of a paper bag," recalled Nick Sevano, Frank's friend from Hoboken, New Jersey, who was then working for him as his valet.

Knowing that Tommy could be brusque and a tough taskmaster, and remembering how he had bolted from the room when he encountered Dorsey during an audition for Bob Chester's band, the young singer was extremely nervous when he met with Dorsey. The first words out of Dorsey's mouth were "Yes, I remember that day when you couldn't get out the words." Tommy asked him to sing "Marie" with the band. Sinatra did, and Dorsey liked what he heard.

Jo Stafford quipped in a recent interview, "Tom was a great patron of excellence." He made Sinatra an offer of $125 a week. Sinatra's wife, Nancy, was pregnant with their first child, and despite his warm feelings toward Harry and the musicians, the James band's future seemed bleak. Frank Sinatra needed money desperately, and he realized that Dorsey showcased his singers like no other bandleader. It was the band every young singer dreamed of joining. Years later, in referring to being given the opportunity to join the Tommy Dorsey band and what it meant to him, Sinatra called the band "the General Motors of the band business."

Sinatra's break with James didn't cause hard feelings. Frank Sinatra went to James's hotel room to discuss with him the offer he had received from Dorsey. When he entered the room, he discovered the bandleader busy reading a magazine. Not wanting to disturb him but needing to get his attention, he walked in and out of the room. Finally, James put down his magazine.

"What's bothering you?" James asked him.

Sinatra told him that he would be happier opening a vein, but that Tommy Dorsey had made him an offer and could pay him fifty dollars a week more. Harry James generously told Sinatra he would not stand in his way. They dissolved their business relationship with a handshake, but a lifetime friendship ensued. Many years later, James recalled in an interview with radio personality Fred Hall that before Sinatra left his hotel room, "I said to Frank, 'If we don't do any better in the next few months or so, try to get me on, too.'"

In December, on the very day her unemployment benefits ran out, Jo Stafford received a collect call at her Glendale, California, apartment from Tommy Dorsey. He told her, "I'd like a singing group in my band, but I can't afford eight people." Jo interjected, "As a matter of fact, we've only got four now." Jo was the lead singer; her three associates in the pared-down Pied Pipers were John Huddleston, Billy Wilson (soon replaced by Clark Yocum, who also later took over the Dorsey band's guitar chair), and Chuck Lowry. They immediately headed east to the Palmer House.

John Huddleston contrasted the four-part harmony of The Pied Pipers to the three-part harmony of the Andrews Sisters: "Jo Stafford singing the lead instead of Patti Andrews made a big difference. Theirs was the sound of three gals. We all sang to fit with Jo. We tried to make it a good section. We sang so much together, but Jo stood out because she was the high voice. She stood out like the lead alto in the sax section."

With the valuable additions of Messrs. Oliver, Rich, and Sinatra plus Jo Stafford and The Pied Pipers, the Dorsey band was now at its very peak. It had style, and now jazz, along with a superb array of vocalists.

On September 1, 1939, Adolph Hilter's *Wehrmacht* marched into Poland; England, and France immediately declared war on Germany, and the United States was heading in that direction. A world war to defeat totalitarianism was looming. As a result of this movement toward armed confrontation and within months the drafting of young American men, uncertainty gripped the country.

Popular music was about to undergo another period of transition, one in which romantic and plaintive ballads expressing the loneliness of women having to deal with their loved ones' going off to an uncertain future in the military were about to become "in." Tommy Dorsey's young, vibrant, and immensely talented band would provide much of the soundtrack for the galvanizing changes ahead.

5

"I'll Never Smile Again"

Real nice, Frank. You're going to go far.
—BING CROSBY

MANY DANCE bands played at the Million Dollar Pier in Atlantic City (now the site of a shopping mall across the boardwalk from the gambling mecca Caesar's Palace) in the spring and summer months throughout the 1920s and 1930s. For example, the Dorsey brothers had worked there for Sam Lanin's band, and the Ben Pollack band had played there with Benny Goodman and Jack Teagarden.

An ex-circus performer turned entrepreneur named George Hamid took over the pier in 1937, and its name changed to Hamid's Pier. Tommy Dorsey first saw Buddy Rich play when Artie Shaw's band was working at Hamid's Pier while the Dorsey band was headlining at the more prestigious Steel Pier in the summer of 1939.

Hamid's son, George, Jr., got to know the Dorseys personally, Jimmy at the Pier and Tommy at the Canadian National Exhibition. He remembered the effect of Tommy's music:

Tommy hit with so many songs . . . and so many beautiful songs . . . and love songs . . . a period when America was in love. That was part of the Tommy Dorsey charisma. Coming out of the Depression, Tommy was well known for his upbeat music, but my God, the ballads! Jack Leonard first with Edythe Wright. They played my junior prom at Princeton in 1938. Tommy carried us

113

through our romantic time. Benny [Goodman] for all of his greatness and power, he did not inspire the romance.

You could just lie there and fall in love with someone you'd pretty soon fall out of love with. On a prom weekend, you'd get your gal and go out in the car and park someplace, and then you'd wait for Tommy Dorsey. The band remotes were on every night. Tommy Dorsey would give you a little help with your newest girlfriend!

With young men being drafted in profusion and some volunteering for military service, big bands found new venues to work: army and air force bases and naval stations. The prewar period had nothing but a favorable effect on the band business because by 1940, dance bands were still big business. Altogether, big bands of every stripe earned $110,000,000 that year.

After undergoing an artistic slump, Duke Ellington was enjoying a resurgence as a result of his having recently hired arranger Billy Strayhorn, tenor saxophonist Ben Webster, and bassist Jimmy Blanton. In early 1940 the Ellington band recorded such significant singles as "Solitude," a new version of "Mood Indigo," "Jack the Bear," and "Concerto for Cootie" (which eventually became "Do Nothing Till You Hear from Me"), earning Ellington a new following.

The phenomenon of the year, however, was the new singer with the Dorsey band, Frank Sinatra. Toward the end of January he made his first appearance with the band in Milwaukee. Dorsey immediately recognized his importance.

Jo Stafford recalled her first impression of Sinatra: "As Frank came up to the mic I just thought, 'Hmmm-kinda thin?' But by the end of eight bars I was thinking, 'This is the greatest sound I've ever heard.'" When asked if his personality was any different then, Stafford replied, "In those years he had ten dollars in his pocket, and in later years he had a thousand dollars. That's the only difference."

John Huddleston noted, "He had something. He sure knew it. I could sense that he was going to do whatever he wanted. You couldn't miss it. He had the confidence that it was going to happen."

Zeke Zarchy recalled, "When I had seen him with Harry James at the Chicago Theater, the audience wouldn't let him off the stage. This scrawny kid had such appeal. I had never seen a vocalist with a band go over like that. He had a certain quality. Jack Leonard was a good singer, but a band singer. Alan DeWitt was a good singer, but a band singer. But for somebody to get up like that! I could sense that he knew that also."

Zarchy added:

People have asked me if Frank was different in those days. . . . My impression was that he was in awe of being where he was. He was in a strange atmosphere, and he didn't know any of the guys. When I say he was standoffish, it's not because he felt that he was better than anybody else. He knew that he was going to be a star because he wanted to be a star. I had that feeling. And I didn't blame him one bit and neither did anybody else because we saw what his appeal was.

One of the tunes he sang in that first show in Milwaukee was "East of the Sun," which was a ballad. It was not up. He swung it at that tempo; we didn't play it at a swing tempo. Later on, I suppose Tommy altered some of the tempos to fit his style of singing.

Along with two Pied Piper selections, the first two of what would total some eighty-three Frank Sinatra tracks with Tommy Dorsey were recorded in Chicago on February 1, 1940. (An incredible total of twenty-three of them reached the top ten on the Billboard Chart during a three-year period.) The first two tunes were "The Sky Fell Down" and "Too Romantic," both arranged by Axel Stordahl. It was not a particularly stirring recording debut. His approach to a ballad was still rather tentative. A year later, however, a "live" recording of the former reveals an emerging stylist with a warm, individual, yet intimate sound, one of the results of an endless skein of one-nighters.

On his first one-nighter Sinatra noticed an empty seat on the bus next to fellow newcomer Buddy Rich. He sat down and chatted with him. When asked why the seat was open, he was later told, "because he's a pain in the ass." After a few days Rich told his seatmate, "I like the way you sing." This soon led to the cocky pair becoming roommates.

Stanley Kay, Rich's longtime personal manager, said, "Buddy told me they had their first argument when Frank started cutting his toenails at two o'clock in the morning. The clicking of the scissors disturbed Buddy and woke him up. An argument started—and no more rooming together."

Jo Stafford remembers that Sinatra formed a closeness with Lee Castle and then with tenor saxophonist Dominic "Don" Lodice (Dominici LoGuidice), who, like Sinatra, was of Sicilian descent, and who had a wonderful sense of humor. Lodice soon was featured on the Dorsey record of

"So What" (not remotely related to the later Miles Davis composition). He and Sinatra later roomed together. For a time, the musicians referred to Frank as "Lady Macbeth" because he was always showering and changing his clothes.

But the budding friendship between Rich and Sinatra was about to become a rivalry. Dorsey watched as an intense conflict developed between his two budding young stars. Apparently, Edythe Wright was a big instigator in the feud between them. She would say things to Rich like, "What an SOB Frank thinks you are," and vice versa. Dorsey kept a firm lid on the growing friction between the two of them, but he beamed as the dancers reacted to the excitement they were creating.

Sinatra had the decided edge, however. First of all, he was a singer and thus communicated directly to the audience. The yearning quality in his voice, so characteristic of his ballad delivery, created an indelible impression, especially with young women. Dorsey sensed that and early on instructed not only Sy Oliver but also Deane Kincaide, alto saxophonist/arranger Freddie Stulce, and particularly Axel Stordahl (Paul Weston had recently departed) to write arrangements that would showcase his slightly built band singer with the prominent curl that fell seductively down over his forehead.

Morris Diamond, who had become Bobby Burns's assistant, recalled the time at the Paramount when Dorsey announced, "And here's our vocalist, Frank Sinatra." The bandleader, forever alert to infractions of what he deemed improper demeanor on the bandstand, stopped the band, which then started vamping. He bellowed loudly so that everyone on the stage could hear him, "Go back there and comb your God Damn hair!" "I was standing in the wings," said Diamond, "when Frank came to me and asked me to get him a comb, which I did, and after combing his hair he went back onstage."

Intent on imparting the musical knowledge he had gained in his more than twenty-one years as a professional musician, Dorsey started spending time with Sinatra. Although he recognized the disparity in their singing styles, he suggested to Sinatra that he listen carefully to what Bing Crosby was doing: "All that matters to him is the words, and that is the only thing that ought to matter to you!" (This was something Harry James had noticed was already important to the young singer.)

As Zeke Zarchy noted earlier, Sinatra was not only an able ballad stylist but equally adept at handling up-tempo arrangements. By listening intently to the essential jazz singer, Billie Holiday, on excursions to Fifty-second Street, Sinatra learned how to bend a note and lag behind the beat, while

exhibiting an impeccable sense of time. Although he had attended Hoboken's A. J. Demarest High School a mere forty-seven days, he had developed a penchant for reading, which gave him a clearer understanding of the
intrinsic meaning of both individual words and phrases, which in time led
to his becoming a storyteller extraordinaire. He had also learned a great
deal in this regard from watching the cabaret singer Mabel Mercer perform
on Fifty-second Street.

In speaking, Sinatra retained his distinctive North Jersey/New York pat-
ois, but in his singing he constantly worked on his diction in order to bring
out the mood and flow of the songs Dorsey assigned him. This underlined
the intensity and emotional honesty with which he interpreted lyrics. The
intimacy of his singing made every woman listening to him feel he was
singing to her and her alone. In time came additional confidence and years
later a sense of elegance that blended with his soft approach to the classic
bel canto singing style he had adopted.

He also learned that the microphone could become his friend, just as
Crosby had, which Dorsey pointed out to him. Using it not only to project
his voice, he saw that it could provide shading to his vocal presentation,
but he used it with economy. He also noticed how Dorsey made use of the
microphone to enhance his own sound, particularly on muted solos.

The most essential ingredient that working with Dorsey brought to Sinatra's singing style, however, was the result of his studiously observing Dorsey effortlessly navigate long musical phrases on the trombone. As he wrote
in *Life* magazine in 1965 (with the assistance of the magazine's then entertainment editor, the late best-selling author Tommy Thompson):

> He would take a musical phrase and play it all the way through seemingly
> without breathing for eight, ten, maybe sixteen bars. How in the hell did he
> do it? I used to sit behind him on the bandstand and watch, trying to see him
> sneak a breath, but I never saw the bellows move in his back. His jacket
> didn't even move. I used to edge my chair to the side a little and peek around
> to watch him. . . . I discovered he had a "sneak" pinhole in the corner of his
> mouth—not an actual pinhole, but a tiny place where he was breathing [this
> was something Pop Dorsey had taught him]. In the middle of the phrase,
> while the tone was still being carried through the trombone [he'd] take a
> quick breath and play another four bars with that breath.
>
> Why couldn't a singer do that, too? . . . It was my idea to make my voice
> work in the same way as a trombone or violin—not sounding like them, but
> "playing" the voice like those instruments.

Reportedly close to a year later, Dorsey finished playing a solo and said to Sinatra, in reference to his discovering his secret of breathing, "Well, Buster, did you find it?" Dorsey also stressed how much he developed his breathing by swimming laps underwater at swimming pools. Sinatra acknowledged that he spent considerable time emulating Dorsey's example by working out at the indoor swimming pool at Stevens Institute in Hoboken. Looking back on this formative period, Richie Lisella succinctly observed, "After he joined the band, Frank phrased exactly like Tommy played. I could tell the difference in his singing in just a few weeks."

Jo Stafford, however, takes a completely contrary view of how Sinatra's phrasing originated. "I do think it's nonsense," she says. "Frank just happened to have a wide rib cage like I've got, which means you take in more air and you learn to use it judiciously with lyrics. Tom [Dorsey] had a good rib cage, too. He knew how to spend it stingily."

In time, Dorsey would become more than Sinatra's musical mentor—he became his hero and a father figure to him. (Sinatra's father, Marty, was thought to be an ineffectual father.) Sinatra asked Dorsey to be the god-father of his first child, Nancy Sandra. Dolly Sinatra, Frank's doting mother, whose own personality was as powerful as Dorsey's, took to him immediately, and Sinatra's wife invited him to their apartment for Italian dinners.

Beyond his musical influence, working with Dorsey intensified personal traits that Sinatra had in common with his mentor. Among them were his impatience; his insistence on exerting a firm control over every situation; his demands to achieve and maintain perfection; his largesse in helping his friends and those in extreme distress; his habit of often treating longtime employees with disdain, while constantly testing both their efficiency and their loyalty; his enjoyment of playing the dedicated host; his spendthrift ways—which didn't always carry over to the paychecks of his underlings; his natural charm (which could be followed by abrupt mood swings); his constant search to associate himself with upper-class people while in the long run finding that he was more comfortable with his own peers; the vengeance aimed at his enemies; and a complete inability to apologize for his actions even when confronted by the fact that he was wrong. The "My Way" aspect of Frank Sinatra's character absolutely emanated from Tommy Dorsey. Why, he even walked like Dorsey!

The similarities could reach the level of absurdity. More than a decade later, after Sinatra had left the Dorsey band, Jess Rand, on a visit to Sinatra's dressing room, discovered a tube of "Dentists Prescribed," a hard-to-find English toothpaste. The only other time he had ever seen that particular brand was resting on a shelf above the sink in Dorsey's office bathroom more than a decade earlier.

As the noted jazz historian Richard Sudhalter cogently observed, "The way it works is when the autodidact looks around and sees a way of doing things, or a way of expressing himself that appeals to him, he makes it his own. . . . And I think that Sinatra as a working-class kid from Hoboken learned that way."

Dorsey knew exactly how important college dates were to the band's popularity. At one time he had his musicians wear blue blazers and brown two-tone saddle shoes on college dates to appeal to that audience. In addition, college dance dates continued to pay well.

On February 20, 1939, after a particularly cold-winter midwestern tour that extended as far west as South Dakota, the Dorsey band was the first orchestra to perform at Frank Dailey's Meadowbrook. The famous dance-band venue, located on Route 23 on the Newark-Pompton Turnpike in Cedar Grove, New Jersey, would later become one of Dorsey's favorite places to work.

An English "bootleg" recording of a concert aired "live" on NBC from the Meadowbrook on Saturday afternoon, March 9, 1940, shows how Dorsey had specifically designed a program to appeal to the enthusiastic college audience. That afternoon opened the festivities with college songs that featured both instrumentals by the band and vocals by The Pied Pipers. The specific college attached to each one of the tunes, as well as the date the band had played there during its rigorous 1936 one-nighter tour, was announced preceding each song. This was followed by a sorority song medley, a fraternity song medley, and an additional college song medley.

It was at the Meadowbrook that Dorsey first gave Sinatra, rather than to Buddy Rich, featured billing. Buddy immediately expressed his anger to Tommy but to no avail. In retaliation, he speeded up the tempo on slow ballads behind Sinatra or played loudly behind him.

This engagement preceded the band's opening in New York for a four-week engagement at the Paramount Theater along with Red Skelton. The first Bob Hope–Bing Crosby comedy opus, *Road to Singapore*, was the film attraction.

During the next several weeks, Frank Sinatra recorded "Shake Down the Stars," "I'll Be Seeing You" (Axel Stordahl arranged this anthem, which fit the uncertainty of the pre–World War II period and went on to become a wartime standby), "Polka Dots and Moonbeams" (which on April 27 became Sinatra's first record to make the Billboard Pop Chart), "Fools Rush In," and "Imagination." These recording sessions took place at night after playing six shows a day, which had started at 9 A.M., at the theater.

In the meantime, Dorsey's domineering personality was still at work. Alto saxophonist Les Robinson remembered that "in between shows sometimes Tommy would go upstairs at the Paramount, and we would rehearse new arrangements. This guy was work, work, work. Unbelievable! He used to say, 'Oh, I got up at six o'clock. I chopped down trees' (which served to maintain his strong physique)."

Les Robinson remembered Tommy coming onstage at the Paramount and not even warming up before playing his theme song. Robinson continued, "I loved Tommy but he used to bug me in a lot of ways. When we went into the Paramount, sometimes he'd come up behind me, and he'd open up one of the keys [on my saxophone] so I couldn't play. Nothing would come out. He thought it was the funniest thing in the world."

Robinson finally couldn't abide the tedious schedule—and Dorsey—so he accepted an offer from Benny Goodman before the Paramount gig was over. Before he left, however, he witnessed the New York bobbysoxers' first reaction to Sinatra: "Frank drove the girls crazy. He used to come out with a big tray of food for the kids in the first row after the show because they'd stay for five shows. [This was something Dorsey had done earlier.] He'd sing those songs with that sound, and the kids would go, 'Ohhhh'. Tommy loved it."

Variety described Sinatra's work as "sock all the way. He's sure of himself, and it shows in his work." *Billboard* said, "He's developing into a first-rate singer." He was still, however, often having to circumvent the loyalty that fans of the Dorsey band had developed to Jack Leonard.

Bunny Berigan's band had gone bankrupt, even though Dorsey's manager, Arthur Michaud, with Dorsey's approval and probable financial backing, had also managed the Berigan orchestra. It had been three years since Berigan had left Dorsey. He rejoined the band at the Meadowbrook on March 3. Artie Shaw pointed out, "Bunny couldn't handle a band. He had no self-discipline. . . . When he got in front of a band, he would get worried, and then he'd start drinking. . . . Pretty soon all the men in the band lost all respect for him. It doesn't work. You have to present a kind of model for the men. When you're standing in front of a band, you have to be the leader, meaning you've got to set the tone. You've got to do what you want the men in the band to do."

Metronome magazine soon jubilantly proclaimed, "Bunny Berigan has made a whale of a difference, musically and psychologically, to Dorsey's band." Tommy recognized that fact and gave him featured billing.

The Paramount booking also marked the hiring of a new girl singer in the person of Connie Haines. This seventeen-year-old, born Yvonne-Marie Antoinette JaMais, whose name had been changed to Haines by Harry James because it almost rhymes with his name, had worked alongside Sinatra in the James band. She had left a few months later when Harry, in his struggle to survive, couldn't afford to carry two vocalists.

A few months earlier, George "Bullets" Durgom (who acquired his moniker for his quickness as a Wall Street "runner"), later a well-known personal manager who represented Haines, caught her singing at the Singac supper club near Frank Dailey's Meadowbrook. He arranged for her to sit in with the intermission band, led by Dailey's brother, so Dorsey could see her perform.

Tommy admired her singing and made her a tentative offer to join the band, but she wasn't allowed to leave the Singac for six weeks. In the meantime, he auditioned a young singer from Nashville, who was appearing on New York radio stations, named Dinah Shore. He noticed that Shore couldn't swing like Haines and also realized that Haines was also a fine ballad singer. Once Haines joined, Dorsey became her legal guardian. She would remain with the band for the next 2½ years.

More than sixty years later, Haines still makes appearances in nightclubs and concerts. She refers to Dorsey as a "star maker," once again alluding to his uncanny ability to nurture and develop talent. "What a heritage! It was Tommy Dorsey who left me that heritage," she said proudly. She related how he showed her breath control in singing ballads. "He'd say, 'Don't take a breath here. You can hold it.' He'd blow his trombone behind me very softly, and when he'd take a breath, I'd take a breath. Tommy put me in a rehearsal hall at Shea's Theater in Buffalo with Buddy Rich and Sy Oliver before we went into the Paramount. For eight hours Sy taught me syncopation, back beat, and all that. That's because Sy wrote those wonderful arrangements Frank and I would sing with The Pied Pipers."

Rich and Sinatra would tease Haines unmercifully. "When they were enemies, they were my friends," she declared. Both of them were several years older and seasoned show business veterans, while Haines was a pert, unsophisticated southern girl, with an accent to match, who was still very much a teenager. "I'd jitterbug and do the Charleston on the last chorus after I sang the middle chorus. They'd say, 'Okay you little cornball.' Frank was the one who did it more. He'd use terms like 'squaresville'; it's a funny term they don't use today."

When Haines and Sinatra recorded "Snootie Little Cutie," they weren't getting along. She remembered, "That was a popular record, but in the studio they had me on one mike and Frank on another at opposite ends of the room. And here we are singing all these cute little bits to each other while I was glaring at him. But that didn't last long, eventually we became friends."

The vivacious singer noted Dorsey's occasional over-the-top lapses in decorum on the bandstand. "I'll never forget the time we were playing the Adams Theater in Newark. Tommy walked over to the side of the stage and turned the fire hose on me, Frank, and The Pied Pipers. (It was Dorsey's way of shaking things up.) By the time I went with Dorsey, Frank had had two or three hits. We had to have a police escort to go from the Paramount Theater to the Astor Hotel, which was around the corner, just to have a hamburger. They were tearing at our clothes—especially Frank's."

To show his own importance, Buddy Rich had a sleek new Lincoln Continental convertible delivered in front of the Astor Hotel with the top down for all to see during the Paramount engagement. Jack Egan did his job getting the newspapers to cover its arrival. Frank Sinatra was shown sitting in the back seat.

Bunny Berigan got his former sideman, Joe Bushkin, the job on piano with Dorsey as well as bassist Sid Weiss. A close friendship soon ensued between Bunny and Frank Sinatra. He came to revere Bunny's trumpet artistry and realized how his commanding trumpet sound enhanced the impact of his singing.

It was then that Dorsey put together a replacement for the Clambake Seven by forming The Sentimentalists, which included himself, Berigan, and Sinatra, along with Freddie Stulce, Johnny Mince, Joe Bushkin, Sid Weiss, Clark Yocum on guitar, and Buddy Rich. The result was a new version of "East of the Sun" and "Head on My Pillow" that featured Berigan, which provided a slightly different setting for Sinatra. The two songs were released as a single on the thirty-five-cent Bluebird label rather than the fifty-cent RCA Victor imprint.

At that same recording session, the band thrice attempted "I'll Never Smile Again," but Dorsey wasn't satisfied with the results. Initially, he had suggested to Sinatra and The Pied Pipers that they approach the song as though they had gathered around a piano at someone's house.

On May 23, this masterpiece finally became a finished recording. Its success was based on that rare combination of the perfect concept together with a high level of performance. Freddie Stulce correctly sketched out a very spare musical setting, and the song was arranged at an appropriate slow tempo, while Axel Stordahl contributed the vocal arrangement. In point of fact, the sound of the orchestra was barely utilized except for Joe Bushkin's meaningful and lyrically bell-like punctuations on the celesta, which, according to Bushkin, was Sinatra's suggestion. Sinatra and The Pied Pipers were in perfect unison with Dorsey's trombone, especially following his muted solo on the final chorus, which restated the plaintive theme. It was Sinatra's solo, which followed his joining The Pied Pipers as the fifth voice midway through the tune, that made it a hit and first established him with the general public.

The impact of the song reached across the Atlantic. Years later, Sinatra became teary-eyed when he was told by Sir Winston Churchill, the savior of Great Britain, "Young man, you belong to my people as well as your own. Yours was the voice that sang us to sleep in that infamous summer of 1940, when people were trying to get comfortable sleeping in the Underground," speaking of the desperate days of the Blitz, when Hitler tried unsuccessfully to destroy the spirit of Londoners with nightly air raids.

According to *Time,* by August 12, 1940, sheet music sales of "I'll Never Smile Again" had surpassed 135,000 copies. Its composer and lyricist, Ruth Lowe, would later write the lyrics of "Put Your Dreams Away," which became the theme song of Sinatra's radio show.

History has long distorted the inspiration for Lowe's song. Its lyrics were not written as a sorrowful tribute to the tragic loss of a loved one in the early part of World War II, contrary to what so many have believed. Instead, Lowe was lamenting the death of her husband, Harold Cohen, a Chicago music publisher. She had been a pianist with Ina Ray Hutton's All-Girl Orchestra, which she left to marry Cohen in 1938, only to lose him the following year. "I'll Never Smile Again" portended the trend of mournful ballads that dominated pop music in the next few years.

The enormity of the Dorsey record of the song is demonstrated by the fact that it became number one on July 27 and remained there for twelve weeks! It proved to be the biggest vocal record of Dorsey's entire career. Yet at the same time that the song was becoming such a huge hit, the Billboard College Poll had Dorsey as the number-three band behind Glenn Miller and Kay Kyser, and Martin Block's *Make Believe Ballroom* poll had Dorsey second to Miller.

From this time forward, Dorsey's sterling cast of singers was given much more time onstage. Sinatra collaborated on fourteen more records with The Pied Pipers. As ever, Tommy knew exactly what the customers wanted.

In retrospect, Artie Shaw remarked, "I never understood why Dorsey started featuring all those singers," which is perhaps Shaw's indirect way of pointing out that his own band had made it on the basis of hit instrumentals. (One could interpret Artie's statement as an expression of musical snobbery.)

The popularity of "I'll Never Smile Again" also led to more recording opportunities for The Pied Pipers, although each one of them received only $82.51 a week as a salary and nothing more for recordings. The country suddenly came to realize the prowess of the group's four-part harmony and the almost perfect pitch of its lead singer, Jo Stafford, who was a coloratura soprano who had had classical training that enabled her to naturally sing falsetto. The shy, highly perceptive Stafford, whom Dorsey called Josie, never encountered a difficult time with him, the reason being he greatly appreciated her astonishing talent.

In recalling her just under three years with Dorsey, Stafford reflected, "It was pretty remarkable because in those days the girl singer was always a cute little bunny. Believe me, I was no cute little bunny; I was a big fat lady, and it didn't make any difference to him! He put me right there at that microphone—'so she ain't cute; she can sing. . . .' I always kind of liked old Tom for sticking with me through fat and thin."

In a 1948 interview with disc jockey Jack Elsworth, Dorsey told an anecdote that reflected Stafford's underestimation of her own talent: "At the Adams Theater one night, Frank was sick. Naturally, the kids were disappointed. . . . I put them on the spot by telling the audience that we had a very good singer who was afraid to sing because she was afraid the audience wouldn't like her. . . . I told them that Jo Stafford was my idea of a very fine vocalist, and I asked if they would like to hear her sing. They said they sure would. So Jo sang 'Little Man with a Candy Cigar.' That was the first time she sang a solo without those three guys standing around her. It took a long time to convince her that she was as good as she is. . . . She's one of the top vocalists of all time."

Stafford rejects the notion of Dorsey as a control freak: "Tom did not control his musicians. The only time he would try to control somebody was when they were messing up." She also summed up what she believed to be Dorsey's attitude toward his employees: "If you did your job, he had no problems with you. An honest mistake was ignored; sloppiness was not. They were two different things." Stafford concluded, "The biggest connection [we had] was through our respect for music. He had a great deal of that."

A brief vacation and a succession of one-nighters preceded the fourteen-week sojourn at the Astor Roof, in Times Square in New York, which began on May 21, 1940. The band proved to be an attraction for the prom season. Its incredible success is demonstrated by the fact that an average of more than thirty-one hundred cover charges were tallied per week. The cover charge was an amazing fifty cents, and "deluxe drinks" from two dollars were advertised. "Men must wear jackets" was the house rule.

Joe Bushkin recalled that on opening night Dorsey stopped the band and ordered Sinatra, "'Just call out the tunes and Joey will play 'em for you.' Frank's high note then was about a C or a D-flat. He was singing up around E-flats and at one point I heard him sing a very clear F, which is really extending your range by a good three notes up above. Dorsey had me do this, because, except on 'Begin the Beguine,' Frank was allowed to sing only one chorus of the song before the band came in. The audience wanted lots more. He sang eight to ten songs and stopped the show. I think the Astor had to have had an effect on the way Dorsey saw Sinatra's importance. You knew it was going to happen. . . . It's strange. I accepted the way he sang as such a natural thing."

Bushkin relished talking about the nights when Dorsey would move up to the trumpet section and play his Louis Armstrong–inspired trumpet solos on "Jeepers Creepers" or a blues by Sy Oliver. Sometimes that would be the signal for Bunny Berigan to toss his trumpet over to the piano for Bushkin to play trumpet: "That would make me play better. I loved chopping Tommy up. I couldn't resist that. I had the whole band rooting for me to level off some of Tommy's egomaniacal personality."

Bushkin contended that his prowess as a trumpeter bothered Dorsey more than his habit of smoking marijuana: "He could put up with booze because he was a lush himself. [That's] before he got into the Nembutals and other pills," referring to the dependencies Tommy would develop. Despite this, the pianist admitted, "The Dorsey band gave every single guy in that band, including myself, a self-discipline. . . . He made you appreciate being disciplined. He would never compliment you, but he'd give you a bad time if one single thing was wrong. That says it all about him. . . . He had to have the best in every area—the house in Bernardsville, the best car, the best chick, the best band."

Regularly scheduled half-hour radio remotes plus the June 25 debut appearance, replacing Bob Hope for the summer on Tuesday nights on his weekly Pepsodent radio show on NBC (the Raleigh-Kool show had gone off the air) helped establish both the surging momentum of the Dorsey band and "I'll Never Smile Again."

On June 14 Dorsey and Berigan joined trumpeters Roy Eldridge and Harry James, Gene Krupa, Count Basie, clarinetist Joe Marsala, Carmen Mastren, and bassist John Kirby for a "Welcome Home from Europe" concert in honor of tenor saxophonist Coleman Hawkins at the Apollo Theater in Harlem. The swing greats reconvened late that afternoon at the WNEW studios to play some more. Though he knew he was not in the same musical league as a jazz soloist, Dorsey realized the importance of being a participant in such events as this and the *Metronome* All Stars recording sessions for RCA Victor.

As a sidelight, during this Astor Roof engagement, the Dorsey band's softball team, often featuring Tommy as pitcher, played the teams of other big bands in Central Park, winning most of the games. One of them was naturally a hotly contested game against Jimmy Dorsey's team, in which the younger Dorsey team came up with three runs in the last two innings to win by a 12–10 score. Joe Bushkin was forbidden to participate in any of the games as the pianist recalled, "Tommy was afraid that I would hurt my hands."

On their Sundays off from the Astor Roof, Dorsey often brought individual members of the band and later on all the musicians and singers down to Bernardsville to enjoy the swimming pool and the tennis courts before playing their radio show. Tommy would also invite various friends down from New York on weekends. He enjoyed playing the role of the gentleman farmer, but more than that he craved companionship after work. Like many public performers, he battled against a deep inner loneliness by socializing extravagantly. He would call Toots to inform her that there would be eighteen for Sunday brunch, and she would automatically tell William (the chef whom Tommy had imported from the Palmer House) to prepare meals for thirty-six visitors.

One of them was Bea Wain, who as vocalist with Larry Clinton's band sang on the best-selling record that made "Deep Purple" a standard in 1939. She and her husband of fifty-three years, the late Andre Baruch, who was one of the supreme voices in radio history and who often was the announcer on Dorsey's NBC remote broadcasts, were then young marrieds. They attended the opening night at the Astor Roof: "I remember Tommy coming over to our table after a set and asking, 'What do you think of the new guy [Frank Sinatra]?' Andre said, 'Uh, he's skinny.' He wasn't very complimentary. And I said, 'He's electric. He is absolutely electric.'"

Dorsey suddenly invited them to come home to Bernardsville with him after the set. They went back to their apartment at the Beresford on Central Park West, got some clothes together, and returned to the Astor. Dorsey drove them down to Bernardsville. "In those days nobody had a swimming pool in New Jersey, but he had one," she exclaimed.

The year before, Dorsey had the band play a benefit for the Bernardsville Fire Department to raise money to buy uniforms so that the Fire Department would fill his newly built Olympic-sized swimming pool. Out of his own pocket he bought enough half-inch tongue-and-groove planking to form a crude dance floor almost an acre in size, purchased a thousand-dollar tent, and then had a bandstand built so the entire town could dance to his music. The event wound up costing him $7,300.

Wain remembered:

We arrived in the middle of the night, and he called out to his wife, Toots, and woke her up, "We got company. Put on some scrambled eggs and put on the coffee and hurry up!" I felt awful. I didn't want to disturb the lady.

After our scrambled eggs and coffee we went to our room, and it was a lovely room. There were a lot of people [there] evidently that we didn't see that night. Anyway, we went to bed. All of a sudden we heard [Wain impersonated the sound of a steam engine] "Whoo! Whoo!" I said, "What the heck is that?" And again, "Whoo! Whoo!" Then we heard a voice saying, "All aboard! All aboard!" We looked up and below the ceiling was a ledge and the train—this really long, fancy electric train—was running along the ledge of the room. It came through the opening in the wall, and this [recorded] voice said, "All aboard! Philadelphia!"

We spent the next day around the pool. Everybody was talking about where they were. We were in Philadelphia. Another was in Milwaukee—there were trains coming through all the rooms. I don't think anybody had a set of trains like Tommy had. And he had a roundhouse. . . . Somewhere in the home he must have had somebody in charge of all the trains.

Paul Canada, a boyhood friend of Skipper Dorsey, and now a Wilmington, North Carolina–based management consultant, said, "The Dorsey train collection covered a huge basement that incorporated many sizes and shapes of Lionel trains with different engines that Skipper and I would sit on and ride. There was one locomotive that was maybe two feet off the floor. Lord knows how many dollars Mr. Dorsey had tied up in those trains." (Dorsey once estimated he had spent $20,000 on his model trains.)

Another band singer, Donna King Conkling, one of the four King Sisters, who were featured with Horace Heidt and then with Alvino Rey's orchestra, formed a close friendship with Tommy. The sisters got to be friendly first with Paul Weston and Axel Stordahl in California and then spent time with them when the Dorsey band played the Commodore Hotel.

"Ah, that wonderful band!" she recalled:

When it was a Sy Oliver arrangement, it sounded like a great black jazz band. When they once worked together, I heard it said that Tommy broke Ella Fitzgerald's heart, whom he loved terrifically. But she would breathe in the middle of a word! He chewed her out, and she was very hurt.

There was a difference between Axel's and Paul's arrangements. Paul's were a little more noveltyish, more rhythmical. Axel's were sweeter, deeper, but very lovely. Even today I would take Tommy's band over Glenn Miller or Benny Goodman.

We had Sundays off and we would go down to Bernardsville and spend the day and stay overnight there. We'd walk out into the acreage and swim. We had some wonderful times. It was so cozy. Tommy was sort of a king, you know. Everyone did what *he* wanted to do. He loved to have fun and laugh. We felt such a kinship with him. He and Paul Weston and Axel. They were our brothers, and we were their sisters.

Paul Canada remembered Bunny Berigan as a "jokester" who enjoyed chasing him up a tree. He also reminisced about how he and Skipper dropped water bombs from an open window down on Times Square on New Year's Eve. This was when Rufus, the Dorseys' chauffeur, drove the boys up to the

Astor in the family station wagon to stay overnight while the band was playing the Paramount.

Canada recalled the action on weekends at Bernardsville:

> I would often stay overnight when we were ten, eleven, twelve years old. The
> limousines would pull in late at night—two, three, four o'clock—to party.
> They were half in the bag, very loud and noisy. Mr. Dorsey and his entourage
> would disembark. There weren't that many from the band, mostly guys like
> Jack Leonard and then later Frank Sinatra, the King Sisters, the Andrews
> Sisters. Jack Leonard had a "Type B" personality; Sinatra had the drive. I
> thought Sinatra was kind of a wise guy, pretty fresh, like he didn't give a
> damn about anything.
>
> We didn't swim in December, January, or February—those were the only
> months the pool wasn't heated. The tennis court was lit up at night. There
> was also a badminton court, a handball court, and a huge barbecue. Those
> were tough years for the country, but that place really jumped.

Canada admitted that it was on one weekend afternoon when the King
Sisters were visiting that he first learned to appreciate the fantasy of the female anatomy: "The girls were lying on chaise lounges at the edge of the
pool. They had their straps off their shoulders. Bunny Berigan came up behind one of them and lifted up the chair and she slid into the water. Every
time she treaded water, her boobs would float to the top of the water. Bunny
and a group of people stood there roaring. He was a very regular guy. Mr.
Dorsey was more aloof."

Within the band, however, the mood was far less fraternal. By this time, the
fierce competition that existed between Rich and Sinatra was very much in
the open. They began having frequent fistfights. Nashville-based saxophonist Jay Patten recalled how his father told him of having seen Sinatra throw
a punch at Rich one night at the Meadowbrook that almost knocked him
off his drum platform.

An equally violent incident took place that the late television producer
Bob Bach, Buddy Rich, Connie Haines, John Huddleston, and Jo Stafford
witnessed. One hot August night during the engagement at the Astor Roof,
at the end of the set, Sinatra was crooning a ballad when Rich abruptly departed from the feathery beat he had established with the brushes and

started playing loudly with his sticks, intentionally throwing off Sinatra's delivery and simultaneously destroying the romantic mood of the song.

After coming offstage, Rich, standing at the door of the musicians' room, began cursing at Sinatra, who was standing across from him in the doorway to the singers' room. Sinatra picked up a pitcher full of ice water from a table next to him and threw it at Rich. Fortunately, Buddy ducked and the pitcher crashed into the wall. John Huddleston recalled, "Chuck Lowry walked over to the wall where pieces of glass were embedded. He put an X on the spot."

Jo Stafford had come offstage earlier with The Pied Pipers. She was in the midst of writing a letter to her parents when the water pitcher whizzed above her. "The next thing I knew there was this tremendous crash and water was running down on the letter," she remembered.

Stafford added, "For the next two years after that, when we played the Astor with Tom, Chuck [Lowry] checked it out and there was still glass embedded in the wall. He wrote some funny comments around the spot." Johnny Mandel, then a teenage Dorsey fan, remembers that one of them was "It can happen here," which was a prewar cautionary slogan warning of the danger of Nazism.

The night after the incident Dorsey sent Sinatra home. This was the first of two firings of his tempestuous band singer. "I can live without a singer tonight, but I need a drummer" was his practical explanation. He sat his two mercurial charges down and told them bluntly that the hostilities had to end immediately, but they didn't.

In a flagrant example of Sinatra's appreciation of La Cosa Nostra and what it could do for him, according to Rich, a few nights later, as he left the Astor after a good night's work, he was approached by two hoodlums, one of whom asked, "Iz your name Rich? . . . We're friends of Frank," before they proceeded to mug him. The front-page story, emblazoned on the September 1, 1940, issue of *DownBeat*, declared, "Buddy Rich Gets Face Bashed In," reporting that it "looked as if it had been smashed in with a shovel."

Bunny Berigan's drinking was *really* getting out of hand. Filling in for him one night, Chris Griffin discovered, "Bunny spilled most of his booze on the music and all the notes were at the bottom of the page. They were just a black blob."

Bunny blew his lines during remote radio broadcasts and the NBC Pepsodent radio show. Dorsey reacted by heckling him, as if that would cause Berigan to cut down his drinking. Other incidents followed. There was a row one night over Berigan's check at the Astor Roof, which Dorsey picked up. It included a ham sandwich and twenty-four scotches! (Presumably, the trumpeter had allowed several of the musicians to be his guests.) On the same night, Bunny fell off the stage right in the middle of the Pepsodent show while soloing on "Marie." (This had happened once before, during the 1937 gig at the Commodore Hotel. When asked why he didn't get rid of Berigan then and there, Dorsey had said, "I can't fire him. He plays too good.")

As Paul Whiteman had done with Bix Beiderbecke, and he had done previously with Dave Tough, Dorsey sent Berigan away for rehabilitation. It didn't work.

The reality was that Dorsey's sidemen and singers were so musically outstanding that he couldn't dominate them. In their performances and in the band's internal dynamics, the focus was on them rather than on his own preeminence. Jo Stafford noted that Tommy often said, "It's a good ork" (the *Variety* word for orchestra).

There were continual contests of will. Berigan began talking back to Dorsey, and their exchanges turned into serious arguments. Dorsey fired and then rehired his troubled trumpeter several times. Finally, on August 20, Bunny was dismissed for good. Ziggy Elman, who had left the temporarily disbanded Goodman band and gone to work for Joe Venuti's band, replaced him. Elman's arrival was the final link in establishing the greatest band Dorsey would ever lead.

Born Harry Aaron Finkelman in South Philadelphia in 1914, the talkative, gregarious trumpeter, seemingly born with a cigar jammed in the side of his mouth, had been a bulwark of the vaunted 1936–1939 Benny Goodman trumpet section, teaming with Harry James and Chris Griffin. His exuberant solo on "Bei Mir Bist Du Schoen," the Yiddish theater song that had been an enormous hit by the Andrews Sisters, was one of many high points of Goodman's historically significant January 1938 Carnegie Hall Jazz Concert. Elman followed up with his Jewish-wedding-band trumpet solos on "Fralich in Swing," arranged by Noni Bernardi, which, with the addition of Johnny Mercer's lyrics and Martha Tilton's vocal, became the well-remembered Goodman hit "And the Angels Sing." When Elman joined Dorsey, the tune was featured with the Dorsey band.

Not only would Ziggy's powerful sound and formidable reputation make him serve as the perfect successor to Bunny Berigan, but in addition, Dorsey enjoyed his zesty personality and his similar drive for achieving perfection. Buddy Rich once admitted, "Ziggy was the most infallible workhorse I ever worked with." Their thundering duet on "Hawaiian War Chant" became a tour de force. The respect Ziggy engendered with Rich also enabled him to stand up to the volatile drummer when Rich's behavior became completely intolerable.

In addition to his solos on "Zonky" and "Swing High," it was Elman's trumpet battle with fellow trumpeter Chuck Peterson (who supplied the high notes) on "Well, Git It!" another Sy Oliver "killer-diller" chart, powered at its core by Buddy Rich's frantic beat, that in 1942 became one of Dorsey's all-time instrumental hits. Unfortunately, Ziggy, like his predecessor, was also a heavy drinker. Jo Stafford remembered how Ziggy would stick a Coke bottle filled with Canadian Club with a straw protruding from it inside his band jacket and take sips while Dorsey wasn't looking.

Soon, Elman led the band in rehearsals and during the first and last sets on certain location gigs, often opening the evening by playing "I'm Getting Sentimental over You" on trombone. On occasion, during final sets on onenighters, he would also stand in front of the band, regaling audiences by playing trombone while Dorsey sat in the trumpet section.

One night during the Astor Roof engagement there was an unexpected reservation. Arturo Toscanini, the eminent conductor of the NBC Symphony, had booked a table with several friends in tow. The demanding Toscanini, who shared Dorsey's standards of perfection, had been quoted as referring to Dorsey as "the world's finest trombonist."

Toscanini's broadcasts emanated from Studio 8H, immediately adjacent to the studio where the Dorsey band was doing the Pepsodent show. Toscanini was well known for his aloofness toward other musicians, although the members of both organizations had long since broken the barriers between the two distinctly different kinds of music by swapping stories as musicians are wont to do.

When Dorsey and the band realized Toscanini was there to see them perform, there was great apprehension about what kind of reaction he would have to their music. With the start of the second set, however, the usually stern demeanor of the maestro seemed to cease as an attentive, pleased look became obvious from the musicians' vantage point on the bandstand.

At the next intermission, Dorsey was invited to his table. After introductions were made, Toscanini declared, "Tommy, the band sounds fine. The boys play with a great deal of feeling, but they play too goddamned loud!" But he said it with a smile. Toscanini's own orchestra had a similar reputation for playing loudly.

The success of the Fred Astaire and Ginger Rogers film musicals, starting with *Flying Down to Rio* in 1933, were a welcome respite from the horror of the Depression. Paul Whiteman and Duke Ellington had made film appearances starting in the 1920s, and by the late 1930s and early 1940s, the popularity of big bands caused them to become a staple of Hollywood musicals and comedies. Producers figured they were a box office plus to their movies, which they often were. They usually served to provide a musical background for the ongoing conflict between the male and female romantic leads; the bandleader was also often cast as the sidekick of the male star.

The Dorsey band's first excursion into Hollywood was Paramount's black-and-white, modestly budgeted *Las Vegas Nights,* which top-lined Phil Regan, Constance Moore, and Bert Wheeler. The film's musical director was none other than Victor Young, in whose orchestra Tommy and Jimmy had played back in the 1920s. In a comedy scene, Tommy played the part of a straight man to Bert Wheeler, the comedian. Wheeler described in great detail how he was an intimate friend of Tommy Dorsey while Dorsey listened. He handled it with the finesse of a veteran actor.

The movie was panned. On its release in March 1941, Bosley Crowther, the film critic of *The New York Times,* wrote, "On account of Tommy Dorsey and his band being hopefully but vainly involved, there may be some mild jitterbug interest in Paramount's "Las Vegas Nights." . . . There is precious little humor, little life, little anything save an excess of dullness in this labored musical show about a troupe of indigent entertainers adrift in the Nevada gambling town."

The musical renditions were uneven. "I'll Never Smile Again" was featured (probably the principal reason the band was actually sought for the movie), although this sequence was rather ineptly staged, with the vocals barely standing out, as was Bert Wheeler's vocal on "Dolores." This latter tune would later become a number-one hit for Sinatra, The Pied Pipers, and the band. "The Trombone Man (Is the Best Man in the Band)" was rendered in a spoofing Spike Jones–like manner before Buddy Rich led the band into a driving final chorus. A splendid version of "Song of India" was featured in its entirety.

Working at Paramount, Tommy saw a great deal of Bing Crosby. (Bing was then the studio's leading star.) Tommy made a guest appearance on *The Kraft Music Hall* radio show, where Bing jokingly introduced him as "Jimmy's brother," just as he had done on Tommy's guest shot on the show five years earlier.

The story goes that one afternoon Bing watched Frank Sinatra film a musical number while dropping by the set of *Las Vegas Nights*. After the scene was designated a "take," he strolled up to Sinatra, shook his hand, and said, "Real nice, Frank. You're going to go far."

Dorsey had used the trip to make *Las Vegas Nights* as an excuse to bring Toots, Patsy, and Skipper to Southern California while the "Brick House" was being remodeled. During their stay at the Hollywood Hotel, Dorsey came down with diphtheria. Toots and the children were forced to leave the hotel and live with Jerry Colonna and his wife while Tommy was quarantined. It was only a mild case of the disease, however, and he quickly recovered and went back to work.

The shooting of *Las Vegas Nights* coincided with an engagement at the new Hollywood Palladium. The Dorsey band's popularity made it a natural for Lawrence ("Larry") Barnett, then the head of MCA's West Coast band department, to book it as the opening attraction for four weeks at the Hollywood Palladium, the mammoth new dance palace, which cost almost a million dollars to build and was located on Sunset Boulevard. It replaced the Palomar, which had been the victim of a devastating fire in 1939 that burned it to the ground.

Barnett, now the retired executive vice president of Chris Craft Industries and vice chairman of United Television, became Dorsey's responsible agent at MCA. He observed:

> Tommy always thought he was running us. You almost had to be a psychiatrist to take care of Dorsey. You were his friend today, and you wouldn't know what you did, but all of a sudden he didn't know you. When we booked him, if you had an open night, he was furious! He wanted to work every night. We went through a lot together, but he and I got along very

well together all through his life. He wanted to be a personality. The band needed a personality. He wanted to be the emcee of the show. [I also think] he wanted to do something else, like even running a business. I think he always had that craving.

The double workload meant the musicians had to endure a difficult schedule with long hours and the resultant lack of sleep. The gig ended well after midnight, and they only slept a few hours as they had to be in makeup by 6 A.M. at the studio. And there was also a lengthy recording session on October 16, 1940.

Besides that, the trip to Southern California hadn't been fun. The night before the opening date at the Palladium, originally set for October 16, the band played Ogden, Utah. The band truck, with considerable equipment, including the instruments and the music, had broken down in Wyoming en route to Ogden. Bobby Burns managed to get the instruments and music to the date in a rented car as well as in the other cars rented by some of the musicians. Buddy Rich had driven cross-country in his new Lincoln convertible, accompanied by his father, Jo Stafford, and her husband, John Huddleston. The truck was repaired and rambled through Salt Lake City and Las Vegas and headed for Los Angeles. In Barstow, California, Burns suddenly realized it was the last day that he could register for the draft, which he accomplished five minutes before closing time.

Larry Barnett secured a booking for the band at the Paramount Theater in downtown Los Angeles in front of the Palladium gig when it was discovered the latter venue wasn't ready to open on time. This infuriated the Palladium's management so much that a lawsuit was filed against MCA and Dorsey for playing this date. The suit was later settled out of court. It has been reported that Dorsey was initially reluctant to play the Paramount date, but MCA told him if he didn't he would lose the deal for *Las Vegas Nights*.

Opening night at the Palladium on Halloween Eve found Bob Hope, comedienne Gracie Fields, and Mickey Rooney in the audience. Tyrone Power, Judy Garland, Errol Flynn, and Lana Turner were there on subsequent nights. Tickets sold for the then astronomical fee of five dollars a head. Neither the price of tickets nor the Paramount booking had any effect on business. The Dorsey band was hot, and the Palladium engagement was an unqualified success.

The extraordinarily talented Rooney sat in on opening night and played an electrifying drum solo that stunned the customers. Buddy Rich complained that Rooney had severely damaged his favorite set of cymbals. On a later return to the Palladium, Rich took his cymbals away before permitting Mickey to use his drum set. After that they became friends.

Also in attendance that opening night on a "busman's holiday" was none other than Artie Shaw, whose band was then on vacation. Between sets, Frank Sinatra solicitously approached Shaw's table and point-blank asked him, "Would you like to hire a male singer?" After nine months with Dorsey, Sinatra was becoming increasingly weary of the leader's demands. Shaw quickly explained, "Frank, I have to have a girl singer. I don't like male singers." "How about Tony Pastor [Shaw's featured singer and saxophonist]?" Shaw shot back, "You call that a singer? He makes me laugh."

The late bandleader referred to Pastor's singing as sounding like a "Soprano Louis Armstrong!" This testy verbal exchange between Sinatra and Shaw marked the start of a lifetime of antagonism between the two celebrated musical figures. As Shaw saw it, "He was jealous that I was there first with Lana and Ava [Gardner]."

During the Palladium gig, on the night of November 11, 1940, after a recording session that included "Star Dust," rendered at a languid tempo by Frank Sinatra and The Pied Pipers, a pianist and singer named Matt Dennis played and sang some of his songs for Dorsey. Dennis recalled, "Jo Stafford had told Tommy about me and Tom Adair [Dennis's lyricist partner]. I had accompanied The Pied Pipers in Los Angeles clubs before they joined Dorsey for the second time. He liked the songs and told me he wanted me, and he said, 'Bring along your lyric writer.' He sent us plane tickets to come to New York in January." Dennis and Adair began writing songs for Dorsey at his new penthouse office in the Brill Building. Dennis recalled, "I was given my own room to write in."

The process of getting Dorsey interested in a song was rather basic. As Dennis explained it, "I would write a love song and Tommy would sit there with Sy Oliver or Axel Stordahl, and if they liked what I played . . . they'd smile and nod their heads in unison. Tommy opened three music [publishing] firms, and each one of them had at least one of my songs."

With his eye for talent and forever the smart businessman, always focused on the "big picture," Dorsey reasoned correctly that the prolific songwriting team could supply first-rate material for his superlative corps of singers to record before anyone else. If their songs became hits (as most of them did), the band would be in even greater demand, and he would publish the songs and thereby reap further financial benefits. His foremost intention, it seems clear, was for the songwriting team to deliver first-rate material that was tailor-made for Frank Sinatra, which would make him an even bigger attraction with the band.

Dennis and Adair wrote eight songs that the Dorsey band recorded during a thirteen-month period in 1941 and 1942. In order, they were Jo Stafford's first solo record with the band, "Little Man with a Candy Cigar"; the magnificent ballad "Everything Happens to Me" by Sinatra; the two-sided record of the festive "Let's Get Away from It All," featuring Sinatra, Connie Haines, and The Pied Pipers," about which Stafford praised Sinatra for exhibiting "a true respect for and knowledge of excellence"; "Will You Still Be Mine?" a vehicle for Haines; The Pied Pipers' "Nine Old Men," which, weeks before he died, Dennis described as "a novelty song that concerned Rip Van Winkle" (Stafford, however, recalls it dealt with the U.S. Supreme Court); the patriotic "Free for All" by Sinatra and the Pipers; "Violets for Your Furs" by Sinatra, a song Dennis said was his favorite composition and was inspired by the songwriters' seeing Billie Holiday perform while wearing a white gardenia at Kelly's Stable on Fifty-second Street and was written on a tablecloth at the club; and Stafford's poignant "The Night We Called It a Day." In 1946, Sinatra introduced their "Angel Eyes," which became another hit and later would be remembered as one of his signature songs.

Dennis spent considerable time around the band while it was touring the East in 1942. He remembers the combustion when, on occasion, Dorsey's renowned Irish temper and Sinatra's formidable Sicilian temper clashed. Dennis contended, "They were stretched to the breaking point because Frank was starting to get offers, and Tommy resented it. He finally settled down enough to realize that Frank was a gem—no doubt about it."

Dennis recalls rehearsals at the Astor Roof in 1941 (where Dorsey got Matt to work with a group of Hawaiian musicians as the relief band), when Tommy provoked the band and vice versa: "I remember one day Tommy threw his horn at Bobby Burns. It missed him. Tommy was drinking pretty good in those days."

To compensate for his drinking, Dorsey's close friend, retired onetime MCA vice president and video company owner Berle Adams, said that Tommy would faithfully go to a Turkish bath on Thirty-fourth Street at two in the morning after his final show at the Paramount. "They knew exactly what to do for him," Adams said. "I would go to the first show the next day. There's Tommy up there—always immaculate! . . . He never had a hangover or anything else—just the sparkling personality he always had."

In describing the atmosphere around the band, Jo Stafford commented, "I would say there was a river of animosity running under the bandstand. Tom and Frank were stuck with that musical respect for each other, and it wound up being a love-hate relationship." Dorsey had helped create a star. Now he was stuck with the ramifications of keeping him happy and the band on an even keel as well.

When asked if he remembered if any of the musicians ever tried to challenge Dorsey or went against his wishes, John Huddleston replied, "I don't think they would have fared very well. If words wouldn't have done it, he would have used his fists."

Sinatra would constantly ask Morris Diamond, who made out the band's payroll, if Buddy Rich was making more than he was. Diamond would tell him, "Frank, I can't tell you!" and then was forced to cover the checkbook with his body. Diamond continued, "But he was making the same amount" ($125 a week).

Diamond recalled Buddy's constantly being short of money: "Hey, Buddy was making that kind of money, and I was making sixteen dollars a week—it wasn't a living wage—and he was borrowing money from me at the end of every road trip! Whenever we came back to town his father would be there and come up to me and ask, 'How much do I owe you?' And he'd pay me then and there." In the years ahead Rich would go through money problems with Dorsey. He saw how high Dorsey lived and used that as his model. Not surprisingly, he declared bankruptcy three times during his long career.

Then, too, there was often trouble not of their own making to confront. In many parts of the country bigotry against Jews and blacks still had the cover of law, or of social convention. Diamond witnessed anti-Semitism at work during his Dorsey days and described Dorsey and Sinatra reacting violently against it: "In Virginia Beach, the manager of the Cavalier Beach Club hotel came up to Tommy as we were checking in and said, 'We can get a room for Mr. Elman at one of the hotels down the street.' Tommy challenged him by saying, 'What are you saying?' The manager replied, 'Well, you understand—Mr. Elman . . .' Tommy pinned him against the wall, grabbed him by the throat with both hands, and said, 'Look, you son of a bitch, if he doesn't stay here we all move out of here right now. What's your choice? . . . I want a suite and his suite is right next to mine!' And so the hotel did it [right away]."

Diamond was present at a party Dorsey hosted to mark the opening of his penthouse office in the Brill Building. He remembers that Edythe Wright was talking to Harry Goodman (Benny's brother and formerly his bassist, who was then his music publisher). Johnny Griffin, owner of the scandal sheet the *New York Inquirer*, said to her, "What are you doing talking to those Jews for? You've got nothing better to do than hang around with Jews? We've got to stick together," within earshot of Sinatra. Diamond recalls that Frank turned around and hit him smack on his mouth when he heard that: "Then I took one leg; Frank's buddy, Hank Sanicola, took the other leg. We dragged Griffin downstairs and dumped him on Broadway. Griffin climbed up the stairs when the elevator operators had left for the night. Dorsey walloped him again."

The still active Diamond added, "I remember that we played the Paramount several times on a Jewish holiday, like Passover. Dorsey would give me twenty dollars and say, 'Go and get some matzos and sour cream and whatever else you have to get so I can have it in the dressing room.' This was so Bob Weitman, the manager of the Paramount, and his assistant, Bob Shapiro, would have something to nosh on." It was gestures like this that caused Diamond to refer to Dorsey as being "kind and thoughtful."

The hits kept coming. Before the brace of recordings of Dennis-Adair material, in early 1941, the triumvirate of Sinatra, Haines, and The Pied Pipers radiated happiness in "Oh! Look at Me Now" (one of Dorsey's most popular records), which Joe Bushkin cowrote with advertising man John DeVries. This was followed by Jo Stafford's solo vocal on "For You" with a Sy Oliver chart, and then there was Sy's treatment of "Without a Song" for Sinatra. Sy wrote the gospel-influenced "Yes, Indeed!" for himself and Stafford to duet on, which featured the rollicking ensemble wailing behind them. (He had originally written it for Jimmie Lunceford, who turned it down, calling it sacrilegious.) This record was released just before Sy's next success, the bracing instrumental "Deep River."

Even after two intense years of working for Dorsey, Oliver's respect and admiration for Dorsey would last until Tommy's death. The breadth of Sy Oliver's talent seemed endless. His importance was central to the band's success. Dorsey had carefully and systematically honed the spirit and musicianship of the band to the point where it "breathed together," in Artie Shaw's descriptive phrase.

In 1941, the band had traveled over a million miles throughout America. Its greatness is well represented in the RCA Victor CD *That Sentimental Gentleman*. The 1940–1942 edition of Tommy Dorsey and His Orchestra was indeed a prime example of *Los Angeles Times* jazz critic Don Heckman's statement that "the big band was the symphony orchestra of the twentieth century."

Johnny Mandel recently remarked that "Dorsey looked ahead, and saw that this is what he wanted to happen. But here's the thing . . . everybody remembers Tommy . . . and Frank Sinatra, Jo Stafford, and The Pied Pipers—and they were wonderful—but nobody noticed the band behind them. It was certainly the best white band of the early 1940s. No question. That was the band."

The highly respected African-American jazz saxophonist Jimmy Heath was a high school student in Wilmington, North Carolina, visiting his father in Philadelphia during the summer of 1941, when he saw the Dorsey band play at the Earle Theater. As he recalled:

Big bands were the sound of the day. There weren't many small groups that were successful at that time. I was a kid who was aspiring to be a member of one of the big bands. You know, Dorsey's theme song, "I'm Getting Sentimental over You," was very impressive to me. Tommy's breath control and the way he sang the melody—he was like a vocalist. When the band did "Well, Git It!"—Ziggy Elman—I was impressed by the cleanliness of the orchestra, the clarity. Tommy Dorsey's orchestra was a precision group.

I was interested in being a composer, an arranger. . . . Sy Oliver, in particular, was able to start an arrangement and develop it to a climax in three minutes. How could you do this? Because there weren't any long, involved, improvisational solos.

Sinatra was a very, very frail guy who had a great voice. He could sing. He was pretty hip singing up-tempo but [his] ballads were the thing. His breath control over the bar lines and the way he held notes and used his instrument were very impressive, too. I was interested in the whole thing—the choir and the harmonies The Pied Pipers used as a quartet in back of Sinatra.

Heath explained why, with all of his respect for Dorsey's band, he preferred Glenn Miller's band: "As a young saxophonist, I liked Miller's music because of the reed section, and the way it was used." He also pointed out that blacks were the originators of the big-band sound: "The white bands had the advantage of the media. They were the ones that everybody thought were setting the style. But not in some black communities . . . There were Erskine Haw-kins, Earl Hines, Andy Kirk, those bands were swinging. . . . There's a direct correlation between the black musicians having started the big-band format with Don Redman and Fletcher Henderson and those people, and Lunceford, of course. You know, that was the real beginning of the stuff."

Theater engagements in places like the Earle and especially dance pavil-ions like Lake Compounce in Bristol, Connecticut, provided lucrative dates for Dorsey's band. This major ballroom first booked the Dorsey Broth-ers Orchestra in 1935. In 1940, after playing a successful date, Tommy asked his friend, the owner, Julian Norton, what band held the attendance record there. When he was told that Glenn Miller had recently set the record, with his determination to outdo Miller Dorsey said, "We've got to do better than that." And he did; when he returned August 24, 1941, Nor-ton's son, "Stretch," who was already working at the ballroom, reported, "Tommy had a guarantee of $1,250 for the night, but with his percentage deal of 60 percent of the door above that figure, he took out a total of $2,696.67. There were five thousand people dancing. That record has never been broken to this day."

ASCAP's acrimonious dispute with the radio networks, which caused the networks to forfeit the programming of ASCAP songs, caused Dorsey to forgo using "I'm Getting Sentimental over You," an ASCAP song, as his theme song. Instead, he began using "Anything," a Broadcast Music Incor-porated (BMI) song, which he had first recorded in 1928 with trumpeter Phil Napoleon.

Because all of Dorsey's publishing companies had been affiliated with ASCAP, as a necessary alternative he opened a BMI company, Essex Music, to publish several new songs that he featured on his NBC show *Fame and Fortune,* which had its debut on October 12, 1940. The show offered ama-teur songwriters the opportunity to compete against each other. The win-ner would get his song published by Essex Music and was paid an advance royalty of one hundred dollars. "Oh, Look at Me Now" was one of the im-portant songs that emanated from *Fame and Fortune.*

"Deep River" was one of several BMI songs that Dorsey suddenly re-corded. Another BMI song, "This Love of Mine," which became one of the most romantic of Frank Sinatra's Dorsey records, was a result of the collab-oration between Sol Parker, Hank Sanicola, and Sinatra. Parker, the only one remaining of the three writers of the song, recalled that it took nine-teen takes to achieve the final version. Parker originally had decided to write a song entitled "For Whom the Bell Tolls," hoping he could couple it with the motion picture that was later adapted from the Ernest Heming-way novel.

Parker recalled:

When I first played it for Hank Sanicola, at Witmark Music in the Radio City Music Hall building, Hank said, "Let's play this for Frank; he's over at the Paramount [with Dorsey]." So we walked over there [and] found a room with a piano. Hank played, I sang, and Frank Sinatra had his arms crossed and his thumb and his forefinger were rubbing his chin while I was singing. When I got through, he made a statement that was beneficial to us all. He said, "Let's make it more commercial." I had written a twelve-bar strain to a forty-eight-bar song. The norm was eight bars to a thirty-two-bar song, so I had written a little Cole Porterish type of a melody.

Two days later Hank went to work for Dorsey's music company. He came to me and said, "This is what we've got so far." They [Hank and Frank] had condensed forty-two or forty-eight bars into thirty-two bars, and someone had written a couple of lyrics opening the song. I said, "This Love of Mine" looks like a good title. I think I'll finish the lyric and wind up the song with the title. Hank played the song on the piano for Tommy. In the contract dated May 20, 1941, Frank Sinatra was given credit for the lyrics and Sol Parker and Hank Sanicola were given credit for the music. [Matt Dennis said that he "corrected" six measures of the original music and that Tom Adair worked on the lyrics of the song, apparently as a favor to Sinatra.]

While the band was at the Astor Hotel, the announcer made a comment that Tommy was going to play a particular song. But then Tommy yelled, "Oh, no, we're going to play Frank's song!" The station soon went blank be-cause of Tommy's problem over the song format with the announcer. After Frank's vocal, Tommy came on and did a minimum of eight bars. It was one of the most impressive solos that you could ever hear. It was fantastic! It was the best part of the record as far as I was concerned.

The song was on the *Lucky Strike Hit Parade* for thirteen weeks. It reached number three. "Chattanooga Choo-Choo" [by Glenn Miller] was number one at the time. We got our first royalty check, which was very nice, probably about fifteen hundred dollars apiece, which was very good money in those days. Jack Johnston, the professional manager of Embassy Music, at first didn't think it was necessary to pay the songwriters for performances earned. When I protested that, Dorsey, without the crescendo of a drum, simply said, "Pay the kid!"

By the fall of 1940, Sinatra was making $250 a week from Dorsey. His confidence had grown commensurate with his newly found status. Tess Dorsey had her own slant on Sinatra's appeal: "He sings pretty fair, but anybody who couldn't be a star singing to my Tommy's trombone ought to be shot."

Buddy Rich continued to bait Sinatra. Between sets one night at the Astor Roof he induced a pretty girl to stand in line to get Sinatra's autograph. After getting it, she said to him, "Thank you very much, Frankie. Now, if I can get three more of these, I can trade them in for one of Bob Eberly's!"

Dorsey fired Sinatra again, this time for causing Connie Haines to break into tears during a Virginia Beach location engagement due to his constant taunting. Dorsey screamed at Sinatra, "You've done that one time too many with her." Dorsey immediately hired Allen Storr as his replacement, who recorded "Only Forever." Storr was soon replaced by Ken Curtis (who later played Festus in "Gunsmoke," the longest-running western series in TV history), who recorded "Love Sends a Gift of Roses." After a few weeks, the obvious difference between them and Sinatra became intolerable to Dorsey. He contacted Sinatra, and according to Haines's recollection, Dorsey told him, "You go and apologize to the little gal. Then you can come back to work."

In the meantime, Dorsey kept the band in the public eye with other novel ideas. In another of his publishing ventures, he wrote a book entitled *The Modern Trombonist*, in which he expressed his ideas on how to become an accomplished trombonist. And then there was the book *Tips on Pop Singing*, written by Sinatra and his vocal coach, the Australian opera singer John Quinlan.

One of the most novel examples of promotion in the history of the band business came from the ingenious Jack Egan. This was a serial that ran daily in most of the Hearst newspapers dealing with two young lovers whose romance unfolds against the backdrop of the Dorsey band. Each episode was illustrated with a photo of individual members of the band, who appeared under their real names. Some time after the story concluded it was published in novelette form.

In the spring of 1941, Jean Bach (then Jean Enzinger), many years later the producer of the Oscar-nominated documentary film *A Great Day in Harlem*, married trumpeter Shorty Sherock. Sherock had been fired by Gene Krupa and replaced by Sherock's musical idol, Roy Eldridge. The newlyweds' plight was alleviated by a sudden Western Union telegram that arrived in their New York apartment from Dorsey, requesting that Sherock join the band in Bluefield, West Virginia.

Bach paints an amusing picture of the band's lineup: "Shorty sat between Ziggy Elman and Chuck Peterson . . . and on the end was Jimmy Blake, who played [almost] silently so he was no problem. But Shorty couldn't hear what he was playing because those [other] guys were playing so loud. Buddy Rich had his bass drum decorated with Lana Turner's picture—getting out his frustrations."

Bach also remembered that Sherock was assigned the "Bob Allen suit" as his band uniform. "The gray flannel suit fit except for the sleeves, which were too short. Dorsey had ordered this uniform for Allen, considering him as a replacement singer when Jack Leonard left. It was kept readily available on the bus in case Sinatra got too uppity," Bach related.

> I had first met Dorsey when I was writing society for the Hearst paper, the *Chicago Herald-American*, in 1938. It was at the Empire Room of the Palmer House opening. All of the people my age I knew were debutantes. Tommy had played at several parties, and so he kind of saw me in that milieu. My first view of him was that of a courtly, polite, but no-nonsense person. He invited me to his recording date. I loved that . . . being on the inside. He was reviewing the sound in the control room and then ordering some baffles for Buddy Rich's drums. At all times, he always seemed to be in command . . . comfortable authority.

She noticed how her relationship with Dorsey would undergo an abrupt change "once I was married to an employee."

Bach vividly recalled a softball game between the Dorsey band and Harry James's band at Dorsey's New Jersey mansion in 1941. The Harry James team was in "grimly serious uniforms," she recalls:

> Everybody in Tommy's band was getting smashed. . . . Being out in the sun and drinking beer, it gets to you. They'd get up to bat and pass out. And they had this Brunswick stew. Not bad—he was pretty proud of it—and beer. I remember nobody was eating. Under the porte cochere he was pouring

champagne for himself. I thought, "Oh man, that would really quench my thirst." You can't drink beer when you're thirsty. Wine seemed a better idea. He never offered it to us. Champagne for himself, while we peasants filed past him to thank him for a lovely afternoon. Please—if you're not going to offer it to your guests, duck into the kitchen for a quick nip.

And that's why Lee Wiley, who was such a snob and who I think had an affair with him at one time, pointed out the bully aspect. She felt that was because of the world he'd been born into. Not no gentleman.

James's band pianist Al Lerner recalled, "Bunny Berigan was the home plate umpire that day. He had some Dixie cups in his back pocket. In another pocket was a bottle of gin, and between each pitch Bunny would toss down a cup of gin. By the third inning, he couldn't even see the batter in front of him, let alone the ball. That made for some very interesting calls. I'll tell you—an outing like this was a gas. To be at an estate like this one for a lot of the guys who, like me, grew up struggling through the Depression!"

James Maher told of a fascinating discovery that was made just before a Sunday softball game in Bernardsville. Phil Giardino, a first-call studio trombonist friend of Dorsey's from his radio days, was the last person out the door as a group of musicians were about to go out and play softball. Tommy asked Giardino to retrieve his favorite baseball bat, which was standing up in the closet. Giardino grabbed it, but before leaving the closet he noticed an old twelve-inch seventy-eight album. Opening it, he found the record worn almost completely white—the shellac had been almost totally obliterated from constant playing. He looked at the label on the record and saw the name "Fritz Kreisler."

Maher thought to himself, "I've got the answer! Fritz Kreisler's phrasing [on the violin] was absolutely stunning. [He could play the long phrases.] You can hear Tommy's breathing and phrasing like you hear Kreisler, and as far as I was concerned, that was all I needed to know. . . . I said to Phil, 'Thank you. That's it. That's the story.' I now know what was happening all these years before Tommy Dorsey became Tommy Dorsey."

By the summer of 1941 the Dorsey band, in the midst of an even more successful Astor Roof engagement than the year before, had taken over the top spot from Glenn Miller in the *Make Believe Ballroom* poll on WNEW. (The Dorseyites referred to Miller's musicians as the "Boy Scouts," while Dorsey, referring to his rival's newly found success, began calling him, "Old Klondike.") But Dorsey was runner-up to Miller in the *Billboard* poll as the favorite college band. In the same poll Sinatra had gone from number twenty-two the previous year to emerge as the nation's favorite band singer. Buddy Rich was also the winner of the *DownBeat* drummers' poll. In spite of all that, Dorsey ordered Jack Egan to extol the virtues of Artie Shaw's band because he feared becoming too popular! As Jo Stafford recalled, "He always said if you're number one, you've got nowhere to go but down."

But he wanted to be at the top; he felt he belonged there. It was exactly what Dorsey had worked for, beginning with his apprenticeship with Jimmy under his father's tutelage in Pennsylvania, the period on the road with Goldkette and Whiteman, the years in New York with Jimmy culminating in the Dorsey Brothers Orchestra, and the struggle in creating his own band. It had been worth it. With this band he had achieved the perfection that he had always dreamed about, and the country saluted him. But the never completely satisfied bandleader wanted more. The repercussions of his way of doing things caused him to make many enemies. That didn't faze Tommy Dorsey in the least. He was now a big success; that's all that really mattered to him.

With it all, life on the Dorsey band bus was always freewheeling and full of humorous moments. Jo Stafford recalled that Carmen Mastren usually stood up much of the time at the front of the bus on the frequent 350-mile jumps between dates. He always was dressed in a red plaid hunter's jacket and a deerstalker (a Sherlock Holmes–type cap, complete with flaps). Since the guitarist had helped develop the original concept for the arrangement of "Song of India," he would face The Pied Pipers and lead them in "singing" the familiar introduction: "Da, da, da, da, rah-dah," and ending it with an amusing "rah-dah." Stafford rememebered:

> Tom sat in the second row on the right side of the bus, and even on the road he was dressed up, always wearing a fedora, but you could see that the back of his neck would get red as a beet. He really couldn't have admonished us because that would have been poor sportsmanship. You had to do something to amuse yourself on those long road trips.
>
> Musicians can be rowdy, but if you're in their good graces and they respect you . . . I wound up with eighteen godfathers. I was pretty well protected from any rowdyism of any sort.

Stafford says she was one of the few people who got along with Buddy Rich: "He let me use his drums to make my bed. I remember his big bass drum. I'd put my feet up on that, with stuff over it, coats and things. I had a whole bedroom set up back there with Buddy's drums! The drums would fill up the aisle. . . . Part of me would be on this side of the aisle. Beer bottles rolled up and down the aisle."

Much of the time Ziggy Elman would be involved in serious poker games. There was always considerable kibitzing going on during the course of these games. And Joe Bushkin was always good for apropos one-liners; once, when the bus was moving along at a snail's pace, he told the bus driver, "Pull over and let the lady in the wheelchair go by."

Bobby Burns recalled the time when after a one-nighter in Pennsylvania Sinatra vowed to beat Dorsey, who had driven his own car, to New York by driving the band bus: "Everybody thought he was nuts as Frank yelled, 'Hold onto your hats. Tommy keeps saying what a wonderful bus this is. Let's prove he's right.' Not that Frank was driving recklessly. But he sure did kick that crate along as briskly as the law allowed. When we finally got to the New York ferry, the car ahead of us belonged to one Tommy Dorsey. I thought he'd have apoplexy when he saw us, especially when he found out that we had burned out various essential parts during the trip. He had to sell the bus after that."

But with all the good times and the band's ongoing success in the spring and summer of 1941, on a personal level Dorsey was headed for trouble. Connie Motko related that one afternoon in Bernardsville, Toots, as well as Tess and Mary Dorsey, who were visiting, discovered Tommy and Edythe Wright in flagrante delicto. Tess and Mary were as appalled as Toots. Tommy's reaction was to immediately vow to stop sending money home to Tess and Tom (although Jimmy continued to do so).

It was the end for Toots, who had withstood not only Tommy's long affair with Wright but also his many dalliances with countless other women (which included Tallulah Bankhead). She had been his anchor, someone whom he could rely on, a homemaker who took care of the children.

Upon discovering Tommy and Wright together, she got into her car and sped off to New York. Forgetting that her car long since had been registered in her name, Dorsey called the state police, attempting to stop her at the Holland Tunnel, informing them that she had stolen his car.

Pat Dorsey Hooker observed, "His ego was such that he could not believe that God had created a woman that could resist him. He was very mad at my mother. He wasn't very nice to her, but she never said a bad word about him at the time. The only derogatory thing she ever said to me was long after I was married. At that time she said that he had expected her to perform the same kinds of things his prostitutes did." Hooker added, "One of the things that I resented and held against him was he moved his current mistress [Wright] in when we moved out."

George Hamid, Jr., was invited for a weekend following his graduation from Princeton. He recalled that Frank Sinatra was there as part of a group one weekend, at which time he remembered his trying to make a move on Edythe Wright, who was there with Dorsey. (Pat Dorsey Hooker also related that Sinatra once made a pass at her one afternoon backstage at the Paramount. She added, "If Daddy had found out, he would have killed him!")

Toots obtained a divorce in New York state on the only possible grounds at the time, adultery, which happened to fit the circumstances completely. Besides catching Dorsey and Wright red-handed, Toots further testified that they had registered in many hotels and auto courts (1940s motels) as husband and wife. She asked the court for five hundred dollars a week in alimony. Hooker once saw her father refuse to sign her mother's alimony checks, saying, "That bitch can wait." With it all, Hooker admitted, "Mother never stopped loving him 'til the day she died."

There were two other serious setbacks to follow. First, the U.S. Treasury Department came after Dorsey for eighty thousand dollars in back taxes. Then Bobby Burns. Being constantly at Dorsey's disposal had begun to take its toll. The hardworking, likable Burns would later became a respected MCA agent. Leonard Vannerson, Benny Goodman's former manager, replaced him.

Snapping under all this pressure, Tommy abruptly walked out on a week-long engagement at Loew's Capitol Theater in Washington, claiming illness. The management paid him for the five days the band worked at the theater. Always seeking to have the edge, Dorsey returned the check and started litigation to get paid for the full week.

The band continued on tour, playing another smash engagement at the Meadowbrook, which included remote broadcasts on NBC, the Mutual Broadcasting System, and CBS. Then the band was off to Los Angeles for another film appearance. Once again, the movie commitment coincided with a booking at the Hollywood Palladium, where several *Spotlight Bands* radio shows also took place.

This time it was a decided step up: MGM's *Ship Ahoy*, which starred the incomparable tap dancer Eleanor Powell and Red Skelton. Powell had sung and tap-danced on the second and third records Tommy's band had ever recorded. The film started production on November 11, 1941. The title of the film was changed from *I'll Take Manila* soon after World War II started, when Manila fell quickly to the invading Japanese army.

Almost midway through the shooting, after finishing work at the Palladium on Saturday night, December 6, Dorsey, Sinatra, and Rich attended an all-night party in the Hollywood Hills home of Lana Turner, with whom Rich was having an affair. Rich had lusted after her for two years, or since the time Artie Shaw had eloped with her. A few months later, Turner drove Joe Bushkin down to March Field in Riverside, California, in her brand-new Lincoln convertible to start his enlistment in the army air corps.

Susan Hayward, Linda Darnell, and other important Hollywood stars were among the guests at Turner's party. Many of them passed out on couches the next afternoon when the party finally broke up. Turner's mother arrived to announce the devastating news of the Japanese attack on Pearl Harbor.

After Dorsey and Rich had ended their relationships with Turner (who today would be rightfully termed a "groupie"), it was Sinatra's turn. As a practical joke, Dorsey bribed a waiter at the Hollywood Plaza Hotel to deposit his dirty dishes under the dome-shaped covers on the dinner cart that Sinatra arranged to have wheeled into his hotel room for a romantic post-midnight supper with Turner.

Among the several notable performances contained in *Ship Ahoy* were Sinatra's vocals on "The Last Call for Love" (which rabid Dorsey fan and film historian Rudy Behlmer informed me was actually based on "Taps") and the rousing "I'll Take Tallulah." (Tallulah Winters was the name of Eleanor Powell's character.) This latter number featured a freewheeling display of both pizzazz and musicality by Eleanor Powell and the band. Powell, after tap-dancing on a table, a chair, and then a diving board, tosses drumsticks and a drum back and forth with Buddy Rich in an incredible finale.

Another spectacular moment centered on "Hawaiian War Chant" in an elongated, magical scene that consisted of Elman and Rich displaying their musical camaraderie on an expanded version of Deane Kincaide's original chart; then the sensational Powell came on for the finale, alluring in a fringed Hawaiian spun-glass skirt.

Also working in Hollywood at that time was Lyle Cedric "Skitch" Henderson, then beginning his long association with NBC as an intermission pianist. He had recently been employed at MGM as a rehearsal pianist, where he first encountered the Dorsey band playing on a soundstage. Henderson recalled, "I was astounded that it was to me, in a way, a small symphony or-chestra, because it had such versatility. And Tommy looked to me like the taskmaster of the world, [which] I think in those years he was."

One day, late that fall before Bobby Burns departed, he asked Henderson to fill in for Joe Bushkin at the Palladium, which was only one block away from NBC. Henderson was told Bushkin "has some problems" (Bushkin had been caught growing marijuana). Henderson related:

> Well, I went. But I was green with fear! I mean, this was the Valhalla of or-chestras! At the Palladium it got to be 12:15 at night and Tommy hadn't even spoken to me. He came over and said, "You read, don't you?" "I cer-tainly do," I replied. "I have a piece of sheet music." It was "Sleepy Lagoon," which Harry James had just recorded. He said, "Maybe later you'll play it with me." And I said, "If you want me to. Yes, sir." He told the band to sit there and I played an arpeggio—y'know, a long E-seventh. I'll never forget it. And Buddy Rich hit a rim shot that could be heard in Peoria, and he said "Waterfall has arrived." Buddy called me "Waterfall" the rest of his life. We ultimately became good friends.

Henderson added, "I had known Sinatra since the mid-1930s when he was on a cross-country Major Bowes tour, and I was working at the Tower Theater in Kansas City. I lasted with Dorsey until things straightened out with Bushkin. In the short time that I was with the band there was always a certain acid communication between Sinatra and Buddy."

And not infrequently, violence. The late *San Francisco Chronicle* colum-nist Herb Caen came upon Rich trying to annihilate Sinatra backstage at the Golden Gate Theater. He recalled, "Buddy was ramming Frank against the wall with his high F cymbal that you play with your foot. Frank was screaming and swinging at him. Finally, Tommy broke it up with the help of a couple of guys in the band."

In the meantime, Frank Sinatra was seriously considering going out on his own. On January 19, 1942, in the midst of the Palladium engagement, after constant prodding by Sinatra, Dorsey agreed to allow him to record four tracks for RCA's Bluebird label. Tommy considered it an experiment to see how Sinatra would sound in a completely different setting outside the context of the band. He also wanted to see if the two records would sell. The answer was affirmative to both questions.

The songs, recorded in Hollywood, were "Night and Day," "The Night We Called It a Day," "The Song Is You," and "Lamplighter's Serenade" with Axel Stordahl as arranger and conductor. The fourteen-piece orchestra that served as his backup consisted of predominantly reeds and strings with no drums. As a harbinger of things to come, Henderson recalled getting a phone call from Sinatra several days before the recording date asking him to play piano for him: "He said to me, 'The old man has goosed me with his trombone for the last time!'"

The next afternoon Sinatra sat in his hotel room playing both sides of his records over and over on his portable record player. Stordahl remembered, "He was so excited you almost believed he had never recorded before. I think this was a turning point in his career. He began to see what he might do on his own."

That evening the singer who believed he had his *own* rendezvous with destiny, told his friend lyricist Sammy Cahn (whose songs he would later record more than any other) that he had to leave Dorsey. Nick Sevano added, "He knew the time had come to move on. I thought he was crazy myself, so did Hank [Sanicola]. Tommy had given him such prominence with the band that Frank had become a star."

Sinatra calculated his timing carefully. Basking in the adulation of female America, swing fans, and critics alike, Sinatra gave Dorsey a year's notice that he planned to leave the band. He analyzed his foremost competition: Perry Como, who was singing with Ted Weems; Ray Eberle, with Glenn Miller; and most of all his prime competitor, Bob Eberly, who was still working for Jimmy Dorsey. Sinatra made it clear that he believed it was mandatory that he start his solo career before Bob Eberly left Jimmy's band.

Art Linkletter, still very active at ninety-three as a lecturer on successful aging, ironically, was then hosting *Young Man with a Band* ("Devoted to the men who make America's dance music") on CBS. Linkletter, an important radio and television personality for seventy years, went backstage at the Golden Gate Theater in San Francisco one day in February 1942 to do a preinterview for that night's show, which was to feature the Dorsey band, and was told by a group of his musicians that Sinatra had just given notice and that this would not be a good time to talk to Dorsey.

Linkletter recalled, "I approached Tommy and said to him how I knew how upset he must be at Frank's decision. He said, 'Yeah, but he's such a damn fool. He's a great singer, but ya know, you can't make it without a band. Every singer has got a band [behind him]. Does he think he can go out on his own as good as he is? . . . It upsets me because he's an important part of our band.'" Linkletter pointed out, "You can understand, at that time nobody thought a soloist [with a band] could go off by himself."

The first year of America's participation in World War II, 1942, was a year of big changes and losses for Tommy Dorsey. Some of those were connected to the war.

Artie Shaw had been the first bandleader to go into the service, entering the navy as a chief petty officer immediately after the attack on Pearl Harbor. Tommy took over Shaw's ten-piece string section (seven violins, two violas, and a cello) and added a harp from the Radio City Music Hall Symphony. This increased the size of the Dorsey band to thirty-one musicians and singers.

The expanded Dorsey aggregation debuted at a Paramount engagement that began on April Fool's Day 1942. The strings provided a further romantic aura to the offerings of Sinatra, Haines, and The Pied Pipers. Perhaps predictably, Buddy Rich objected to their inclusion. He felt the strings made the orchestra less of a jazz orchestra and more of a dance band, which was exactly what Dorsey intended.

A U.S. Treasury Department–sponsored radio broadcast aired on NBC's Blue Network during this engagement reveals the authority with which Dorsey read a script, while Sinatra and Stafford showed how inexperienced they were in that department. Tommy's intense hatred of the Japanese and Hitler, as well as his strong sense of patriotism, is also evident in his passionate delivery of a message to sell war bonds.

As was the usual practice, the Astor Roof booking for the eight-week-long prom season followed a four-week gig at the Paramount. Jimmy Dorsey, then headlining with his band at the Strand, was in attendance on May 3, 1942, the opening night. And in another reprise, Tommy and Jimmy had a fistfight. Tommy started it by insulting several of Jimmy's associates. That led to an instant argument between the brothers. Tommy threw the first punch, hitting Jimmy on the jaw; his brother quickly retaliated. Jimmy Gardner, a young jazz fan and good friend of Jimmy's, stepped between him and got a right planted on his nose for his peacemaking effort. After more punching and shouting the fight was over. For the next few performances at the neighboring theater, Jimmy wore sunglasses.

Dorsey's inability to stay sober continued. One episode that reflected the effect it had on him sounds like a slapstick comedy routine in the retelling. One night during the Astor run, he began playing the ascending opening melody line of the arrangement of "Sleepy Lagoon." When he reached the top note, he muffed it. When that happened, as was the usual practice, he said to the band, "Take it from the top." On his second attempt, he blew it again. This elicited laughter from two of the violinists. His immediate response was "You two! Get the hell out of here. You're fired!" Four unsuccessful tries brought forth even more derisive laughter from the band. Entire sections were summarily fired, until only six musicians were left on the bandstand. The laughter spilled over to the audience, and the entire room was filled with merriment. Dorsey looked at the near-empty bandstand, saw the humor in what he had generated, and burst into laughter. The next day all the fired musicians were rehired.

In another booze-induced incident, Chuck Peterson, weary of being overshadowed by Ziggy Elman's work in Dorsey's eyes, and about to be drafted, showed up drunk one night at the Astor Roof. Dorsey ordered him off the bandstand. In retaliation, he stuck his tongue out at Dorsey, which led to the leader's charging after him. Peterson left before a remote radio broadcast went on the air. Billy Butterfield was available, but when he showed up, he, too, had had too much to drink. Dorsey was left having to put up with the best of a bad situation.

After entering the army, Peterson told fellow trumpeter and arranger Billy May that his ambition was to join the American Legion upon his discharge. "I'm going to get one of those hats and I'm going to find where Dorsey's playing. I'm going to drive a motorcycle up on the bandstand. They can't hurt you when you've got that hat on." Years later Peterson did return for another round with Dorsey. This time Tommy was more tolerant of Peterson's drinking.

While Dorsey was having his own drinking problem, it was an ongoing dilemma with many musicians. Their various personal hang-ups, combined with the constant strain of one-nighters, led to booze and marijuana serving as their escape from reality. There were few certified rehab centers at the time that could effectively cope with these ongoing problems. As Paul Whiteman had done with Bix Beiderbecke, and Tommy had done with Dave Tough, Dorsey had sent Bunny Berigan away for alcoholic rehabilitation, but it hadn't worked.

On June 2, 1942, Tommy was at Polyclinic Hospital as Bunny Berigan passed away, having spent much of the time during his last days at his bedside. Bunny was just thirty-three years old. Despite their past differences, the sentimental part of Dorsey had maintained a soft spot for Bunny. Their association dated back to the radio and recording days, and Bunny had been an integral part of the Dorsey Brothers Orchestra. Tommy paid all the funeral expenses and, along with Harry James, set up a trust fund for Berigan's children. Bunny's reputation as one of the essential jazz trumpeters endures, and his record of "I Can't Get Started" remains a classic.

Then, on July 12, after a series of strokes, Pop Dorsey died at the age of seventy at Friends Hospital in Philadelphia. His career as a music teacher in Lansford had lasted nineteen years. More important, he had been responsible for launching the careers of the most significant brother-band-leader combination in American musical history. His funeral, held in Shenandoah, was a major event.

Attending the funeral resulted in Tommy and Jimmy's umpteenth reconciliation. In August, Dorsey Brothers, Inc., headed by George Marlo, became a new music-publishing entity. They both had the right of refusal on all the material considered for publication. Their first song was "I Don't Care What You Think of Me," written by Ruth Lowe, Steve Weiss, Phil Mann, and Fred Jay. Both brothers planned to record it, but the recording ban imposed on August 1 by James C. Petrillo, the head of American Federation of Musicians, prevented them from doing so. The song was never recorded.

In typical Dorsey family fashion, on September 19, there was Tommy, along with Tess and Mary Dorsey, attending Jimmy Dorsey's opening at the Palladium. They all looked radiantly happy. Mickey Rooney once again sat in on drums, and Ziggy Elman and pianist Bob Zurke jammed with him while Milton Berle served as emcee.

Dorsey didn't take Sinatra's decision to leave the band easily. At first, he played the role of disappointed father. But on August 15, during the band's summer tour of the Midwest, *DownBeat* broke the story that Sinatra was planning to leave in September. The singer was still working under a three-year contract that he had signed in January 1940 that extended to the end of 1942. (It didn't bother Dorsey in the least that Frank had broken his contract originally with Harry James to join *his* band.) Tommy continued to refuse to discuss the situation with Sinatra and for months thereafter had little to say to him.

This had no adverse effect on Sinatra's work with the band. Among his most compelling hit recordings with Dorsey, "Street of Dreams," "In the Blue of Evening," and the magnificent "There Are Such Things" were all recorded that spring and summer. The latter, which also featured The Pied Pipers, had much of the charm and pathos of "I'll Never Smile Again."

"Frank had a drive I've never seen in anybody," stressed Nick Sevano. "Nothing meant anything to him but his career." Sinatra's first wife, the former Nancy Barbato, in describing Frank's determination to succeed, said:

Oh, Frank always had it. . . . Before he even joined Harry [James] . . . he was focused, which you know is important, and it took a lot of work. He used to be very tired when he got through working because he put everything he had into it. You've got to work awfully hard to acquire and attain.

. . . Tommy was a good teacher because he had a great band, and he had wonderful vocalists with him, and they were great together. . . . But without Tommy I know it still would have happened. . . . Frank had a master plan for himself, and he worked at getting there. I think he always had it in the back of his mind that this was a stepping stone.

But in order to establish himself as a solo performer it was important for Sinatra to seek out an important agent at a major talent agency to represent him. He found him in Frank Cooper, the head of the radio department at General Amusement Corporation (GAC), which had formerly been Rockwell-O'Keefe.

At ninety-three, the outgoing and still very involved agent remembered, "I had met Frank when he was with Harry James. I used to visit him then and afterward when he went with Dorsey. . . . I got pretty close to him. We got to talking about his leaving the band. After he told Dorsey he wanted to leave, he called me and said, 'Frank, go to work.' The guys at GAC thought I was crazy. They didn't think Frank was going to make it. I thought he was a poet."

When Sinatra got back to New York, he told Cooper that he had made a deal with Dorsey and Leonard Vannerson releasing him from his contract. Cooper, shocked, asked to see it. Cooper recalled:

He showed me the papers, and then I saw that he gave Tommy Dorsey 33⅓ percent of his gross earnings and 10 percent to Vannerson on top of that! [The latter was commission for Vannerson's having secured him a Columbia Records contract.] Then he had to pay 10 percent more to us as his agent! I said, "We can't do this! This is crazy. You'll be broke all your life because there's a thing called income taxes on top of that!" And so he said to me, "I wanted to get out. Don't worry. I'm not paying him a quarter. He can do whatever he pleases."

At Sinatra's "official" farewell to the band on a radio broadcast, he announced that Dick Haymes would be his successor and sang "The Song Is You." This was on September 3, but he didn't actually leave until September 30, following a date at the Circle Theater in Indianapolis. (Bob Eberly was still singing with Jimmy Dorsey's band.)

He immediately hired Axel Stordahl to be his arranger and musical conductor at a salary of $650 a month, reportedly five times what Dorsey had been paying him. It was the best musical decision he could possibly have made at the time. Stordahl knew exactly what and how to write for "The Voice."

Sinatra's first post-Dorsey job was singing "Night and Day" in Columbia Pictures *Reveille with Beverly* before heading back to New York to appear on a twice-weekly CBS radio show called *Singers*. That was arranged by Manie Sachs, his selfless and devoted friend and former MCA agent, who was head of A&R at Columbia Records, then a division of CBS.

Dorsey, too, post-Sinatra's exit, headed for Hollywood, where he was now under contract to MGM, the leading studio that produced musicals. His band was about to start work on the Technicolor musical version of Cole Porter's Broadway musical *DuBarry Was a Lady*. Lucille Ball, Red Skelton, and Gene Kelly were the stars.

The band played in a few requisite nightclub scenes, one of which included "Well, Git It!" Ziggy Elman and Jimmy Zito (who took over Chuck Peterson's solo) on trumpet, Heinie Beau on clarinet, Don Lodice, and Buddy Rich all played brilliant solos. There was also extended piano playing by Milt Raskin, who had succeeded Joe Bushkin; Raskin is joined on camera by another piano player facing him. Presumably it was a studio piano player. The prerecording for the number was actually done by Bushkin, on leave from the army air corps, and Raskin.

One of the most spectacular and bizarre settings imaginable for a big band to be presented in has to be the palace of King Louis XV, played by

Red Skelton. In a dream sequence, the band is adorned in long eighteenth-century red coats (while Dorsey is in powder blue), blue knee pants, light blue silk stockings, and brass-buckled shoes. Each musician wears a white powdered wig. The song, played by the band and sung by The Pied Pipers along with Dick Haymes (in similar costumes), is "Katie Went to Haiti," in a sanitized version of Porter's original risqué lyrics. Ziggy Elman is unintentionally laughable wearing a furrowed bouffant wig while playing one of his rambunctious trumpet solos.

The finale of the film brings back the three leads, along with featured player Virginia O'Brien, performing the comedy dance number "Friendship." Dorsey joins them looking a bit out of his league in supplying a brief dance turn.

With the completion of filming in November, the studio rushed the band into a Judy Garland opus, *Presenting Lily Mars*. Just before filming commenced on the movie, Dorsey got into an argument with Clark Yocum, the band's guitarist and a member of The Pied Pipers, during a train ride to Los Angeles from Oregon. Mistakenly, Yocum had given Dorsey wrong information on which train to board before they got on the right train. Tommy abruptly told him he was through. John Huddleston then said to Jo Stafford, "C'mon Jo." Yocum and Chuck Lowry left with them at the next station. "I knew we could find something," reasoned Huddleston, and they did for a time. They were a successful recording group even after Stafford departed to go out on her own in 1944.

Bullets Durgom had left Glenn Miller to become Dorsey's record promotion man. Durgom saw that the disk jockeys seemed more interested in Sinatra's vocal records with Dorsey than in Dorsey's instrumental records. His enthusiasm helped "There Are Such Things" to spend six weeks at number one to close out the year. In 1942, one major hit on the nation's 400,000 jukeboxes would do as much for a dance band as six solid weeks on radio.

Frank Cooper had a master plan in mind for his new client. He recalled:

I had a good friend Frank went to—Bob Weitman at the Paramount. He, too, wasn't certain that Frank could make it on his own, but he liked Frank, and he said to me, "I'll tell you what we do. I have booked Benny Goodman into the Paramount. I will put Frank into the Mosque Theater in Newark for a weekend to see how he does, and if he does well you will have a deal [to work with Benny Goodman] for a thousand a week at the Paramount." I said, "Okay." But Bob didn't know that Newark and Frank were close—very close!

He was a New Jersey boy. Well, in Newark they went crazy for him! So he went into the Paramount directly from there and Tommy [Dorsey], of course, was expecting to be paid.

Meanwhile, Sinatra worked a theater date in Hartford with Duke Ellington's band late that fall just before playing the Mosque. This engagement was the start of a mutual respect between them that culminated in their finally recording together twenty-five years later. At the Mosque, the glowing reaction was mainly from Sinatra's devoted female fan base. That was nothing, however, compared to what transpired at the Paramount on Wednesday, December 30, 1942.

Billed as an "Extra Added Attraction," Sinatra came onstage right after Benny Goodman and His Orchestra wound up their first set of the day. Benny's introduction merely consisted of, "And now, Frank Sinatra." The bobbysox brigade that had been breathlessly awaiting his appearance went into complete ecstasy. A barrage of screams swept the theater. Goodman turned around in complete bewilderment and said, "What the hell was that?" as Sinatra opened with "For Me and My Gal," while his band accompanied him.

Seven years after his own epic breakthrough, Goodman was there at the birth of America's next pop culture hero. The effect of that initial four-week engagement, followed by a four-week extension, would mark the beginning of the end of the Swing Era. Within a few years, as a result of Frank Sinatra's unprecedented rise to stardom, the popularity of singers would completely eclipse that of the big bands.

6

"Opus #1"

The sound of a winner.
—PHOEBE JACOBS

IN 1942 and 1943, the most significant influences on events in Tommy Dorsey's life would be the war, the split with Frank Sinatra, and Hollywood. The war drew many musicians into military service, necessitating frequent personnel changes and gasoline rationing, which caused serious travel problems. There was also the overall problem of finding the right musicians in order to maintain the high level of musicianship Dorsey demanded.

The split with Sinatra would have a dramatic legal aftermath and serve as a test of Dorsey's competitiveness. In Hollywood, Dorsey made a series of movies under contract to MGM. Hollywood also brought a fortuitous change in Dorsey's personal life. By 1944, a fourth driving influence would challenge Dorsey's ability to dominate circumstances. A new form of jazz, bebop, would define a new musical era, making swing the music of yesterday.

When Glenn Miller formally left his Chesterfield radio show on September 24, 1942 (a job Dorsey had coveted), to accept a captaincy in the army air corps, Tommy Dorsey and His Orchestra became the leading dance band in the country. The *DownBeat* poll had designated his orchestra the number one "sweet band" for the first time since 1939, attributing the victory to his addition of a string section.

Dorsey himself was too old to serve in the armed forces. His band continued to be much sought-after for war bond benefits and V-disks, which were recorded specifically for the armed forces. Earlier that year, as part of his commitment to the war effort, Dorsey had donated his salary, approximately $7,500, from his final week at the Paramount to the Navy Relief Fund. He played many camp and hospital shows for the USO, which were aired on Armed Forces Radio. This was in addition to exposure on other radio shows like *Command Performers*, *One Night Stand*, *Mail Call*, and some 250 appearances on Coca Cola's *Spotlight Bands*—more than any other bandleader.

A total of thirty-nine bandleaders served in the military during World War II. Besides Dorsey, Benny Goodman and Harry James were also rejected by their draft boards. This was central to their ability to maintain their importance as major bandleaders during the war.

Harry Friedman, a prominent MCA movie agent, saw how well Dorsey's last two movie appearances had registered at MGM and secured a studio contract for him in 1942. Dorsey was included in the famous double truck color photograph in *Life* magazine showing the studio's contract players. There were soon rumors concerning the studio's possibly venturing into the record business by establishing its own label with Tommy as its first artist. This was supposedly after Dorsey had discussed the potential profits from phonograph records with Louis B. Mayer, the studio's head.

Within a month, however, such talk was stymied by the seriousness and length of Petrillo's union recording ban, which affected all musicians. Vocal groups took the place of bands in backing singers, as in Sinatra's romantic 1943 single records for Columbia. The ban led to furthering the popularity of singers at the expense of big bands. This was in addition to the shortage of the shellac used to make records, which would have made the MGM venture chancy. As a result, Tommy re-signed with RCA Victor. MGM Records did become a recording entity, but not until after the end of World War II.

The recording ban didn't affect Dorsey nearly as much as it did other bandleaders; he saw it coming and had purposely stockpiled a series of records for systematic release. "There Are Such Things" reached its peak of popularity, ultimately becoming Dorsey's third million-selling single record. And then Sinatra's record of "It Started All over Again," backed with "Mandy, Make Up Your Mind," was released for the first time and became a double-sided hit. Soon after that, "Boogie Woogie" was rereleased by RCA and became a gold record.

The astounding reality of Sinatra's impending dispute with Dorsey would soon become a major show-business cause célèbre. For, as Frank Cooper had observed earlier, Dorsey wanted his substantial piece of the Sinatra action based on the terms of their September 1942 contract.

There were other varied factors at hand, however. MCA desperately wanted Sinatra, but of course, Frank Cooper had signed him to a GAC contract months earlier. And then there was another important ingredient to deal with: Dorsey was a longtime MCA client; he had to be placated as well.

Intricate negotiations that involved the keenest minds in the talent agency business coupled with the knowhow of various experienced show business lawyers took place over an eight-month period commencing in early 1943. It has long been speculated that La Cosa Nostra forced Dorsey to finally settle the contract, as in Mario Puzo's famous line from his best-selling novel *The Godfather:* "He made him an offer he couldn't refuse." This oft-quoted remark referred to a prominent don's purportedly shoving a pistol in a major bandleader's mouth and demanding that he let his popular singer out of his contract. It was supposedly based on the actions of Willie Moretti aka Willie Moore, the padrino of North Jersey, who was then close to Sinatra.

Retired New Jersey *Bergen Record* entertainment editor and syndicated writer Dan Lewis knew Moretti personally until Moretti was "clipped" in 1954. He once asked Moretti if there was any truth to these reports. Moretti smiled and, in a rare departure from omerta, answered, "Well Dan, let's just say we took very good care of Sinatra."

Pat Hooker vividly remembers her father telling her about getting a threatening telephone call at dinnertime early in the Sinatra-Dorsey contretemps. The anonymous caller implied ominous consequences if Dorsey didn't "cooperate" by letting Sinatra out of his contract. He was reminding Dorsey that he had two children, and that he wouldn't want anything to happen to them. That's when Dorsey responded by putting up barbed wire atop the wall surrounding the Brick House, installed sweeping searchlights that bathed the property on a nightly basis, and constructed an elaborate electric fence at the entrance to the property.

"I can tell you that Frank had a great love of gangsters," said Frank Cooper. "We would go out to dinner, and when I arrived at the restaurant to meet him, it wasn't just Frank; it was maybe six other guys [with him]. There were gangsters [around him] all the time I knew him. And I'm sure he had relationships with those people."

It's not surprising that Francis Albert (Frank) Sinatra (named for St. Francis of Assisi!) was drawn to the "Men of Respect," often Sicilian like himself, whom he first encountered in his native Hoboken and Jersey City environs. Early in his singing career, he discovered that they owned the nightclubs and other entertainment venues where he performed. These men were tough and successful and had unquestioned power. That appealed to the skinny and determined singer. He wanted success, and he wanted power badly. At a young age he had developed a contempt for authority and for many of the rules of conventional society that drew him to these men who could make things happen for him.

To him size did matter. He often wore "elevator shoes" to disguise the fact that he was only five feet seven and a half inches tall. His lack of height was a key factor in his often bizarre behavior and led to his developing a decided Napoleon complex. From an early age he believed he must always assert himself like the big guys did; otherwise he might be buried. (Decades later, Sammy Cahn and Jimmy Van Heusen knowingly wrote a song for him to sing as part of the *Robin and the Seven Hoods* score called "I Like to Lead When I Dance.")

Dorsey may have originally appealed to Sinatra because of his toughness. At five feet ten inches (without *his* elevator shoes), his ramrod-straight posture made him appear like a big man to Sinatra. His dynamic presence, the unquestioned authority that he exuded, his mercurial temper, and his combativeness made him resemble even more the Mafia men Sinatra admired.

The severity of Dorsey's 1942 one-sided signed agreement with Sinatra, drawn up in exchange for a loan of seventeen thousand dollars to get his solo career under way, further reflected Dorsey's power. Frank Cooper pointed out that this contract was invalid, for as he stated, "In a court of law, it [would have been] illegal. It was easier for MCA, which was composed of a group of very, very tough guys, to start negotiating." A court fight would have taken many months if not longer; it was essential for Jules Stein and Lew Wasserman, who ran MCA, to seize the moment when Sinatra was so much in demand.

At this juncture, Cooper bowed out of the Sinatra-Dorsey fracas. He contended that Tommy Rockwell (then head of GAC) was anti-Semitic and resented him, despite the loyalty Sinatra showed him in Rockwell's presence one day backstage at the Paramount. As Cooper explained it, "I could not win because, as much as Frank and I loved each other, it just wasn't going to be."

But before he left GAC, after supervising the booking of Sinatra into the Riobamba in New York to show that the young singer could register with an adult audience, Cooper provided him his first important national exposure by getting him a spot on the popular *Your Hit Parade* radio show. Cooper went on to start his own agency, whose first important client was the comedian Alan Young (later the star of the TV series *Mr. Ed*), who was then in the Canadian navy. Cooper sold Young as host of what turned out to be a popular radio show. An offer from Twentieth Century Fox for Young to star in a movie would bring Cooper to Hollywood in 1945.

The Dorsey siblings as toddlers: Tommy, Jimmy, Mary, and Edward. Photo taken circa 1911 in Shenandoah, Pennsylvania. Edward was scalded to death in a tub of lye later that year.

(SOURCE: FROM THE COLLECTION OF JOE SCOCCO)

The Dorsey Saxophone Quartet in 1916: Pop Dorsey, 44, with his sons Jimmy, 12, and Tommy, 10, and daughter, Mary, 8.

(SOURCE: FROM THE COLLECTION OF CONNIE MOTKO)

Dorsey's Wild Canaries, the first band led by the Dorsey brothers. Jimmy is second from the left and Tommy on the far right. Photo presumably taken in 1921.

(SOURCE: FROM THE COLLECTION OF JOE SCOCCO)

Bix Beiderbecke's first recording session in early 1925. Bix is shown with his arms around clarinetist Don Murray and trombonist Tommy Dorsey. To the left are banjoist Howdy Quicksell, drummer Tom Gargano, and pianist Paul Mertz. (SOURCE: FROM THE COLLECTION OF DUNCAN SCHIEDT)

Jean Goldkette Orchestra, Detroit, 1924. Back row: Dewey Bergman (piano), Joe Venuti (violin), unknown, Irish Henry (tuba), Tommy Dorsey and Bill Rank (trombones), Fuzzy Farrar and Tex Brewster (trumpets). Front row: Charlie Horvath (drums), Dock Ryker, Jimmy Dorsey and Don Murray (saxes), Howdy Quicksell (banjo). Goldkette is pictured in the inset. (SOURCE: FROM THE COLLECTION OF JOE SCOCCO)

1938—The Palais Royal at 40th and Broadway, New York. Kay Weber is the vocalist with Tommy Dorsey waving the baton in front of The Dorsey Brothers Orchestra. Jimmy Dorsey is at center of the sax section. (SOURCE: FROM THE COLLECTION OF JANIE NEW DORSEY)

Bandboy Richie Lisella surveying the damage after The Tommy Dorsey Band bus collided with an automobile on a snowy highway in Pennsylvania in the 1930s. The band then went on to the next job and right to work. (SOURCE: FROM THE COLLECTION OF RICHIE LISELLA)

Richie Lisella and Tommy Dorsey with the driver at the accident scene. Note Dorsey's ever-present take-charge posture. (SOURCE: FROM THE COLLECTION OF RICHIE LISELLA)

Tommy Dorsey's greatest band. Clockwise, outer circle,
beginning upper left: Clark Yokom (Pied Piper and guitar),
Connie Haines and Frank Sinatra (vocalists), Jo Stafford (Pied
Piper), Chuck Lowry (Pied Piper), George Arus (trombone),
Chuck Peterson (trumpet), Heinie Beau (saxophone), Johnny
Mince (clarinet and saxophone), Freddie Stulce (saxophone),
Don Lodice (saxophone), Paul Mason (saxophone), Ray Linn
(trumpet), Buddy Rich (drums), John Huddleston (Pied Piper).
Inner circle, beginning upper right: Lowell Martin (trombone),
Les Jenkins (trombone), Jimmy Blake (trumpet), Ziggy Elman
(trumpet), Sid Weiss (bass), Joe Bushkin (piano). Dorsey at center
of photo. (SOURCE: FROM THE COLLECTION OF WALTER C. SCOTT)

ASSIGNMENT OF WAGES, S
OR OTHER COMPENSATI

WHEREAS, I, the undersi
act with TOMMY DORSEY, w
ain agreement dated on o
, which said agreement r
es and contained a negat
rforming for others; and

WHEREAS, in consid
ay to the said TOMMY DOR
all wages, salary, commi
due me or hereafter to
from any employer.

NOW, THEREFORE
said TOMMY DORSEY, hi
assigns, until the p
agreement dated the
been made and paid
wages, salary, com
due me or hereaft
from any present

OR OTHER COMPENSATION FOR WAGES.

Dated, New York, September 3rd, 1942.

Frank Sinatra

Tommy Dorsey's usurious contract with Frank Sinatra,
which gave Dorsey 33⅓ percent of Sinatra's earnings.
(SOURCE: FROM THE COLLECTION OF THOMAS F. DORSEY, III)

Dorsey playing a muted trombone solo while his band singer, Frank Sinatra, appears captivated by someone in the audience. (SOURCE: FROM THE COLLECTION OF JANIE NEW DORSEY)

Trumpeter Ziggy Elman, with his proverbial cigar, and assistant band manager Morris I. Diamond flank Frank Sinatra during a Sunday outing at Dorsey's mansion, "The Brick House," in Bernardsville, New Jersey in 1941. (SOURCE: FROM THE COLLECTION OF MORRIS I. DIAMOND)

The marquee at Atlantic City's Steel Pier, "The showplace of the nation," during the summer of 1941, with the Andrews Sisters and Tommy Dorsey and His Band.

The slide of Dorsey's trombone encompasses his friends The King Sisters. Left to right: Yvonne, Donna, Alyce, and Luise. Photo taken at a rehearsal for an RCA Victor radio special in 1942.

Backstage at the Capitol Theatre in New York in 1947. Dorsey cuts the "Happy Anniversary" cake with Frank Sinatra, Jo Stafford, "Mom" Dorsey, and Tommy's second wife, Pat Dane. The Dorsey/Dane marriage dissolved later that year.

Dorsey in repose, presumably at a recording session, still looking immaculate. The bandleader had a habit of falling asleep on a moment's notice, only to awaken and pick up a conversation precisely where he left off.

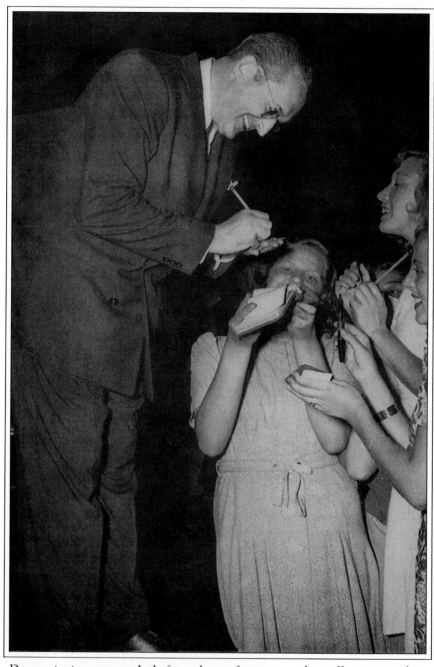

Dorsey signing autographs before a bevy of teenagers who well represent the bobbysoxers of the World War II generation. (SOURCE: FROM THE COLLECTION OF JANIE NEW DORSEY)

A distinguished turnout of bandleaders from the 1930s and 1940s, paying homage to the Dorseys' reunion at the Statler Hotel in New York in 1955. Left to right first row: George Auld, Woody Herman, Tommy Dorsey, Jimmy Dorsey, Jimmy Palmer, Tommy Reynolds, and Sonny Dunham. Left to right back row: Les Elgart, Johnny Long, Frankie Carle, and Art Mooney. (SOURCE: PHOTO BY BEN RAAST, NEW YORK, COURTESY OF JANIE NEW DORSEY)

Tommy Dorsey in the Movies

Dorsey with leggy tap dancer Eleanor Powell at the culmination of the astounding "Hawaiian War Chant" number in *Ship Ahoy*, 1942.
(SOURCE: FROM THE COLLECTION OF JANIE NEW DORSEY)

Mickey Rooney, Judy Garland, and Dorsey, with his orchestra, "put on a show" in MGM's 1943 *Girl Crazy*.
(SOURCE: COURTESY OF THE ACADEMY OF MOTION PICTURE ARTS AND SCIENCES)

Frank Sinatra yells out encouragement as saxophonist Don Lodice, singer Connie Haines, trumpeter Ziggy Elman, drummer Buddy Rich, and Dorsey jam during a musical number in Paramount's 1941 musical *Las Vegas Nights*. (SOURCE: FROM THE COLLECTION OF CONNIE HAINES)

Comedienne Nancy Walker, comedian Ben Blue, and Dorsey and His Orchestra perform "Milkman, Keep Those Bottles Quiet" from MGM's 1944 *Broadway Rhythm*.

The court of Louis XV never had it as good as Tommy Dorsey and his Orchestra (note Buddy Rich on the left) in resplendent eighteenth-century garb in MGM's 1943 musical *Du Barry Was a Lady*.
(SOURCE: COURTESY OF THE ACADEMY OF MOTION PICTURE ARTS AND SCIENCES)

Tommy Dorsey away from the Bandstand

Dorsey and his family in happy times. Photo taken at a Denver hotel in 1940 while the Dorseys were en route to California: Pat Dorsey, Tommy, "Skipper" (Thomas F. Dorsey, III), and jubilant "Toots" Dorsey.

(SOURCE: FROM THE COLLECTION OF PAT DORSEY HOOKER)

A Dorsey family reunion at the Surf Club at Virginia Beach in 1947. Left to right: Lester Hooker, Jr.; Pat Dorsey Hooker; the Wilson Ameses (friends of Pat and Lester); Pat Dane; Tommy; and "Mom" Dorsey.

(SOURCE: FROM THE COLLECTION OF PAT DORSEY HOOKER)

A band party at Dorsey's Greenwich home in October 1956. Back row: Drummer Tommy Widdicomb, Dorsey, television personality Bert Parks (a neighbor), property manager Abe "Bibsy" Mosler, bassist Billy Cronk, trombonist "Tak" Takvorian. Front row: Alto saxophonist Gail Curtis, trumpeter Lee Castle, tenor saxophonist Fred Savarese, saxophonist Babe Fresk, trumpeter Charlie Shavers, unidentified person, bus driver "Whitey" Sutherland. (SOURCE: FROM THE COLLECTION OF SMITTY CARBONE)

Singer Lynn Roberts has her ponytail groomed by Dorsey one afternoon at the Frontier Hotel in Las Vegas in 1955. Note Dorsey's white hair and paunch, the results of 35 years on the road.

(SOURCE: FROM THE COLLECTION OF LYNN ROBERTS)

Photo taken at a rehearsal for the first national television appearance of Elvis Presley on January 28, 1956, on the CBS-TV variety show *Stage Show*, hosted by Tommy and Jimmy Dorsey.

Tommy and Jimmy Dorsey in their very first appearance after reuniting on April 17, 1953, at the "Easters" concert at the University of Virginia. Drummer Jackie Mills is at right.
(SOURCE: FROM THE COLLECTION OF JACKIE MILLS)

Frank Sinatra adjusts the microphone on August 12, 1956, at the Paramount Theater in New York. Sinatra and the Dorsey brothers headlined for a week-long engagement. Note Tommy Dorsey about to give the downbeat at left, saxophonist Babe Fresk is seen through the strings of the harp, and Sinatra's pianist Bill Miller is at right. (SOURCE: FROM THE COLLECTION OF WALTER C. SCOTT)

Jimmy and Tommy Dorsey flank "The Great One"—Jackie Gleason. He was a great benefactor of the Dorseys, giving them their own CBS-TV show, *Stage Show*.
(SOURCE: FROM THE COLLECTION OF JOE SCOCCO)

Photo taken on the night of November 26, 1956, as the band played on at the Statler Hotel in New York after Dorsey's death. The leader's trombone was left on a chair in front of the band. (SOURCE: FROM THE COLLECTION OF JOE SCOCCO)

Perhaps the last photo ever taken of Dorsey, at the October 1956 band party at his Greenwich home. He looks like a man at peace with himself and happy to be in the company of his musicians.

Throughout all these machinations, Dorsey kept his cool, firmly believing he had an enforceable contract with the most talked-about personality to capture the attention of the entertainment business in years. He wasn't sure just how long the Sinatra phenomenon would last, but he knew those who wanted Sinatra would eventually have to deal directly with him.

The highly skilled publicist George Evans, whom Frank Cooper had initially brought to Sinatra's attention, who had staged the lovefests at the Paramount, showed another aspect of his genius. It was not publicity as much as public relations at work when, as part of his campaign to paint Dorsey as the villain, Evans had Sinatra's young fans parade in front of the Earle Theater in Philadelphia on the day of Sinatra's opening, holding various signs decrying how their hero was being treated unfairly by Tommy Dorsey.

Manie Sachs suggested to Sinatra that he retain Henry Jaffe as his attorney. This was after Sachs had taken Sinatra to see Harold Medina, then a prominent lawyer who eventually became famous as Justice Medina, when he ordered John L. Lewis's United Mine Workers back to work and severely fined the union for its prolonged strike. Medina had turned Sinatra down as a client.

Jaffe took charge of the multifaceted situation. He contacted Leonard Vannerson, who explained that Dorsey didn't want to talk; he wanted his money. Nonetheless, Jaffe, who was then also secretary of the American Federation of Radio Artists (AFRA), went to see Dorsey. As perhaps a hollow threat, Jaffe asked Vannerson if Dorsey wanted to continue broadcasting on NBC. He suggested they talk further about his dispute with his new client. Nothing, however, came of it.

Jaffe proceeded to confer with Jules Stein. They started discussing ways that might lead to a possible settlement with Dorsey. Manie Sachs, as a former MCA agent, was brought into subsequent meetings. In an attempt to free him from GAC, presumably Jaffe suggested to Sinatra that he turn down any work the agency offered him. All the while, MCA agents tried to convince Sinatra that he was being undersold by GAC.

In the meantime, on May 26, 1943, Sinatra followed up his earlier success with Benny Goodman at the Paramount by headlining his own engagement there. Dorsey commented to the press, "I treated him like a son, and I made him. I hope he falls on his ass." His wishes were not realized; it was another smash engagement for his former singer.

Finally, Jaffe went to Los Angeles in August 1943 to meet with N. Joseph "Joe" Ross, Dorsey's lawyer. It was finally agreed that Dorsey would receive sixty thousand dollars to end the dispute with Sinatra. Thirty-five thousand of the settlement amount was paid by MCA, which took over Sinatra's career. As further compensation, a separate substantial payment was made by Jules Stein to Tom Rockwell at GAC. Manie Sachs arranged to have Columbia Records pay the remaining twenty-five thousand as an advance against Sinatra's future record royalties.

I asked Larry Barnett for further comment on the final disposition of the conflict. His reply was "The guy who really knows what happened is Lew Wasserman, and he's not going to tell you."

Sinatra had reportedly paid Dorsey only a thousand dollars in commissions under the terms of his September 1942 contract. Dorsey nonetheless had made a profit of forty-three thousand dollars on top of the loan he had made to Sinatra a year earlier. All of the participants seemed to have come out well on the deal, although in time MCA and Columbia Records came out best. For the next year or so, on radio and in the press, there was a standing joke about what percentage Sinatra actually owned of himself.

After Dorsey first believed he had made "a hell of a deal," Arthur Michaud, Dorsey's former business adviser, had returned as his manager. Michaud told him he should have accepted twenty thousand with an additional 2½ percent or 3½ percent of Sinatra's income for the next seven years as a settlement. This caused Dorsey to believe that once again MCA had looked out for its own interests considerably more than his.

As a postscript to the Sinatra contretemps, in 1951 Dorsey revealed in an *American Mercury Magazine* article that after negotiations with Sinatra had at first bogged down, he had indeed been approached by three tough-looking men who told him in no uncertain terms that he had better let Sinatra out of his contract or else.

While a steady supply of patriotic, uplifting war movies were being made to inspire the home front, musicals were also being produced for pure entertainment value as an escape from the uncertainties of the time. Making movies in a stress-free environment for Dorsey was a welcome respite from his ongoing dispute with Sinatra and his attempts to keep his band together.

In *Girl Crazy*, director Busby Berkeley attempted a reprise of the magic he'd created five years earlier in the Warner Brothers 1937 musical *Hollywood Hotel*. One of the most captivating presentations of a big band on film had involved the spectacular appearance of Benny Goodman and members of his band sitting atop the boot of individual chauffeured white Austin convertibles driving along in section formation "playing" the Richard Whiting–Johnny Mercer Oscar-nominated song "Hooray for Hollywood."

In the spring of 1943, the so-called Arthur Freed Unit began production of *Girl Crazy*, starring the unbeatable combination of Mickey Rooney and Judy Garland, along with Tommy Dorsey and His Orchestra with Berkeley directing. The movie still stacks up well among the finest of this genre in the "golden age of MGM musicals." In addition, it was both one of the best and the last of the duo's "Let's put on a show" movies and was one of the leading box office films of that year. It was the second film version of the 1930 Gershwin Broadway show in which Tommy and Jimmy Dorsey had worked as pit band musicians.

Tommy, in one of several scenes in which he was alone on camera, shows his natural bent as an emcee while welcoming Mickey Rooney to a western college dance. The band then tears into "Fascinating Rhythm" in jump tempo with solos by Ziggy Elman, Don Lodice, and Heinie Beau. The bite of the Dorsey brass section is miraculous. Rooney intercedes to showcase the melody with a compelling piano solo. (It wasn't Rooney's artistry on display, however; onetime Dorsey musical cohort Arthur Schutt was Mickey's sound-track piano "double.")

Berkeley's astounding "I Got Rhythm" number was arranged by Sy Oliver and featured Garland singing with the band. The Dorsey band in cowboy attire marches up and down in formation while playing the classic song in tempo behind Rooney and Garland, led by Dorsey in a flat cowboy hat (close to a Lester Young–type pork pie lid), a bandana, a western shirt, and cowboy boots. A chorus of cowboy and cowgirl beauties suddenly appear, who step lively while carrying poles adorned with bright banners. (Unfortunately, the film was shot in black-and-white.) This leads into a barrage of six-guns going off and finally a cannon exploding, the perfect device to close both this spectacularly staged number and the picture itself.

Exactly sixty years after the shooting of *Girl Crazy*, Rooney reminisced fondly about Dorsey: "It's a sad thing that he isn't around anymore because there's no music like Tommy Dorsey's. . . . But, of course, music changes and you've got to go along with it." And speaking of Tommy's natural bent for film acting, Rooney observed, "He was a natural at anything he did. I think he had a great presence."

Berkeley's "Fascinating Rhythm" number was actually directed by Norman Taurog. This was after Berkeley had already gone over budget (and apparently had problems with Garland) and was taken off the picture by Arthur Freed a month into shooting.

In the interim, after the scene in *Presenting Lily Mars* featuring Garland and the Dorsey band received an adverse reaction in a preview screening, the studio decided to reshoot the finale. A new production number was filmed with Garland singing and dancing (with Charles Walters), "Broadway Rhythm," as part of a medley backed by the Dorsey band, which was shown descending on a circular platform behind her.

In the meantime, Buddy Rich had endured a painful breakup of his romance with Lana Turner. He played on the soundtrack of both *Girl Crazy* and *Presenting Lily Mars*, but Glenn Miller's former drummer Moe Purtill (who had replaced Dave Tough years before with Dorsey) was seated behind the drums in both movies, miming Buddy's playing. Rich was so upset by being on the MGM lot where Turner was queen, even for recording purposes, that he had asked Dorsey for permission not to appear during the several days required to shoot the band for the two movies.

But then, in an example of his ceaseless craving for stardom on his own, Rich accepted an offer from Universal Pictures to appear in a "B" picture, *How's About It,* starring the Andrews Sisters. His billing in the movie read, "Buddy Rich and His Orchestra." He had accepted this offer without Dorsey's permission, which brought Tommy's wrath down upon him even more. In Dorsey's mind, Buddy Rich was *his* property; this example of ingratitude renewed the on-again–off-again problems between them.

Shortly after that, during 1943, Ziggy Elman was drafted and entered the army air corps, and Rich finally joined the marine corps at Camp Pendleton, California. Actually, Buddy had been all set to enter the marine corps at the time *DuBarry Was a Lady* was in production, but Dorsey and MGM asked a certain recruiting officer to conveniently hide Rich's papers until the picture was completed.

The months ahead were difficult for Dorsey, as they were for all bandleaders, in attempting to hire good musicians. The draft had taken away the best players, who exchanged horns for rifles. During World War II, a total of forty-two Dorsey alumni served in the armed forces.

Alto saxophonist Larry Elgart, who in the 1970s recorded the huge-selling *Hooked on Swing* album and who coled a successful band with his brother, trumpeter Les Elgart, starting in the mid-1950s, spent seven months with the Dorsey band in 1943 into 1944. "Tommy Dorsey was the best bandleader I ever worked for," Elgart contends. "He knew exactly what he wanted, and most of the guys didn't know what they wanted. He was totally in control of sixteen musicians. He's listening, he's looking, he moves his body to tell them what to do because he's playing while he's conducting."

Elgart had his own serious problems with his brother regarding the musical direction of their band. It was Larry who created the famous "sophisticated swing" sound of their band. He added, "When we hit, I remember Tommy saying to me, 'Larry, I'm very glad for you. I'm so happy this thing is happening for you.'" (Did Dorsey perhaps see in the Elgarts' success exactly what should have happened with him and Jimmy?)

In these uncertain times, when promising young musicians were indeed at a premium, Dorsey met a soft-spoken, talented pianist and arranger named Charlie Wick, who led a five-piece dance band at the Petite Café in the Carter Hotel in his hometown of Cleveland. Wick had already graduated from the University of Michigan with a degree in music and was in the midst of seeking his law degree from Case Western in Cleveland.

Try as he might, Wick couldn't get accepted by any branches of the armed forces as a volunteer due to his acute problems with allergies. When he was finally drafted in October 1942, he was rejected because he was allergic to wool.

Dorsey came into the Carter one night during the band's Palace Theater engagement in Cleveland. Wick recalled, "I gave him an arrangement of 'I've Only Been Dreaming Again,' a tune I had written when I was in high school, which Fred Waring had been playing on his Chesterfield radio show. Dorsey didn't record it, but he was impressed by the fact that I played some of the tunes he liked and the way I did them."

Dorsey saw that this young man had other talents in addition to his musical abilities. He kept in touch with him. By the end of 1943, Wick had passed the bar exam, and in April 1944 Dorsey asked Wick to join his band to coach The Sentimentalists (the singing group that had followed The Pied Pipers) and write occasional arrangements. Essentially, however, he wanted Wick to get involved in his business.

Wick noted, "I frankly didn't realize that he enjoyed business that much. He had that wonderful viewpoint toward me that wasn't realistically credible, but that was his perspective. He felt that there were intangibles in a legal relationship, as far as musicians were concerned, that lawyers generally wouldn't understand, but that I, as a musician, possibly could."

At this juncture, Nick Sevano, who had recently left Sinatra's employ, entered the picture. Dorsey had welcomed him back to the band and had given him the job of advance publicity man. Wick recalled, "I told Nick about Tommy's offer, but I said I felt that I'd rather stay in Cleveland and practice law. Nick said to me, 'You're crazy. You've got to do this.' Nick really changed my life."

Wick joined the band in Milwaukee, en route to the West Coast, and was soon listed as one of the arrangers contributing to the "Dorsey Concert Orchestra." Dorsey had something more specific in mind, however. He yearned to own his own ballroom, which had the potential of being a significant financial success. Owning a ballroom would also allow him to keep the band off the road and thus provide a respite from the attendant difficulties.

He told Wick he wanted him to negotiate a deal to purchase the Casino Gardens from its owner, Bernie Cohen. (As Larry Barnett remembered, "That was because the Palladium wouldn't pay him what he wanted.") This was in addition to the management's refusal to offer him a guarantee plus a percentage agreement to dance bands.

The Casino Gardens (now gone) was located on Ocean Park Pier in Ocean Park, California (later incorporated into Santa Monica), and could handle thirty-seven hundred dancers at full capacity. The purchase price was fifty thousand dollars, according to *Variety*; *Metronome* said the figure was sixty-five thousand. Jimmy Dorsey was Tommy's principal partner, and Harry James, who had suddenly assumed the position of the nation's number-one bandleader, had a smaller financial participation. Opening night was set for September 1944, with a "battle of the bands" between the two Dorsey orchestras.

"I had offices upstairs in the ballroom," Wick remembered. "Tommy's band played there for a long while. I remember some of the big stars used to come in—Judy Garland, Lucille Ball and Desi Arnaz, Mickey Rooney. They all loved his music. Tommy also insisted I stay at the Sunset Plaza in [West] Hollywood, where he and Pat Dane [Dorsey's second wife] were living."

Business remained brisk. Swing was still very much in vogue. Los Angeles was full of servicemen who enjoyed dancing to name bands. And then there was the defense industry that was going twenty-four hours a day with workers, working in shifts, who were also eager to go out and dance.

When engagements were booked in the East, Dorsey wanted Wick to come back there with the band, but Wick wanted to remain in Los Angeles and take the California bar exam. Though he passed it, he never worked a day as a lawyer. He had started to invest in California real estate.

Wick went on to run the William Morris Agency's band department for five years before he left to start his own law firm, which represented musical and variety stars such as Rudy Vallee, Ken Murray, Horace Heidt, James

Melton, Arthur Murray, Don Ameche, and others who hosted weekly network radio shows.

Wick later made a successful transition into other areas, which included
making the publishing deal for Winston Churchill's epic series *History of the
English-Speaking Peoples* and advising Ronald Reagan in his gubernatorial bid
in California. Later, he served in the Reagan administration for two terms as
director of the U.S. Information Agency (USIA).

During the shooting of *Girl Crazy*, in February 1943, Pat Dorsey became
Pat Hooker when she married midway through her first year as a student at
William and Mary. She was only seventeen years old. Her bridegroom,
Lester Hooker, had recently left college to enter the army air corps. Years
later, Lester became a highly respected basketball coach, first at William
and Mary and then for over a decade at the University of Richmond.

Pat's troubled relationship with her father stemmed from the way she felt
her mother was treated during and after their marriage was dissolved. As
she saw it, "The judge said, 'This woman should be supported in the manner to which she has been accustomed.' She never was. She had to sell her
silver to send Skipper and me to college. Every time he got behind in paying the monthly alimony money, our lawyer would make his lawyer have
Daddy take out another insurance policy on his life and pay for it." She also
stated, "I would say he was not an ideal father. He was very strict, he had a
grand ego, and there was not much room in his life except for himself."

Tommy flew from Los Angeles to Richmond, Virginia, to give his daughter away at her wedding. It was the first time he and Toots had seen one another since their abrupt split-up two years earlier. Since their daughter was
a minor, both of them had to give their permission for Pat and Lester to
marry. Tommy made his feelings known when he said, "Toots, if this doesn't
work I'm holding you responsible." His apprehension was ill founded. Pat
and Lester had an extremely successful marriage that produced three children and lasted fifty-six years until Lester passed away in 1999.

Although Dorsey may have been dubious about his daughter's marriage
and didn't much like paying alimony and child support, it didn't sour him on
the subject of marriage. Larry Barnett referred to Toots as "a nice lady. She
was a homebody who loved to cook a meal for Tommy. She didn't belong
married to a show business person." Dorsey's second wife was another story.

Pat Dane (Thelma Patricia Ann Byrnes-Gray), tall and slim, with chestnut hair and flashing licorice eyes, was an MGM starlet when Dorsey met her at the studio. Born in Jacksonville, Florida, she had attended the University of Alabama for almost three years before moving to Los Angeles. In 1941 she was signed to an MGM contract, which, with options, lasted until 1945. Her first film appearance was as one of thirty-two "blue ribbon" beauties in *Ziegfeld Girl*. Although she had had no previous acting experience, she was soon cast in an important featured role in *Life Begins for Andy Hardy*, opposite the original Hardy boy, Mickey Rooney. Dane segued into *I'll Wait for You*, and director Mervyn LeRoy signed her for a memorable role in *Johnny Eager* with Robert Taylor and Lana Turner. The starlet looked delectable in a bathing suit, which kept MGM staff photographers busy so that the publicity department could continue planting cheesecake pictures of her in newspapers and magazines.

Pat Dane and Tommy Dorsey seemed made for each other. Dane had an exhibitionist's streak that appealed to Tommy's own in-your-face personality. Neither one of them cared what other people thought of them. They reveled in being a part of the glamour that big-band stardom represented and in addition what being signed to MGM represented to the world. (One must not forget that the slogan of Louis B. Mayer's empire was "More Stars Than There Are in the Heavens.") At last Dorsey had the showpiece he had always wanted in a wife.

They eloped to Las Vegas on April 8, 1943. Dane gave her age as twenty-two, but she was actually twenty-four, and Dorsey was thirty-seven. It was the second marriage for Dane as well as for Tommy. As a wedding gift Tommy bought his bride a new Lincoln Continental convertible. It pleased him to see her driving it; he believed it was a reflection on him.

At that time, Dane was shooting a Red Skelton comic vehicle, *I Dood It*, as second female lead to Eleanor Powell. Jimmy Dorsey's band had a starring role in the picture. Tommy insisted he have a cameo role as well. Jimmy apparently didn't like Dane. He had dated her a few times before Tommy met her. A few years later, when presenting a birthday cake to Tommy at the Indianapolis Theater, Jimmy shoved the cake in Dane's face, and another Dorsey brothers fracas followed.

Retired Los Angeles radio and television sports commentator Gil Stratton played the part of Mickey Rooney's roommate in *Girl Crazy*. He recalled meeting Dane at the studio. She was asked, "How could you marry a bandleader?" She replied, "He was the only guy in the business who wasn't a 'center fielder,'" referring to the fact that most men, upon meeting her, hit on her immediately, but Dorsey apparently didn't.

Tommy enjoyed showing off his new bride to his musicians and to his friends in his own inimitable fashion. She wasn't shy about showing herself off either. Singer Peter Marshall, who would later host the long-running television show *Password*, was once the brother-in-law of Dick Haymes through Haymes's marriage to his sister, the actress Joanne Dru. Haymes told him that Dane enjoyed flashing her bare breasts from the wings at the Hollywood Palladium while Haymes was onstage singing with the Dorsey band. Tommy watched his bride's antics with unrestrained glee, beaming with pride.

Singer Mel Torme, who was also an accomplished drummer, sometime later was considered by Dorsey to replace Buddy Rich. Torme recalled meeting with Dorsey at his apartment on Sunset Plaza Drive. Dorsey poured himself a tumblerful of scotch; Torme, at twenty-one, was a nondrinker and settled for a Coca-Cola. Torme's career was then well on its way to becoming successful; he tried to explain to Dorsey how impractical it would be for him to join his band as drummer.

Pat Dane, wearing a halter and shorts, swept into the living room from the kitchen with a trayful of Danish pastries. Dorsey remarked, "Greatest tits in town. Show 'em, hon!" With a slightly exasperated shrug of her shoulders, Dane put the tray down, reached with both hands toward the back of her neck, untied the bow on her halter, and revealed her gloriously formed breasts. "How about those, huh, kid?" Dorsey remarked. Torme stammered, "Very nice," while his eyes bored holes in Dane's chest. Calmly the actress retied the halter and went back to the kitchen.

Berle Adams recalled an even more extreme display of their lack of inhibition. Dorsey invited Adams to have dinner with him and Pat Dane in Chicago. "He came into town and called me up telling me he wanted me to meet his new mate. She arrived wearing a white turban [a 1940s fashion statement favored by other Hollywood glamour girls like Lana Turner and Maria Montez]. She was a very beautiful girl. We were sitting there having dinner, and out of the clear blue sky she says, 'Tommy, who's the greatest cocksucker you ever met?' Tommy says, 'You are, darling.'" Adams laughed at the recollection, "I fell under the chair."

This was hardly the only time that Dorsey proudly spoke of his wife's prowess at oral sex. Clarinetist Buddy DeFranco's first night in the Dorsey band in December 1943 found him being welcomed by the bandleader backstage at the Palace Theater in Cleveland. "Hey, you stale shitheel, come in here," said Dorsey. "I want you to meet my old lady, Pat. She is the greatest cocksucker in the world." On hearing Dorsey's declaration, DeFranco was completely shocked, but even more so when Dane boasted, "You're fucking right I am!" He recalled, "He didn't think that was offensive at all, and neither did she." DeFranco added, "I later learned that the reason she was wearing dark glasses that night was to cover up the black eye Tommy had given her."

Child star, actor, and director Jackie Cooper, in his autobiography, *Please Don't Shoot My Dog*, remembered being jolted by Dorsey and Dane one day. Dorsey said to him, "Wanna see a real fan?" whereupon Dorsey hoisted her skirt and pulled her panties down to show that the initials *TD* had been shaved into her pubic hair.

Besides being a vibrant, sexy young woman whom Dorsey relished showing off as his wife, Dane enjoyed making the rounds of Hollywood nightclubs with Tommy. She was the complete opposite of what Toots had represented to Tommy.

In the next years while he was a contract player at MGM, the studio made maximum use of Dorsey's talents. In a scene in MGM's patriotic war drama *Bataan*, starring Robert Taylor and George Murphy, the Dorsey band is heard but not seen playing "Well, Git It!" Listening intently to the radio broadcast on the doomed Philippine peninsula, the actor exclaimed, "That's Tommy Dorsey from Hollywood."

Following a spate of back-to-back films, Benny Thau, who ran the talent department at the studio, ordered more appearances by Tommy Dorsey and His Orchestra. Next up was *Broadway Rhythm*, top-lining George Murphy, Ginny Simms, Charles Winninger, Gloria DeHaven, and Nancy Walker.

This musical comedy was loosely based on Jerome Kern and Oscar Hammerstein II's *Very Warm for May*. The movie opens with the Dorsey orchestra playing the familiar "National Emblem March" in a large gazebo. The band is bedecked in crimson red marching-band uniforms complete with gold braid. As the camera pulls back, it is revealed that it is actually a scene in rehearsal onstage from an upcoming Broadway musical produced by actor George Murphy's character. Later, in real life, Murphy became a Republican senator from California.

Charles Winninger, who portrays Murphy's father, plays an out-of-tune trombone solo in a duet with Tommy. After Winninger's painful licks, Dorsey illustrates his mastery of the instrument. Later on, the two of them join up to sing a duet about the good old days in "I Love Corny Music." They proceed to play a second trombone duet as Dorsey this time demonstrates his Dixieland chops.

In another memorable production number toward the end of the picture, Tommy and his musicians are dressed in white, complete with clip-on black bow ties and white hats with black visors and black shoes—perfect 1940s milkman outfits. The studio thought this was the proper garb for them to play "Milkman, Keep Those Bottles Quiet," backing musical comedy star Nancy Walker, years later remembered for her "quicker picker-upper" television commercials. Walker sings and dances the number along with comedian Ben Blue.

After completing his work on the picture, Dorsey returned to New York and rehearsed a new band, which included some holdovers. Tommy opened with the band on October 4 at the Café Rouge at the Hotel Pennsylvania. Soon, as ever-vigilant Dorsey expert George T. Simon reported, Dorsey "improved his band once again."

Tom Sheils, fresh out of Notre Dame, who began his show business career by working for Glenn Miller in his office and later represented a myriad of important performers, including Johnny Carson, attended a Dorsey performance one night at the Café Rouge with Glenn and Helen Miller, Don Haynes (Sheils's boss, who was Miller's manager), and Polly Haynes. This was shortly after Captain Miller and his band had finished their army air force radio show *I Sustain the Wings*. Sheils said, "I recall Tommy lamenting the fact to Glenn that he was losing a lot of his best men to the military service. Tommy was saying something like 'Guys who were just mediocre are asking for big salaries, but they're not worth it. That's the way it is these days.'"

In December 1943, Dorsey hired Gene Krupa away from Benny Goodman more than a year after Krupa had been busted for marijuana possession in a sting in San Francisco. Drum expert Burt Korall said, "Dorsey was convinced that Krupa could reestablish himself with the public by not just playing one-nighters and hotel gigs as he had been doing with Goodman. He insisted that MCA get the band back in the Paramount to showcase Krupa. The result was instantaneous. Gene was a sensation all over again. His future was secure."

According to a saxophonist in the band, Dorsey's largesse toward Krupa included his sanctioning Pat Dane's interest in going to bed with Krupa. It was all part of keeping both his wife and his star drummer contented!

While Tommy was at the Paramount with Krupa for four weeks, Jimmy's band was at the nearby Roxy. Jimmy outgrossed Tommy $113,000 to $80,000 in the first week. Both bands played to capacity audiences, but the Roxy was a much larger theater, with two thousand seats more than the Paramount. On New Year's Eve, after an argument with him on the bandstand, Tommy fired the veteran baritone saxophonist Ernie Caceres and explained precisely why to the audience as the humiliated Caceres left the stage.

On February 29, 1944, when Jimmy was celebrating his fortieth birthday, Tommy, along with Gene Krupa and fellow bandleader Jan Savitt, came to Minneapolis, where Jimmy's band was headlining at the Circle Theater. It was the first time in twelve years Tommy had been there to observe "The Brother's" birthday.

Important new additions to Tommy's band were clarinetist and alto saxophonist Buddy DeFranco and pianist Michael "Dodo" Marmarosa. Shortly after that, Bob Allen, himself a former bandleader, finally took over as the band's male singer. His female counterpart was Bonnie Lou Williams. Several months earlier, The Sentimentalists, made up of the four real-life, petite Clark sisters (Mary, Peggy, Ann, and Jean), ranging from seventeen to twenty-three years old, who hailed from Grand Forks, North Dakota, joined the band, replacing The Pied Pipers. The Sentimentalists had been with Major Bowes Amateur Hour and had toured with the USO.

I asked Peggy (Clark) Schwartz, widow of clarinetist Willie Schwartz, who became one of the most successful Hollywood recording-studio musicians following his early success with Glenn Miller, how she and her sisters could keep up an attractive appearance (a prerequisite for all female band singers) and also maintain their voices while putting up with the constant traveling and sometimes lecherous musicians along with alternately cold and overheated buses. Schwartz's succinct laughing reply: "In those days you had to be young and stupid. You also had to be pretty needy. . . . It was almost comical when you look back at it; it was part of the growing-up process."

The sisters had auditioned for Dorsey in their West Forty-fifth Street apartment and were hired on the spot. The four bubbly as well as talented Clark sisters knew full well that the prestige of working for Tommy Dorsey would be their main compensation. "I think we got thirty-five or forty dollars apiece a week, and we had to pay for our own room, meals, clothes, and cleaning. Every week it was hand to mouth," Schwartz recalled. They made friends with Dorsey's musicians, lead alto saxophonist and arranger Sid

Cooper, guitarist Bob Bain, trombonist and arranger Nelson Riddle, and Buddy DeFranco. Except for the deceased Riddle, Schwartz maintains a close relationship with all of them to the present.

The Sentimentalists had to learn The Pied Pipers' songs just as Bob Allen and later Stuart Foster sang the songs Sinatra had performed with the band and Bonnie Williams sang many of the Connie Haines and Edythe Wright songs. But they also had new tunes, some of which became big hits, like "On the Sunny Side of the Street," "I Should Care" (with Bonnie Lou Williams), "Nevada" (with Stuart Foster), "On the Atchison, Topeka, and the Santa Fe," "Chicago" (with Sy Oliver), "The Moment I Met You," and "Why Do I Love You?" from *Show Boat* (with Stuart Foster).

Schwartz made it clear that she and her sisters were on strictly business terms with Dorsey. "It was just a job," she related. "I thought he was cheap the way he paid us, but we thought, 'God, we're lucky to be here. We're having a great time.' We finally went to Dave Jacobs, the road manager. He got us a raise of fifty dollars each when housing prices went up."

The time spent with Dorsey also gave them a keen appreciation of Sy Oliver, whose charts sometimes featured the group. This led to a close friendship with Sy. "He really helped us. If anybody had a hang-up, he'd level with you and say, 'What are you talking about? How big a deal is that?' I just loved him."

In 1942 Sy Oliver was drafted into the army. By 1944 he had been promoted to staff sergeant. He was only able to write for Dorsey on a part-time basis, so Dorsey was forced to hire other arrangers. Sid Cooper and Nelson Riddle took up some of the slack.

Early in 1944, Sid Cooper came on the band (replacing Larry Elgart) to play lead alto and write arrangements. A few months later, twenty-three-year-old Nelson Riddle became a member of the brass section. In time, Riddle became more than an acceptable trombone player, but at that time Dorsey contended he held his jaw too rigidly when he played. Riddle had been with Charlie Spivak's band for over two years, during which he wrote the chart of "White Christmas," which was the big-band hit of the tune, although it was far surpassed in sales by Bing Crosby's famous record of the Irving Berlin classic.

From the start, Dorsey greatly respected Cooper. He also saw great potential in Riddle. He teamed Cooper with Riddle in order that Nelson could absorb the style of arranging that he wanted. Their first coendeavor was the chart of "Top Hat, White Tie, and Tails" to feature The Sentimentalists on the *All Time Hit Parade* radio show. "There was a noticeable difference in style between us," Cooper recalled, "but it seemed to work out all right."

Sid Cooper recognized the influence of Bill Finegan's teaching (Finegan was Riddle's original mentor) on the first two charts Riddle wrote alone for Dorsey, "Like Someone in Love" and "Sleigh Ride in July." Others included cover versions of hit songs like "There's No You." Another chart that Dorsey never recorded but continued to play was Nelson's perfect vehicle for his particular way of playing ballads, "Laura."

Buddy DeFranco remarked:

Even though Nelson kept the basic "Laura" structure and the basic harmonic, he chose in some areas to throw in a few altered chords. It gave an ethereal effect to the song and to the arrangement. The guys in the band loved it, but Tommy said, "Get that out of here. That's not the 'Laura' I know." He then trimmed it down pretty good. I think that's when he began calling Nelson, "The Cloud," and sometimes "Cloud 9."

Tommy used to scream at almost all the arrangers for writing too much and trying to get too far out. Nelson and Finegan were the guys who wrote what they wanted to write, and it was way ahead of its time. Tommy would say, "No, take that out." Bill and Nelson would get bent out of shape because they were proud of what they had written. But Tommy, like most bandleaders, knew what the public wanted, and he tailored those arrangements to suit it. Tommy's idea of a good arrangement was more like Sy Oliver—ya know, blood-and-guts-type arrangements.

Working for Dorsey gave Riddle easy access to strings, since Dorsey's band had an even larger string section than the Maritime Service Orchestra, where Riddle had worked just before joining Dorsey. As Riddle described it, "I had enough time to try out different string voicings and thus was able to add to my 'tool box' proportionately."

Dorsey referred to the strings as the "mice." After Riddle wrote his first arrangements for him, one night Dorsey suggested they have dinner together. He told the young arranger, "I like your writing, but you're relying too heavily on the 'mice.' You're making them too important. I'm thinking of getting rid of them soon. They're basically a tax deduction so I want to keep that flexibility, but when I get rid of them I want to have arrangements that the band can still play." Riddle recalled that he was crushed by Dorsey's pronouncement, "But I revised my plans so that I started writing without leaning on the strings. It was just as well. I then learned to write both ways."

All told, Sid Cooper believes Riddle wrote about a dozen charts for Dorsey in the eleven months he was a member of the band, starting at twenty dollars an arrangement. The time Riddle spent with Tommy Dorsey had a profound effect on his later career.

Diane Atkins, the widow of Lenny Atkins, who played violin for Dorsey from 1942 to 1945, pointed out the high quality of the string section during the time Riddle was arranging for the band: "Lenny started out on the viola with Tommy and then replaced Leonard Posner on lead violin. Bernard Tinterow and Lenny Posner on violin, my Lenny on viola, and George Ricci on cello played chamber music for Frank Sinatra when he said he wanted to hear chamber music and to learn about some of the finer nuances of classical music."

Within months eight more strings were added to the section—another example of Dorsey's ever-changing ideas to achieve a more romantic sound for his orchestra. From December 1944 until June 1945 Dorsey led his "Big Bertha Band," which comprised forty-six musicians. During this latter period, because of attrition from the draft, the entire string section consisted of female musicians. The absence of draft-free musicians provided opportunities for women to play in various big bands. (After the war, the strings were gone.)

In addition to Cooper and Riddle, Dorsey also employed arrangers Hugo Winterhalter (later known for his sometimes overly dramatic arrangements for Eddie Fisher's records in the 1950s, on which Sid Cooper often participated as a flutist), Eddie Sauter (formerly Benny Goodman's ace arranger), and Freddie Norman. All of them were quite different in their musical approaches.

Bob Bain, the band's guitarist, explained, "Tommy always knew who the right arranger was to assign each piece of new material." He was also not against hiring well-established arrangers like David Rose. Upon playing the stringmeister's chart of "Smoke Gets in Your Eyes" for the first time, Dorsey told the band, "Guess how much that arrangement cost me—a thousand bucks . . . but it was worth it."

At this time of his life, Dorsey felt invincible. His unqualified success on records, on radio, and in personal appearances had propelled him into movies, where he was signed to the leading studio. He also had a spectacular-looking wife. He was exempt from being drafted into military service, so he didn't have to face the same risks as younger men.

By 1944, Dorsey could boast of having two thousand fan clubs. He declared, "Radio and records are fine, but it's the 'face to face' contacts that hold fans. You can't fluff off kids and tell them what kind of music to like. They tell you." (He would live to see the validity of his comment and witness how it adversely affected his future.)

His trombone virtuosity had long ago brought him to the attention of the classical world. It was only natural that eventually he would be showcased in a New York concert by a major conductor. All of this was good publicity that even his young fans appreciated.

Dorsey's considerable appeal to young people was never better shown than at his February 15, 1945, concert appearance at City Center with the seventy-five-piece New York City Symphony Orchestra, conducted by the famous Leopold Stokowski. In the audience were twenty-three hundred schoolchildren. This concert marked Dorsey's classical music debut. (He had previously recorded pop versions of Schubert's "Ave Maria" as well as works by Rimsky-Korsakov, Mendelssohn, Brahms, and others.) The occasion was a premiere by his old boss from the late 1920s, Nathaniel "Nat" Shilkret's Concerto for Trombone and Orchestra. It was said to be the first classical concerto ever written for the trombone.

"I'm very enthused, but I've never worked so hard in my life. . . . I've been practicing more than I've practiced in the last fifteen years," said Dorsey during rehearsals. Continuing in a self-deprecating manner, he added, "I hope they like it. But I don't know much about [concert] halls. Now if it was the Arcadia Ballroom or Roseland." At one afternoon rehearsal he asked Stokowski, who had first marveled at his playing when he saw him perform at the Hollywood Palladium, if a solo he had just played was correct in its concept. The maestro facetiously, yet candidly, replied, "Just a little bit sharp, . . . Tommy."

When Dorsey came out onstage and walked through the orchestra to begin performing without being announced, he was greeted with the kind of reception usually given to a singing rage like Sinatra. The concerto received a very enthusiastic reception. This was especially true after the playing of the third and final movement, with its quasi-Gershwin passages and its brief reference to "I'm Getting Sentimental over You," along with an overall rhythmic feel. Stokowski sternly lectured the teenagers, however, after the completion of the second movement, threatening not to play the final movement unless they stopped squealing.

Miles Anderson, the well-regarded classical trombonist and also a one-time member of Les Brown's "Band of Renown," has a keen appreciation of Dorsey's work. He related, "I was amazed by his classical technique. Much of the [Shilkret] piece is played in the upper register, where Tommy was very much at ease. There are several minithemes throughout the piece. The opening is basically more classical, but Tommy plays it lyrical. The piece is certainly valuable in the trombone world."

Anderson went on to praise Dorsey's staccato technique: "He played in a way as if he knew about traditional trombone playing a bit. He sounds like if he wanted to he could have had a career playing in a symphony orchestra."

The late George Frazier was one of the most urbane observers of pop culture from the 1940s to the 1980s. One of his memorable *Boston Globe* columns consisted of short, pithy judgments regarding various bandleaders and jazz musicians. Included in his comments were "Tommy Dorsey has the quickest temper in the business. . . . Russ Morgan is the handiest with his fists."

Late in his literary career, after years writing for *Life* and *Esquire*, Frazier coined the English use of the Spanish term *duende*, which became a favorite expression of his. It was the catchword for his column, always leaving an air of mystery surrounding its definition. He insisted it was a word that was better defined by example than by language, pointing out that it was a definite and unique quality that only certain *special* artists possessed.

Duende is actually an Andalusian word, meaning "hobgoblin or ghost" in the original Spanish, but translated it means a special force or characteristic that makes one irresistibly attractive. The word has also been translated as "soul—the spirit of the earth, and the power to attract through personal magnetism."

Frazier concluded that Miles Davis personified duende. It would seem that Tommy Dorsey's very presence in front of his band—his magnetism, the intensity of his leadership, his volcanic temperament, his matchless ballad playing, and yes, his clothes (which always meant a great deal to Frazier)— would have also caused him to label "The Sentimental Gentleman" as indeed representing duende.

Dorsey on film, as well as on audiotapes of studio or live recordings, comes across as very much of a "man's man." He was masculine and profane, enjoyed the company of women, and was a zealous sports fan. Although he always displayed an abundance of energy, he required little sleep. According to Larry Barnett, he had the uncanny ability to fall asleep momentarily during business meetings, only to quickly regain consciousness and pick up where he had left off. He laughed easily and had an abundance of charm. He willingly helped musicians in financial trouble and didn't want anyone to know about it. And, as has been revealed, he couldn't do enough for musicians whose work he admired. As a perfect example, when alto saxophonist Hymie Schertzer told him he was planning to get married, Dorsey had a jeweler bring over a tray full of rings to pick from and then insisted on paying for the wedding ring.

As part of his Gaelic heritage, he enjoyed telling jokes and humorous stories to a rapt audience made up of fellow musicians or old friends. Though he never lost sight of his humble Eastern Pennsylvania coal-mining-town origins, with frequent references to his youth, he enjoyed the high living style of the wealthy, who often hired his band. He adopted their way of dressing, their manners, and their free-spending ways. Living well was his way of proving that he both was successful and deserved respect.

Bill Finegan summed up his impressions of Dorsey as "a volatile character who generated an aura of excitement about himself. You got within three feet of him and there was electricity in the air." He remarked on the force of Tommy's personality, "Anyone who got in a position of power after being around Tommy acted like Tommy."

Tommy's contentious relationship with Jimmy would last to their final days together. But despite that, as Larry Barnett observed, "He really loved Jimmy." The dual aspects of their fractious relationship by now had become a shtick they joked about in their performances. In a trumpet duel heard on a radio remote from the Meadowbrook in 1943, the competition over who was the more accomplished trumpeter is second to the fun they have in purposely playing clams (wrong notes) and missing high notes in order to keep their musical exchange entertaining. The "hard-fought" contest was labeled a draw.

There was a nasal, yet gravelly sound to Dorsey's voice. He sometimes spoke rapidly out of the side of his mouth. His rough edges were never completely smoothed over. He displayed a pronounced confidence that also revealed his unyielding manner. His eyesight was so bad that Pat Hooker said, "If he didn't have his glasses on, he couldn't see the food that was put in front of him." The people he liked he called "Harv," just as Benny Goodman, who forgot everyone's names, referred to them as "Pops." (Artie Shaw claimed that Dorsey lifted the moniker "Harv" from Fulton "Fidgey" McGrath, an accomplished jazz pianist/arranger who had recorded with the Dorsey Brothers Orchestra in the early 1930s.) Bores who approached him he referred to as "stiffs." Another favorite expression of his was, "That bird doesn't come from the same parrot."

The pride of ownership he felt with regard to Pat Dane, along with his lack of reluctance to use his fists when he felt it was necessary, combined to get Dorsey into the biggest scandal of his life. It was just off the Sunset Strip in West Hollywood on the night of August 5, 1944, that the so-called Battle of the Balcony took place. Sixty years later, Charlie Wick, then running Casino Gardens, still remembered the date.

It started at 4:30 in the morning at the Sunset Plaza Apartments during a party in honor of Pat Dane's twenty-sixth birthday. The main participants in the fracas were film star Jon Hall; Jane Churchill; Dane; Allen Smiley (Aaron Smehoff), then a codefendant with Bugsy Siegel, the notorious mob figure, in a bookmaking case; and—Tommy Dorsey.

It all started at the Dorseys' apartment when Hall returned to the premises to retrieve a handbag belonging to Jane Churchill, Winston Churchill's third cousin, an attractive Kansas City socialite. Hall apparently put his arms around Dane, in what he later described as a playful but chaste manner. Dorsey objected strenuously to Hall's familiarity with his wife, and though Hall apologized, Dorsey landed a punch to his chin, which knocked Hall to the floor of the balcony.

The actor Eddie Norris, former husband of film star Ann Sheridan ("The Oomph Girl"), and Churchill had been waiting outside the apartment house in a car for Hall's return. The three of them had met earlier that evening at the Clover Club and had been invited by the Dorseys to their apartment for a nightcap. Other partygoers suddenly ran out to inform them that Hall had been seriously injured in a fight. They quickly returned to the Dorsey apartment and found Hall bleeding profusely from severe wounds to his face, nose, and right ear. Three men, one of whom was Allen Smiley, who lived in the next apartment, were armed with knives and bottles. Reportedly, when Norris pulled them off Hall he was kicked in the face.

Churchill, in an attempt to help Norris, managed to push the assailants away from Hall. Meanwhile, Dane grabbed Churchill's hair and with her other arm held her head in a hammerlock. In the impending scuffle, Dane's clothes were ripped. Despite the severity of his injuries, Hall drove himself to the emergency room of a nearby hospital, where he had thirty-two stitches in his head and sixteen stitches in his neck. Dane called the police, who made no formal report.

Churchill was interviewed the next night while dancing at the Trocadero. She said she had been threatened and told not to say anything further about the incident. The night after that Hall, in an interview with the Los Angeles *Daily News*, claimed he had merely "patted [Miss Dane] on the shoulder." He also said that the person who he thought had wielded the knife that had worked him over belonged to Allen Smiley. In a companion story in the same newspaper, Dorsey speculated that possibly a shard from a broken flower pot had caused the knifelike incisions on Hall's face! On August 9, Hall exposed his brutalized features to *Los Angeles Examiner* writer James Murray and said, "Does that look to you as if it were made by a flower pot?"

As speculation about a series of upcoming arrests mounted, the Los Angeles and New York newspapers, as well as the wire services, reveled in la scandale Dorsey. Again in the Los Angeles *Daily News*, Dorsey admitted that he had thrown the first punch, which had put things into motion, but that according to him this was after Hall had first made contact with him. He denied that knives had been involved and repeated his denial after another guest at the party, Panamanian sailor Antonio Icaza, accused him of having attacked him with a knife and a bottle. Meanwhile, in another interview, Norris claimed that Dorsey had been insulting him earlier at the party and had told him "to get the hell out of here!" He was now willing to forget the entire incident, saying as peacemaker, "I got just what was coming to me."

Almost a year to the day after Joe Ross had settled the contract dispute with Frank Sinatra, he was pressed into service to defend Dorsey against the suit for forty thousand dollars in damages made by Icaza. Meanwhile, Hall and Jane Churchill were cooperating with District Attorney Fred N. Howser. In a bizarre twist, Churchill was said to have been spotted at a local restaurant dining with Allen Smiley. But the final surprise came about two weeks after the Battle of the Balcony when Jon Hall decided not to press charges against Dorsey, Dane, or Smiley!

After some deliberation, Howser, nevertheless, felt he *had* a case against the three participants. They were indicted for felonious assault. The attorney Isaac Pacht defended the Dorseys.

According to a *DownBeat* story, Pacht got the bail for Dorsey and Dane reduced from ten thousand dollars each to five thousand. In spite of the success he was then enjoying, Dorsey obviously had cash flow problems in view of the fact that a commercial bonding firm wound up posting bail for him and Dane. The trial date was quickly set for September 26, three days before the band was to open at the Casino Gardens.

Smiley hired Jerry Giesler to represent him. Over the intervening years, the expression "Get me Giesler!" has become a familiar slogan in Hollywood history, and with good reason. Among several famous trials, Giesler would get Errol Flynn off on statutory rape charges, represent Robert Mitchum after his marijuana arrest, handle Marilyn Monroe's divorce action against Joe DiMaggio, and defend Lana Turner and her daughter, Cheryl Crane, in the infamous murder of Johnny Stompanato.

After a postponement, the trial proceedings in California Superior Court commenced on November 30, 1944. The thrust of the defense's case was that Dorsey was protecting the privacy of his own home and had acted in self-defense. This claim was made in hopes of getting the charges against Dorsey and Smiley dismissed.

During a recess Dorsey was handed a telegram addressed to Tommy ("Slugger") Dorsey that read, "Following your trial with great interest. Hope it comes out in your favor. We fight for our wimmin [sic] too." It was signed, "Fifteen Weary Marines in San Diego."

The preliminary part of the trial began in circuslike circumstances. Two women jurists were removed after requesting and getting Dorsey's autograph. In court, Tess Dorsey was seen smiling in support of "my Tommy." Pat Dane disclosed she had purchased fourteen pairs of nylons to encase her exquisite legs, "but before the shortage" of nylons due to the war. Finally, after some deliberation eleven women and one man were selected to constitute the jury.

Wearing a protective translucent sheath on his nose, the first witness, Jon Hall, was asked to demonstrate how and where he had placed his arm around Pat Dane. In his testimony he was unable to specify whether it was Dorsey or Dane who had actually cut him with a knife. Giesler and Pacht cross-examined Hall ferociously. In her testimony that followed, Jane Churchill was unable to state unequivocally if she saw weapons in the hands of any of the defendants. When Bugsy Siegel's name was injected into the proceedings, the two defense attorneys tried unsuccessfully to seek a mistrial.

The testimony of Panamanian seaman Antonio Icaza over the next two days was vague at best, since he had obvious problems with English. More important, however, Judge Arthur Crum grew increasingly angry at Icaza's constant "I don't remember," after some forty of such answers. Giesler then informed the court that he had discovered various immigration violations in Icaza's background.

Jesus "Chuey" Castalon, the guitarist at the Clover Club, another guest at the party, testified it was he who had gone next door to get Allen Smiley to intervene when he and others were unable to separate Dorsey and Hall. He went on to state that once Smiley entered the Dorsey apartment, Hall went after Smiley.

In view of all this haphazard and conflicting testimony, Edwin Meyers, who argued the case for the prosecution, made a move for a dismissal, something unprecedented in Los Angeles criminal court history. The defense made a similar motion, but Judge Crum ordered the trial to proceed. Pacht and Giesler then tried hard to establish Hall as a perjurer. They pointed out the various discrepancies in his and Icaza's testimony.

Two days later, on December 6, after the state had rested its case, Judge Crum dismissed all charges. In his decision, he said, "To further protract this trial, with its heavy expense to the taxpayers, would serve no useful purpose whatsoever." He further ruled that instead of having Antonio Icaza jailed for perjury he ordered him thrown out of the country in view of his prior immigration convictions.

The photo of Dane kissing a highly pleased Giesler on the cheek with the grinning Dorsey and Smiley on either side of him was published everywhere. Three years to the day after the Japanese surprise attack on Pearl Harbor, Tommy Dorsey's surprise attack on Jon Hall resulted in his being completely exonerated. A week later Hollywood gossip columnist Jimmie Tarantino prophetically wrote, "There will always be a Hollywood as long as we have a Jerry Giesler."

Jon Hall, in a statement issued through his attorney, Grant Cooper of the well-known firm of Loeb and Loeb, pronounced himself "very pleased," saying, "The entire affair arose out of a misunderstanding. At no time did I have the slightest desire to institute proceedings against anyone."

Whether through a blatantly poor prosecution case, the luck of the Irish, or other factors, Dorsey got off scot-free. He himself pronounced, "I'm glad it's over. Now I can go to Chicago [the Chicago Theater] and catch up with my band. But I was never worried about the outcome." (Because of the case, Dorsey had been forbidden to leave Los Angeles County.) Benny Benson, Tex Satterwhite, and Nelson Riddle had taken turns playing his solos during the first few days of the Chicago gig.

Did money change hands behind the scenes? Was there studio influence from MGM and Hall's advisers? The answers to these questions may never be known, but the likelihood is yes on both counts. We shall probably never know the answers to these questions. Too many people involved in the violent confrontation suddenly became "forgetful." In those years, it is certainly true that the movie studios had tremendous influence in this company town.

There were some compelling consequences to the case for Dorsey. Before the indictment took place the band had prerecorded and filmed its work in the MGM musical *Thrill of a Romance*, which starred Van Johnson; Esther Williams in the role that further established that "wet she was a star;" and Metropolitan Opera star Lauritz Melchior. Louis B. Mayer, always seriously concerned with the good behavior and morality of his stars (if not his own), must have been extremely apprehensive about the outcome of the trial since the film had been essentially finished by the time the trial began.

There were reports that Dorsey's acting scenes and the band's musical numbers would be excised from the film. Whether it was due to the unfavorable publicity that surrounded the trial, Dorsey's earlier complaint to the studio that his band was only paid for the days it performed on a picture (as against the Harry James band being paid from the day it reported for work), or the fact that bandleaders were suddenly losing some of their luster as screen attractions, the next option on Dorsey's services was not picked up by MGM. In addition, an almost-signed deal for a major cigarette commercial, built around the Dorsey band, was canceled after his indictment.

George T. Simon noted, "So much bad publicity ensued . . . and the future of the band seemed to be in jeopardy." But as he had throughout the trial, Dorsey seemed unscathed and up for any challenge.

The ill-conceived recording ban was finally lifted in November 1944. It was finally obvious to James C. Petrillo that the ban on recordings using musicians didn't result in more work for them in other areas. On the contrary, it provided less employment.

Shortly before he was to go on trial for assault, Dorsey began recording anew at the RCA Victor studio on Sycamore in Hollywood on November 14, 20, and 22, 1944. From these three recording sessions came two immortal big-band records. The first was Sy Oliver's miraculous arrangement of his composition "Opus #1," which the band had been playing for several months, including featuring it in a rather bland version in *Broadway Rhythm*.

The record of "Opus #1" contains memorable solos by Buddy DeFranco on clarinet, Milt Golden (a substitute) on piano, and Bruce Branson on baritone saxophone. The arrangement is driven by the masterful drumming of Buddy Rich, who had recently replaced Gene Krupa. During the recording process, Dorsey saw the need for a pronounced opening drum break to kick the tune off; Rich knew exactly what was required. "Opus #1" was an immediate hit and quickly became a gold record. For several years afterward, it seemed as though Dorsey's record of the tune and Billy May's zesty arrangement of "Cherokee" for Charlie Barnet's band were the theme songs of choice for a multitude of important disk jockey radio shows.

In retrospect, the spirit that pervades "Opus #1," starting with Rich's drum solo, is so happy and uplifting that recently publicist Phoebe Jacobs aptly called it "the sound of a winner." Its release coincided with General Eisenhower's forces crossing the Rhine and on the verge of defeating the German army in its homeland while MacArthur's "I shall return" landing on Leyte in the Philippines marked the turning of the tide in the war against Japan. It appeared obvious that America and its allies were about to become victors in this worldwide conflict. "Opus #1" reflected that fact, although, strangely enough, Oliver had written it during the early part of the war, when news from the front was extremely grim.

The other side of the record was Sy's version of "On the Sunny Side of the Street," which later became still another gold record. It featured The Sentimentalists and Branson and has a Luncefordian flavor with its harmonic richness. Guitarist Bob Bain considers its introduction "one of the greatest ever written." At the bridge of the arrangement there is a memorable muted trombone chorus—played by the entire Dorsey trombone section—which restates the theme and serves to introduce the engaging four-part harmony of The Sentimentalists.

Contrary to Buddy DeFranco's wish to express himself like any creative jazz musician, Dorsey demanded that he play his familiar solo on "Opus #1" exactly the same way at every performance. This fact further rankled the clarinetist because there had been several takes of the tune recorded, each with a different solo of his. As the leader, Dorsey, however, had the privilege of choosing the version he wanted. Due to the popularity of "Opus," Buddy sometimes had to play it several times a night. After an especially deviant solo on the tune, Dorsey fired him, but he had to give him eight weeks' notice because of the lack of available able musicians. In the interim, Dorsey cut off all of his former solo opportunities.

DeFranco's cardinal sin in Dorsey's eyes, and the source of their growing alienation, was his increasing interest in playing and perpetuating bebop. This revolutionary, more intellectual brand of jazz, conceived by African-American musicians, was a form of protest against swing music and the musical expression of a new black nationalism, and perhaps in truth the precursor of the modern civil rights movement.

Bebop (or bop) was solidly grounded in earlier styles of jazz, such as New Orleans jazz and swing. However, it represented a marked increase in complexity. Perhaps its most significant characteristic was the highly diversified texture created by the rhythm section—a considerable contrast to the insistent four-beat approach by swing musicians. In bebop, the basic beat was stated by the bass player and elaborated by the drummer on the ride cymbals and hi hat, while a variety of on-and-off beat punctuations were added by the piano, bass, and snare drum. The best bebop soloists, spurred on by a strong rhythm section, could play rapid melodies based on the harmonic structures of various popular songs. ("I Got Rhythm" was a particular favorite.) Bop musicians for the most part rejected the elaborate written arrangements of swing for a straightforward pattern: a unison statement of the themes followed by a string of improvised solos and concluding with a unison statement.

Bebop had been inaugurated at Harlem's Minton's Playhouse and Clark Monroe's Uptown House in 1940 and 1941 by such principal practitioners as trumpeter Dizzy Gillespie, alto saxophonist Charlie "Bird" Parker, pianists Thelonious Monk and Bud Powell, guitarist Charlie Christian, and drummers Kenny "Klook" Clarke and Max Roach. It was transported by Gillespie to Fifty-second Street in 1944 with his first starring engagement at the Onyx.

The Dorsey brothers responded to the new music in their characteristic ways. Jimmy Dorsey had seen Gillespie at work at the Onyx and at first couldn't abide what he saw. He left the club in a drunken fit. He returned, however, and saw the value of Gillespie's originality, so much so that he tentatively offered him a job with his band, an offer which was never fulfilled. Stanley Kay said that Buddy Rich brought Dizzy to Tommy's attention, but his reaction was, "What is that—Chinese music?"

Soon afterward, Gillespie began working with Parker, the jazz world's Mozart, a true musical genius, in perpetuating bop. Interestingly enough, Parker acknowledged Jimmy Dorsey as one of his major influences on alto saxophone. Earlier, in 1940, Parker and Gillespie had met at the Booker T. Washington Hotel in Kansas City, had played together in Earl Hines's band, and had helped incorporate bebop into Billy Eckstine's big band.

By the mid-1940s it had already begun seeping into the mainstream of jazz. Most swing musicians strongly resisted its oncoming impact; "Melody seemed to be beside the point," as the fledgling swing pianist George Wein saw it. Woody Herman's adventuresome Second Herd and Boyd Raeburn's band gave bebop its first acceptance among white big-bands.

Thomas Francis Dorsey, Jr., however, would have none of that! Behind the self-assured front was basically a very conservative man who resisted change. But then, why should he depart from his long-established pattern of success, which featured himself and a corps of first-rate musicians and singers performing danceable renditions of romantic ballads along with a generous supply of swing instrumentals? Besides that, learning to play bebop would have meant a difficult adjustment for him. He never had been much of a jazz soloist. How was he going to learn and attempt to master the complexities and intricacies of bebop? The thought of learning a new musical language after all these years must have terrified him, although he would never acknowledge it. Perhaps Dorsey's old friend Eddie Condon summed up the sentiments of both Dixielanders and swing musicians versus beboppers when he said, "They flat their fifths, we drink ours."

In response to Tommy's antibebop stance, Woody Herman, who always displayed an excellent sense of humor, once bought the squarest sports jacket he could find at a San Francisco men's shop and sent it to Dorsey along with a card that read, "If you want to play that way, why not dress that way?"

Some of Dorsey's musicians were more adventurous. DeFranco, Dodo Marmarosa, and Sid Cooper marveled at what Parker was doing after having seen him play in Harlem. Cooper was so inspired that he wrote a batch of bebop arrangements of Parker's tunes like "Koko," which were tried out over a period of several days between shows in the basement of the Strand Theater. (This predated what the group Supersax attempted almost thirty years later.)

Dorsey heard about the new music his saxophone section was experimenting with and wanted to see for himself. He walked in right in the middle of an arrangement and told the musicians, "Keep playing. I just wanted to hear what you guys are up to." Afterward, he asked, "What *is* that stuff? I really like it." When informed that it was called bebop, he angrily left the room and slammed the door. This bizarre incident was just another example of the enigmatic Dorsey.

Not long after that, Dorsey fired Marmarosa for incorporating bebop into his solos during the band's engagement at the Capitol Theater. Pianist Jess Stacy was brought in to play the next show. Bob Bain remembered that Dorsey had Stacy play four choruses on "Boogie Woogie" during his first set. They were far afield from Marmarosa's treatment of the Dorsey classic: "It completely threw off the entire feeling of the rhythm section, the way Jess played it." But Stacy's swing concept was exactly what Dorsey wanted; therefore, he remained with the band for the next several months.

What Dorsey hadn't realized was that months before—in one of the last scenes in *Thrill of a Romance,* Marmarosa's composition, "Battle of the Balcony Jive," was essentially bebop. This riff tune starts out with DeFranco (sporting a serious 1940s cone-shaped pompadour) soloing, backed by the band's rhythm section of Marmarosa, bassist Sandy Block, Bob Bain, and Buddy Rich. This leads into a dazzling drum solo by Rich, before Dorsey walks into the scene smiling approvingly at the musical festivities and plays a half chorus as the other horns in the band join in.

Tommy Dorsey may not have cared for bebop, but Lauritz Melchior, who was equally egotistical and temperamental, loathed jazz, period. He grew increasingly disturbed at the impromptu jam sessions that took place off the set between takes. One day he walked up to Buddy Rich and said, "Have you had enough of that rotten music? I have." Buddy's reply was a quick, "Fuck you!" In point of fact, Dorsey himself and the band had more total exposure in this film than in any movie heretofore. There were three additional musical numbers featuring the band (one of which included the King Sisters) that were removed from the final cut.

In *Thrill of a Romance,* Dorsey once again showed his mettle as an actor in a scene in which he asks Melchior if he would consent to sing with his band. Melchior agrees to do it if Dorsey will first bring him a steak. Dorsey proved to be the perfect comedic foil for the tenor. Unlike Benny Goodman and Glenn Miller, Dorsey was once again completely at ease on film being a straight man in a comedy scene, feeding his costars the appropriate lines, or merely showing his charm.

The ludicrous finale of the picture makes use of a Cyrano de Bergerac device; Van Johnson sings Sammy Fain and Ralph Freed's ballad "Please Don't Say No" to Esther Williams, who is leaning out of the window of her aunt and uncle's house looking down at him standing pleadingly on the lawn below. Johnson is lip-synching to Melchior's voice with the bombastic tenor standing next to him. The Dorsey band provided the background accompaniment.

DeFranco left the band at the end of February 1945, at the conclusion of the 400 Club engagement in New York. He looked forward to getting away from the big-band atmosphere to concentrate on the evolving small-group scene in jazz. Although he had been second in the *DownBeat* Poll the previous year, he found few employment opportunities. In May, he hooked onto an opportunity with Gene Krupa's new band.

Dorsey checked on what was happening to DeFranco in the interim. A month later Dorsey called him saying, "Okay, you stale shitheel. Got enough wrinkles in your belly? Are you ready to come back?" In one of the few times a sideman outfoxed Dorsey, DeFranco explained to him that he was doing well on his own. When Dorsey asked him how much he wanted to return to the band, DeFranco demanded a new weekly salary of $350 plus extras for recording and any other work not on the regular schedule. He also said he wanted Dorsey to wire him $500. The bandleader yelled at someone in the room where he was calling from, "I knew it. DeFranco is broke. That son of a bitch is broke!"

The atmosphere between them changed on DeFranco's return. In Nelson Riddle's arrangements of "There's No You" there is evidence of his recognition of the musical validity of bebop. Buddy noticed a chord structure that was reminiscent of Gillespie and Parker. Naturally, he and Tommy argued over that. Buddy got Dorsey to finally admit that he wasn't able to handle anything musically advanced.

DeFranco noted, "He loved exchange. He liked to talk to people who had the [strength of] character to stand up to him. For example, Buddy Rich was just as quick tempered as Tommy, and they managed to get along in spite of their volatile tempers, because they had mutual respect."

DeFranco and Dodo Marmarosa, who were then roommates, severely tested Dorsey's patience in a hilarious incident that ended in the triumph of gumption over temper. One day in 1945 they overslept in their hotel room in Louisville and missed the early-morning train to St. Louis with the band. Discovering that scheduled airlines and trains would not get them to St. Louis in time, they called the Civil Air Patrol. A pilot at the Louisville airport agreed to fly them in his small plane for $350; unfortunately, the two musicians had only a combined total of $200 with them.

Nevertheless, the pilot agreed to take them. But he lost his bearings and instead of following the Ohio River to the Mississippi, ended up in Springfield, Illinois. The two itinerant musicians were already late for the gig that was taking place 120 miles away. Since they didn't have the agreed-upon fare, the pilot seized their luggage and locked it up. DeFranco and Marmarosa got on the phone and frantically called Louis Zito, Dorsey's road manager, who demanded, "Where the hell are you guys?" Zito added, "You better get the train going to New York or California because if you come here it's death! The Old Man is so mad that he's just left the stage and he's in his dressing room and won't talk to anybody." They pleaded to have Zito wire them $250 so they could retrieve their luggage.

The money arrived, the pilot was placated, and they then took a train from Springfield to St. Louis. On their arrival, they went to the Mark Twain Hotel and were told the hotel had no rooms for them. They were forced to sleep in the mezzanine and at 7:00 A.M. took their bags down to the lobby en route to the train station. Louis Zito, waiting for them, told them, "You'll probably get fired. Four days in the electric chair or something like that. But, since you're here, you might as well come along."

The train was filled with servicemen, forcing DeFranco and Marmarosa to put their bags in the aisle. Before they got on the train, they had stopped in a bar and had five quick beers, which resulted in their having upset stomachs. Hungry, they headed for the dining car, only to come upon Dorsey. The "Sentimental Gentleman" got up from his seat and approached them, the veins standing out on his forehead, his face crimson red; he glared at them for a long time before saying, "You guys are ridiculous! You remind me of *me* when I was a kid. I can't get mad at you. You tried to get there. You hired a plane. Stick around. I'll give you both a raise."

As DeFranco reflected, "We never expected *that* in a million years. But that was Dorsey. You never knew one minute from the next what his attitude was going to be."

Despite their rancorous parting, when there was money involved and promotional advantages to be gained from it, Tommy Dorsey and Frank Sinatra made personal appearances together several times in the years ahead. The first was on Sunday, September 17, 1944, on a broadcast of the Lucky Strike *All Time Hit Parade* radio show, on which Sinatra sang "I'll Walk Alone" and "If You Are But a Dream" with the band. A tape recording of that show reveals a jaunty Sinatra, cockily reflecting his newly found success, along with a feeling that he enjoyed no longer being treated like a Dorsey hired hand. He jokingly refers to Dorsey as "The Arm" for his emphatic method of giving an abrupt downbeat to his musicians.

There is an exhilaration evident in the sound of the band. Dorsey may have constantly complained about the shortage of first-rate available musicians during these years, but he was not about to allow the high musical level of his band to suffer.

Included in Dorsey's trombone section on the *All Time Hit Parade* was Nelson Riddle. Nine years later, Sinatra and Riddle would begin collaborating on a collective body of work that would include some of the most sophisticated and meaningful popular work ever recorded. Not by accident, Riddle would use such fellow 1944–1945 Dorseyites as Mickey Mangano on trumpet, Bob Bain on guitar, and violinists Al Beller and Lenny Atkins in these initial recording sessions. As Bill Finegan pointed out, "There is a straight line between Nelson's sitting in that Dorsey trombone chair playing those Sy Oliver charts, which had real identity, and the up-tempo arrangements that years later he started writing for Frank Sinatra."

On October 24, 1945, opening his CBS radio show *Songs by Sinatra,* "The Voice" remarked, "I was walking down Fifth Avenue when I heard a familiar sound," which was followed by the opening bars of Dorsey's famous theme. An underlying edge to the proceedings begins almost immediately when Sinatra tells the audience of encountering "my old boss, Dorsey, at a huge nightclub [the 400 Club]. Wondering, Would he speak to me? I went up to him and said, 'Hi Tom!' Whereupon Dorsey barks out, 'I knew you'd come crawling back one of these days!'" Sinatra goes on to remark, "Life on the Dorsey band was not at all times as sweet as 'Apple Honey'" (the title of a then-popular Woody Herman instrumental). The famous twosome served and volleyed while introducing sometimes truncated versions of some of the songs that had made their association so special—"There Are Such Things," "I'll Never Smile Again," "Marie," et al. The palpable feeling of rancor on both sides built during the course of the show.

And then at the 400 Club on November 21, 1945, Sinatra helped celebrate the tenth anniversary of Tommy Dorsey and His Orchestra. Testimonials were given by cowboy star Roy Rogers and bandleaders Cab Calloway and Gene Krupa. Sinatra sang "Blue Skies," which he had recorded with Dorsey several years earlier. There is a marked difference in his approach to this swing arrangement—the influence of jazz along with an even greater confidence has shown itself. He introduces Dorsey's bright new trumpet star Charlie Shavers's solo by shouting out, "Take it, Charlie!" following his vocal.

The arrival of Charlie Shavers in February 1945 to play the jazz chair and sometimes lead trumpet marked the first time an African-American musician had became a regular member of the Dorsey band. (Sy Oliver had only been a replacement in the trumpet section.) Charlie soon established himself as one of the foremost brass players ever to work for Dorsey. (Bill Finegan affirmed, "Unfortunately, the public never knew it.")

With his happy-go-lucky personality, iron chops, and brilliant swing concept (as both a trumpeter and a vocalist), Shavers should have been a major jazz star. One has to wonder what a creative personal manager like Norman Granz, who was also a successful concert and record producer, could have done to make Shavers the success he deserved to be. But as it turned out, Charlie would be merely a sideman who was in and out of the Dorsey band several times over the better part of the next decade.

Peggy Schwartz remembers that despite his importance to the band, "Charlie still had to go through the back door of hotels on the road. He could never eat with the rest of the band. We'd bring him whatever he wanted from restaurants and diners."

Shavers's musicianship was a highlight of the March 15, 1946, record date George T. Simon put together at the acoustically perfect East Fifty-eighth Street studio Liederkranz Hall in New York. The two Dorsey orchestras combined forces to record a V-disk consisting of "Brotherly Jump" and "More Than You Know," which were arranged and conducted by Sy Oliver. Both tracks featured solos by Shavers and the Dorseys.

The prestige of Dorsey's band during the war years was an important consideration in the eminent director Martin Scorsese's choosing to stage a fictitious opening scene showing a facsimile of the Dorsey band in his 1977 MGM musical, *New York, New York,* which starred Robert De Niro and Liza Minnelli. Trombonist Bill Tole, cast as Dorsey, was shot in a tight closeup playing the theme, followed by the band's rendition of "Song of India" and "Opus #1." The performance supposedly takes place on VJ Day at the Hotel Pennsylvania. In attempting to be completely accurate, there was even a black trumpeter in the band representing Charlie Shavers.

Dorsey's prestige led to the Mutual Radio Network (whose flagship station was WOR in New York) announcing him as its musical director in the fall of 1945. His salary was $300,000 a year. He was given his own Monday-through-Friday radio show, in which he showed that he was a natural as a disk jockey, playing records and delivering pointed comments on various musical selections. His shows were broadcast from various cities as the band toured the country. (A year and a half earlier Tommy had signed a deal with Henry Ford for Ford to sponsor a similar kind of a show, but Ford had changed his mind and settled the contract before the show began airing.)

Roger Carroll, the retired longtime radio personality on KMPC in Los Angeles first encountered Dorsey on radio. He remembered, "I was living in Baltimore as a kid of twelve or thirteen listening to those band remotes. So two or three o'clock in the morning was midnight in California, I'd get up to listen to Dorsey broadcasting from the Casino Gardens. I noticed he, rather than other orchestra leaders, always listened to the announcer. A lot of the bandleaders would just say, 'Thank you, here's the song.' Dorsey gave the impression to the audience 'Hey, this guy's a friend of mine.' It wasn't 'I'm better than you. I'm not on the same level as you are. I'm here to entertain you!'"

Carroll says that ability translated to Dorsey, the radio personality. "When I first heard him on Mutual, I was impressed," he said. "Here's a guy who's one of my favorite bandleaders and look how easy this is to him. He's up there talking and every word he says I'm listening to him. He would say nice things about people—short, to the point, say what you have to say—and play the music. Dick Whittinghill (also on KMPC and a onetime Pied Piper) and Arthur Godfrey had the same thing. When they talked on the air, they sounded like they were talking to you, even if they were reading [a script]. They related to the audience."

The obvious connection Tommy Dorsey made with his admirers as a musician and bandleader perhaps compensated for his inability to connect with his home life and more especially with his children. The bandstand was his real home. That was the place where he received the acclaim he coveted.

With all his years as a successful bandleader that had made him a household name, he looked to the immediate postwar period without any fear or trepidation. He saw no reason to worry about what lay ahead. Why should he? He had already triumphed during the nation's worst economic downturn and a cataclysmic world war, both of which had put serious obstacles in front of him.

But throughout the war years, Dorsey continued to have his on-and-off problems with alcohol. As Bob Bain pointed out, "Sometimes he would drink, and when he drank he was a lot more jovial. He would point to Buddy Rich on "Well, Git It!" and let him loose. He'd walk offstage and have a drink. You'd see a maniacal grin on his face."

Buddy DeFranco remembered, "When he quit drinking, which he did for about a year when I was with him [after the Jon Hall incident], things got worse. Everybody used to wish he'd go back to drinking again."

"When he went on the wagon," Bob Bain said, "he really became Mr. Business. At two-thirty in the morning after the job, he wanted to have a rehearsal, but everybody learned to live with it. Of course, there was no overtime pay."

Codeine and turpenhydrate, found in cough medicine, which he used when he had a cold, he discovered could also give him a high and became his replacement for alcohol. Middle age and his love of good eating also affected his waistline. Because of that, according to Bain, "He had two wardrobes. That would take care of the period when he put on weight."

Through the years, Dorsey really didn't much care about how much a musician drank if it didn't adversely affect his playing. Following the precedent set in the band previously by Sterling Bose, Bunny Berigan, and Ziggy Elman, Bain explained, "The drinkers were basically in the brass section—like the trumpeters George Seaberg and Solly LaPerche. Solly also liked to smoke marijuana. I remember the night Tommy spotted Solly smoking a joint when the band opened the new 400 Club at Forty-third and Fifth Avenue in the early part of 1945. Dorsey ran him off the bandstand and up a flight of stairs." Bain added, "You've got to remember, however, you also had a bunch of fiddle players in the band. All they did was eat oranges!"

Bain was paid $125 a week. The string section players got $115 a week. Buddy Rich was the highest-paid musician at reportedly $1,500 a week, with George Seaberg, who played lead trumpet, the second highest paid at $400 a week. The musicians were responsible for their own room and board. I asked the guitarist if Dorsey's musicians felt they were an integral part of the pantheon of big bands. "No, I wouldn't say that. It was a good band; it played together and had good arrangements. But if somebody offered you more money, you'd go to the next band."

Dorsey had long maintained a profound respect for Duke Ellington. He recruited him to guest-star on Sy Oliver's "The Minor Goes Muggin'," which was recorded on May 26, 1945, at the RCA Victor studio in New York. This was part of a reciprocal agreement which eleven days earlier had allowed Tommy to be featured with the Ellington band on "Tonight I Shall Sleep," another RCA recording.

Bob Bain was an Ellington devotee. He and the other members of the band were given no advance notice of Ellington's appearance at the recording session. "The arrangement changes keys and goes right into Duke's piano solo," Bain recalled. Duke's familiar puckish sense of humor was in evidence when, as Bain continued, "let's just say that the band was playing in F minor, and then there's a drum break or something, and then it starts out with a piano solo in B-flat minor. Duke, to me, was still playing in F minor. After we rehearsed, I went over [to him] and said, 'You know that . . . ' And he said, 'I know that now but it sounded kind of outside didn't it?'"

In reference to Dorsey's appearance on the Ellington record, *Metronome's* unnamed critic complained, "The double feature idea produces nothing that couldn't have been done as well or better, musically speaking, by leaving it to the Duke's own Lawrence Brown." As to the Dorsey record, which featured Ellington, he wrote, "The pert, lively Duke chorus is the best thing in a generally noisy performance." Buddy Rich, for his remarkable playing on the tune, went unpraised.

Bain had to be content playing rhythm guitar in the band, which meant no solos for him:

> Tommy was not interested in the guitar other than as a rhythm instrument. He hated the electric guitar. He didn't want to know about it. And this was after Charlie Christian had done all that stuff with Benny Goodman.
>
> He would raise his hands up and down with one finger in each hand while conducting the band. Trying to play rhythm guitar while watching him was like pulling teeth because it was hard. It wasn't relaxed.

Sitting to the right of Buddy Rich meant being close to Rich's sock cymbal. Bain recalled, "Buddy could swing a band, but he didn't have to play loud to do it. The other thing about Buddy was that he couldn't read music. He would hear the arrangement played once, and the next time we rehearsed it he'd catch anything that was worth catching. He'd just remember it like that."

Bain would go on to play guitar in Doc Severinsen's band on the *Tonight Show with Johnny Carson* for twenty-one years. He played alongside Rich on most of Rich's many guest appearances on the show.

Contrary to Buddy DeFranco's observation, the hostility between Rich and Dorsey was endless, chiefly because in many ways they were so much alike. As Buddy DeFranco contended, "Buddy Rich's whole living countenance he lifted directly from Tommy Dorsey. So did Frank Sinatra."

There were countless incidents that defined the Dorsey-Rich relationship. Bill Finegan remembered a rehearsal in Hollywood at the theater where the popular radio show *The Lux Radio Theatre* and the Dorsey radio show, sponsored by Raleigh Cigarettes, were produced. Finegan had been discharged from the army air corps and had come out from New York by train and brought a batch of new arrangements for the band. After running down the first tune, Dorsey suggested to Rich that he should make a slight change in his approach to the arrangement. Buddy objected to Dorsey's direction and responded with an untoward remark. Dorsey immediately went after Rich, chasing him off the bandstand, back and forth through the rows of seats, working their way to the back of the theater, out the front door and onto Vine Street.

The truth of the matter was that Rich's temper was perhaps even quicker than Dorsey's. Before rejoining Dorsey, Rich had been thrown into the stockade for hitting an officer and later dishonorably discharged from the marine corps. He claimed to have come home from the corps only to find his girlfriend in bed with another man. "I left her and him for dead," he said.

Gene Krupa's decision to leave Dorsey to start up his own band again fit perfectly with Rich's sudden availability. In 1944, he began his second of several extended stints with Dorsey.

Nelson Riddle told of a subsequent date the band played at an army air force base in Arizona:

We had been flown from LA to a big airfield in Phoenix. Then we had to take a bus to where we were going to play the concert. As we drove along, Buddy kept seeing telephone poles with placards saying, "Tommy Dorsey and His Orchestra Featuring Gene Krupa," that were left over from when the date was originally booked. Buddy was getting madder and madder. We got to the field and started rehearsing. Halfway through it, Buddy slammed down his drumsticks. "I'm walking out. I'm not going to sit here and play notes for another drummer." Tommy turned [around] and looked at him and said, "You'd better stick around. Because if you don't, you're not going to get off this base alive." And he meant it!

By the fall of 1945 Rich had had enough of Dorsey and left the band. The following year Frank Sinatra, despite their troubled past, came up with two $25,000 checks to fund Buddy's new orchestra. Bygones meant nothing. They had never lost the high esteem for the other's remarkable talent. Stanley Kay remembers being at Toots Shor's midtown joint when Sinatra said to Rich, "I'll have you working so hard you'll be begging to get off."

On Nelson Riddle's recommendation, Alvin Stoller took over the drum chair with Dorsey. He and Dorsey also had their disagreements, which led Dorsey to remark to Stoller, "There are three rotten bums in this world— Buddy Rich, you and Hitler—and I have had two of them in my band."

The members of any Dorsey band had to maintain a level of musical consistency. Newcomers had to get up to speed quickly. Karl DeKarske, who joined in March 1945, explained, "I was playing third trombone. Boy, was he a hard taskmaster! He expected you to know the book, as well as the trombone parts, inside of two weeks. That meant learning three to four hundred arrangements. . . . He gave everybody a bad time. Cracking a note, splitting a note, or missing a note—that didn't bother him. But coming in wrong, not paying attention—the guy didn't miss anything. He had eyes in the back of his head."

Conversely, an example of his ability to laugh at himself and again handle comical situations was shown when he guested on a 1945 Spike Jones radio show. He asked the musically irreverent leader of the "City Slickers," "What's all this junk doing in the studio . . . like washboards? What's the wheelbarrow doing there?" Jones answered, "That's for carrying the tune." A series of crashing cymbals precedes Dorsey's trombone solo as a vocal chorus romantically sings "I'm Getting Sentimental over You" behind him. The mood abruptly changes at the end of the first chorus with a cascade of gunshots, whereupon the singers descend into a true Spike Jones free-for-all motif and begin hiccuping. This is followed by a whistle, clanging bells, and a notoriously out-of-tune trombone solo to complete this most unusual rendition.

Dorsey's own musical confidence was tested on the January 15, 1946, *Metronome* All Stars recording session. Despite the fact that Sy Oliver had written two arrangements that called for a jazz trombone solo, Dorsey said, "No, no, I'm not the jazz player. Bill Harris is the jazz player. With a player like him around, I'm not going to embarrass myself!" Buddy DeFranco said, "This was really surprising, coming as it did from a guy with such an inflated ego."

Dorsey for years had expressed animosity toward Billy Burton, Jimmy Dorsey's manager. His initial problems with Burton stemmed from his belief that Burton was stealing from Jimmy. His feelings were compounded by Burton's having convinced another client of his, Dick Haymes, that he should leave Tommy's band to go out on his own back in 1943. Burton obtained a Decca contract for Haymes and a succession of hit records followed.

Milt Ebbins, the veteran personal manager who represented Count Basie for twelve years beginning in the war years, remembers being with Basie in the presence of both Dorsey and Billy Burton in 1943. "Tommy made a disparaging remark about Jimmy. Billy agreed with his assessment of Jimmy. Then Tommy said, 'Listen, let me tell you something: What I say is what I say, but don't you ever say anything against him. You understand it?! I don't want to hear it. Period!' I thought he was going to hit him."

Tommy's resentment of Burton had increased when Jimmy and Burton turned down a film offer brought to Tommy when he was under contract to MGM. It called for a film biography of the Dorsey brothers that would concern their rise to national prominence, starting with their humble beginnings in Pennsylvania. Under the terms of the proposed deal, both of the Dorseys would get $62,500 for themselves and their orchestras. Burton pointed out, however, that Jimmy and his band (without Helen O'Connell and Bob Eberly, who were important attractions in themselves) had been paid $50,000 for their work in *The Fleet's In*. He then told the press he had made the studio a counteroffer of $90,000 for the services of each of the brothers and their bands, which the studio had accepted. Tommy wanted no part of Burton's deal, despite the fact that Burton agreed to waive his commission.

As happens so often in Hollywood, a film property is never totally rejected. In time, someone else picks it up and puts it into production. United Artists chose to go ahead with the project, originally titled *My Brother Leads the Band*, and shooting began on July 15, 1946. Charles R. Rogers was the producer and Alfred E. Green was the director of the movie.

Tommy and Jimmy played themselves in *The Fabulous Dorseys* (the final title) and handled their acting responsibilities adequately. Once again, Tommy's confident air about himself stood out. Janet Blair (who once sang with Hal Kemp's band) and William Lundigan provided the romantic interest, essaying the roles of a singer and a piano player who hail from Shenandoah and follow the brothers on their musical journey. Arthur Shields and Sara Allgood, both veterans of the famous Abbey Theatre, were splendid as Tom and Tess Dorsey.

Richard English wrote the initial script. In a *Saturday Evening Post* article called "The Battling Dorsey Brothers," English reported that the two Dorsey brothers orchestras had grossed over $6 million in the preceding five years. The final shooting script, by Art Arthur and Curtis Kenyon, was riddled with total fabrications and clichés that destroyed the impact of the incredible story it attempted to tell. With it all, the early part of the picture, which encapsulated the struggle of the Dorsey family to survive and the dedication of Tom Dorsey, Sr., in making his sons succeed as musicians, was well scripted.

In 2003, Janie New, Dorsey's third wife, observed, "It was full of untruths, it was in black-and-white, it was the first of the movie biographies of band-leaders, and it didn't have Jimmy Stewart." The latter part of New's quote referred to the fact that *The Glenn Miller Story* was a highly popular movie due in large part to Stewart's starring as Miller. Dorsey had been offered a role in the film but had turned it down, telling columnist Tony Zoppi, "That was no more 'The Glenn Miller Story' than 'Jack in the Beanstalk.'"

The music in *The Fabulous Dorseys* was exemplary throughout. That was because the brothers, Ziggy Elman, tenor saxophonist Charlie Barnet, trumpeter Henry Busse, Bob Eberly, drummer Ray Bauduc, Art Tatum, and Tommy's sterling new band and his new vocalist, Stuart Foster, made noteworthy appearances. Paul Whiteman, playing himself, also had an important acting role.

The constant friction between the brothers formed the movie's recurring theme. Their feuding finally ends with their reconciliation upon Pop Dorsey's death at a Whiteman reunion in which they contribute solos to Leo Shuken's "Dorsey Concerto," which ends the picture.

Bing Crosby and Frank Sinatra, who obviously were important figures in the Dorseys' story, were conspicuous by their absence. It seems obvious, however, that the two superstars recognized the fact that this film was in no way an "A" production, and it would not be wise to appear in it.

Bill Finegan arranged a medley of Tommy's and Jimmy's many hits for the picture. He remembered, "There was a shot on the screen of the two bands in a ballroom, side by side. The camera would go to Tommy's band and you'd hear a few bars of 'Marie'; then it would pan to Jimmy's band and you'd hear 'Tangerine.' It was a bitch to get it to be precise. We recorded it at night, all in one take through this whole medley with Tommy's band playing all the music."

Finegan describes a bit of reality imitating art imitating reality: "Jimmy arrived with a load on. Tommy was furious and started giving him holy hell, but Jimmy kept laughing and wouldn't take it seriously. The band just sat there listening to all of this. The two of them walked out. They were gone quite a while, and when they came back, Jimmy had sobered up enough to record. Eventually, we got it done because we had to have both of them there."

In July 1946, just before work began on *The Fabulous Dorseys*, saxophonist and clarinetist Abe Most replaced Buddy DeFranco. "Tommy was off everything when I got there," Most remembered. "He was all sweetness and light. I thought this was really the top. It was the kind of band I'd always wanted to play with."

Three days before the road tour began that fall, Most married Gussie Snider. Their honeymoon was spent traveling with the band on the bus. Pat Dane, who traveled with Dorsey in his car, would play poker at a dollar limit with Gussie and some of the musicians after the nightly jobs.

Soon, Most saw more than sweetness and light. He recalled, "We played a college date once and the president of the class came up on the bandstand and said, 'Mr. Dorsey, would you please play . . . ' Tommy said, 'Get off the stand. I'm playing what I want to play. After I've finished what I want to play we'll be able to play something for you.' I don't know if he added that, but usually we had a set routine." Most remembered that Ziggy Elman, who had returned in March, ran the band on the last set.

Starting on September 13, Tommy arranged for both Dorsey bands to play alternate sets twice a night for two weekends at the Casino Gardens, doubling from the shooting of *The Fabulous Dorseys*. Jack Egan was brought out from New York to raise Tommy's publicity profile during the making of the movie. As a gimmick, he saw to it that a gigantic pair of boxing gloves was on prominent display above the bandstand and also had the brothers photographed shaking hands while holding a six-inch-long ax before they started playing on opening night. Frank Sinatra showed up to sing "I Don't Know Why" on a remote broadcast and stayed to sing with both bands.

Veteran trombonist Chauncey Welsch was then a member of the Jimmy Dorsey band. Welsch recalled, "He and Jimmy were getting along famously, and they continued that way during the time I was with Jimmy's band, which was from March 1946 through 1947."

Welsch had left Benny Goodman's band to join Jimmy's band. He explained why musicians would expose themselves to the wrath and mental anguish that came with the Goodman and Tommy Dorsey territory: "There was a feeling of elitism. If you could work for Benny or Tommy and actually last, it could do wonders for your career. If you could satisfy them, you gained a reputation for yourself. Those guys were easy to work for unless you became complacent and didn't perform up to the level which they hired you for."

Welsch also believes firmly that Jimmy was much more attuned to harmonic structure than Tommy: "He was more deep than Tommy was. I heard all three of them [Goodman plus the Dorseys] play trumpet, and the best was really Jimmy. He played the cornet better than Tommy, and of course they started on the cornet. I also had the feeling that Jimmy was more flexible and was able to transfer what the new music might be. More important, he engaged people in the band who were attuned to that sort of thing." With Charlie Parker having paid homage to Jimmy's playing, it's perhaps easy to understand Jimmy's adaptability and appreciation of bebop.

Welsch describes the regimented effect Tommy's conducting had on the musicians:

> The one thing that stands out about Tommy's band is that often he'd be holding the last note with the band, and his cutoff was the downbeat for the next song. His musicians would have to memorize certain parts of the arrangements so that they could handle those cutoffs and downbeats, and then when you got a couple of bars you could open up the music. Jimmy never did anything like that at all. Tommy's band generated huge excitement, but we had the sense there was a lot more tension in his band. We could somehow flaunt the ease with which we were able to get through the night without any of the extra stress—we're with the easy guy, they're with the hard guy.

Welsch, an avid student of the trombone's history, brought out the fact that Arthur Pryor, the virtuoso trombone soloist with John Philip Sousa's famous band in the early 1900s, initiated the heritage of the instrument. He believes that Pop Dorsey followed that model in teaching Tommy how to play the instrument: "Tommy heard Dixieland from his contemporaries, who showed him some of the great strains of that music in the 1920s, when there was nothing else. The next step was when Tommy took the instrument to another level and, in doing so, became the first successful lyrical trombone player."

Welsch recalls instances when Tommy, not Jimmy, was the underdog. "Tommy would sit in with Jimmy's band in places like the Chase Hotel in St. Louis when he'd stop in to see Jimmy," said Welsch. "He was always very sweet to me, nothing but engaging and encouraging. Jimmy always liked to flaunt some other kind of trombone player in his face—it was kind of a one-upmanship attitude. I was playing some pretty fast things at different points. If Tommy were around he would call the arrangement that I would be featured on. There was a bit of teasing that went on. Jimmy was showing things . . . a different set of dinnerware."

Welsch also marveled at the fact that at a prerecording session for *The Fabulous Dorseys*, when Tommy couldn't find his horn: "Somebody went out on a scavenger hunt and came back with a prop horn, which was an old

Conn 6H. He put this piece of junk up to his face and sounded exactly the same as he always did. This was an amazing thing to witness."

Jack Egan's arrival at the Casino Gardens coincided with the slump that hit dance bands throughout America in May 1946. Tommy believed his incredible promotional ability would somehow change the sagging business climate. Jimmy, as well as Harry James, pulled out of the Casino Gardens operation while Tommy's band was working there, leaving Tommy as the sole owner.

It wasn't only the ballrooms that were suffering: Attendance at one-nighters in general and at nightclubs declined sharply. Wartime prosperity had fueled interest in big bands. Suddenly, the returning veterans, the so-called Greatest Generation, was using the GI Bill to return to finishing high school or to start college. The number of marriages zoomed to the highest rate in the nation's history. Soon, the first so-called baby boomers were born. The young marrieds began saving their money for their future together. Buying a house and appliances for the home was suddenly more important than spending money to go out to a ballroom to dance. There were numerous other factors at work that contributed to the decline.

Harry James observed at the time, "Today's younger generation doesn't dig the dance jive. Until a big, fat majority of young people get the urge to dance again, instead of standing in a trance watching a singer, there won't be any appreciable upswing in the band business." Vocalists had completely taken over popular music.

Tommy Dorsey would not stand by passively and watch the business that he loved and excelled at go down the drain. He lowered his ballroom guarantee from $3,500 to $1,500, insisted admissions be cut to $1.80, and donated a portion of the receipts above the guarantee to the promoter for expenses. However, he continued to rail at MCA for not booking the band properly. There were some bright spots: The combination of Ziggy Elman and Charlie Shavers in the trumpet section was a big treat for Tommy as well as for the customers.

Trombonist Karl DeKarske remembers Dorsey saying, "There's the right way, the wrong way, and the way Ziggy plays." Fellow Atlantic City trumpeter Dave Sheetz explained, "Ziggy's embouchure deficiency in effect gave birth to an original style of playing."

After the completion of *The Fabulous Dorseys* and the Casino Gardens gig with Jimmy, the band flew to Texas for a successful two weeks at the Texas

State Fair in Dallas starting on October 5, 1946. Sharing the stage with the Dorsey band at the fair were the famous fan dancer Sally Rand and a comedian named Jackie Gleason, who had previously appeared in small parts in the Twentieth Century Fox musicals *Springtime in the Rockies,* which starred Harry James, and *Orchestra Wives,* in which he played Glenn Miller's bassist. In his act, Gleason played trumpet in addition to telling jokes and stories. He opened up by saying, "I just flew in from Oklahoma City, and boy, are my arms tired!" This trite kind of material would seem to indicate that Gleason was headed for oblivion; nonetheless, he and Dorsey struck up a rapport.

Trombonist Charlie LaRue had joined the band in June. He remembered Charlie Shavers looking at the tour schedule that showed dates in North Carolina at the end of the tour and remarking, "NC—that means No Charlie." This was about as vocal a protest as black musicians could make about conditions in the South that prevented appearances by mixed bands. LaRue said:

> But Charlie went out on the tour anyway. When we got to the last date, which was two days at the University of North Carolina in Chapel Hill, the student buyer for the college prom wouldn't permit Charlie on the bandstand with the rest of the band. Tommy said, "If he can't play in the band, the band won't play!" They finally compromised and Charlie was allowed to come up onstage and play his solos, but he had to go backstage after that. He still wasn't permitted to sit with the band during the rest of the performance. There weren't any problems on the rest of the dates. Charlie and Ziggy would swap solos on tunes like "Well, Git It!" and Charlie would sing and play "At the Fat Man's."

Dorsey couldn't manufacture a demand where there was none. However, in the midst of this tour, he came to the realization that not only were the guarantees down significantly from those of less than two years earlier, but fans just weren't turning out in the same numbers. He notified his musicians that the band was finished after the completion of the tour in late November. They saw the reality of the moment. Jobs for dance band musicians became scarce.

He put together a new band to play a four-week-long Capitol Theater engagement starting December 26 that had already been booked. It featured holdovers like Boomie Richman on tenor, Charlie Shavers, and Abe Most. Carmen Mastren came back to play guitar, and Cliff Leeman returned on drums. Johnny Rotella, fresh from a stint with Benny Goodman, replaced Sid Cooper and was delighted at being part of such a formidable lineup.

He remembered, "Playing for Tommy, I saw perfection on an instrument few people have ever seen. His taste for songs was unbelievable, his tempos were right on the money, and the sound he got on his instrument speaks for itself. When you'd look at him, you'd feel a sense of confidence."

Two tracks recorded in late December with that short-lived Dorsey band were Bill Finegan's charts of "How Are Things in Glocca Morra?" and "When I'm Not Near the Girl I Love," with vocals by Stuart Foster and The Sentimentalists, from the new Broadway musical *Finian's Rainbow*. This show's blatant satire on racism with music by Burton Lane and lyrics by E. Y. "Yip" Harburg had a sparkling score. The former record was the first top-ten hit Dorsey had enjoyed in a year and a half, although he had enjoyed a number two hit with the songs from the *Show Boat* album and had five singles in the top twenty-five between January and June 1946.

Tommy's last hurrah wasn't the only one that season. Benny Goodman, Harry James, Les Brown, Woody Herman, Jack Teagarden, Benny Carter, and Ina Ray Hutton also disbanded their orchestras that December. The Swing Era had lasted eleven years and four months, and now it was over.

7

The Rules of the Road

I thought Tommy was the George Steinbrenner
of the bandleaders, but he was fair.
—DANNY TRIMBOLI

T HE YEAR of 1947 was a time of reappraisal. America had already
entered a new epoch as its war veterans returned to pursue educational
and business opportunities. And by the look of the pop charts, recordings
by singers were what was popular.

The trend in popular music was turning away from the inspired romantic
ballads of Berlin, Gershwin, Kern, Porter, et al. and veering toward frivolous
novelty songs featuring singers, such as "The Dickey-Bird Song," "Woody
Woodpecker," and "Civilization" ("Bongo, Bongo, Bongo, I Don't Want to
Leave the Congo"). These song titles and the nature of these songs reflected
the brassiness and frivolity of the time.

In such an atmosphere Tommy Dorsey's legendary status would help to
maintain his visibility in changing times, but it wouldn't keep his career going indefinitely. Dorsey fully realized that the halcyon years for big bands
were over, but he also believed that his band could remain an attraction if
he continued to be resourceful. As ever, although he retained various personal managers, the most important business decisions emanated from him.
His hour-long radio show was still being heard daily on 450 Mutual stations, but hit records continued to be the real key to lasting success.

In order to continue feeding the band with new songs, and in particular to provide material for his band singers to record, Dorsey hired Jack Johnstone to run his publishing companies. Former employees Richie Lisella, Morris Diamond, and Nick Sevano returned.

Following up his own successful 1946 records with Stuart Foster, Dorsey started out the new year by recording more songs for RCA Victor that featured Foster—"A Thousand and One Nights," "Time After Time," "It's the Same Old Dream," and "My Love For You." Johnny Rotella remarked, "What a great ballad singer Stuart was. He had the feeling for a song like Frank [Sinatra] did. His treatment of a ballad was warm, tender, and he had a lot of feeling."

The handsome Foster, born Tamer Aswad, was of Lebanese descent. He had spent a grim five months in 1944 singing with Guy Lombardo and His Royal Canadians at the Hotel Roosevelt in New York. Foster simply couldn't abide Lombardo's famous "businessman's bounce" brand of dance music. Carmen Lombardo, Guy's saxophone-playing brother, sensed how unhappy Foster was and informed him that Dorsey was looking for a male singer.

Guy Lombardo was a longtime friend of Dorsey's. Carmen brought Foster over to the 400 Club in early 1945 and introduced him to Dorsey. Tommy had him sit in for one song and hired him immediately. He quickly dispatched Sid Cooper to write arrangements to feature his new singer. Foster made an impression with his first record with the band, "A Friend of Yours."

Although Dorsey was against wives' traveling with their husbands, Foster and his wife, Pat, a member of the singing act the Kim Loo Sisters, and Cooper and his wife, Ethel, became inseparable. And in a fairy-tale ending, Kim Loo married Sid Cooper in 1989, years after they both had lost their respective spouses.

Kim Loo recently related, "Stuart's breathing improved so much. . . . It came to him through Tommy. He loved the band. He loved everything about being there." Dorsey held him in equal regard. Kim Loo feels Foster's most important records with the Dorsey band were "Ol' Man River," from the *Show Boat* album, and the single record, "Out of This World." Bill Finegan pointed out, "Stuart didn't have that one-dimensional crooner approach." The richness of his voice and the compelling way he handled lyrics caused many to consider Foster in the same league with Jack Leonard as being the best male singer Dorsey ever developed next to Sinatra.

After 3½ years, Foster left Dorsey to go on his own and to start a family. He never became a bona fide star but rather was a working singer on such radio shows as Percy Faith's and had his own CBS show before branching into television. He died suddenly in 1968 of a heart attack while on tour in Japan at the age of forty-nine.

Both Dorseys got a brief publicity boost early in the year with the opening of *The Fabulous Dorseys* on February 26. The movie's world premiere was held at Loew's Regent Theater in Pennsylvania's capital city of Harrisburg. Throughout the brothers' home state, an official proclamation designated that week as "Dorsey Week."

Unfortunately, the movie was a flop, critically and commercially. When it opened in New York on May 30, Bosley Crowther of the *New York Times* offered, "Whatever convinced producer Charles Rogers that the Dorseys' life would make good screen material is one of those unfathomable Hollywood mysteries." *Time* said, "The famed Dorsey feud, which absorbs a good deal of the story, finally becomes as tedious to sit in on as any other family quarrel."

There were no profits resulting from the box office receipts of the movie. Three years later, the Bank of America sued Charles R. Rogers and United Artists, among others, for an $817,500 production loan plus interest. Tommy and Jimmy were well aware that their life story had not been made into an epic movie.

Days before the world premiere, Pat Dane and Dorsey separated. Dane was having difficulties living Tommy's kind of life, which included constant traveling. Within days, however, Hollywood gossip columnist Louella Parsons, admitting Dorsey was "a fabulous character," announced that they had reconciled in New York. Soon after that Tommy attempted a fresh start personally and professionally. Dorsey spent the month of March with Pat in Miami. It marked his first extended vacation in years. It was also a second honeymoon for them.

He had sold the Brick House in November 1944, since he was spending most of his time in Los Angeles. While in Miami, he purchased another status symbol, a ninety-eight-foot yacht, after turning in a forty-two-foot craft that he had purchased only weeks before. He bought it from Edgar Garbisch and the daughter of Walter Chrysler (the president of Chrysler Motors). Borrowing one of his favorite musical titles associated with the band, he dubbed it *The Sentimentalist*.

In April, the Dorseys headed for Los Angeles. Tommy enjoyed living there. The pace of life was easier in Southern California. *The Sentimentalist*, with its new silverware inscribed with a trombone, as well as a nine-man crew, which included a cook and an engineer, sailed through the Panama Canal and up to Santa Monica to meet them.

It was now time for Tommy to put a new band together. No one figured he could ever stay away.

Nothing changed much. He wanted Ziggy Elman (who had considered starting his own band at the end of 1946) and Charlie Shavers to come back. He also convinced Harry James's tenor saxophonist star, Corky Corcoran, to join his new band, though Corky's laid-back personality didn't gibe with Dorsey's firm discipline; he only lasted a few months before he returned to the James band. Dorsey's most important acquisition was drummer Louis Bellson (Luigi Paulino Alfredo Francisco Antonio Balassoni), whom he induced to leave Benny Goodman. He also sported a new vocal group, The Town Criers (Lucy Ann, Alva, Gordon, and Vernon Polk), to serve the same role as The Pied Pipers and The Sentimentalists. After the Casino Gardens opening, he was glad he had a home base, especially since one-nighters weren't paying what they once had and the jumps between them were getting longer and longer.

The new Dorsey aggregation debuted on May 16 at—where else?—the Casino Gardens. Harry Schooler, an experienced ballroom entrepreneur, was brought in by Dorsey as his partner in the Casino Gardens operation. Schooler had owned the Aragon Ballroom in Santa Monica, promoted big bands at the Municipal Auditorium in Long Beach (where the Dorsey band had once drawn sixty-seven hundred people one night), as well as dances for black patrons at the Shrine Auditorium. He also had customers who danced to records in Burbank at the Elks Auditorium.

Schooler convinced Dorsey that the ballroom had to come up with a well-planned promotional program if the Casino Gardens operation was to succeed. He conceived a series of themes that were established nightly on a weekly basis. Monday nights the ballroom was closed, but Tuesdays were devoted to Tuno-O, a game using bingo cards to guess the titles of songs that the band would play; Wednesdays, Winston Pottery was given away; Thursdays were pizza nights, when free slices were given to the first one hundred customers; Fridays were designated as collegiate night, providing free admission to those showing their college identification cards; Saturdays, of course, were the nights to make money, so there were no promotional gimmicks on that night, but on Sunday nights six diamond rings were given away by Kaye's Jewelers.

As an added promotion, Schooler and Dorsey set up the Miss Santa Monica beauty contest as a franchise from the Miss America organization.

Dorsey bought a Kaiser automobile when the new car was introduced in 1947 and installed it in front of the ballroom. (Schooler cautioned him, however, not to invest in the company, stressing that the company was not set up to mass-manufacture its product.) Soon, according to Schooler, Dorsey was grossing fifteen thousand a week.

Schooler, now a retired rancher living in Helendale, California, believes pizza was actually first introduced in California at the Casino Gardens. In typical Dorsey fashion, Tommy brought a favorite pizza baker from New York to install a pizza oven and kitchen. One account says the pizza operation was a failure because most of it was actually consumed by the musicians.

On a nightly basis Dorsey and Schooler would dine at a table on the balcony that overlooked the dance floor and watch a five-piece band led by his old friend from the 1920s, cornetist Red Nichols play, from 7 to 9 P.M., which preceded the Dorsey band. Nichols was attempting a comeback, having been forced to work in a defense plant during World War II to survive. When Dorsey realized that KMPC was carrying remote broadcasts of Nichols's band, he sat in before his own nightly sets. "He didn't want to miss the opportunity to get added plugs for the Casino Gardens!" pointed out Schooler.

Despite the change of scene, personal problems continued between Dorsey and Pat Dane. On July 3, Dane filed for divorce in Nevada, charging "extreme mental cruelty," but it was an essentially amicable parting. She said in an interview, "There was no home life. I couldn't take the night life. Tommy, like all musicians, slept by day." They had separated three times before she decided on the divorce.

Dane spent the necessary six weeks' residency in Reno. As a parting gift, Dorsey gave her a new Cadillac convertible. Their union had lasted four years and four months. On her August 17 return to Los Angeles, she proudly told the Associated Press that her date that night was with her ex-husband! They would continue to have various rendezvous in the years ahead.

On Independence Day of 1947, at the Dunes Hotel in Las Vegas, Dorsey presented Frank Sinatra, backed by the Dorsey band, in two shows, at 10:00 P.M. and midnight. Once again, it was a business matter that could benefit them both. Tickets were priced at $4.50 and $3.75, plus free parking. Despite the fact that their first movie was called *Las Vegas Nights* (which was actually shot on the Paramount lot), it's believed that night at the Dunes was the first time either Dorsey or Sinatra had ever worked in the soon-to-become-famous gambling mecca.

That summer, Dorsey himself was back on the movie screens—at least with a featured role in Sam Goldwyn's production of *A Song Is Born*, starring

Danny Kaye and Virginia Mayo and directed by the highly respected Howard Hawks. (It was a remake of the Gary Cooper–Barbara Stanwyck–Gene Krupa vehicle *Ball of Fire*, which had been released in 1941.) Working alongside Tommy in a jam session number playing "Flyin' Home" was the formidable lineup of Benny Goodman, Louis Armstrong, Lionel Hampton, Charlie Barnet, Mel Powell on piano, Harry Babasin on bass, and Louis Bellson. Only Goodman and Dorsey got separate card billing in the opening credits, probably because they had major agencies representing them.

Bellson remembered that during rehearsals for the jam session sequence, "Goodman would frequently arrive late and then he'd walk over to the piano. Mel Powell would pick out a tempo for him. Harry Babasin would start playing fast, and I'd come in on drums, and we would begin playing. We had a little jam session because there was nothing else going on. . . . When you're making movies, there's a lot of time to fool around."

After a series of late arrivals by Goodman, according to Bellson, "Dorsey told Benny, 'C'mon, stop fooling around. Let's get on with the movie.' So Benny said, 'I'm ready, but you're not ready for us.' It kept building. Finally, one day Tommy walked over to Benny and grabbed him by the arm and stopped him as he was playing. Benny turned around. He was shocked and said, 'What do you want from me?' Tommy said, 'I'm sick and tired of this!' He swung and missed him. Then Louis Armstrong got in between them; . . . Lionel was back there still playing his vibes. There could be an earthquake, and he'd still be playing."

Aline Mosley of United Press International, in her perhaps slightly overzealous account, reported that Goodman had shown up two hours late, having caught Armstrong's performance the previous night at a club. She also reported that a studio employee had to be sent to get Goodman out of bed. Goodman had apparently called Dorsey "a five-letter name" in the course of the rehearsal. Their instruments and music stands fell to the floor when Dorsey and Goodman "made a few passes at each other." After they were pulled apart, Goodman and Dorsey cursed at each other and Goodman kicked Dorsey, whereupon Dorsey threw a right-hand punch. Goodman left the soundstage and went home. He said he didn't fight back because "I'm not a pugilist."

The newly divorced bandleader didn't lack for women in his life. Dorsey was now living at the nearby Miramar Hotel in Santa Monica. Harry Schooler recalled, "The women would come by the Casino Gardens during the last set. I remember seeing Doris Day there." The former Bob Crosby and

Les Brown band singer was then separated from her husband and was about to make her screen debut in *Romance on the High Seas* at Warner Brothers.

One night Dorsey met chorine Janie New at the Casino Gardens. She was there with Sam Weiss, a song plugger, and Jill Meredith, New's good friend, with whom she was staying in Los Angeles. She and Meredith had danced together in the chorus line at the Colonial Inn in Miramar, Florida, near Miami.

The vivacious twenty-two-year-old blond, at five feet four inches, was too small to be a showgirl. After completing high school in Dublin, Georgia, New had gone up to New York, where she spent a year at the Albiene School of the Theatre. She was in the chorus of a Ziegfeld Follies revival at the Winter Garden Theater on Broadway that starred Milton Berle. During its almost two-year run, she became a specialty dancer and was the understudy to the lead singer.

New's short-term marriage to Bob Mizzy, who had previously been married to Gypsy Rose Lee, the grand burlesque star, ended in divorce in Miami where she danced in the chorus line at the Colonial Inn. She had spent three winter seasons there and worked at the Copacabana in the interim.

When Dorsey came over to the table to confer with Weiss, New pointed out to him that the tent card on the table spelled Dorsey "D'orsey." Provocatively, New asked, "Are you so busy that you can't even look at the programs you've made up?" Dorsey said, "Let me see that." He took it in his hand and exclaimed, "I'll be damned! I can't oversee everything." New added, "This is a big oversight. You must have 350 to 400 tables in here." Dorsey said, "Close to 500" and facetiously added, "Do you want the job? The job is open." New explained that it wasn't her line of work.

The bandleader-proprietor was intrigued by New's sassy personality. Dorsey and New left together in his car. In the midst of heavy traffic, he abruptly jumped out to speak to a friend in another car. New accidentally put her foot on the wrong pedal. The motor was still running, which caused her to hit an object on the side of the road. Dorsey ran back to his car and yelled, "Can't you drive?" She admitted she couldn't but accused him of being negligent in jumping out of his car and leaving her alone with the motor running. Dorsey said, "I didn't know there were any at all like you." She countered with "At least I don't have my name spelled incorrectly."

The great Dorsey was not used to a woman talking back to him, much less a woman he had just met. They began dating four weeks after that convoluted beginning. One night New had another date, Tom Baker, a man she knew from New York, whom she was kissing goodnight on the doorstep of Jill Meredith's apartment. Suddenly, she heard footsteps behind her. She knew it must be Dorsey. He saw them embracing and quickly ad-libbed, "Is Jill at home?" New and Meredith wound up getting bit parts in the jam session scene of *A Song Is Born*.

New returned to New York and the Copacabana, where she had previously danced in the chorus line. (Eddie Fisher was then the production singer.) She saw Dorsey subsequently in New York. In a 2003 interview, she related, "I would put 'TD is coming' on my calendar when he was to be in town." She would work it out to switch nights off with the other girls so she could arrange to have two nights off in order to meet him in other cities. This routine lasted for several months.

In September 1947, Dorsey went out on his first national tour in almost a year. The five-month-long tour would again end at the Capitol Theater in New York.

Looking for another big score, Dorsey recorded "Boogie Woogie Revisited." That, and the likes of his new version of "Mississippi Mud," featuring Gordon Polk singing the old Bing Crosby–Rhythm Boys tune with Paul Whiteman (on which the Dorsey brothers and Bix Beiderbecke had originally soloed) in a comical vein, was uninspiring. The one important recording the band made that year was "Trombonology," Sid Cooper's arrangement of a Dorsey composition. This recording vividly displays Dorsey's phenomenal technique, especially his facility in the upper register.

In December, Buddy DeFranco rejoined Dorsey. DeFranco, who had placed at or near the top of the *DownBeat* and *Metronome* polls for the previous few years, had left the band for the second time in the summer of 1946 determined to establish himself in Hollywood as a studio musician. Dorsey insisted to him that he would never find work there.

In eight months, DeFranco worked only one studio job. This was despite his obvious stature and promises of various opportunities by such influential people as music contractor Dave Klein and Andre Previn, who as a teenager had already established himself as a staff composer and arranger at MGM. Years later, DeFranco would find out that Dorsey himself made sure his prediction would prove accurate. DeFranco learned from talking to Ziggy Elman, by this time himself a busy studio musician, that Dorsey had effectively blackballed him in Hollywood. He had informed the many contacts he had made while making movies and recording there during the 1942–1946 period that DeFranco was completely unreliable.

In desperation, DeFranco joined Boyd Raeburn's band, whose modern jazz sensibility he greatly admired. He had no choice but to return to the Dorsey band in December 1947. No bandleader was more vindictive than the "Sentimental Gentleman of Swing," one of whose favorite expressions was "Nobody leaves this band on their own. I only fire people!"

On his return to the band, DeFranco resumed his friendship with Charlie Shavers, whom Dorsey considered "the greatest trumpeter of them all." Although no one realized it at the time (including Shavers), he suffered from narcolepsy, a completely unknown disease in the 1940s, as well as diabetes. His tendency to nod off in the middle of a set caused some people to think that he was a junkie, which was absolutely not the case. When he fell asleep, he even managed to sleep through Louis Bellson's drum solos!

Despite his predilection for perfectionism, Dorsey enjoyed having a good time on the bandstand, and a sense of humor was central to achieving it. In line with that he began awakening Charlie Shavers by squirting him with a water pistol. Eventually, in retaliation, Shavers would squirt Dorsey back with his own water pistol and once filled up the bell of Dorsey's trombone with water as it sat on the bandstand before a gig. This in turn led to Dorsey's squirting water at the entire band. As a result, all the musicians armed themselves with water pistols, and frequent water fights took place. Dorsey then went one giant step further and came up with a large weapon that resembled a tommy gun that could shoot water.

Bellson came up with the idea of hitting Shavers, who was sitting close to him, with a drumstick eight bars before it was time for his trumpet solo. Later, Dorsey arranged to have Shavers's chair wired, which gave him a mild electric shock as he awoke. Another time, during the course of a recording session, when Shavers fell into a deep sleep, Dorsey had all the microphones and the recording machines turned on as he asked Shavers a series of raunchy questions, which Charlie answered with a snore.

After a succession of such antics, Dorsey reverted to his usual regimen but went even further, forbidding giggling and laughing onstage. Smiling wasn't even permitted. During a performance, any band members who were caught looking at their watches were liable to be nicked by the slide on Dorsey's trombone. Twenty-dollar fines were levied for all such violations. DeFranco and Boomie Richman sometimes got giddy but were never caught. All of this merriment made the tedious, never-ending sameness of life on the road a trifle more bearable.

There was a lively feeling on the band fueled by the likes of the drinkers, such as Elman, Shavers, and Gordon Polk, interspersed with the exciting musicianship displayed by the light drinkers or teetotalers like pianist Paul Smith, Cooper, DeFranco, Richman, and Bellson. Besides that, there was a strong sense of showmanship on display as there was with all Dorsey bands.

Bellson's colorful presentation included his simultaneous use of two bass drums. In addition, he had devised a revolving platform that weighed 450 pounds and that required hiring a separate band boy to set it up on the bandstand, take it apart after the gig, and install it on the bus. As Bellson recalled, "The platform revolved, which Tommy controlled with a button. I did a bit with my hands, and then I'd do the same bit with my feet so the audience could see what I was doing. In the theaters, the lights would go out and a black light came on. I had drumsticks that lit up in the dark and flashed on and off. I also had a separate light on each of my drums."

Retired tenor saxophonist Henry Crawford replaced Boomie Richman for a few weeks in the fall of 1947. "I sometimes sat directly in front of Louis and his twin bass drums. When he played one of his spectacular solos, the pressure on my ears was so great that I had to open my mouth and silently scream to relieve it. I also remember when Louie refused to stay in a hotel where we were booked because the hotel wouldn't allow Charlie Shavers to stay there; he went with Charlie to another place where Jim Crow wasn't practiced."

Bellson and Dorsey formed a mutual appreciation society, as did many of the first-rank musicians who worked for Dorsey. Their association included three more stints with the band: "Tommy came up with the idea of the lights. Theatrically, he was a genius—he knew what would sell. When I first joined the band, he saw me set up—I had over ten drums. When I finished about an hour later he said to me, 'All you need is a brush up your ass for a swish beat and you'll be all right.'" In time, Dorsey realized that Bellson was the only drummer who had followed Buddy Rich who could fully satisfy him.

Bellson also noted how hard Dorsey drove the musicians:

I think of all the bands I ever worked with that [Dorsey] band was the hardest-working band of them all. We did five months of one-nighters in one stretch with no days off, five hundred miles on the bus a day. That meant we played a gig from nine to one, but he always played nine to one-thirty. He wanted to impress the promoter by playing an extra half hour. We'd pack up the bus, make a food stop, and then travel all night and get to the next stop about twelve noon. After sleeping on the bus during the night, we'd check into a motel and sleep for three or four more hours, then get up, get ourselves ready, and have dinner on the gig. Now you worked three hours on the gig without stopping from nine to twelve midnight. Then you took about a twenty-minute break and played until one-thirty. If he was mad at the guys— which he pretty often was—the cutoff would be the downbeat for the next tune. In other words, you're playing straight through without a break; you've actually kept going. And he'd be playing right along with you. I looked back at the trumpet section—Doc Severinsen was there, Charlie Shavers, and Ziggy Elman were on the band [together] for a while—they were bleeding from their lips. That's how hard they were playing! And Tommy was saying, "C'mon you guys! What's the matter with you?"

But one thing about him, you knew what he was getting mad at—it was always for a good reason, and it was very obvious. Dorsey would sometimes turn crimson, foam at the corners of his mouth, and then would suddenly cool off and laugh at himself. He wanted you to come onstage dressed right. You couldn't wear a tuxedo and white socks; otherwise back in the dressing room and get straight. And he wanted you to play your best every night.

But there were always dates to be played at home in the Panther Valley. The decided interest in entertainment that pervaded the area also extended to the theater. From 1949 to 1953, John Kenley, the theatrical impresario, ran a very successful summer theater operation, bringing stars from Broadway and Hollywood to headline there. There Tess Dorsey persuaded Kenley to move his operation to Lakewood from Deer Lake.

Kenley remembered, "When either of her sons played Lakewood, she would complain to me, 'All they do is spend their money. They don't know how to save!' And then she would regale the audience that night when people came to dance. The old people loved it, but the young people hated it. And her sons couldn't get her off the stage. But she evidently had a vast influence on them. She would say, 'They're here because of me. I made them study. I made them learn.' She was the earth mother of that region."

Dr. Stephen Botek recalled, "When Tommy would play at Lakewood, it was like playing in his kitchen at home. He would loosen up. He knew what people liked. He had pride in his band: 'Look who I have—Ziggy Elman, Charlie Shavers, Boomie Richman,' and he would show them off. Buddy DeFranco would play all those wonderful solos for, like, ten choruses.

Tommy was in his glory. He was a [hometown] hero. When he played a solo, even the band listened. Lakewood was a paradise and for only a buck and a quarter. It was so inspirational."

Alto saxophonist and clarinetist Hugo Loewenstern, who played with Dorsey from 1948 to 1952 and went on to work for Jack Teagarden and Harry James, among others, recalled, "The next year the band did 125,000 miles. He could make a lot more money on one-nighters. We had some really long jumps between dates—Key West one night and then onto a transport plane to Tempe, Arizona, the next night."

Bellson recalled that there were frequent unfortunate racial confrontations on the road because of Shavers's presence in the band:

> Somewhere down South—North Carolina or South Carolina—segregation, of course, was going on. Tommy told the buyer [on one date], "He's in my band. He's an artist. He's featured in the band." He was told, "You can't have him play here." The governor was called. When we arrived at the gig, there was dinner for the band and way over there was a little table for Charlie—way separate. Tommy said, "What's that for? No, Charlie eats with us!"
>
> That night on the bandstand, about an hour and a half into the dance, here came five big guys. A couple of them had baseball bats. They wandered right up to the bandstand. Charlie and I said, "Uh oh, here it is. What are we going to do now?" Tommy went down to the edge of the bandstand, looked at them, and said, "If you guys don't get out of here I'm going to wrap this trombone right around all your necks." When we heard that we said, "Whoa," and about that time the police arrived. Tommy wasn't afraid of anybody. He had feelings. . . . He stood up for Charlie.

Bellson, during his long career, has worked for Duke Ellington, Count Basie, Benny Goodman, and Harry James. He ranked Tommy's musicianship extremely high: "I sat behind Tommy for three years, and when he played those ballads, I actually had tears in my eyes. . . . I don't know of any bandleader or instrumentalist that came close. Dorsey had as much going on with his instrument as Goodman had on clarinet. Those guys had one thing—they were geniuses. They knew the right tempos to play for the audience. When they played a dance they played the right tempo. When they played a concert—different tempo."

Of the five immortal big-band leaders, Bellson concluded that Dorsey was probably the smartest of them all—for his ability to lead a band, to get things done, to be able to handle any situation, and to be able to look into the future. But when Bellson left Dorsey in 1949 to move to Los Angeles, where he planned to study composition with Buddy Baker, Dorsey once again showed his vindictiveness when a favorite musician gave notice. He retaliated by immediately cutting off Bellson's drum solos.

"One night he pressed the button that controlled the drum platform to turn me around and left me out there," Bellson recalled. "There was only so much you could do with your feet. I turned around to him and said, 'Even Shakespeare had an ending.' He looked at me and said, 'Smart ass, huh?' He kept me out there for another five minutes. But I can honestly say the entire experience with Dorsey was phenomenal."

Another superb musician who could handle Dorsey's musical as well as personal challenges was pianist Paul Smith. Surely one of the most underrated jazz pianists, Smith would go on to become Ella Fitzgerald's accompanist during four different tenures dating from the early 1960s to the early 1990s.

The six-foot-five-inch-tall Smith started working for Dorsey at the beginning of the 1947–1948 tour. Frank Riordan said that Dorsey once told him, "He's the best piano player ever to work for me." In one of his patented uses of the vernacular, Dorsey said to his musicians, "Paul can play chicken salad and chicken shit at the same time."

Smith remembered how he joined Dorsey: "It was at the Pacific Square Ballroom in San Diego, where I lived. I sat in one night with the band. He had just fired his piano player. I had just come off working with the Les Paul Trio. Les could play some horrendous tempos so I was used to playing extremely fast. When Tommy had a new guy in the band, he usually would burn him out on the first tune by having him play a lot of choruses. His idea of a fast tune was like a ballad to me after working with Les. After twenty choruses he hadn't burned me out. There was a difference between trying out for his band and being asked to join the band."

Midway through the tour, Smith returned to San Diego to pick up an old Chrysler convertible, which he drove to Miami with trumpeter Vern Arslan to rejoin the band after its short hiatus. He drove his convertible the rest of the tour. "Louie Bellson used to sit in the back seat with a drum pad on his lap to practice, which certainly paid off," Smith recalled.

Interestingly, Smith said that the last half hour of the last set on dance dates, as in the past, Dorsey devoted to playing jazz. "He'd pull out the Finegan stuff, the stuff I'd written, and stuff Charlie Shavers and Louie had written. The kids used to stand around the bandstand 'cause everybody was playing choruses, and he had some pretty good soloists."

Smith had been a military policeman in the army during World War II. His motto was "You leave me alone; I'll leave you alone." Several months later, on a ferryboat ride from Windsor, Ontario, to Detroit, Dorsey gathered all the musicians around him. He remarked, "Look at 'Little Abner' (his nickname for Smith) with his pie and milk!" Smith sternly replied, "Tom, you lead your band, and I'll eat my pie. Do we understand each other?" According to Smith, "We looked at each other for about ten seconds, and then he said, 'You're okay, kid!' We were friends from then on."

Smith remembers that although Dorsey and Buddy DeFranco never got along, Dorsey would say, "But he can play in my band anytime," after calling DeFranco names. DeFranco stated, "If you were sick and needed help, Dorsey would take care of you. I had asthma in those days. It wasn't until I went for therapy that I got rid of it. He would tolerate my asthmatic seizures. I would go away for four or five days or go to the hospital. . . . I never got fired for that. . . . I once had a terrible strep throat. He had his doctor flown down from New York. . . . He was that kind of guy. In spite of his tremendous ego, he was really sensible and humble."

DeFranco made plans to work in Chicago during the band's time off at the Preview with an all-star quartet, which he would colead with George Shearing. It included Chubby Jackson on bass and Bellson on drums. It seems likely that Dorsey, being so territorial, induced Charlie Shavers to call DeFranco and tearfully ask him, "What have you done with my boy, Louie?" and hang up. Not long afterward, DeFranco got a call from a man who introduced himself as a private detective. He informed DeFranco there was a warrant out for his arrest for kidnapping Louis Bellson! (Was this another example of Dorsey's vindictiveness, his playing a practical joke, or both?)

After the Dorsey band got back together in Florida, Dorsey took the musicians on a minicruise to the Keys on *The Sentimentalist*. The band was routed up the Atlantic Coast to New York, traveling, as usual, by bus. *The Sentimentalist* was sailed up to New York simultaneously and fitted with new diesel engines, which reportedly cost Dorsey twenty-five thousand dollars.

Joining the band in North Carolina on its way to New York, on Arthur Michaud's suggestion, was a new girl singer named Audrey Young. She found life on the road very difficult, but she fortunately made friends early on with Ziggy Elman, whom she described as "my pal. He was so sweet. He used to call me 'Bagelhead' because I wore my hair pulled back, and I had a bun at the back of my head." Paul Smith remembered her as "a nice lady who had a very good sound for a band singer." Louis Bellson described her as "a lovely person who made a nice appearance and could sing ballads well."

The Broadway columnist Earl Wilson quoted Dorsey's own appraisal of Young's performance at the Capitol Theater: "When she came out in the low cut beaded gown, you couldn't hear her first number with the guys all whistling and the women tearing her apart. She's the first beautiful girl I ever knew who could open her mouth onstage. Most of them can't carry a tune—even in printed form."

While Young was on the road she would call collect to her ardent admirer in Hollywood, Billy Wilder, the small-in-stature but giant-in-talent writer and director, who wondered when she was ever coming off the road. Young married Wilder in 1949 and quit singing.

Although Dorsey would often meet up with Janie New on the road, he began simultaneously seeing Candy Toxton (Florence Anna Tockstein), whom he had met at the College Inn of the Hotel Sherman, where she modeled in a fashion show. He saw her in New York and then in Los Angeles, where she was working as an actress at MGM during the period *The Fabulous Dorseys* was in production.

Toxton recalled, "I had a big crush on him, and it grew to love on my part. I thought it grew to love on his part, too, 'cause he said, 'I love you' very easily. He was a very jealous man, constantly checking [on me]. He would call my mother looking for me and would call different people to find out where I was, and then when he finally reached me, he would ask me questions to try and catch me in a lie. It was 'cat and mouse.'"

Toxton was twenty years younger than Dorsey; she says her mother's strenuous opposition to their relationship brought her closer to Tommy because she was defending him all the time. She didn't know about New: "He said to me, 'Believe in me, trust in me, I love you. I really am through with her,'" referring not to New, but to Pat Dane, from whom he was separated but to whom he was still married.

Toxton related an incident that reveals an insensitivity typical of Tommy in his dealings with women: "He was very difficult, and I think being difficult was part of his attraction. Once I drove his Chrysler station wagon from LA to the Midwest to where he was playing. I had an accident and was badly bruised when I hit a plow in a field. The car was destroyed. When I called

Tommy, instead of saying, 'How are you?' I remember his first line was 'Did you ruin the car?'"

At the same time, Toxton says, Dorsey could be very romantic and charming. She recalled how Dorsey would play songs from the stage that he knew meant a lot to her and then give her "the look."

Toxton subsequently signed a contract with Columbia Pictures, reporting directly to Harry Cohn, the hateful president of Columbia. She was scheduled to work in *The Jolson Story*. During that time, she says, she and Tommy starting having problems.

There was no *People* magazine, *Entertainment Tonight*, *Access Hollywood*, *The Insider,* or *Extra* at that time to fan the flames of celebrities' private lives. Movie magazines were the 1940s and 1950s counterparts. But the most powerful forces were the gossip columnists, many of whom had their own radio shows, like those of Walter Winchell, Hedda Hopper, Louella Parsons, and Jimmy Fidler.

By the winter of 1948, the Dorsey-Toxton relationship had turned extremely serious—or at least Hollywood gossip columnist Jimmy Fidler would have the country believe it was. He told his nationwide Sunday-night radio audience that Toxton had picked out her trousseau and that she and Dorsey might possibly sail to the Bahamas any day now in his yacht and get married.

Dorsey told her, "I want you to notify the studio that we're going on a vacation so there's no problem . . . Maybe we'll make it legal."

Dorsey wasn't necessarily on the rebound from his divorce from Pat Dane. The plain fact was that he had a strong sex drive that had to be satisfied. However, he did want to remarry and wanted a place to go home to.

When Toxton arrived in Miami, she found Dorsey extremely proud of *The Sentimentalist*: "Jackie Gleason came over to look at it. They were buddies and had a lot of fun together. We were having cocktails in the living room of the yacht when Tommy mentioned that the Henry Fords were coming down to be his guests on the boat. I was nervous about that, hoping that I wouldn't embarrass Tommy. I was only nineteen or twenty at that point, but everything was fine."

Meanwhile, Janie New had heard Fidler's broadcast in Georgia while visiting her parents. She was sporting a five-carat diamond ring that Dorsey had given her; she had seen Dorsey only recently in Atlanta. He had asked her to come down to Miami; he told her about his new boat and said, "We'll get married in Miami."

"That's why I had given my notice opening night at the Colonial Inn," New recalled. "I stopped off at my mother and father's first."

New's experience in show business had taught her to think twice about the veracity of publicity. Not jumping to conclusions, she said, "I took the ring off my left hand, and I put it on my right hand. I said [to myself], 'You're going to do something about this! There goes your trip to Miami because it's obvious that this girl [Toxton] wouldn't have gone down there unless she was invited.'"

According to New, Dorsey kept phoning her, but her mother was instructed to say she wasn't in, which only increased his pursuit. She finally decided to call Roy Evans, a friend of hers, as well as Dorsey's, who had his own yacht at the Miami Yacht Basin, called *For Evans Sake*. She wanted to see if Fidler's report was accurate. Evans, completely unaware of her relationship with Dorsey, invited her to come down to attend a big party that was taking place the next night.

New was escorted by Evans and Walter Troutman, who owned the Jockey Club in Miami. Dorsey and Candy Toxton were also in attendance at the party. Dorsey saw New from afar but merely waved to her.

The next night New was accompanied by the same two men to see singer Tony Martin on his opening at the Latin Quarter. They could see Dorsey, Toxton, his attorney Lee Eastman, and his accountant Phil Braunstein sitting at ringside. As he was leaving, Dorsey came by their table, saw New, and quickly saw that the ring he had given her was not on her left hand. Evans introduced her to Dorsey.

The next day Dorsey sent his valet, Kenny Drew, over to *For Evans Sake* to see if New was onboard, and if so, he was instructed to find out how long she planned on staying there. He inquired of New when it would be convenient for him to talk to her. Shortly thereafter Dorsey arrived by speedboat. He told New, "I can't chase you all over the country. You're always a few steps ahead of me, and then you're gone. I've got to know where you are, and this is the only way I can keep track of you. So I want to marry you." He told her to make plans for their wedding a week later in Atlanta.

Meanwhile, Toxton was still onboard *The Sentimentalist*, living with her rather sentimentally dishonest boyfriend. She recalled an evening of arguing followed by a late-night phone call which Tommy took in another room. "I had a funny feeling about it," Toxton said, "but I didn't suspect another woman. He was on the phone for quite some time. I asked who it was. He said it was none of my business. We had another argument, and I went to sleep. In the morning we started up again. It wasn't getting any better. I said, 'I'm going to go home. This is ridiculous.' And he said, 'Fine. If that's what you feel you have to do, then you do it. I'll have my man Kenny take you to the airport.'"

Toxton expected to be paged at the airport, or if not, she thought she would at least get a phone call on her arrival home in Los Angeles "because that's what he used to do. We never fought, but if there was a disagreement of any kind, a jealousy or anything like that, we always made up. When I walked into the apartment—I lived on Olympic Boulevard—I called Ava Gardner, who lived upstairs. I asked her if anybody had been calling me. She said, 'No, I never heard the phone ringing.'"

Several days later, it was Toxton's turn to get the news about *her* private life in the media. She read in the newspaper, "Tommy Dorsey Weds." "I passed out," she recalled.

New, twenty-four, and Dorsey, nineteen years her senior, were married in Atlanta on March 27, 1948, at the Fulton County Courthouse. His bride was two years older than his daughter, Pat. Mom Dorsey made her first airplane flight, all the way from Los Angeles, where she was then living, to attend the ceremony. Pat Dane even sent a congratulatory telegram.

Dorsey told an *Atlanta Journal* reporter, "This is the last marriage for me." The newlyweds spent their several-days-long honeymoon on *The Sentimentalist*, then got into his Cadillac and hit the road for the band's tour, which was routed toward Texas before heading northeastward toward New York, where they would settle in Dorsey's penthouse apartment at Seventy-third Street and Park Avenue.

Dorsey's attorney, Lee Eastman, traveled by train from Chicago to Los Angeles with the agent Berle Adams following Eastman's visit to Florida to see Dorsey. Adams recalled, "Lee said to me, 'Tommy's given up women. He's now got the boat and no women.' We got to Salt Lake City, and they bring the newspaper on the train. Lee saw the headline, 'Tommy Dorsey Marries.' He said, 'That's impossible! They're wrong. What the hell did he marry her for?'"

Three weeks passed before Toxton heard from Tommy at the home of Shirley and Johnny Johnston in Beverly Hills: "Johnny got a phone call. It was Tommy. He asked if I was there. When I got on the phone, he immediately said, 'How are you, Happy Hambo?' his nickname for me. I didn't say anything, and he said, 'Can we talk?' And for the first time I said, 'No, we can't talk, you son-of-a-bitch! How dare you do that to me!' I started crying, said a few other things, and hung up on him." Dorsey tried calling again, but that was their last conversation.

Decades afterward, Toxton was philosophical about Dorsey but still flinched at his memory: "He had the world at his feet, so maybe he was typical in many ways of a successful man who can do anything he wants any-time he wants to . . . ”

After the shattering split from Dorsey, Candy Toxton briefly dated Frank Sinatra, and then Mel Torme, whom she had originally met at a cocktail party at Tommy's apartment. She married Torme on February 11, 1949, in Chicago.

“I wasn't interested in Frank because he had gone with everybody,” Toxton remarked. “I didn't find that interesting. Tommy and Frank were a lot alike in character. They were both their own man. Tommy had much more class than Frank. Tommy could be his own man without having six or seven yes-men around him. I don't think Mel was in that league. But I think Mel made a better husband as a result of not being in that league. I don't think Tommy could ever have been a great husband, and I thank God that God knew that for me.”

Immediately after marrying Toxton, Torme was offered a concert tour with Dorsey. Toxton demanded that he turn it down, but Torme explained that the money was too good for him not to accept. Since they were still on their honeymoon, Torme insisted his wife sit in the first row of the theater at their first concert. “Tommy was on stage watching me the whole time,” Toxton recalled. “It was painful. He didn't bother me. It's just that I had to be there as long as Mel was onstage with him. . . . I didn't go backstage.”

Now past forty, Dorsey was drawn to women almost half his age, but he wasn't able to embrace the brand of jazz that had emerged from that same generation. He seemed to regard bebop as a terrible indignity foisted upon the dance band business in its decline.

During this period, Tommy enjoyed guest-performing at Dixieland concerts presented at Town Hall by his old friend Eddie Condon, where he could play with musicians he respected, like cornetist Bobby Hackett and clarinetist Peanuts Hucko. This music still had an audience; it was akin to swing music.

Commercial success was always his main goal; everything his orchestra did after “Marie” and “Song of India” was with that idea in mind. If elements of jazz that entered into the band's presentation through the writing of Oliver, Finegan, Kincaide, and a few others he hired proved to be commercial—or at least praised by critics and audiences—so much the better.

His insistence on stating the melody, and more-or-less adhering to it, was illustrated by an encounter with the jazz pianist Marian McPartland. The longtime host of *Piano Jazz,* the popular NPR radio show, who had met Dorsey through his longtime relationship with her husband, Jimmy McPartland, brought a tune she had written to a Dorsey band rehearsal. As McPartland recalled, "The tune was quite a pretty ballad, and I started to play it. I guess I must have been improvising or playing around with the melody because all I can remember was him saying, 'Marian, for God's sake, play the God damn tune.'"

McPartland figured she might possibly have included some bebop licks: "However, what I was doing was not sticking to the melody, which I knew you should do if you're doing a demo for somebody. He never took the tune, but that's all he said to me about it. I guess I went back to playing it straight, and he said, 'Oh, that was nice,' or 'Thank you,' or something quite polite."

Gunther Schuller, in his 1989 scholarly volume *The Swing Era,* wrote, "Good examples of the [Dorsey] band's postwar work abound, although they are rarely innovative or highly creative. . . . Except for Woody Herman, and Stan Kenton, most surviving white bands spent their energies to revive, in one way or another, the late Swing Era—Dorsey included. Always a traditionalist, Dorsey would . . . allow a Bill Finegan to introduce a few bitonal harmonies and modern chord substitutions. Dorsey could never think of jazz in creative terms or as instantaneous creative composing, equating it with Dixieland, already an essentially anachronistic style when Dorsey started his orchestra." Schuller's observations were essentially correct. But the creativity his arrangers brought to his music wasn't an incidental thing for Dorsey.

Tenor saxophonist Loren Schoenberg, who later became a teacher of graduate courses at Juilliard and Manhattan School of Music and also played in Bobby Short's orchestra, offers a generous appraisal of Tommy's musical progress:

"Let's put it this way. If you take the recordings that Tommy Dorsey made at the beginning of his bandleading career . . . like 1935 and then if you contrast them with the late Deccas or, let's say, even the last Bill Finegan things he recorded in 1953—'Blue Room' . . . and 'Comin' Through the Rye'— with the content of what Tommy Dorsey was when he began, I think there's a greater amount of growth in the music that he did than the music that Benny [Goodman] did. . . . Look who was in Tommy Dorsey's band. Listen to the records now and then make your judgments, just from the music.

... What I'm talking about [is] the rhythm and the harmony and the melody." He added the praise for Finegan, "I've never heard a [big-band] record of Dizzy Gillespie of any writer—it could be George Russell or John Lewis or even Todd Dameron—who had half of the craft and the sophistication of orchestration and composition that Bill Finegan did."

After another Petrillo-induced recording ban in 1948 and 1949 was lifted, Dorsey recorded Finegan's instrumental "Drumology," written specifically for Bellson, and "Pussy Willow," predominantly an ensemble showcase. And then there was his intricate reworking of songs like "It's Delovely" and "I Get a Kick out of You" in a popular Cole Porter album.

Charlie Shavers's top-ten record of "The Hucklebuck," in which both his singing and his trumpeting were on display, made Dorsey especially happy. At the recording session, it took approximately twenty takes for Shavers to pronounce the word *sacroiliac*, a key word in the lyrics. The melody had been freely adapted by the arranger, Andy Gibson, from Charlie Parker's bebop anthem "Now's the Time."

Dorsey's continuing rants against bebop began appearing in the jazz press. Among them were "Booze and bebop don't agree with me," "I admire Dizzy and Bird, but young musicians can't play it [bebop] well. They need seasoning [*sic*]." He explained, "Dizzy's big band was booked into ballrooms in the Midwest, and it didn't do well. They called it dance music, and it wasn't. Bebop isn't accepted by the masses—it doesn't have the beat. I can't tell if it's a five-bar or eight-bar phrase." He further complained, "Jazz has to have melody," citing the Original Dixieland Jazz Band, Bix Beiderbecke, and Bunny Berigan. He pointed out that Louis Armstrong's All Stars featuring Jack Teagarden had just done record-breaking business at New York's Bop City—one of the principal temples of his most unfavorite music. He also told Earl Wilson, "Bebop stinks. It's set music back twenty years."

Not surprisingly, these rancorous comments brought retaliation. Mike Levin of *DownBeat* said, "What is this campaign on the part of a lot of big bandleaders to put down bop? . . . All this noise puts those who like good music in a very uncomfortable position. They recognize that Tommy Dorsey is a poor excuse for a jazz musician."

In a KNBC Los Angeles radio symposium devoted to bebop, Nat "King" Cole said, "I don't know what to say about Tommy. I should think a man who has led the way like he has would be glad to see something new come along. . . . I think anyone who professes to hate bebop to the extent he does just doesn't know anything about it." Mel Torme rashly commented, "I think

Tommy kind of signed his musical obituary when he rapped progressive jazz." Woody Herman, who once said, "Dorsey made stars out of other bandleaders," offered, "Socially, Tommy and I have had a beautiful friendship, and I'm sure it will continue, but musically we have not seen eye to eye on too many occasions. I, for one, feel Tommy isn't doing music justice by making statements [about bop]."

Two of Dorsey's contemporaries, Goodman and James, had tried to "get with the new thing" in the late 1940s, but after rather brief flirtations with bop, they returned to their swing roots. Aside from Dorsey's basic resistance to change, as Buddy DeFranco pointed out, there was another important factor: "Bebop was a listening kind of music, and Tommy ran a dance band."

Perhaps due to the diatribes from critics haranguing him for his unwillingness to accept change, or perhaps because he saw bebop as possibly becoming more of a mass music, on the afternoon of his opening night at the Astor Roof on July 11, 1950, when the band was dressed in their band uniforms for a New York *Daily News* photo shoot, Dorsey announced he wanted to give the band a bebop flavor. Boomie Richman recalled, "He said, 'If we can't lick 'em, we've gotta join 'em.' I remember it well. My son was born that day. That's why I had given him my notice."

Dorsey now had first-rate bebop soloists in pianist Lou Levy and vibist Terry Gibbs, along with Louis Bellson, who had easily adapted to the new music. "But that didn't last long. That was just his idea of the moment," Richman said.

Richman's replacement was none other than the great Zoot Sims. But his concept was too advanced for Dorsey. Right in the middle of playing a twenty-two-bar solo on what had been a showcase for Richman, "Dry Bones," at the Astor Roof, Sims was fired.

In a change from his old policy, Tommy had wanted Richman to stay on and have his family travel with the band. Richman recalled, "He wanted to get me a trailer, like his, which we called 'The Silver Bullet,' so I could live in it with my wife and son while doing one-nighters. The only thing was, [he and Janie] traveled like that, but he had a chauffeur and a chef and a maid!"

There was strife in the marriage to New from the beginning. During the summer of 1948, when he worked for Dorsey as band boy, the late Artie Mogull remembered, "He and Janie had a big fight on the phone. We were up in New Bedford, Massachusetts, playing a concert. He told me to get on a bus to New York and to go up to his apartment and get all the silverware [which he prized]. He wanted me to get it before she came back to the apartment. I called him to tell him that I had it all. He said, 'Jesus Christ, she's on her way back to the apartment with me. Get the silverware back before she gets there!'"

Both Tommy and Janie were extremely strong-willed individuals. Among other things, Janie couldn't bear his mood swings, infidelities, and inability to see anyone else's point of view.

As everyone who knew him realized, however, Dorsey's unpredictability worked both ways. New never forgot an instance of his spontaneous kindness and generosity. They were driving through Georgia when Tommy realized they were not far from Warm Springs, which President Franklin D. Roosevelt had often visited in order to use the therapeutic baths. He decided to swing over there and take a look. When he saw children being treated, he decided to do a show for them. He had the state police track down the band on the bus. The musicians grudgingly came to the hospital, gave their performance, and ended up with tears in their eyes and not wanting to leave. "Tommy insisted on going to every room to sign autographs," New said. "Afterward, the hospital wrote to him and said that normally the lights went out at a certain time, but it was actually two or three hours later that night because all the kids started writing letters to their parents about the wonderful show they had just seen. It was so heartwarming."

George Thompson was Dorsey's road manager during the late 1940s. Thompson observed, "He had a way of talking to people from the lowest class to the highest—he was at home in any strata of society, like the so-called high class or financial people like Neiman Marcus in Dallas. He was like a king to those people. When we played for Harvey Firestone of the Firestone Tire Company, at Meyers Park in Canton, Ohio, Firestone was in a wheelchair, but he would be there all the time. He loved Dorsey."

Another one of his associations with the moneyed class dated back to 1935, when he played the coming-out party for the daughter of Roy Chapin, the president of the Hudson car company. In 1951, the band played a date for the Hudson company at the Detroit Yacht Club. *The Sentimentalist* was sailed through the inland waterways to Detroit and docked at the Detroit Yacht Club, where the vessel was sold.

Thompson added, "Whenever he played New York or even outside New York, he had priests and nuns in the audience. He would take care of them and pay all their expenses and do anything for them. He didn't look for publicity. He didn't want anybody to know about such things."

Thompson was amazed by Dorsey's stamina: "He would sleep four hours a night, and he wanted everybody else to do the same. He always liked people around him. Sometimes I'd have to be with him until four o'clock in the morning. After a gig on the road, we'd go to eat. He'd buy a piece of pie, and he'd drink half a pint of milk. The bill might come to thirty-five or forty cents. He'd leave the waitress five dollars. If we played a theater or the Café Rouge, he would leave me money for everybody from the bus boy all the way up to the maître d'."

Baritone saxophonist Sol Schlinger recalled the resourceful thinking Thompson did to save Schlinger's job with Dorsey:

> George had told me what a great job I was doing after two weeks on the job. Then he came up to me at intermission right after that and said, "The old man told me to give you your notice. But do me a favor, for the next few nights, come in early, get on the bandstand, open the book, and look it over. When he comes in and sees you on the bandstand like that, I'm pretty sure it will [all] work out."
>
>   I know I did that for probably a couple of days. As I did it, I was sort of laughing to myself—what am I doing here? At any rate, I wound up staying with the band for another year. I would say that's where Tommy was at. It was like being in the marines.

Schlinger laughed as he related that tenor saxophonist Sal Collura was on notice while the band was playing in San Francisco: "We were playing softball against a hotel team or something. Tom wasn't playing, he was the coach. Sal was playing center field. He made a shoestring catch for the out, and Tom says, 'Take his notice off!'"

During the Christmas period, when Tommy's band was off, Schlinger worked for Jimmy Dorsey's band and recalls very clearly how different the experiences were musically. When he left, he told Jimmy, "I've worked with The Brother, and all I can say is that any professional musician would know the difference." He added, "I was implying that he was the better of the two. He looked at me and said, 'Get out of here, kid.' It was as if he had heard that before."

For Tommy, this seems to have been a period of satisfaction. Thompson said that shortly after he joined the band Dorsey said, "George, this is the best band I've ever had." This was the period when either Louis Bellson or Buddy Rich was with him. Finegan's arrangements were continually praised, though the sound of the RCA recordings failed to capture the vitality this Dorsey band had. As Finegan pointed out, "You had to hear it in person to hear the real sonority."

(Over the years this has been true of other great bands. For some reason, the pressure involved in that recording process sometimes inhibited the performance level of musicians.)

"Finegan's an original. He was one of the first modern arrangers," observed Johnny Mandel recently. "He spread things out in his voicings. The lines all made sense, the inner voices—he just wrote beautifully. He worried about modulations and things." Writer Burt Korall added, "The Finegan [Dorsey] band in many ways was more musically inventive than the Oliver [Dorsey] band. Finegan is a genius."

There continued to be a revolving door to the band for Buddy Rich. After his first band failed, he toured with Norman Granz's Jazz at the Philharmonic and spent several months with Les Brown before he returned to the Dorsey band for the third time in 1950. Three months later, while on tour in Texas, he informed Dorsey he was leaving in order to back Frank Sinatra with a new band at the Paramount. Dorsey responded by telling Rich he could take him to the musician's union for failure to give proper notice. Instead, he said, "This is the last time you will ever see a check signed 'Thomas F. Dorsey, Jr.'" As ever, it wasn't; Rich would return again in November 1954.

Like Louis Bellson, drummer Ed Shaughnessy featured two bass drums in his presentation. He joined the band at the Capitol Theater following a European tour with Benny Goodman. Former Dorsey bassist Sandy Block suggested Shaughnessy to Dorsey as Rich's replacement.

"I think I had a really firm relationship going with Tommy because I would play bebop records in the third-floor dressing room between shows," said Shaughnessy.

> His dressing room was on the second floor. He'd yell up, "Turn that shit off," and I'd say, "Maybe if you listened you would learn something!" And he used to laugh. I played some Yma Sumac ["The Voice of the Xtabay"]. He would come out and yell, "That's worse than the other shit—turn that off."
>
> I was always impressed by his professionalism, as I was with the performance he could get out of a band. When the guys weren't playing something quite right, he always seemed to have the right thing to say. He said to me once, "You have a natural feel like Buddy does. There's one thing I can help you with. As you play faster, play a little lighter, but don't lose the intensity." I asked him, "Did you get that from your own horn?" "Yes," he said, "but it works on drums, too." I was a lucky fellow. Five years prior to that I was out

in the audience with a sandwich in a brown paper bag listening to this band for two and three shows. This had to be at the Capitol Theater.

Shaughnessy felt, "The only musicians I ever saw him kick in the can from time to time were lazy players. Discipline was absolutely paramount. I liked that because I think you should always play your best. I think that's the reason I didn't have a bit of trouble with him. He even gave me two raises."

Dorsey wanted to manage Shaughnessy and offered him a three-year contract. The drummer begged off, explaining that he had to leave the band to work around New York because of the grave condition of his mother's health, and the two parted amicably. Shaughnessy would go on to play on Steve Allen's first network show, which was on CBS, and then on NBC for twenty-nine years with the *Tonight Show* band under the direction of another Dorsey alumnus, Doc Severinsen.

One of the best trumpet players ever to play in a big band, Carl "Doc" Severinsen joined the Dorsey band in 1949. Severinsen could play with power and a swinging feeling. He had been brought to Dorsey's attention seven years earlier during the war when Dorsey was first starting to encounter problems finding good musicians due to the draft. Severinsen was only fourteen at the time, and although Dorsey was duly impressed, he felt he was too young to join the band. It was then that the young Oregonian first saw the Dorsey band in performance. "Ziggy Elman stood up and played first. He was one of the loudest trumpet players who ever lived. And that changed my life," Doc recalled.

Severinsen joined Dorsey at the Shamrock Hotel in Houston. He remembers his emotion that night. "The first set, which was the dinner set, the band played without Tommy. Then we started playing the next set, and Tommy walked out on the stand and didn't say hello. Nothing. Just walked over, picked up his horn and played the theme. I broke into tears. . . . All you ever had to do, if you were a brass player, was to look at his embouchure and listen to how he breathed and how he played things. Today, I watch Direct TV and study Dorsey. There was a completeness surrounding his band that nobody else had."

Severinsen left the band when Dorsey announced in 1951 that he was taking Janie on a seven-month-long belated honeymoon, which actually ended after a little over a month in Europe. Severinsen later came to the band for a second time but left after only a few months. He went back to New York and settled there: "But, I'll tell you, once you've played with

Tommy's band for any period of time, you're a Tommy Dorsey guy. . . . There was one way to play it and it was *his way*."

Another Dorsey drummer was Irv Kluger, who had played with Stan Kenton, Artie Shaw, and several other name bands. He replaced Buddy Rich with the Dorsey band several times. "Seven, eight times, sometimes three weeks, sometimes four months," as Kluger remembered.

In a rather startling observation, Kluger contended that Dorsey could have been successful playing bebop on a regular basis. "What the hell is bebop," Kluger stressed, "except the ability to have velocity? Bud Powell wasn't really into bebop. He was a one-three-fiver and beautiful, but he wasn't into bebop yet. Bud just extended his ability to do a five, a seven, a nine, and thirteenth, which Artie Shaw ate alive because he was always broad-based. [Kluger also played drums on Shaw's bop-influenced *Last Recordings* CDs.] I think it was more than fear; it was drunken laziness that kept Dorsey from going forward," referring to the World War II period, when he first worked for Dorsey. Working for Dorsey was wearing: "I enjoyed leaving because, you know, the song 'The Thrill Is Gone'? Enough was enough."

At the 1949 Shamrock Hotel gig in Houston, due to segregation, Charlie Shavers once again wasn't permitted to appear as part of the Dorsey band. Charlie led a small group comprising black musicians at the El Dorado Club, in the Houston ghetto. This was something Shavers often did when he wasn't permitted to play dates with Dorsey in the south.

E. C. Holland, the longtime head of the Houston musician's local and himself a well-respected trumpeter and bandleader there for many years, remembered, "When Tommy finished at the Shamrock, he came over to play with Charlie. On a borrowed trombone he traded fours [exchanged four-bar solos] with him, and then Tommy copied Charlie's fast bebop stuff. Ray Wetzel and the guys from Tommy's band came over to see Tommy really play jazz. He would never do it on a record because that's not where he made his money. It was really amazing to hear."

The grandiose opening-night festivities from which Shavers was barred at the Shamrock in 1949 were well depicted by the eminent film director George Stevens in the Warner Brothers film version of Edna Ferber's novel *Giant*. The role of the flamboyant owner of the hotel was portrayed by James Dean, who goes into a drunken rampage in front of a room of his celebrated guests. Dean's character was based on Glenn McCarthy, one of the first highly publicized Texas oil millionaires.

Dorsey was drawn to McCarthy, a successful industrialist, and began socializing with him. McCarthy encouraged Dorsey to invest in some of his oil well sites, and Dorsey, in turn, notified the band about his investment and suggested they put their money in as well. According to trumpeter Art Depew, now leader of the Harry James Orchestra and a former Dorsey trumpeter, "One share was three thousand dollars. Some of the guys did it. Turns out the fields went dry. Tommy felt badly about it and bought the guys out."

Also joining the band at the Shamrock Hotel in 1949 was the statuesque red-haired singer Frances Irvin. She was to spend the next three years as the band's vocalist. It was at the Shamrock that she met her future husband, saxophonist Gene Cipriano, who years later became a highly successful Hollywood recording-studio musician. Hugo Loewenstern had recommended her to Dorsey.

Irvin remembered the glamour of the Shamrock: "It was top drawer—the microphones, the lighting, the whole place. It was like being on a movie set. I worked the last two nights of the engagement. The next night we drove 365 miles to a little place in Louisiana. It was a big letdown. I said to myself, 'This is the road.' I had never been outside of Amarillo. I used to be a drum majorette there."

When the band reached New York's Capitol Theater, Irvin got a banner review, "Redhead Sparks Show." This had been preceded by another notice on the road in which Irvin had been called the "Texas Tornado." Dorsey couldn't handle this kind of attention being given to his new girl singer. "He called me on the carpet and bawled me out. One of the old timers on the band said, 'Don't you know why he did that? Just so he can control you.'" In retrospect, Irvin speculated, "Maybe he didn't want me to get a big head and ask for a raise or something."

Hugo Loewenstern said, "Janie New taught Frances a great deal about stage presence." Irvin recalled that New interviewed her, very aware that her husband had had a long-term sexual relationship with his first band singer, Edythe Wright. "She found out I was a Texas hick who knew nothing."

While Irvin was driving to gigs with Dorsey in his car, Dorsey insisted that she listen to various female singers so that she could identify them: "He was training my ear, and that would help my phrasing. He told me to go see Lena Horne perform. He wanted me to learn something from her whole presentation."

For a time Dorsey tried to put together another singing group like The Pied Pipers with Irvin in the Jo Stafford role: "I had a [wide] vibrato, so we let it go. I didn't enjoy that at all. We also went through about twelve boy singers while I was there." (Dorsey seems to have been looking for the impossible dream—another Stuart Foster, much less a Jack Leonard or a Frank Sinatra.)

As with Sinatra, when Irvin was about to leave, Dorsey signed her to a seven-year contract as her manager. She was offered the female singer's job on the *Tonight Show* with Steve Allen, but Dorsey turned it down. Dorsey contended, "I'm afraid if it doesn't work out you'll be associated with failure." The slot was taken by Eydie Gorme, which led to her eventual stardom. Eventually, when the Ciprianos moved to Los Angeles, Irwin was able to get out of her management contract with Dorsey.

In 1949, after all the money he had poured into his West Coast home base, the Casino Gardens proved to be a money-losing proposition, and Dorsey sold it for $150,000. Now he had to spend even more time on the road. A year later, with one-nighters in the United States getting even more difficult to book, MCA came up with a prize booking—three weeks in Havana.

Dorsey had featured a few Latin dance numbers like other bands. He looked upon the Cuban gig, however, as just another well-paying location engagement.

Leonardo Timor, who would become a refugee from Castro's Cuba and now lives in North Miami Beach, played lead trumpet in the Rafael Ortega Orchestra at the San Souci, where the Dorsey band headlined and played for dancing. Buddy Rich, who had started in vaudeville as an act billed as "Traps, the Boy Wonder," was given the opportunity to do a tap dance number and sing with the band in the nightly show that began at midnight. Timor recalled that Rich was ill one night and the great Cuban drummer Guillermo Barreto took his place, adapting to the Dorsey band's style. "We had a lot of Dorsey's records, and he could read music quite well," he explained.

Timor struck up a friendship with Ray Wetzel, who gave him a Parduba mouthpiece that he played as long as he played trumpet. In recent years Timor has stopped playing the trumpet and begun learning to play the trombone. "I want to learn to play like Tommy," he said.

During the Havana engagement, Wetzel got a letter from Stan Kenton, asking him to leave Dorsey immediately in order to rejoin the Kenton band. When Wetzel told Dorsey, he was furious and insisted that Wetzel stay.

(Tragically, the trumpeter was killed in August 1951 changing a tire on a roadside while he was traveling with Charlie Shavers on tour with the Dorsey band.)

Boomie Richman recalls the trip to Havana with great fondness. Perhaps one reason was that he spoke fluent Spanish: "I think it was about the happiest engagement the band ever had [when I was there] because every day [the guys] availed themselves of the Baccardi rum afterward, and they had a lot of freebies."

Twenty-four-year-old Tino Barzie, a Pittsfield, Massachusetts, native and former clarinetist and saxophonist with Tex Beneke and the Glenn Miller Orchestra, aspired to become a band manager. Barzie's mentor was John O'Leary, who had been road manager for Glenn Miller and the Beneke band. Barzie had previously met with Gene Krupa about managing his new band. The meeting with Krupa went well. It had been arranged by Larry Barnett, who had also suggested Barzie to Dorsey.

"I was living at the Piccadilly Hotel," Barzie recalled. "I got a person-to-person call from Tommy Dorsey one day in November 1950. He said, 'I need some help for a couple of weeks. I just fired my manager [Leonard Vannerson]. Can you meet me tomorrow in Canton, Ohio?'"

Barzie got himself out to Ohio, met Dorsey, and went over the contracts with him for the dates ahead. The next day he drove with Dorsey in his Cadillac convertible to Akron: "This guy drove like a maniac. . . . He was going seventy-five miles an hour. He plugged his electric shaver into the cigarette lighter with one hand and begins shaving. He's driving with the other!" They discussed the status of the current band.

Barzie remembers his tryout for the job: "At the date in Akron, he asks me how I liked the band. I told him it was great. Then he tells me to give notice to a trombonist, a saxophonist, and two trumpeters—and to get them out of there. I asked him if he had some replacements coming in. 'No, you get them,' he said. I got it done, and that impressed him. At the end of two weeks, I showed him all the receipts. Then he said, 'You're not going to leave. You're going to stay here.' 'What about Gene?' I asked. 'I'll straighten that out with Barnett in the morning.' Sure enough, he called Larry the next morning and said, 'I'm keeping this guy. Tell Gene I owe him one.'"

Barzie, whose enthusiastic manner and way of speaking are reminiscent of the actor Robert Duvall, would remain with Dorsey until the very end of his life. His detractors say, "He would have you believe he invented Tommy Dorsey." The fact remains that Barzie made an important contribution to the success the band enjoyed, particularly in Dorsey's last years. He quickly grasped the way Dorsey thought and saw where the band's fortunes were headed. He had to walk the fine line between doing what Dorsey wanted and seeing how it might affect the morale of the band.

The United States had endured a depression and helped win a second world war. Tommy's music had helped express that era's optimism and heart. In the five years since the end of World War II in 1945, America had shifted from a feeling of optimism to a deep-set paranoia about its former ally, the Soviet Union. As an example, the House Un-American Activities Committee (HUAC) began hunting communists in everything from politics to entertainment. Senator Joe McCarthy of Wisconsin took advantage of this national apprehension. In 1950 he accused the State Department of being filled with communists without any tangible proof. McCarthyism was born.

American military forces entered into an armed conflict with North Korea when its army invaded South Korea on June 25, 1950. Within a few months American and South Korean forces found themselves holding on for dear life to a small perimeter in the southernmost part of the Korean peninsula. These significant developments had little effect, however, on the music in the early 1950s, which remained nondescript.

Dorsey was then confronted with the fact that two of the major companies—RCA Victor Records and MCA—that had helped pave his pathway to stardom were becoming disillusioned with him. That both worried and angered him more than he would ever admit.

In that eventful year of 1950, after fifteen years, RCA Victor parted company with Dorsey on August 17. He recorded his last tracks on July 11, the culmination of a grand total of almost three hundred single records, which included seventeen number-one records. Sales of his records totaled a reported 37 million records sold, including 13 million in the previous five years. The latter was an especially surprising figure in view of the decline of the band business. But then again, the sales of several significant reissues had helped swell these figures.

These significant sales totals led to Decca Records' signing an unrealistic three-year contract with Dorsey that guaranteed him a minimum of fifty-two thousand dollars a year for fifty records per year. Decca thought there was still magic in the Dorsey name. He began by recording "T.D.'s Boogie Woo-gie" (his third version of this instrumental) and then a sequel, "Opus #2." There were recording sessions for instrumental albums by Victor Young and Gordon Jenkins, which featured Tommy as guest star. He also recorded four tracks with Bing Crosby for old times' sake. Jack Leonard and Dick Haymes guested with the Dorsey band on other records.

Continuing the trend of pairing singers with name bands, Don Cherry, not the jazz pocket trumpet player, but the singer and pro golf player, recorded "Music Maestro" and "Strangers" with the band. "Tommy made it so easy since I couldn't read music," said Cherry. "He had a great sense of humor and was a very nice man." As a golfer, Cherry said, "Tommy wasn't that good. He had an eighteen handicap."

Dorsey's second important contract, with MCA, expired that fall. Over the years he had paid the company more than a million dollars in commis-sions. He expressed his feelings toward the agency when he had a special li-cense plate made, "4Q MCA," a not-so-subtle nose-thumbing at the agency. Dorsey was reluctant to sign a contract renewal. What was left of the band business was slowly but surely fading away. Dorsey had been at odds with the agency for some time, often complaining to Larry Barnett about the long jumps between dates and the smaller guarantees.

But with all the factors that affected the slump of the band business, the most significant was the impact of television. "Uncle Miltie" (Milton Berle), seen on NBC, had become "Mr. Television." Major personalities like him created such a following that it was easier for the public to sit at home and be entertained for free than to go out to a ballroom to dance.

Laura Jons Collins, who sang briefly with the band in 1949 under the name of Jeanne Carroll, remembered Dorsey's telling her, "Those god-damned television antennas are going to ruin the music business." They al-ready had helped kill the band business by 1949.

By this time, Barnett had assumed the presidency of the parent company, MCA, at the time when the agency had become such a significant force in the motion picture and the television businesses that it had inaugurated other companies, such as MCA-TV and MCA Artists. Its power and influ-ence would cause it to be labeled the octopus, not so much from envy as from fear. For swing musicians, the dominance of MCA loomed large enough to inspire a blues lyric sung by Jack Teagarden: "I started up to see Bud Freeman, but I lost my way/and I thought for a minute I was on the road for MCA."

Perhaps in Dorsey's eyes the incredible success of the company, which had started out booking small dance orchestras, in the long run worked against it. He firmly believed he wasn't being given the same kind of attention from the agency that he had received years earlier. The reality was that the big band was fast becoming a nonentity in pop culture.

In a much-talked-about bold statement that let the industry know his opinion of where his future lay, Dorsey took out a full-page advertisement in *Billboard* in its December 16, 1950, issue. In large letters it read, "PHEW! After 15 years I am finally out of the clutches of YOU KNOW WHO!!! I am booked exclusively by . . . TOMDOR ENTERPRISES, Inc. For all available dates, please contact the above." It was signed by Tommy Dorsey.

In spite of his animosity toward the agency, however, Dorsey continued his friendship with Berle Adams, who had joined MCA the year before and who by this time was an MCA vice president and later became a member of its board of directors. Dorsey would telephone Adams using the pseudonym of Harry Bluestone (a violinist and one-time member of the Dorsey Brothers Orchestra) to ask Adams to meet him for dinner in New York. He did this in order to protect Adams from embarrassment at the agency.

Adams recalled that Tommy constantly referred to Jimmy as "The Little Brother." He also noted how much Dorsey enjoyed playing one-nighters. Dorsey said, "When you're a star and you play a one-nighter, you come into a town, and you're a hero, you get the adulation. It's amazing. . . . They've been advertising you for weeks. They worship you. They tell you how wonderful you are on the road." Adams added, "Dorsey was fabulous—he could make them eat out of his hands."

With MCA out of the picture, a twenty-nine-year-old former Glenn Miller Air Force Band tenor saxophonist, Vince Carbone, a decent man in a business that never had many, began booking the band from Dorsey's longtime office suite at 1619 Broadway. He and Tino Barzie had worked together in the saxophone section of the Beneke band. Carbone began referring to Dorsey as the "smiling Irishman." Barzie remained on the road with the precarious job of satisfying Dorsey's various whims while managing the band.

Dorsey spent much of the first half of 1951 in Hollywood, where the band performed in a nondescript eponymously titled short subject, at Universal Pictures, the kind that featured big bands. Following that there was an appearance in an Allied Artists "B" picture, *Disc Jockey*, in which the band played "Oh, Look at Me Now." The radio personalities depicted in the film had no resemblance to the Al Jarvis–Martin Block types synony-mous with big bands, and the Dorsey band's music was incongruous with the contemporary musical outlook of the film.

On the band's return to the East, in the midst of a tour, Dorsey fired Tino Barzie one night in Waterville, Maine. Barzie contended it was because he didn't want to go out to the bus to retrieve a picture for Dorsey to autograph for an attractive woman fan, afraid he might wake up the bus driver. Barzie was by now used to Dorsey's often irrational behavior. After the gig, Dorsey threw a fit, grabbed Barzie by the throat, and started to bang his head against the wall. He told Barzie he wanted to fight him, but the young manager refused, saying, "You're old enough to be my father. I wouldn't want to fight with my father." Dorsey ordered the band boy to take Barzie's gear off the bus. Dorsey chased him down the street and then got into his own car and left town.

Barzie found a local limousine service to drive him to Boston. From there he went down to New York. At Tomdor Enterprises he dropped off money and tickets for the band's upcoming flight to Chicago.

Janie New Dorsey, acting as intermediary, called to invite Barzie to have dinner with her a few days later. New realized that her husband's outbursts sometimes were based on a momentary fit of temper rather than his overall disapproval of that person. Over dinner, according to Barzie, she said, "Tommy really misses you." He told her he wasn't sure what he wanted to do and went home to Pittsfield to see his family. When he returned to New York, he had a second dinner with Janie, who encouraged him to come back to the band.

The next day, at the Picadilly, he got a message from the hotel operator that someone had called him from Hartford, Connecticut. Knowing the band's itinerary, he knew the call was from Dorsey. Returning the call, Barzie was met by, "You little shithead! You get your goddamned ass back here!" His almost month-long hiatus from the band ended.

Events in the following months got worse. If the trip to Havana in 1950 had been the high point for several of the members of the band—and in that case it was a trip to a foreign country—the next overseas excursion, coinci-dentally to another Latin country, was perhaps the nadir of the band's tour-ing experiences. Starting on Thanksgiving Day of 1951, the band embarked on an almost two-month-long tour of Brazil. Fifty-two years later, for two surviving band members it's still a bad memory.

Dorsey got off to a mischievous start on the trip to Miami with his new bassist Phil Leshin, who had joined the band in Toronto. Knowing that Leshin had most recently been with Buddy Rich's band, Dorsey said to him, "How could God give so much talent to such an evil son of a bitch?" Leshin remembers his own reply, "That's exactly what Buddy said about you, when I told him I was joining your band."

The tour itself was difficult from its inception. Trumpeter Buddy Childers, himself a licensed pilot, recalls the problems began because of Dorsey's clothes fetish: "It all started out with the fact that the airplane had to take care of Dorsey's six wardrobe trunks, each of which was about six feet high. There wasn't room for the trunks in the Chicago and Southern DC-4's baggage compartment. Tommy insisted they weren't going unless the trunks were put on the plane, so the airline had to bump about ten passengers and take out some seats. That meant the band had to fly from Miami and then to the Dominican Republic, en route to Venezuela, and finally to Rio de Janeiro. Dorsey was accompanied by his wife, Janie; their two-year-old baby daughter, Susan; and a nurse. We had to sit around the Miami airport all night as we were in quarantine. On the second attempt to take off, at three or four in the afternoon, we took off on cruise power, which meant flying only three hundred feet over Miami Beach. We finally got up to ten thousand feet and then started going down to two hundred feet again, thirty to forty miles out in the ocean."

En route, Leshin says there was an announcement that the pilot had just been informed that after 8 P.M. all planes flying over Venezuela would be shot down, which meant their plane couldn't fly over Venezuela that night.

The band was welcomed warmly on the stopovers, but there were also delays. In Santo Domingo, a local band at the hotel, thrilled by the news that Tommy Dorsey and His Orchestra were staying there, got the Dorsey musicians to jam with a contingent of Latin musicians until 5:30 in the morning. In Trinidad, the passengers were met with trays of rum punch. From there, it was on to Venezuela before stopping in Belem, Brazil, and then on to Rio. They arrived at four o'clock in the morning on the third day, already a day late. Leshin recalled their being picked up by Jorge Guinle, reputed to be the richest man in Brazil, in six Rolls-Royces. Guinle later sat in on drums on one of the Dorsey band's appearances in Rio.

Ill feelings dominated in the band from the time they arrived. Tommy was in a bullying mode, his familiar reaction when events weren't going the way he wanted.

"We played at different places all over town," Childers remembered. "We were supposed to play from ten in the morning until five o'clock the next morning. The band had a meeting. Everybody was miserable, bitching about how much we were working."

It was when the band did a TV show in Rio that Tommy started laying into Charlie Shavers for being drunk, "which he wasn't," Leshin said and added, "I'd wake him up and he'd play the most beautiful music in the world." When Childers told Dorsey to lay off Charlie, that he hadn't been drinking, that he and the whole band were all extremely tired, Tommy stomped out of the studio and walked back to the hotel, about seven or eight miles away. The band did the show without him with trombonist Nick Di-Maio acting as leader.

It was quite unusual for two such musicians to stand up against Dorsey, but there was a price for their show of solidarity. "The next week we were docked a day's pay," Childers recalled. When he asked Tommy why they were being docked in their pay, Dorsey replied, "Take it up with Petrillo when you get back to New York." Childers informed him that he didn't do business that way.

The touring within Brazil was extensive. The band flew north to Recife for four weeks and did a daily radio broadcast. Two or three days a week there were flights to and from Belem and to several other cities in northern Brazil to play dance dates.

Dorsey decided Frances Irvin should learn to sing "C'Est Si Bon," then a hot pop song, in Portuguese. A Brazilian film actor worked with her to teach her how to sing it phonetically. When the audience laughed at her rendition, Dorsey told her to sing it again.

During a radio broadcast by the band on Christmas Eve, Childers responded to an order from Dorsey by screaming back at him and held his trumpet like a club threateningly: "I was mad at the way Tommy was treating Phil, Eddie Grady [the drummer], and several of the other musicians. I figured out that if somebody like Tommy respected you musically, he had to test you as a man." As if in copycat response, a commotion ensued in the audience, provoked by the scion of one of two warring families' saying something unmentionable about the mother of the other family. A fight broke out and the broadcast was terminated. In a conciliatory move, Dorsey threw a Christmas party for his musicians the next day.

By now, Dorsey was fed up with the traveling, the food, the people. Communication was difficult—English was barely spoken in Brazil at that time, and no one in the band spoke Portuguese. There were also more personal strains. Susie was sick during the entire trip, and Janie was constantly irritable.

But what was of paramount importance was the fact that Dorsey hadn't been paid for the next four weeks of the tour up front, according to the terms of the contract. The entire tour was supposed to be worth $200,000. After waiting a week, he and his family abruptly left for Miami, leaving the band stranded without pay.

"Sam Donahue [the tenor saxophonist] led the band at some private parties," Leshin remembered. "This was after the government took the instruments away from the musicians and then gave them back."

Fortunately, the hotel in Rio allowed the musicians to sign for everything. "After about a week, two truckloads of militia escorted us to the airport. We left on a C-46 for Miami," added Leshin. Tino Barzie, winging it, assured the musicians they would be straightened out financially once the band arrived back in New York.

"When I got to Miami, I had a dollar seventy-five in my pocket," said Childers. "Phil, another musician from the band, and I slept on the beach in Miami Beach that night. The airline that sponsored the tour brought us back to New York. I had a dime left when we got there. I called Eddie Safranski, the bass player, who came and got me at LaGuardia Airport." Soon afterward, Leshin filed a union claim against Dorsey and months later received a check for a thousand dollars.

Despite this nightmare, Childers said, "The band was so good. I loved the way Tommy did everything except when he was nasty to people. It was fun playing with that band—much more fun than the Kenton band had been for me." (Both Childers and the bassist Norm Seelig, who preceded Leshin, remembered that one of Dorsey's favorite lines, when told a musician who was a nice guy was available to join the band, said, "Send me a prick that can blow.")

Starting slightly over a decade later, American musicians looked forward to going to Brazil—the women, the sun, the beaches, and the music. Musicians like flutist Herbie Mann and alto saxophonist Bud Shank discovered the new form of the samba called the bossa nova during their tours. A few years later the jazz tenor saxophonist master Stan Getz and guitarist Charlie Byrd enjoyed a worldwide hit album, *Jazz Samba*, which featured the bossa nova music of Antonio Carlos Jobim.

Childers's final words on Dorsey were "Buddy Rich tried all his life to be Tommy Dorsey, but he never quite made it. Sinatra [whom Childers worked for during his last years on the road] tried to be Tommy Dorsey. Neither of them made it. There was only one Tommy Dorsey."

The friction between Tommy and Charlie Shavers continued once they were home. Gene Cipriano, who joined the band soon after the disastrous Brazilian trip, remembers being both shocked and amused one night in Newfoundland when Shavers and Dorsey had one of their periodic rows: "Tommy said to Tino Barzie, 'Fire this guy!!' Charlie then said to Dorsey, 'You can kiss my big fat black ass!' Dorsey then threw him off the bus and snarled, 'Get to New York your own way.' I threw a twenty dollar bill out the window to Charlie and several other guys threw money out the window to him. It was cold. Snow was on the ground. Two weeks later Charlie was back on the band."

The Shavers-Dorsey relationship defied explanation. Baritone saxophonist Harvey Estrin believed, "Charlie probably respected Dorsey as a person, plus Tommy was paying him four hundred dollars a week, and he featured Charlie a lot."

Cipriano had great admiration for both men's musicianship. "When I took up the oboe," said Cipriano, "It was all air and wind. I'd see what Tommy would do—how he'd play a phrase. For any woodwind instrument, but especially the oboe, you really have to control it because there's only a small hole you put the air through. Charlie Shavers could do that, too— inhale and breathe at the same time. That's hard. I loved Charlie—playing with him was like a concert every night."

As with all musicians Dorsey respected, he couldn't do enough for Cipriano: "I drove with him in his Caddy once from New York to Boston. I had to take my draft physical in New Haven. He waited for me for an hour or two, and then we headed for Boston."

Cipriano also admired Dorsey's sense of humor. Dorsey, he recalls "wound up hating that car. He had picked it up new when we were in Detroit on a one-nighter tour. He had a big sign made up, which he had installed on the side of the car saying, 'This car is a lemon,' which included a drawing of a lemon. He told Lonnie [his band boy] to drive around Los Angeles so people could see it. It got back to Cadillac. They came and took it and gave him a brand-new car."

Cipriano laughed as he told of how lead alto Eddie Scalsi, who was also a barber, would panic whenever he cut Dorsey's hair. By the early 1950s, Dorsey had let his hair go gray and wore it in a crew cut, which was the style of the day: "He'd say, 'Eddie, you'd better do a good job or you're gone, man.' Eddie would get uptight and come back on the bandstand and say, 'I just cut his hair. I don't know if I did a good job or not.' Tommy knew he could get to you. He always liked to have somebody in the band he could pick on."

There were other signs of aging besides Tommy's graying hair; by the 1950s, Dorsey was no longer pitching in the hotly contested softball games with other big bands. The outcomes of the games were still very important to him. Les Brown's brother, Stumpy, a trombonist, related that after losing the fifth game of a deadlocked series with the Brown team in North Hollywood, Dorsey fired off a telegram to Harry James: "Would you be interested in two trumpet players for two outfielders?"

Even after his marriage to New and the beginnings of their family, however, Dorsey continued pursuing other women. New was very aware of that fact. She could no longer tour with him because she had to stay at home raising Susie and their little son, Steve.

New also understood that girl singers were often the target for bandleaders. Over the years, Dorsey had had affairs with various girl singers. Once, in Chicago, at the Stevens Hotel, where there were several towers, Dorsey ordered the band manager to aim a movie camera with a long lens directly from his room across the airshaft toward his room in a neighboring tower in order that he could shoot Dorsey having sex with the current girl singer!

Life on the road was hard for girl singers who had romantic involvements at home. This was the situation that faced Marietta Cox, who was secretly married to stage director Bob Marich when she joined the Dorsey band in 1952. Cox, who has enjoyed a continuing career as an actor on television and in movies and who serves as artistic director of the Houston Theater Center, said, "Fortunately, Bob came to see me when we were playing for any length of time on a location. We've been married fifty-one years so it didn't hurt the lifetime of the marriage."

Like many Dorsey veterans, she speaks of Dorsey's perfectionism: "I loved him. I'll tell you why—he was a very fastidious man. He didn't like anything sloppy. Why, he used to send his laundry to a cleaner in New York [the Bluebird Hand Laundry on Lexington Avenue] and to other ones in Boston and Philadelphia! If Tommy had been head of the CIA, September 11 never would have happened!"

Cox recalls Tommy's reaction when she tried imitating the singing style of Sarah Vaughan, who had become a star in the early 1950s. Cox recalled:

Tommy said to me, "Why do you come in behind the beat?" I said, "Well, that's the way Sarah Vaughan does it." "That's her style, not yours," he exclaimed. Then he said, "I don't want that. That's lazy, and it's sloppy. Hit it right!" I respected that because he was such a wonderful musician. . . . He also said, "Don't slide up on the notes. Just hit it right on. . . . You create your own phrasing by being truthful and real in interpreting the lyrics your own way. The way you speak is the way you should sing. It isn't someone else's feelings that you're expressing." I thought that was wonderful advice.

There was one thing I argued with him about. The people kept asking for "Jambalaya," which was a Jo Stafford hit. I didn't have the sense to learn the song. I hated it, but he told me, "I want you to learn it." He called my bluff one night and called the tune. I came up to the mic, and I kept singing, "Jambalaya, Jambalaya, Jambalaya"—I might have thrown in a "crawfish pie" or something. I was faking it. And he just fell out. He thought that was so funny.

Cox also pointed out, "He didn't like people who talked hip talk, jazz talk. He said, 'That's because usually they can't play.' He said they tried to talk like musicians instead of being musicians. If somebody got real carried away with themselves he'd say, 'Tino, get rid of that ace!'"

Cox credits working with Tommy with teaching her the things she needed to become a good director: "to tell a story, to get a style, and to be meticulous." Cox gave dancer and Broadway director Tommy Tune his first directing jobs, and she taught the noted actors Patrick Swayze, Dennis Quaid, and JoBeth Williams.

She was replaced by a seventeen-year-old singer named Lynn Roberts. Roberts had started singing in vaudeville theaters at the age of eight and was with Charlie Spivak at the age of fifteen. Barzie hired her the night he saw her singing at the Taft Hotel in New York with Vincent Lopez. A week later, she took the train to Fayetteville, North Carolina, to start working with the band.

The effervescent blond Roberts was a good singer who over a two-year period became an accomplished band singer under Dorsey's tutelage. She still is today. He once told her, "Get hurt a couple of times, then you'll know how to sing a love song." Roberts found her own way. She fell in love with Daryl "Flea" Campbell, the band's lead trumpeter, and they were married on March 2, 1954.

Roberts remembered how intimidating Dorsey was: "Just his voice. He asked if I knew certain tunes. The next day we were on the bus and on tour." This group of one-nighters led to the Roosevelt Hotel in New Orleans, the first of several hotel engagements that would include the Statler (formerly the Pennsylvania) in New York, the Claridge in Memphis, the Edgewater Beach in Chicago, and eventually the Last Frontier in Las Vegas. By now the girl singer's job paid $125 a week. Trumpeter Johnny Amarosa doubled as the boy singer for a while. He recorded some twenty-three records with Dorsey as a vocalist, including an especially good version of the 1950s ballad "How Do You Speak to an Angel," in addition to many more tracks as a trumpeter.

Eddie Fisher, Vic Damone, Johnny Ray, Patti Page, and Teresa Brewer now claimed the hearts and minds of young America. Young people then thought band singers were old-fashioned. Roberts kept up with what was then fashionable by wearing her blond hair in a ponytail.

On the night of her first wedding anniversary, while the band was playing at the Saxony Hotel in Miami Beach, she decided to wear her hair down, against Flea Campbell's advice. When Dorsey saw her, he said nothing but walked up to the trumpet section and said to Campbell, "I guess she doesn't care what anybody says, huh." Campbell explained that it was their anniversary. Dorsey replied, "You tell her that from tomorrow on she can wear her hair down—she's fired." Campbell automatically gave his notice. He worked out his remaining time with the band while Roberts sat at a table every night with her ponytail down.

She recalled, "Dorsey looked at me as if I didn't exist. I would flip my ponytail around like a little brat." But like all those with real talent, with Dorsey there was always the possibility of their eventual return.

With Dorsey it seems there was always the flip side. For all the instances of pettiness, there were other displays of generosity and respect. Several of Dorsey's musicians of the early 1950s who had played in other important big bands offered revealing comparisons of the ways Benny Goodman, Harry James, Glenn Miller, Charlie Barnet, Woody Herman, Les Brown, or Jimmy Dorsey, for instance, led their respective bands and the way Tommy Dorsey operated.

Drummer Jackie Mills, who spent two tenures during the 1950s with Dorsey, also worked for Harry James three times. As Mills remembered:

> During the year and a half I first worked for Dorsey, I got bronchitis and I stayed in Chicago. I was pretty sick. He called my hotel room and said, "I just want you to know [that] when you're better you've always got a job on this band." That made me feel wonderful. Just before that, I knew that a baritone saxophonist [Babe Fresk] got seriously injured in Louisiana. Tommy called

doctors all over the country that he knew and made sure that he got the best medical care. He wouldn't leave it alone until he was absolutely okay. He never forgot that kid. It made me feel he really cared about his guys, no matter how nasty he could get.

I don't mean to run anybody down, but if somebody had gotten injured like that on Harry's band, Harry wouldn't have lifted a finger. Harry would have said, "Pee Wee [Monte, his manager], take care of it." I don't think Harry was really close to anybody, whereas Tommy really got close to people.

Mills also said, "People like Tommy Dorsey and Charlie Barnet put the musical part ahead of the personal part. It was more important to them to respect how you played, your attitude, and your focus on music than it was whether you were a nice guy or on drugs or screwing somebody's wife. All they cared about was what kind of job you were doing."

Clarinetist and alto saxophonist Danny Tromboli remarked, "I remember Dorsey once saying, 'The four hours on the bandstand you owe me. What you do with the rest of your time is your business.' He expected the same perfection or near perfection that he expected of himself. There was no doubt that he was the boss. Tommy was the George Steinbrenner of the bandleaders, but I thought he was fair. I loved him."

Tromboli, who withstood the Brazilian debacle and spent fifteen months with the band, heard various examples of gratuitous cruelty on Benny Goodman's part, though he added, "In Benny's defense, his presence is still felt today in the clarinet world, and his technique is being challenged by Paquito D'Rivera, Eddie Daniels, and Ken Peplowski, and perhaps one or two others. Benny Goodman could not have played so lovingly on ballads if he was all bad. Surely, the same could be said of Tommy Dorsey."

Baritone saxophonist Danny Banks had a different slant on Dorsey and Goodman: "Tommy didn't get rich gracefully. . . . He had a similar background to Benny Goodman. Benny was brought up in the Jewish ghetto in Chicago. Tommy was from the coal-mining area. They didn't have much. Tommy all of a sudden was rich, and he was famous, and he didn't do it as well as his brother. He separated himself from the band. He began to treat the band like employees, wallpaper." Of other bandleaders, Banks observed, "In working for Jimmy, I noticed he was warmer. He cared more for the guys. . . . Among the leaders, I think my biggest influences really were Benny Goodman and Charlie Barnet. They really turned me out. There wasn't a problem adapting to Dorsey, having worked for them first, and besides that, he paid well."

The bassist Greig Stewart "Chubby" Jackson also recalled Dorsey's mean streak. The jovial Jackson had made his mark as the cheerleader of Woody Herman's Second and Third Herds, joined Dorsey during the fall of 1951 in another engagement that the band played at the Shamrock Hotel. Shortly afterward, he participated in a national radio show with the band. In reading a script for the show he played a character and feigned a Jewish accent. That irritated Dorsey, and a battle of words ensued.

Jackson recalled, "I don't believe in my entire life in the music business I had ever been talked to like that. This was despite the fact that the whole band broke up at what I was doing. My impression was that the reason he didn't like what I did was because he was anti-Semitic." (In Dorsey's defense, it must be pointed out that he had many Jewish musicians in his band throughout the years. They included Ziggy Elman, one of his all-time favorites, and Buddy Rich; despite the endless antagonism between Dorsey and Rich, anti-Semitism never seemed to be at the root of it.)

Jackson continued:

Tommy was an originator on trombone. I respected the fact that he had the pretty sound, and he never made many mistakes. But what he did play was always the same. He played what I call "music comfortable." I had come from Bill Harris [the trombone star of the Herman Herd]. What I saw in Tommy was a tremendous ego. It was his personal life, the way he handled himself and other people—that was terribly annoying to a certain sense of humanity.

With Woody's band, he would take advice from all of us. I would recommend different players. I was responsible for getting quite a few guys on that band. Woody would let the band make up those "head" arrangements. He was very aware of our being human beings. He once said to me, "You guys owned the band, but you know something, it was my band." The difference between Dorsey and Herman wasn't even talkable. It was that different.

For Art Depew, too, Dorsey was less interesting musically than other bandleaders: "The band I enjoyed the most was Charlie Barnet's because of Charlie's personality, and Harry's [James] band was very, very broad musically. Tommy Dorsey was about number 3. It was sophisticated, and we played good jazz, which was good for trumpet players, [but to me] Dorsey was number 3 because Barnet was a bit more modern. He was getting into some bebop, and then he still had the old. And the Harry James band, because of Harry, we played a lot of things that were crossovers, too. I must say, though,

Dorsey was always in command of the situation. Harry was, in his own way, but Harry was like a sideman down in front of the band."

Alto saxophonist Red Press remarked, "The thing you felt with Tommy was that this was royalty. When I got to play with Benny Goodman, it was a complete downer. Tommy was up, the energy was up. Benny was in his own fog. If you were asked, 'What do you like best about Benny Goodman,' it would have to be his playing. But if I had to be around either one of them, I'd rather be around Tommy Dorsey with all his hatred and stuff." (The "hatred" Press referred to was when Dorsey called Press a communist when it was suggested that Press was available to return to the band; Press acknowledges he was "a troublemaker in those days.")

Press, who is now in charge of the contract negotiations for the musicians' union on Broadway, once asked Dorsey in the middle of a performance, "How long do I have to be with the band before I can relax?" Dorsey answered, "When you're an alumnus you'll relax!"

Press didn't feel there was a pulsation—a swinging feeling—that a Goodman band had and the Dorsey band lacked: "I thought Benny's bands really swung a lot, but don't forget that with Tommy at the end I was playing Ernie Wilkins's charts. We were swinging, really swinging. With Benny you had a conductor with absolutely zero personality, zero energy."

Alto saxophonist and clarinetist Sal Libero joined Dorsey in 1955, directly after spending "almost nine very satisfying years with Les Brown." He said Brown, who hailed from Riverton, just west of Pottsville, once said to him, "I'm proud of my arrangements; I was just a fair clarinet player and alto player."

Libero had been one of the initial members of the Glenn Miller Air Force Band. As he saw it, "Glenn was a decent guy. To him music was more of a business-type thing. To Tommy the music was more important." (Miller once said to John Hammond, "Why do you judge me as a musician? All I'm interested in is making money.")

Speaking of Dorsey's greatness as a trombonist, Libero called him no less than "the messiah of the horn": "As a leader he also had a God-given talent." However, when asked by Dorsey which band he preferred, his or Les Brown's, Libero had to admit to Dorsey, "I think there's a little more fire in Les's band." In one of Dorsey's more candid moments, he declared, "That's what happens when your personnel [Brown's band] is more intact and it's been [that way] since the beginning." The sad truth was that Tommy's personal volatility and musical rigidity had denied him a similar stability in his own band. At this point he was also starting to feel an impermanence about his stardom and the future of his band. The precarious condition of the business was getting to him.

Maynard Ferguson, at seventy-seven, is still leading his Big Bop Nouveau band and still possesses much of the energy of a much younger bandleader, but he speaks with the wisdom of long experience and reflection. Ferguson started playing in American big bands after coming down from Montreal in 1949. He became a mainstay with Boyd Raeburn and Charlie Barnet and made a substantial name for himself playing incredible high-note solos with the Stan Kenton band of the early 1950s. He also spent some time with Jimmy Dorsey's band.

He recalled Jimmy's inviting him to have dinner with him one night. He was meeting Tommy at the Café Rouge at the Statler Hotel after Tommy's gig:

> Tommy came over to our booth, and he starts flattering me: "Jimmy told me you're a hell of a trumpet player. You had to abandon Canada?" I explained to him that I had opened for his band at the Montreal Forum with my band when I was fourteen years old. Sinatra, Ziggy Elman, and Buddy Rich were with him then. After the gig, I went over to this hangout for bands. Dorsey's guys were in their uniforms eating pastrami sandwiches. I ask this one guy, "Which one is Ziggy Elman?" He says, "He's the ugly son of a bitch, over there." The guy I asked was Sinatra, who I didn't recognize nor did I have any use for what the hell—a band singer. Come on! Where's the jazz trumpet player? And of course, Ziggy heard everything he said, and all the musicians laughed.
>
> Jimmy proceeded to tell his brother, "You ought to hear him play." Then Tommy said, "Well, listen, kid. Jimmy was telling me that you're probably going to end up having your own band in this country. Let me give you a little advice: First of all, you're the star of that goddamn band, do you understand? I hear that you go over well with the audience. I don't give a fuck whether it's a singer or a saxophone player or a drummer, when they start killing the audience, you get rid of them right then."

Ferguson recalled, "I was too inexperienced to realize what he was saying was 'Look at all the guys I have lost.' Whatever the direction of his conversation, you can draw your own conclusion. At the same time, Jimmy's looking at me, shaking his head like, 'Oh boy. Tommy's on a tangent again!'"

Dorsey's words to Maynard Ferguson on bandleading sound like the ravings of a tired old man. He was only in his mid-forties, far from an old man, but having spent the better part of thirty years on the road was starting to take its toll. He looked like a beaten gray fox. In another example of his iron will, he had stopped smoking cold turkey after about a quarter of a century of smoking two packs a day.

But Tommy was never really "clean." His use of uppers, as well as codeine and turpenhydrate, which had by then replaced alcohol on a daily basis for the better part of a decade, certainly contributed to his excessive mood swings. (They also, Sol Schlinger observed, "made him yak a lot and got him from town to town.")

In the winter of 1952, in the midst of a Statler engagement, Tommy checked into a Manhattan hospital for removal of his gall bladder. Trombonist Sammy Nestico, later an outstanding arranger for the Count Basie band in the 1970s and 1980s, was hired to play Dorsey's solos. Nestico took a leave from his air force duties at Bolling Air Force Base, where he was a technical sergeant. He remembered, "Tommy was my idol. I had memorized all his solos."

Pianist Doug Talbert declared, "Sammy played with such beauty and gorgeous tonality; we were all mesmerized by his superb talent. Naturally, Dorsey heard the news of Nestico's high level of performance. This led him to return to the bandstand quicker than anticipated."

Tommy's jealousy began to taunt him. It wasn't about Jimmy now. There was a new group of bandleaders emerging: Ray Anthony, Ralph Flanagan, Ralph Marterie, Billy May, and Buddy Morrow, all of whom had come into recent prominence. Doug Talbert remembered that in the midst of one tour Dorsey instructed the bus driver to turn off a disk jockey show that happened to be programming several of Morrow's popular RCA records, which was being piped throughout the bus. It obviously bothered him that one of his best former sidemen was now more popular on records than he was.

As a result, he wanted to hire Morrow's popular band singer, Frankie Lester, who turned him down. "I had worked for him for two months in 1945," Lester recalled, "But he fired me, saying, 'Kid, I have a lot of things I want to do. I don't have time to train you.'" Tino Barzie told Lester, "You're the only singer who ever turned down Tommy Dorsey."

In the fall of 1952, a concert date in Bridgeport, Connecticut, included the Dorsey band in a "battle of the bands" with those of Les Brown, Ray Anthony, and Ralph Marterie. "Tommy was worried and bitching," Talbert recalled. "He put us through hell for about ten days before the date, rehearsing and rehearsing [after a night of playing a job] from one to three or four in the morning on a Bill Finegan chart or some other wild arrangement to get ready. In my opinion, Les Brown turned out to be the winner of the battle."

By 1953, Tommy Dorsey had been leading his own band for almost eighteen years. Dedication, leadership, extraordinary musicianship, and an eye for new talent had carried him and the band through countless triumphs and only a few down times. He had created a unique approach to the trombone and could caress a melody like no one else. Among musicians he had a solid reputation for always leading first-rate orchestras. To the American public he was a household name. Fame had brought him as close, after all these years, as he would ever get to personal and artistic fulfillment.

8

The Final Reunion

Thomas, you must help The Brother!
—MOM DORSEY

WITH THE inauguration of Dwight D. "Ike" Eisenhower on January 20, 1953, America had a president who perfectly fit the times. The smiling former general, who had led the "Crusade in Europe" to defeat Nazi Germany in World War II, attempted to alter the status quo domestically as little as possible so as not to run counter to the conformity that pervaded the decade. Until he was compelled to send federal troops to enforce the integration of public schools in Little Rock, Arkansas, in 1957, he and the country had for the most part avoided the serious social problems that were festering underneath the placid surface.

The 1950s were indeed dedicated to banishing the shadows—real, exaggerated, or imaginary. Nevertheless, the decade led to McCarthyism on the one hand and the Korean War on the other. The placidity of the decade was described by Joe Klein, in his best-selling biography of Bill Clinton, *The Natural*, as "the deep narcotic prosperity that enveloped the nation after World War II." These regressive aspects of the epoch in some way provided a natural environment for Tommy Dorsey to prosper playing the music of the previous era.

At the same time, a new and revolutionary jazz movement was emerging in California under the umbrella of "West Coast Jazz." Such instruments as the flute, oboe, bassoon, and even the cello were brought into use in a jazz

255

context. Eschewing the hard-bop movement then developing in New York, in Los Angeles, Gerry Mulligan, the baritone saxophonist, led an almost chamber-music-like, pianoless quartet that featured trumpeter Chet Baker. In San Francisco, the classically oriented jazz pianist Dave Brubeck introduced further-out time signatures, such as six-eight, seven-eight, and eight-nine, with his octet, his trio, and later his quartet, which featured alto saxophonist Paul Desmond.

It's been said that there was Paris in the '20s and New York in the '50s. The early 1950s could also justifiably be termed the "Jazz Age," insofar as it encompassed *the* music of the hip college crowd. It was also the last decade in which various forms of pure jazz were commercial. New York continued as the center of the existence of jazz, but now, college students made up an important segment of the weekend audience.

On Fifty-first Street between Broadway and Seventh Avenue, the commercial jazz nightclub Basin Street featured the likes of the Benny Goodman Septet. Around the corner and up Broadway a block and a half was Birdland, the center of the bebop culture, where Count Basie's New Testament band displayed its bluesy wares featuring Joe Williams, who was equally adept at singing blues or ballads. For piano rooms there were the Composer, where Billy Taylor and Phineas Newborn held forth, and the Embers. Situated directly across the street from the nighttime home of the "swells," El Morocco, the Embers was where the free-swinging Erroll Garner began to reach commercial acceptance. At the Hickory House, pianist/composer Marian McPartland made her initial impact in New York.

On weekends downtown, the Central Plaza and the Stuyvesant Casino were the home of traditional jazz. Ex-swing-band stars and Dixieland stalwarts (Buck Clayton, Jo Jones, J. C. Higginbotham, and Miff Mole) worked in tandem in a jam session format. At Eddie Condon's, on West Third Street in Greenwich Village, Wild Bill Davison and his mob, which included Condon playing guitar, was a mainstay for Dixieland fans.

Mabel Mercer, although not really a jazz singer, appealed to the sprinkling of collegians who were a bit more sophisticated, through her appearances at various East Side boites. Singing ballads, seated in a chair and accompanied only by pianist Jimmy Lyons, she could interpret Cole Porter and many others better than anyone else.

And for those who still enjoyed dancing to a big band that also featured some jazz, there was the Café Rouge of the Statler Hotel at Thirty-third Street and Seventh Avenue, where Tommy Dorsey and His Orchestra held forth.

With all of this wide diversion in the various types of jazz, Dorsey, Woody Herman, Stan Kenton, and, of course, Count Basie and Duke Ellington still believed in the validity of the big band. It was what they knew how to lead.

Meanwhile, black urban teenagers were discovering a new music called rhythm and blues (R&B), which had originated in the South and in the black ghettos. DJs played R&B tunes like "Cryin' in the Chapel" by the Orioles and "Money, Honey" by the Drifters, which introduced young whites to this emerging black music. Beginning in 1954, R&B would move away from its blues base in several distinct directions. Its randy side was exemplified by Big Joe Turner's powerful anthem "Shake, Rattle, and Roll," Big Mama Thornton's "Hound Dog," and Faye Adams's "Shake a Hand"; it's smooth side in records like the Moonglows' "Sincerely," "Earth Angel" by the Penguins, and Johnny Ace's "Pledging My Love," songs which used street corner harmony, in what would become known as doo-wop. A succession of Ruth Brown hits like "Mama, He Treats Your Daughter Mean" and Chuck Berry's number-one R&B hit "Maybeline" began crossing over to become popular with white teenagers.

Phil Gallo, associate editor of *Variety*, recently commented, "I would say that the young white audience looked for something more in their music than what their parents listened to, so they turned toward black music. And what they found was a wide variety of music. What really opened things up was the last pure blues smash hit, 'Things That I Used to Do' by Guitar Slim, arranged by Ray Charles, and most important, Charles's 'I Got a Woman,' which became a pop hit in 1955. This was the first gospel tune adapted into R&B and made popular."

Less than a year later, a young white performer would emerge and change pop music forever. Tommy Dorsey's radar would eventually pick up on the phenomenon of Elvis Presley, but he couldn't have possibly fathomed the profound impact the new pop music would have on his own career.

Meanwhile, Tommy Dorsey maintained his devoted following. During a two-week booking at the Statler in March 1953, a host of bandleaders came in to see the Dorsey band—Harry James, Ray Anthony, Duke Ellington, Stan Kenton, Woody Herman, Johnny Long, and Neal Hefti. Hefti, a versatile arranger who had previously played in the Dorsey trumpet section, wrote the "The Most Beautiful Girl in the World" chart, which later became the last of Tommy Dorsey's 186 pop chart hits.

Pianist Doug Talbert was given the honorary title of "assistant leader" by Dorsey as he led the band on a nightly basis during the dinner set at the

Statler. He wrote an arrangement of "September Song," an appropriate tune to play for the early audience. Talbert recalled seeing Mom Dorsey there frequently. He noticed that Jackie Gleason would often join her: "Once or twice a night Jackie would borrow Lee Castle's trumpet to play with the band. I was expecting to hear a beautiful solo after he requested a twelve-bar blues in B-flat. He started blowing intermittently—nothing but B-flats at strange intervals with no conception of time or feeling. That's when I knew the 'Great One' had no musical talent whatsoever, but he was an absolute master of comedy and creativity that was unmatched on television."

Gleason could neither read nor write music, but playing one-fingered piano he had an uncanny feel for a melody, exemplified by the beautiful and haunting theme he composed (with the aid of arranger Pete King), "Melancholy Serenade," which became the familiar signature of his television shows. An incurable romantic, he also conducted a series of highly successful "mood" albums of standards for Capitol Records, starting with *Music For Lovers Only*, in which Bobby Hackett played a series of brilliant melancholy solos on cornet. Gleason's love for big bands led to other former big-band soloists, such as alto saxophonist Toots Mondello, being featured on subsequent albums.

Gleason's various theater and nightclub engagements with the Dorseys, and various drinking escapades with them, led to a friendship, which had become close by the early 1950s. They often ran into each other at various show business haunts, such as Frankie and Johnny's, in the theater district, but especially at Toots Shor's, where la crème de la crème of the nation's sports and entertainment figures spent considerable off time. Shor's was the place where Gleason reigned supreme.

Gleason's friendship with the Dorseys also owed considerable to their common Irish heritage. Once they became bosom buddies, Gleason would make unexpected excursions to dance dates in New England to see his favorite band perform. Janie New contended that much of Gleason's bigger-than-life personality was more than a little based on Tommy Dorsey.

Mike Dann, who would be CBS's head of programming from 1963 to 1970, at that time was director of program sales for the network, which put him in direct contact with Gleason. Dann said, "Tommy was an idol in Gleason's eyes because of his importance in music. He felt that Tommy Dorsey was the greatest bandleader of the 1930s and 1940s, and that there was no one like him. Since Gleason really did have nine lives, if he came back as a musician, he would have been Tommy Dorsey—there's no doubt about it!"

Talbert remembers hearing talk around the band that Tommy and Jimmy were going to get back together. Jackie Gleason had a future television show in mind for them. He wanted the brothers to reunite as "The Fabulous Dorseys." Initially, Tommy was opposed to the idea since the two brothers hardly ever spoke, but toward the end of the Statler engagement, Gleason, Tino Barzie, Tommy, and Jimmy Dorsey agreed in principle to the idea of a show. Presumably, Mom Dorsey also had a say in this matter. (Tommy might not have always agreed with her, but he was always open to her counsel.) *Billboard* and *DownBeat* soon began speculating about whether the Dorseys might get back together.

In fact, Tess may have pushed the idea of a reunion more than anyone. She was financially dependent on her two sons—Tommy paid the rent of $135 a month on her East Eighty-first Street, New York apartment, and Jimmy paid her living expenses and gave her $25 a week to help pay for a nurse companion. There was more to it than this. In her mind, family was inseparable and her sons' interests were her own.

She recognized that Jimmy was in dire straits at this juncture. He had just had most of his stomach removed after a severe case of ulcers. He was drinking heavily, the Internal Revenue Service was after him for back taxes, and he was bankrupt, partly due to his last manager's having stolen from him. He had also been forced to close down his orchestra.

Tommy sent Tino Barzie to New York to check on Jimmy, who was living at the Warwick Hotel now that he was divorced. Barzie remembered, "Cigarette smoke, empty bottles all over the place. He had a beard, and his hair looked terrible. Jimmy was totally gray. He always dyed his hair." Tommy instructed Barzie to get Jimmy out of the hotel and to pay his overdue bill, as well as the rent on his Cadillac. Barzie flew with Jimmy down to Atlanta, where Tommy's band was headlining at a new club, Joe Cotton's Steak Ranch. "After a few days in the hotel he began traveling with us on the bus, and he started to feel better," Barzie recalled.

Tommy may have ordered Barzie to straighten out Jimmy's affairs, but Connie Motko and her husband, Bill, contend that Tommy's orders to Barzie stemmed directly from Tess Dorsey. As Bill recalled it, "She talked to Tommy on the phone and told him, 'Thomas, you must help The Brother!'"

Almost eighteen years after their celebrated split on the bandstand of the Glen Island Casino, the Dorsey brothers were indeed back working together. Their complicated brand of brotherly love and the strong maternal influence were the determining factors.

Tommy and Barzie devised a plan to get Jimmy back in good playing form on a nightly basis. Publicity would help establish a new fan base, and then Jackie Gleason had big plans for the brothers. Their reunion began with two dances and a concert at the University of Virginia on April 17 and 18, 1953, as part of Easters, the University's biggest party weekend of the year. The Saturday-afternoon concerts on these major weekends more often than not consisted of students drinking whiskey from a paper cup or swigging from a bottle while sitting on blankets on the floor along with their dates, digging the music.

During the weekend, Tommy was given a plaque for being selected as the favorite bandleader to ever play at the University of Virginia. He had made numerous appearances at the university over the years (including two in the last three years) and had created a sterling reputation with the successive dance chairmen who bought the bands for the three major weekends. Jo Stafford, who had worked there with Dorsey in the early 1940s, recalled, "Oh, what a beautiful place. I can still remember it after all these years."

At the Saturday-afternoon Memorial Gymnasium concert, which I witnessed, the beauty and pathos of the way Tommy delivered his theme song and "Quiet Please," a vehicle for Jackie Mills's drum solo, were thrilling to hear. Jimmy Dorsey was essentially a guest star, playing only a few songs, while Tommy offered a program of his greatest hits.

Barzie recalled how Tommy introduced his brother: "He'd say, 'We've got a little extra surprise for you. We've got somebody in the audience tonight we're going to bring up here. In my estimation, he's the world's greatest alto saxophonist. I want you to say hello to my brother Jimmy.' The people went crazy. Jimmy would come up onstage with his horns, play a couple of tunes with Tommy, and then do a Dixieland number. We started out with 'Sweet Georgia Brown,' I think it was." Doug Talbert recalled, "When he joined us, the only chart we had was 'Ruby,' the theme from the [Jennifer Jones] movie, which featured both Tommy and Jimmy."

In one of their next gigs, Tommy and Jimmy sat in with Ray Anthony's band at a Duke University concert. Anthony had worked for Jimmy's band after leaving Glenn Miller, when he was only nineteen years old. The trumpeter, who continues to lead a big band that works in Los Angeles, Las Vegas, and occasionally on cruises, refers to Tommy Dorsey as "the reigning king of the big-band era." He added, "I don't think Jimmy wanted to be out front [just] like Tex Beneke—never bandleaders, always sidemen. Some guys wanted to be out front. Tommy was one—'This is my band. This is my thing.' There was never any doubt as to who was in charge."

The band headed to New York to rehearse the libraries of both Dorsey orchestras before starting out on a midwestern tour. Adhering to Tommy's wishes, Jimmy had to get rid of all the members of *his* last band except for trombonist Jimmy Henderson (later the leader of the Glenn Miller Orchestra during the 1980s) and saxophonist Buzz Brauner, who replaced two of Tommy's sidemen. In a telling aside, Danny Banks remembered, "Jimmy Dorsey once told me, 'Anybody that I hire or Tommy hires, [it] automatically means they're going to work for both of us, and one of them will steal from the other.'"

Veteran Dorsey trombonist Valey "Tak" Takvorian believes, "The band got better with those few personnel changes. The writing also got better [when people like] Deane Kincaide, Ernie Wilkins, and Howard Gibeling began delivering new charts."

Soon it was abundantly clear that time hadn't changed the power relationship between the brothers. Jimmy was essentially a high-paid sideman— Tommy started Jimmy at $500 a week, eventually raising him to $1,200 a week—but he got no piece of the gross earnings of the band. At first, Barzie came up with the highfalutin billing of "The Sentimental Gentleman— Tommy Dorsey and His Orchestra Featuring the World's Greatest Saxophonist, Jimmy Dorsey." It soon became "The Fabulous Dorseys, Tommy Dorsey and His Orchestra Featuring Jimmy Dorsey." To the public, the billing didn't matter; they were pleased to have Tommy and Jimmy back together.

Tommy had "The Brother" right where he wanted him—obligated to him. In my view, he felt there was no injustice in this. He remembered that early on, Jimmy was the guy with the talent. He knew he had to work on developing his legato approach on the trombone while Jimmy was out amusing himself on the golf links. He knew Jimmy didn't know how to run a band like he did. Tommy also knew that Jimmy wanted everybody to like him. He knew full well that that's not the way to lead a successful band. He realized that you can't let your musicians ever have the upper hand.

When he and Jimmy first split up, Bing Crosby gave him a great opportunity, but he knew he had made it all happen by himself with *his* band. Sure, Jimmy had made it with his own band, but he couldn't sustain it, especially when the business turned bad after the war. Tommy knew he could handle things much better; it was time to show Jimmy who had really turned out on top. He was willing to take care of the little son of a bitch, like mom wanted, but he knew it was really his band, and it would succeed because of him alone.

In an attempt to keep their appearances together peaceful, on a typical dance date Tommy worked out a format whereby Jimmy would lead the band for the first thirty minutes of the opening set with a series of swing arrangements to get the evening under way, while Tommy remained in his dressing room. Tommy then came onstage to take over the band and play his arrangements. That way they circumvented their age-old disagreement about tempos. It also allowed them each to please their fans by playing their individual hits. Occasionally, the brothers would break out their trumpets and play duets.

Despite Tommy's clear dominance, his jealousy of Jimmy still flared up on occasion. Doug Talbert recalled that on one of their first gigs after the reconciliation, when Jimmy got an especially enthusiastic reception from the audience, Tommy came up to him and said, "Doug, who pays you?" Talbert replied, "You do, Tom." Dorsey then said irritably, "Remember that!" The pianist added, "Tommy preferred I play once in a while with the feeling of Fats Waller or Count Basie, but he didn't want me to get too far out with my jazz; Jimmy was so free [when he was on the bandstand] the band sounded completely different. When Tommy took over, everybody would stiffen up."

A national television audience was now made aware of the Dorseys' reunion on May 23, 1953, when The Fabulous Dorseys debuted on CBS-TV's number-one Saturday-night program, *The Jackie Gleason Show*. On the show, which aired from 8 to 9 P.M., the band was featured in the classic "Honeymooners" segment with Ralph Kramden (Gleason) and his sidekick Norton (played by the brilliant Art Carney), who described himself as "a subterranean engineer." The incomparable twosome paraded about in their coonskin caps. (This was during the Davey Crockett craze following the success of *that* television show.)

The premise of the sketch was that Kramden had decided to hire Tommy Dorsey to play for the bus drivers' benefit ball while his wife, Alice (Audrey Meadows), had booked Jimmy's band. Both brothers show up, wind up mending their long-standing feud, and play together with the band "Dry Bones," "Ruby," and finally "South Rampart Street Parade," which called for a Dixieland free-for-all. CBS saw that the Dorseys' appearance created a favorable rating.

The band continued to tour. The night before and the night after the Gleason show, The Fabulous Dorseys, with returning singers Gordon Polk and Lynn Roberts, drew twenty-six hundred adoring fans at the Rustic Cabin (the club where Harry James had discovered Frank Sinatra), across the Hudson River, near the George Washington Bridge. Traffic jams around the club caused the local police to be called. *Variety* spread the news of the successful weekend engagement.

Later that spring, the band returned to the Midwest on a one-nighter tour, and after playing the venerable Claridge Hotel Memphis, where new arrangements were tried out, it headed for Texas, then still the source of many one-nighters. Finally reaching Los Angeles in August, Tommy recorded several single records for Decca. Since Jimmy was under contract to Columbia, he couldn't be included. (In those years recording contracts were truly exclusive; artists signed to one label weren't allowed to participate in records on another label.)

Tommy and the band also recorded eight selections adapted from classical pieces, including "Fruit Cocktail" (Tchaikovsky's "Dance of the Sugar Plum Fairy"), "Grieg's Grotto" ("Anitra's Dance"), and so on for an album. While at work on another Dorsey album, Bill Finegan contributed some of the arrangements. Nelson Riddle (then starting to write for Frank Sinatra) helped Finegan finish work on a new version of "I'm Getting Sentimental over You" when Finegan experienced an acute case of writer's block.

While in Hollywood, the Dorseys filmed another inane Universal band short subject called "Dorsey Brothers Encore." Early on in the story line, the contentious brothers break into an argument in the producer's office.

This activity in Hollywood was followed by a string of successful one-nighters, filled with adoring fans. When Doug Talbert left in 1953, Tommy made Lee Castle assistant leader of the band, while also featuring him on Dixieland tunes. Tommy treated trumpeter Castle like a godson (Tess Dorsey called him "my Italian son"). After leaving Tommy's band years before, Castle had established himself with Glenn Miller, Artie Shaw, and Benny Goodman; when he tried to make it with his own band, Tommy pointedly made an effort to help him in his new venture. When, surprisingly, it failed and he returned to the Dorsey band, Tommy said to him, "I was a pretty smart guy." Castle asked, "What do you mean?" He replied, "You're here, aren't you?"

Paul Cohen, Flea Campbell, and John McCormick were Castle's trumpet section mates. With the band's expansion to four trumpets, and when Johnny Amarosa was doubling as a singer, for a time there were five trumpets. For years, Paul Cohen had been regarded as an exceptional lead trumpeter. This was his third stint with Dorsey. Charlie Shavers had originally recommended him to Dorsey. During one of his several hiatuses from Dorsey, Shavers had distinguished himself playing both open horn and muted solos as a member of Oscar Peterson's sextet, which backed Fred Astaire in the classic album *The Fred Astaire Story* in 1952.

Cohen recalled the second time Dorsey fired Shavers; it stemmed once again from Shavers's falling asleep on a gig: "He said, 'Hey Charlie, get off the bandstand.' Then there was Tommy's famous harangue, 'Tino, warm up that airplane! Get off! You're through.' I felt bad for Charlie—the way Tommy did it—no class."

At seventy-eight, Cohen, who continues to lead a big band in south Florida, candidly remarked, "I learned to play first trumpet with Dorsey, so I could last because he was such a taskmaster. I learned how to go from nine to one [the hours of most dance dates] because that was the ultimate test of a lead trumpet player in a band. After a while he got to like me a little bit—not too much, just enough to say, 'Hey Callahan, what's up with that number?' That was his nickname for me 'cause Cohen was too much for him to slur. I achieved status—he made me an Irishman!"

Though Janie New was steadfast in claims that Tommy didn't abuse pills, Cohen recalls Tommy giving him some uppers in the midst of a long and grueling tour: "I was kind of beat. He tried to either do me a good thing or a bad thing, which turned out to be a bad thing. I took that pill, and man I was praying to God for me to come down and let me stay down! I had never experienced this feeling! Jesus, it was awful! But he never said anything to me." However, when Cohen gave his notice, Dorsey was furious and chased him around the Café Rouge.

Cohen remembered Flea Campbell as "a very good trumpet player." (His nickname, acquired during a stint in the Air Force, stemmed from his slight build.) Campbell, then married to Lynn Roberts, split the lead chair with John Frosk when Cohen departed. Dorsey paid him two hundred dollars a week.

Eventually, Charlie Shavers came back to the band. Flea Campbell related that a few months later, during an engagement at the Cal Neva Lodge in Lake Tahoe, Charlie started drinking in the bar at two in the afternoon and climbed on the bandstand at 8 P.M. in his tuxedo and yellow shoes. Dorsey ordered him to leave and told him to get some coffee. "No, Man. I'm cool," Shavers replied. Dorsey called, "Someone to Watch over Me," but Shavers was so wrecked he couldn't play his solo. Dorsey then instructed Campbell that Shavers was not to play anymore that night. Every time Shavers picked up his horn, Dorsey would push his arms down with the slide of his trombone.

The next morning the band prepared to leave on the bus at 10 A.M. Dorsey was in the driver's seat. Shavers came out from the motel with his bag and his horn. "You don't work here anymore," said Dorsey as he shut the door and the bus took off. But Shavers returned again a month later.

Campbell observed that Tommy constantly looked out for "The Brother." "He bent over backward for him," he contended. "Jimmy was hurting. He felt like he was a charity case. Tommy said to him, 'You don't have to ride on the bus.' He got him a car and had the band boy drive him. Sometimes they got into a shouting match, as happened one night in Las Vegas over some arrangements. Tommy started to have stuff written for both of them. Every week two or three came in. Tommy would come out after Jimmy did an hour after intermission, and they finished together. But they didn't agree musically at all."

As a leader, Tommy continued to inspire the same mix of feelings. Campbell said:

> I still think of Tommy a lot, [all these] years later. You couldn't get close to him. Only once or twice did I have a one-on-one conversation with him. When he was on the stage, you knew everything was taken care of. . . . He worked us hard, but he was working hard, too. . . . My whole life has been the big bands, and to me he personified what a big-band leader should be like. Every once in a while the band would have a lapse. The guys weren't paying attention or they'd start what he called "goofing." He'd say, "I'm going to show you how to goof. I'm not signing the checks." He did that quite often, which was kind of funny. You eventually got paid, but he made it uncomfortable for a while, and Tino had to bail everyone out of the motels.

Campbell said that despite all the money being made from *Stage Show*, recordings, and the regular gigs, there wasn't a great spirit in the band: "I would say most of the guys were professionals, and they knew they had a good thing, but I don't think many guys liked him. I liked him."

Trumpeter John Frosk, whom Tommy called Cyclops because of the thick glasses he wore then, said, "We used to live in fear. In the winter, when we slept on the bus, sometimes the guys would hang their clothes on the windows. He hated that. He used to follow us in his car, stop the bus, and have an inspection."

On Friday, December 4, 1953, the band opened at the Statler Hotel. Despite the fact that there was a week-long newspaper strike taking place, radio and television exposure caused the opening night to be a sellout and reminiscent of the prewar era. NBC was so enamored of the Dorseys that six radio remote broadcasts took place from the hotel during December.

Jackie Gleason continued his fervent interest in the Dorsey brothers by booking them on his last CBS-TV show of 1953. Two years earlier Gleason had appeared six times as a guest on Sinatra's ill-fated 1951–1952 CBS-TV show during the time when Jackie was starring in his own *Dumont Cavalcade of Stars* show. This show brought Gleason to the attention of Bill Paley, president of CBS, who signed him to an unprecedented $11 million contract in 1952 and gave him his own show. The "Great One" (the label Orson Welles and then Lucille Ball bestowed upon him) soon coined the phrases "How sweet it is!" and "Away we go!" The latter became the signal for festivities to begin on his weekly television show.

The December 26, 1953, telecast found the Dorsey brothers and the band as the centerpiece of a forty-five-minute segment of "The Honeymooners." The premise was that Alice has found a briefcase belonging to Tommy on the bus. She in turn gets in touch with Tino Barzie in order to let him know that she has found it. Soon after that, Tommy and Jimmy come to the Kramdens' apartment to retrieve the briefcase. Jimmy mentions how much trouble he and Tommy had in finding the place until they heard Ralph's booming voice. After a few minutes of pleasantries, Norton suddenly enters the apartment and asks if the Dorseys will play for the upcoming Sewer Workers Union dance. As Norton explains it, "We hold the dance outside. No one would rent us a hall."

In appreciation for finding the briefcase, which contains "most of our new arrangements," according to Tommy, the Dorseys invite Ralph and Alice to be their guests New Year's Eve at the Statler. Ralph feigns stomach pains as an excuse from having to drive his normal bus route on New Year's Eve. In a throwback to an old burlesque skit, Ralph's boss, who is also attending the performance at the Statler, is appalled to discover Kramden and Norton after the three of them read newspapers and converse back and forth while waiting outside the Café Rouge. The boss immediately fires Kramden, but the boss's wife intervenes and smoothes things over.

The Dorsey band then begins playing "Ain't She Sweet?" when suddenly Gordon Polk falls down during his rendition of the song. The camera catches Tommy seething as Polk falls. This is followed by the band's playing "Puddle Wump," featuring Tommy's fast trombone chorus, followed by Jimmy's choruses on alto saxophone and clarinet. Tommy remarks how this tune has been a sensation in every ballroom they've played. The show closes with the inevitable "Auld Lang Syne."

Here was a rare combination of masterful situation comedy that segued seamlessly into an intelligently framed presentation of a big band. This was live television that well represented the era.

Aside from Jackie Gleason's shows, almost no other television shows were providing big bands with any exposure. Moreover, TV continued to keep people at home and out of the few ballrooms, theaters, and hotels that still featured them. NBC, after showing favorable ratings from its various radio broadcasts from the Statler with the Dorseys, took a further step against the onslaught of television by making a further attempt to feature "live" entertainment featuring big bands. It was called *The NBC Monitor All Star Parade of Bands* and began with the Dorseys broadcasting from the Statler on January 2, 1954, and after that from various locations on the road.

Decca Records had seen the error of its ways in expecting Tommy's records to sell and decided not to re-sign Tommy; the possibility of adding Jimmy offered absolutely no attraction to the company. The disaffection was mutual. One day Tommy moaned, "Jesus Christ, my records aren't released; they escape." Another one of his complaints was "If they had put the secret of the atomic bomb on Decca, the Russians never would have got it!" It was his way of explaining that the company wasn't promoting or distributing his records properly.

Tommy's business sense came to his aid. He developed his own idea about future recording contracts. He wanted to own his masters and lease them to whatever company signed him. In January 1954, despite the severely limited market for dance bands, he and Jimmy were able to make a deal with a new record company, Bell Records, a subsidiary of Pocket Books, Inc. (owned by Simon & Schuster), to release single records. That left the door open for Tommy to seek an album deal. In search of a new market for its singles, Bell sold them on newsstands for a mere thirty-nine cents. The Dorseys' record of "My Friend, the Ghost," made the pop chart as number thirty for a week in April 1954.

Phoebe Jacobs, now vice president of the Louis Armstrong Educational Foundation, involved in perpetuating the importance of the heritage of jazz immortals, worked at Bell Records in the early 1950s. She recalled the recording session when Sy Oliver altered the lyrics of the Leonard Bernstein–Comden and Green song "Sisters," from the Rosalind Russell musical Broadway hit *Wonderful Town*, to "Brothers," for Tommy and Jimmy to sing and play together: "Mom Dorsey came to the recording session with a priest friend of hers. The two guys were absolutely like two boys. You would never know they had [ever] had an argument. As soon as they were handed the lead sheets by Sy, they were sensational together."

Jacobs remembers how attractive Tommy was: "He wasn't particularly what you'd call ravishingly handsome like Clark Gable, or one of those guys, but he was very macho. Oh my God, his clothes! This man always used aftershave lotion [Green Water], and he always looked so clean. And he knew how to be extremely courteous and wonderful to women." She recalled his devotion to his mother: "He constantly called his mother. He was so family-oriented. . . . It was just unbelievable."

Jacobs knew Sy Oliver, who was then vice president of A&R (artists and repertoire) at Decca, an astonishing position for any black executive to hold in any business during the 1950s. Jacobs spoke of Oliver's vulnerability: "Despite being married to a white woman [the former Lillian Ventimiglia, an Italian woman who replaced Mary Clark in The Sentimentalists], he did not wear his color and society's treatment of color well. Sy Oliver was bruised. He didn't function with great self-esteem even though he walked like a warrior. His body language was 'Man! I'm a winner.' Inside, he was crumbling and hurting." She remembers the Dorsey band's run at the Statler: "Tommy had some sensational solos with Charlie Shavers. The band played for dancing, and everybody adored it. . . . Tommy conducted his orchestra as if he were John Philip Sousa."

Like others, Jacobs remembered Dorsey's deep respect for Oliver:

Tommy treated Sy as if he was a hero. I remember once in an elevator at 711 Fifth Avenue he almost clobbered a man who told Sy he had to use the service entrance. I was frightened because Tommy was like a machine gun. Sy had such humility and dignity. He dressed beautifully and had beautiful manners. I recognized that Sy was smitten with his relationship with Tommy. Tommy would always bring out the best in Sy. He'd always come through for Tommy, and Tommy knew he would. In fact, I always relished the challenge 'cause he was anxious to prove to Tommy that he could do anything he asked him to do. I would say that Tommy Dorsey had a greater appreciation of Sy Oliver than Sy had of himself.

On the single records for Bell, the Dorseys revisited the past with new, two-sided versions of their respective hits from the 1930s and 1940s, "Marie" (with a Gordon Polk vocal) and "Green Eyes" (with Lynn Roberts attempting to duplicate Helen O'Connell's definitive version). These were among a grand total of twenty-six tracks the Dorseys recorded for the label.

Arthur Shimkin, president of Bell, sent a complimentary copy of "Marie" and another Irving Berlin song, "Love You Didn't Do Right by Me," to the composer. Like Richard Rodgers and other famous composers, Berlin was adamant about the way his songs were recorded. In an angry telephone call to Shimkin, Berlin bellowed out, "Tell that Irish bastard not to fuck around with my song." He demanded that "Love" be rerecorded without a change in the ending. Shimkin, in turn, called Dorsey to inform him of Berlin's unhappiness over the recording. Dorsey countered with "Tell that Jew bastard that I fucked around with 'Marie' and without that there wouldn't have been any song." Despite his usual bravado, Dorsey did, in fact, rerecord the song. After all of that, it didn't much matter. Both versions flopped. There would be no more hit single records for the Dorseys.

Herbert John "Jackie" Gleason proved to be the best friend any bandleader could ever have. Decades later, he told Morley Safer during the course of a *60 Minutes* profile, "When you're number one, number two, or number three, there's nothing that your little heart desires that you can't get." Gleason took full advantage of that fact and got exactly what he wanted in 1954 with *Stage Show*, the CBS-TV variety show, as his summer replacement. The network probably considered it as a trial run for a possible fall show for the Dorseys. It was the perfect showcase for the Dorseys and was seen from July 3 to September 18.

Jack Gould, the TV critic of the *New York Times*, in reviewing the opening show, however, sniffed, "The staging was unbelievably old fashioned. The aim, apparently, was to do nothing more than follow the format of the band show that once was a feature of larger motion picture houses."

Leonard Stern, one of the mainstays of Gleason's writing staff, believes the idea for *Stage Show* originated from Gleason's New Year's Eve Show in late 1953 that had featured the Dorsey brothers. To Stern, Tommy came across as a "gentle, almost professorial kind of man": "It might have been the glasses that did it. The teacher element was that he was the authoritarian, he was in charge, but he wasn't the type who exploited it. He had a kind of patience and took his time in making a point."

When Gleason broached the idea of having Tommy and Jimmy occupy his time slot for a summer show, Tommy asked Gleason how he and Jimmy could possibly headline his summer show on a Saturday night, the night when the band had to have its biggest payday. Tino Barzie interjected that the answer might be for Frank Dailey to book the band for most of the summer.

Dailey wound up giving the Dorseys permission to be a half hour late on Saturday night in order that they could perform on *Stage Show*. In exchange, the Dorseys' engagement at the Meadowbrook got several plugs on the television show. As Barzie pointed out, "The power of television [even] at that time, when it was in its infancy, was remarkable."

Stage Show was predominantly stocked with traditional recording artists as guest stars. They included The Four Aces, The DeMarco Sisters, The McGuire Sisters, Eileen Barton, Lillian Roth, and Roy Hamilton. Jazz musicians such as Louis Armstrong, Lionel Hampton, drummer Cozy Cole, and trumpeter Henry "Red" Allen were other guest stars. The show with Armstrong was highlighted by the Dorseys' spirited version of "That's A-Plenty," on which they traded solos with their old friend. Each program opened with the camera entering Studio 50 at Broadway and Fifty-third Street (then the home of the *Ed Sullivan Show* and now the *David Letterman Show*), taking the home viewers down the aisle to their "seats." Gleason supervised the entire production.

There was sometimes a residual from being a guest star on *Stage Show* for the Dorsey orchestra. After her appearance, singer Eileen Barton insisted on having the Dorsey band appear with her on a USO tour, and she volunteered to replace it at a Miami Beach hotel engagement when the band unexpectedly had to fly to New York to do *Stage Show*. But long before her big record of "If I Knew You Were Comin' I'd 'a' Baked a Cake" had led to her booking on *Stage Show*, Frank Sinatra, who was then partnered with her father, Ben Barton, and Hank Sanicola in Barton Music, called her to say that Dorsey wanted her to become his band singer. "I turned it down," said Barton regretfully. "I was wrong because if I'd had his backing and his arrangements, there were no heights I couldn't have reached. I was doing a single and didn't want to get on the bus and all that stuff."

Without question, Jackie Gleason emerged as one of the towering show business talents of the last century—a far cry from where his career had been stranded during the 1940s. *The Honeymooners* series also was arguably the best television situation comedy ever produced. Gleason's incredible prowess as a serious actor was revealed in the television version of William Saroyan's *The Time of Your Life* and later in such films as *The Hustler, Requiem for a*

Heavyweight, Gigot, Soldier in the Rain, and *Nothing in Common* before he became a caricature of himself in *Smokey and the Bandit* and its two sequels.

Now that he was a superstar, he exerted his newly found power by also being extremely difficult at every turn. Like Tommy Dorsey and Frank Sinatra, he firmly believed his way was the only way. Gleason refused to rehearse but made one compensation: He refrained from drinking on the day of the show. Despite his incredible success in television, he never won an Emmy, although he did win a Tony for his performance in the musical *Take Me Along* on Broadway.

Leonard Stern surmised, "The various characters Gleason portrayed were extensions of beliefs he held that if you're good you get exploited. If you don't give a damn about anything—Reggie Van Gleason—the world is your oyster."

Despite his carefully conceived ideas on how to keep the band in its newfound cycle of success, Tommy never thought twice about how he treated musicians whose playing didn't meet his high standards. This was merely another symptom of his restlessness and his ferocious competitiveness, which would never cease. Even with establishing his new band with Jimmy, Tommy's familiar sadistic habits remained.

As the trombonist George Monte related, "If you played saxophone and made a mistake, you got Dorsey's slide in your back." Speaking of the leader's knee-jerk impulse to fire musicians, Monte added, "You knew right away whether he was going to settle in with them. He kind of gave the band a whitewash every so often. I think he just wanted a change, maybe for freshness."

It wasn't always easy for a musician who joined the band based on Jimmy's recommendation. Pat Chartrand's experience serves as a perfect case in point. He was first seen by Jimmy (then on vacation) when Chartrand was playing tenor saxophone with Harry James's band at the Hollywood Palladium. After the gig, Jimmy invited James to play golf with him the next day. Harry begged off, saying, "I can't. Why don't you play with this new kid with the band?" Chartrand remembered, "I had a good round with Jimmy that day. He said to me, 'Why don't you join our band? We'll play golf all the time!'"

In the year Chartrand stayed with the band, Tommy didn't leave him alone. Chartrand avowed, "Tommy didn't leave anybody alone. He always had something to say to somebody—anybody. There was always a tenseness in the band. My problem, more than anything else, was that I was Jimmy's boy. I played golf with him a lot and [as a result] I got a little browbeaten by Tommy. . . . I don't think Jimmy really felt at ease with 'The Brother.'"

Chartrand put his feelings in perspective when he described a gig one night in Evansville, Indiana:

> Jimmy got on the microphone and told the audience about how well I had played golf that afternoon. That pissed Tommy off. He called "Well, Git It!" just before the break. There's a very long tenor solo. Tommy made me play twenty, thirty choruses, which was a little more than normal, in fact, three or four times more than normal! I was bleeding out of my mouth. He said, "Do you want to be a golf player or a saxophone player? Play another chorus!" He was right behind me shouting into my ear. I just finally had had it up to my eyebrows with Tommy. I told him, and then Tino, "Why don't you fire me so I can go back home?" That was it. I quit.

Some people looked the other way when Tommy behaved badly. Other people only saw his good side, and former MCA agent Eddie Collins was one of them. He lived a good bachelor life in New York during the 1950s. He initially met Tommy at the Meadowbrook during the summer of 1954, when Tino Barzie invited him to come out and see the band. Tommy admired Collins's date, a tall, blond fashion model named Gretchen Harris, who was dancing with Collins close to the bandstand. Collins introduced Harris to Tommy, which led to an immediate rapport with him. Collins soon became a regular at the Statler when the Dorsey band was in New York. "I saw the Dorsey band seventy to eighty times in those years," he claimed. "After work I used to go see Tommy in his suite at 6:45 P.M., before he went downstairs to work."

Although Dorsey, as well as other former MCA clients, had vowed never to work any location where MCA booked its bands (and lived to see the foolishness of such an edict), he had no problem with the fact that Collins worked for the agency. It helped that Collins did some of the booking for Tommy's good friend Guy Lombardo. One night he brought Dorsey out to Jones Beach to see the *Arabian Nights* show Carmen Lombardo had written. Collins recalled:

> Afterward, Tommy reminisced with Lauritz Melchior, who was the lead in the show, about their days together at MGM. Then Guy and the Royal Canadians played for dancing.

On the way back to New York he was driving his black Cadillac, and we went through several little towns. He showed me where he had lived in the early 1930s when he was so much in demand playing on radio shows. He was going down memory lane and really seemed to enjoy that.

Of course, when I was fired from MCA, that made my friendship with Tommy even better. We would go down to Broome Street and have dinner at the Grotto Azurra, and sometimes at Goldie's New York up on East Fifty-third Street—the most wonderful bar in the world, with those two pianos going all the time. I brought Tommy and Johnny Mercer there. Tommy also enjoyed Ed Wynn's Harvwyn Club. Tommy loved to talk about the old days, and how much he admired Jack Teagarden. He said that when he and Jimmy first arrived in New York at Penn Station they had little bags, almost like little see-through things that were round, made from wicker. He talked about how they scrounged around until they got a little gig here and there.

For Collins, what stood out about Dorsey was his warm and outgoing personality as much as his stature as a musician and bandleader: "Tommy would have been a great Irish politician. He could talk to people and charm them. When you'd walk into a restaurant with Tommy he knew so many people, and he knew all their names. When he walked into a room, you knew he was there—he had that kind of personality. People liked Tommy, and they should have. I never saw the mean side of him. I found him very humorous. Tommy was a good dancer. He was also a gentleman. He would get up when a woman came to the table, and right away he'd pull a chair out so she could sit down."

Collins spoke of the nights he spent with Dorsey and Gleason at Toots Shor's and how they reveled in each other's success: "I think Jackie always wanted to be a musician, and I think he probably worshipped Tommy's ability to play the trombone. On weekends in the fall I'd spend Sundays with Tommy watching the Giants games on his small black-and-white TV set. Sometimes we'd meet Tino, Jackie, and Frank Satinstein, the director of his show, at La Cremallere in Banksville, New York, just over the New York line from Greenwich for Sunday night dinners."

Collins recalled introducing Tommy to that year's Miss Rheingold. (Rheingold was a popular beer.) "Her name was Rita Daigle. Janie wasn't home that much. I brought Rita up to Tommy's house. Later, I went downstairs and looked out the window, and there was Tommy kissing Rita. He was very interested in her for a while."

In addition to playing the role of unfaithful husband, Tommy still wasn't much of a father. Patsy had made her sentiments clear when she described her home life before she left home to attend college at William and Mary. Patsy's younger brother, Skipper, was another victim of Toots's divorce from Tommy. Skipper was shuttled off to boarding schools (the Harvey School and Hotchkiss) before matriculating at Williams.

In the fall of 1951, Williams was playing football at Princeton on its home field, Palmer Stadium. Tommy came down from New York with Tino Barzie and Vince Carbone to cheer on his son, who was playing halfback. A fan of his sitting next to him asked Dorsey, "How long has your son been playing football?" and then, "What fraternity is he in at Williams?" Dorsey didn't know the answer to either question. The fan reprimanded him for not knowing the answers to his questions by saying, "You should. I have all your records." The reason he didn't was simply "because he didn't know what the hell I was doing at Williams," Skipper recently admitted.

Skipper does acknowledge, however, that his father offered his connections to help him get into flight school after he entered the navy in the fall of 1953. His father told him to approach a certain admiral he knew at the Naval Air Station outside Boston and inform him that he was Tommy's son. The mention of Tommy Dorsey's name got immediate results: "Because of Dad's friendship with the Admiral, I got into flight school instead of having to go to naval OCS at Newport."

Suzie and Steve Dorsey spent time with their father mostly during the band's frequent engagements at the Statler in New York. The Dorsey home in Greenwich, Connecticut, was only an hour's drive away. When Tommy was home, he made attempts to be a loving, attentive father, but unfortunately, it just wasn't in him. His family life was essentially spent with his real family, the sixteen-piece band he led.

Dorsey's highly involved relationships with some of his best musicians continued, but without their former drawn-out melodramas. In mid-November 1954, on a southern tour, which preceded another long engagement at the Statler, Buddy Rich came back to the band for the fourth time. A few months earlier, the IRS had indicted Rich for not reporting over thirteen thousand dollars in taxable income. He needed money desperately. In addition to using Tommy's way of life as his modus operandi, he never did get over his obsession of trying to emulate the free-spending ways of his hero, Frank Sinatra. Dorsey guaranteed him at least the thirty-five thousand dollars a year in salary that Harry James had been paying him (if not more) and gave him featured billing.

On his return, Rich was quoted as saying, "We've both calmed down some . . . so I know [that] Tommy and I will get along fine now." Their antics, if they can be called that, continued. John Frosk remembered that the night before Rich joined the band at Andrews Air Force Base, Tommy called the band together: "He wanted us to be real polite to [Rich] and not to get him agitated. Ten minutes before the first date we heard a crash. When Buddy saw the drums weren't set up right, he picked up the whole set and threw it down on the dance floor. The first day!"

Eileen Barton delighted in passing along the story about the temperamental drummer related to her by Tino Barzie that apparently took place on this tour. One night Rich got up from his drum kit at the end of a set, threw his drumsticks in the air, said, "That's it! I'm through being a nice guy," and walked off the bandstand. This time Dorsey broke into fits of laughter.

On an outdoor date at the Connally Air Force Base in Waco, Texas, a swarm of mosquitoes attacked the band. At first Dorsey was amused, but amusement gave way to anger when he realized Buddy wasn't handling the problem with alacrity. In his frustration he threw a trombone mute at him, and Rich left the bandstand in the middle of the performance. Trumpeter Bitsy Mullens took over on drums.

Rich called Lee Castle from his Miami home and told him to inform Tommy that he wouldn't be returning to the band. Dorsey's response was "Tell him if he decides to change his mind he won't have a drum set. I've just given it to Rocky Marciano [the heavyweight champion]!" Louis Bellson was called about finishing the tour. After Tommy realized he had a contract in place with Rich, and highly aware of the inspiration his drumming gave to the band, another reconciliation took place.

It was on this same tour that Dorsey had a serendipitous musical encounter with his old idol, Jack Teagarden. After an appearance in a Pittsburgh suburb that preceded a date in Aliquippa, Pennsylvania, in early December, en route to New York for five weeks at the Statler, the band bus was driving through Brentwood, Pennsylvania. All of a sudden Tommy saw a sign out front of the Bali Keo nightclub—"Jack Teagarden and His Band"—and exclaimed to the bus driver, "Stop! Everybody out of the bus! Jack's playing here!"

Tommy and his musicians sat in the audience during Teagarden's last set. Then Tommy instructed the band boy, "Bring in all the music stands and set up." That was the signal for the Dorsey band to play an impromptu set, with Jack Teagarden playing Tommy's parts; his clarinetist, Kenny Davern, and another formidable trombonist, Tommy Turk, who happened to be there to see Teagarden, joined in. That was followed by Tommy, Jimmy, Lee Castle, and Buddy Rich jamming with Teagarden's band. Jack and Tommy recapitulated their blues duet on the 1939 *Metronome* All-Stars record. The session lasted until 4:30 A.M.

A tape of the performance furnished by Bitsy Mullens recorded a rare expression of pure, unguarded admiration in Tommy's enthusiastic introduction of Teagarden: "I've been copying him since 1928 and never came close." One realizes how much that night meant to Dorsey and captures the thrill he got from playing with the jazz trombonist he knew he could never be. Teagarden showed his appreciation for Tommy's impromptu visit, declaring at the end of the evening, "This is the best Christmas present I've ever had."

Stage Show was reborn when Gleason took a two-week vacation, which encompassed the January 1 and 8, 1955, programs. For the first show the Dorseys' guest stars were Duke Ellington and singers Johnny Ray and Mindy Carson, and then again Ray and the biggest female recording star of the 1950s, Patti Page, on the second show. The reaction from the network was so strong that plans were made to schedule *Stage Show* on a regular basis for the start of the fall season with three sponsors already set.

There were three other memorable events surrounding the Dorsey band during the first three months of 1955. In January, a celebration at the Statler commemorated the twentieth anniversary of the year the Dorsey brothers had started their own bands. On February 3, Martin Block's *Make Believe Ballroom* on WNEW threw a party at Manhattan Center celebrating both the show's twentieth anniversary and the inauguration of Tommy's and Jimmy's bands as well.

Frank Sinatra dropped by during a break from his engagement at the Copacabana. Almost eight years had passed since they had last worked together. Sinatra had suffered through a mostly self-induced career burnout after leaving his wife, Nancy, marrying screen siren Ava Gardner, and then breaking up with her. He had made a miraculous comeback after winning the Best Supporting Actor Oscar for his performance in *From Here to Eternity*.

The merry-go-round began moving again at full speed with the release of Sinatra's emotional *In the Wee Small Hours* album. Its impact caused the leading music critics to suddenly acknowledge him as a truly brilliant artist. Referring to the importance of this album, John Rockwell, of the *New York Times*, in his *Sinatra, an American Classic*, noted, "A public that had at first been titillated, then offended, by the Gardner-Sinatra relationship was now ready to recognize its validity once they heard it expressed as poignantly and painfully as this."

The banter between Dorsey and Sinatra on the *Make Believe Ballroom* anniversary show was nervous and edgy. When Dorsey said to Sinatra, "I don't want to be too presumptuous, but would you mind singing . . . " Sinatra interrupted him with "I'd be happy to sing a song . . . only because Toots Shor begged me not to." Dorsey laughed nervously and countered with "I remember fifteen years ago when I said *you had to sing!*" Sinatra wound up singing four songs. When Sinatra left the bandstand, Dorsey acknowledged, "I always get a charge hearing him."

It was obvious that the role reversal was difficult for Tommy to accept: His former band singer had long since eclipsed him in popularity. Referring to the enthusiastic response to Sinatra singing, he recomposed himself and said, "Nothing can top that—even though we got stuff in our book to move these walls. I guess on that we'll take five."

On March 12, during still another Gleason vacation, the brothers doubled between *Stage Show* and the Meadowbrook. That night Count Basie, Kate Smith, and the DeMarco Sisters were the three disparate guest stars. Bitsy Mullens, in his down-home Arkansas manner, noted, "I can remember standing close to Basie and watching those little, short fingers when he was comping. Man, it lifted me right off the floor. It was kind of like getting a prostate massage from an octopus."

Charlie Parker watched the show that night from the suite of the Baroness de Koenigswarter in the Stanhope Hotel. Reportedly, at 8:30 P.M., during the Dorsey band's playing of "South Rampart Street Parade," Parker began to laugh, then suddenly collapsed and died a few minutes later of a massive heart attack at the age of thirty-five. This tragic event, which included showing Parker's watching *Stage Show*, was reenacted by director Clint Eastwood in the 1988 Warner Brothers film *Bird*, his film biography of Parker.

The combination of successful engagements at the Statler, the many radio remotes emanating from the hotel, Armed Forces Radio shows, and their television appearances on *Stage Show* made the Dorseys once again a significant draw on the road. Buddy Rich's return further enhanced their appeal, but it was by now clearly a retro appeal.

In a three-page article that *Look* magazine (the rival to *Life* as the leading weekly picture magazine) ran under the banner of "The Dorseys Bring Back the Swing Era," George B. Leonard, Jr., described a college dance at Virginia Polytechnic Institute: "On the bandstand was a man more familiar to the late '30s than to the middle '50s. Tommy Dorsey's hair was gray now, but his gestures were as vehement as ever, his trombone notes as impeccable and glossy. At one side, facing away from the rest of the band, was Brother Jimmy, absorbed in his own private world as he delicately fingered his clarinet. High on a platform at the back, surrounded by a cluster of drums and cymbals, sat Buddy Rich. He was chewing gum, counting two beats with his body and three with his jaws for every one he played."

Leonard went on to say, "There are those who would call the Dorseys musical reactionaries; some musicians say the Brothers play the music of the '30s because that's all they can play. Others look upon Tommy Dorsey . . . as primarily a businessman whose garage in Greenwich, Conn. will never be empty for lack of a Cadillac."

The magazine piece cited Tommy's antibebop stance; he was quoted as calling boppers "musical communists." Buddy Rich made a jab at Dave Brubeck: "You ever see that funny bored, puzzled look on the faces of the people listening to Brubeck? They're puzzled because they don't know what they're listening for." The Swing Era veterans were only deluding themselves; within a year or two Dave Brubeck would take over the college concert market.

For a brief time a good feeling prevailed between Rich and Dorsey. The bandleader told Stanley Kay, "If he will just behave himself I will give him a band. I will back him." Kay then told Rich, "B, you know that guy really loves you, and he loves your playing." Anyone with only a soupçon of insight into the psyches of Tommy Dorsey and Buddy Rich, however, knew that this latest association couldn't possibly last. The good old days of the Dorsey band were gone, and how could Buddy Rich possibly adhere to Tommy's demands when he had led various bands of his own in the interim?

In mid-April, Rich left Dorsey for the last time. In retaliation, Dorsey carried out his previous threat to report him to the American Federation of Musicians. The charge was failing to give proper notice when he left the band. Dorsey also revealed that he had been paying off Rich's debts and had doled out more money on those debts than Rich was due under their salary agreement. He seized Rich's drum kit and gave it to Vinnie Forrest (Vince

Forchetti), the other superb trombone soloist in the band, who could also play drums.

In Orlando, Florida, during this same tour, Mickey McDermott, the southpaw pitcher who knew Dorsey through Tino Barzie, brought his roommate, Michael Dante, with him to Tommy's hotel room. Dante, then a shortstop trying out for the Washington Senators, who had been studying acting at the University of Miami in the off season, was wowed by Tommy: "What a star presence he had. He was charismatic, authoritative, intelligent, and fastidious. His toothbrush had to be folded a certain way and everything he did was [geared] to perfection. . . . He also loved baseball."

Dorsey remarked to Dante, "You've got to be probably the handsomest ballplayer in the big leagues." Dante discussed how he wanted to be an actor when his playing days were over. He figured that might be sooner than later because he was recovering from an operation on his shoulder. "Tommy wanted us to come see the band perform. It was fantastic—Jimmy Dorsey, Charlie Shavers, Buddy Rich . . . and a lot of wonderful musicians. The next day Tommy put on a [Senators] uniform and worked out with us. He took infield. He was in seventh heaven." A budding friendship developed between Dorsey and Dante. Dorsey left him with the band's itinerary for their forthcoming trip to Las Vegas and California and promised to send him a ticket anytime Dante wanted to join him. He also promised to arrange a screen test for Dante at MGM. He told Dante, "There's only one guy I did something for, and he did okay. His name was Frank Sinatra."

Dante recalled, "He would call me every three or four days to check on me. 'How's it going, pal?' He got that from Gleason. The Senators were breaking camp. I told Calvin Griffith, the owner, I wanted to take a leave of absence for two weeks. Tommy sent me a ticket, and I joined him in Las Vegas, where the band was playing at the Last Frontier in the main room. He said, 'Tino will pay you a couple hundred dollars a week and expenses, and you'll have some fun with us.' One night Tommy and Bobby Layne, the great pro football quarterback, made a bundle of money gambling."

In Los Angeles, Tommy got in touch with the producer Jack Cummings, whom he knew from the days when he was under contract to MGM. Dante took acting lessons at the studio before undergoing a screen test and became friendly with Clark Gable, Greer Garson, Vic Damone, and Gene Kelly. Tommy left town before the studio signed Dante to a contract, and the two never met again, but Tommy kept in touch with him from the road.

Dante recalled, "*Somebody Up There Likes Me*, Rocky Graziano's biography [which starred Paul Newman], was my first picture, as it was for Steve

McQueen and Sal Mineo. Tommy was excited about that." Dante would continue as a working actor in Hollywood for the next forty years.

Dorsey's friendship with Michael Dante was reminiscent of his association with Charlie Wick. The results were also similar. He saw something in both individuals and used his business acumen to further his friends' careers. He obviously enjoyed playing the role of mentor. Underneath the mask of the egotistical perfectionist, the enigmatic bandleader also had a heart and a sincere interest in helping others.

Before Buddy Rich left, the band began recording a series of instrumentals, which were eventually included in two albums released posthumously on Columbia Records. The first, *Tommy and Jimmy Dorsey in Hi-Fi*, demonstrates the precise section work of the band driven by Rich and then Louis Bellson, who returned in August 1955 along with his old roommate, Charlie Shavers. (Bitsy Mullens explained, "Louie idolized Buddy and played a lot like him; Buddy played heavy, Louie played light.")

The trademark Columbia sound, complete with considerable echo, enhances the impact of the Dorseys' solos on the albums. One of the most spectacular examples of their excellent musicianship is found in their individual as well as unison solos on "Melancholy Serenade" because fundamentally they were both supreme melodists. The tune was a tailor-made for them. And in an attempt to give the band a more swinging image, Tommy hired Ernie Wilkins, the saxophonist turned talented arranger, whose writing was of considerable importance in the return to prominence of Count Basie's band during this same period. He began contributing to the Dorsey book, as did bebop arranger Todd Dameron. Knowing Dorsey's antipathy to that musical idiom, Dameron kept his writing simple.

Wilkins's modern saxophone voicings and modern swing writing provided a different flavor to the band with such originals as "Flagler Drive" (named after the street where Tommy lived in Greenwich), "Peace Pipe," "Skirts and Sweaters," and "Stereophonic," the latter named for a new recording process that would soon become the standard. Deane Kincaide returned to writing for Tommy with several stirring gospel-oriented compositions like "We've Crossed the Widest River," "How Far Is It to Jordan," "This Is What Gabriel Said," and "Judgment Is Coming."

But in deciding what would make up the bulk of the Dorsey Brothers Orchestra's recorded output, it seems evident that Tommy considered the benefit to *his* publishing companies from the material on this and the album *Live in '55 at the Holiday Ballroom* (a ballroom outside of Chicago), which was released as a CD in 2004, rather than how Jimmy's interests could best be served. The result of the priority given to commercial considerations was dramatically uneven. The band's repertoire that night included "Nevada," "It Started All Over Again," "This Love of Mine," "There Are Such Things," "Swanee River," "Opus #1," and so on from Tommy's book, against "Maria Elena" and "Perfidia," which had been previously associated with Jimmy.

The Dorsey band's version of Ernie Wilkins's famous arrangement of "April in Paris" ("One More Time"), written for Basie, which he gave to Dorsey, illustrated the essential difference between an outstanding jazz orchestra and a good dance band. When Tommy discovered that Wilkins was selling some of the same arrangements to both bands, he fired him.

Jimmy's ability as an improviser on both alto sax and clarinet, particularly in the Holiday Ballroom CD, stands out. The sound of his alto saxophone, with its wide vibrato, is indeed unique, as is the loose, dancing quality of his clarinet playing. And how he could swing! Based on these live recordings, it's apparent that Jimmy Dorsey was unquestionably the superior jazz soloist of the Dorsey brothers.

The brothers disagreed, as usual, about the music and how it should be played. Bitsy Mullens, who played on both of these albums, recalled a serious argument between Tommy and Jimmy toward the end of the recording of the first of the two Columbia albums: "Everything that Jimmy would say he'd kind of move himself forward, but Tommy stood his ground. Jimmy got red in the face and left the studio. Toots Mondello was called in to solo on the remaining tunes. Jimmy stayed in his room at the Statler for a day and a half. I really think, as the older son, he saw Tommy as the interloper, stealing what was rightfully his."

Yet, as always, an attack on his brother from anyone else brought Tommy to his defense. Mullens recalled a brawl that took place in the ballroom of the Bradford Hotel in Boston: "Some of these South Boston Irish cats started yelling at Jimmy—things like, 'Your brother had to rescue you.' Jimmy lashed back at them. A big fight got going on the dance floor. Those guys were going to charge the bandstand."

Singer Bill Raymond added, "Tommy sent Tino to get rid of those guys, to get them out of the ballroom. He had his jaw broken for his efforts. Then Tommy said, 'Help him out.' Before I knew it, I was on the floor."

Mullens picked up the story, "At intermission, Tommy called them 'yellow sons of bitches.' Then those cats started after our drummer, Jo Jones [who was African-American]: 'Hey, you've got your nigger with you!' The word was that after the job these guys were waiting for Tommy. Finally the cops came. Those drunks staggered down the street. I was glad to leave Boston that night."

For Gleason's replacement slot during the summer of 1955, instead of the Dorseys he chose their old boss, Paul Whiteman, to host *America's Greatest Bands*. The Whiteman show featured four different name bands each week. Although collegians were embracing jazz and there was a strong interest in rhythm 'n' blues by teenagers, which in 1955 had turned into the white world's version called rock 'n' roll, with the gigantic hit record "Rock Around the Clock" by Bill Haley and the Comets, the network television programming executives paid absolutely no attention. This was years before Madison Avenue chose to recognize the buying potential of the emerging youth market. Interest in programming big bands on radio, much less on television, however, was waning fast.

The Dorseys again took to the road. The Holiday Ballroom date in Chicago was part of a late spring and summer tour, which also included their second engagement in the main room at the Last Frontier in Las Vegas, followed by one-nighters in the Northwest before heading for Southern California.

While in Vegas, Vince Carbone and his fiancé, Evelyn "Smitty" Smith, a flight attendant, decided to get married. Since Smitty's father was against her marrying a Catholic, Tommy, a lapsed Catholic, insisted on giving her away at their wedding ceremony at the St. Joan of Arc chapel. While walking Smitty down the aisle, Tommy said to her, "You're marrying a dago. Remember we are two good Irish people." "I almost fell down laughing as we strolled down the aisle," she remembered.

As the band ventured into British Columbia, Jimmy told Tommy that he was growing tired of doing one-nighters, and he wasn't sure how many more he could take. In Winnipeg, Tommy had his valet, Sonny Tate, and Lee Castle escort Jimmy to a well-established local medical clinic, where a growth was discovered on one of Jimmy's lungs. Jimmy's many years of heavy drinking and smoking had taken a severe toll. Jimmy would much rather have been on vacation playing golf, but he continued as the band returned east and toured New England.

That fall the Dorseys returned to New York City to appear weekly once again under the auspices of Jackie Gleason on CBS from Studio 50. But this time *Stage Show* was cut to a half-hour show airing from 8:00 to 8:30 P.M. It preceded the Gleason show, which consisted of a half-hour version of *The Honeymooners* and debuted on October 29, 1955. The band also resumed a weekend schedule at the Meadowbrook, which extended through New Year's Eve.

Viewed today, the episodes of *Stage Show*, in its various incarnations (there were sixty-seven in all), provide the distinct feeling that the 1950s represented a much simpler time. These were standard variety shows of the time, complete with gaudy sets and banal scripts. In retrospect, one might think of them as "junior" Ed Sullivan shows with limited budgets. Throughout, however, Tommy reveals a show business veteran's sense of how to introduce acts. Jimmy is not nearly so facile. It's easy to see he is forever reading from cue cards.

There were usually two guest stars on *Stage Show*. Tommy continued to show a keen ear for new talent: Among those who went on to prominence were Bobby Darin, Connie Francis, and Della Reese. The band provided excellent support for such newly emerging singers as Sarah Vaughan and Tony Bennett, who even then exhibited their signature styles and polish.

At least one of Tommy's or Jimmy's favorite hit tunes was included each week, sometimes played by the band, and sometimes as background for the June Taylor Dancers. During the dancers' number, there are always camera shots from the top of the theater stage, copying the camera work on a standard Busby Berkeley routine. The Dorsey band, always well rehearsed, played its music with a decided zest. Tommy's decisive downbeats and cutoffs were highly noticeable. The trumpet section had a pronounced bite and was highlighted by Charlie Shavers's solos. Louis Bellson's time-keeping was immaculate. The brothers' solo spots were continually exhilarating.

Singer Bea Wain greatly admired Dorsey's playing: "When I did a guest shot on *Stage Show*, I sang 'Blow, Gabriel, Blow.' The arrangement that I had had a horn coming in. I would sing to the horn—and Tommy would answer me vocally. And then he would play the interval. God it was a thrill! When Andre Baruch and I had a disk jockey show in New York on WMCA called *Mr. and Mrs. Music*, we had guests. We had a trio, and Tommy played an obligato with me, and that, too, was a real kick."

On a show devoted to Irving Berlin's music, Tommy's poignant version of "Remember" stands out after all these years. On this same show, Tommy and Jimmy once again exhibited their Dixieland chops on "Alexander's Ragtime Band." On more than one of the shows, the combination of Bob Eberly and Helen O'Connell was brought back to reprise their "Green Eyes" and "Tangerine" hits of yesteryear with Jimmy. On another show, O'Connell sang her memorable version of "When the Sun Comes Out."

With his renewed success, Tommy continued to display his longtime generosity. Lee Castle told of the time he pulled up in a taxi at the front door of Studio 50 with Tommy:

> We sat in the cab. I noticed Tommy putting hundred-dollar bills in his fingers. All of his cronies, guys you hadn't seen in years, who had seen hard times, would wait there for him. Tommy would shake hands with each one of them and give him one of his hundred-dollar bills. He did that all the time. Sinatra did the same thing. It had rubbed off from Tommy.
>
> At Christmastime, I would go with him to send food and clothes to a lot of people. He used to say to me, "If word of this leaks out about this, I'll know it was you. You keep your mouth shut!" The hard years in Shenandoah and his memories of the Great Depression were never far from his thoughts.

Mike Dann believes that it was some sort of record for the Dorsey brothers to have lasted what turned out to be three years with Gleason and still remain close to him: "There were very few people Tommy had respect for. Benny Goodman wouldn't have gotten through lunch with Gleason. Eventually, I think Tommy would have left Gleason. That's true of anybody in his life. Gleason was a cruel man. He was cruel to himself."

Dann recognized Tommy's managerial aptitude: "I always said that I thought Tommy Dorsey could have been the chairman of the Chase Bank. He really could handle most people and situations well, and he could cover up mistakes. He was a problem solver. Jackie was a problem creator! They [the Dorseys] could mesh with Gleason because there was never a creative problem on [Tommy] Dorsey's side. Jackie Gleason as a performer operated on his own potential on a scale of six or seven. Dorsey as an orchestra leader and musician operated on a scale of ten, and that made him number one. Gleason was the greatest all-around performer I ever knew, and yet he never fully achieved what he could do."

Dann made several other pungent observations: "Jackie Gleason was a phenomenon from the very start. You combine Gleason with a number-one bandleader, and remember radio had been built on bandleaders, and the bandleader was king. As a matter of fact, radio built two things. It built radio, and it built MCA. And as a consequence, you couldn't be on radio unless you went through Jules Stein and Larry Barnett—they owned it. Radio was for the masses. Music was the backbone of [both] radio and early television."

Dann made it very clear that while Jack Philbin might have been billed as the executive producer of *Stage Show* for Gleason's Peekskill Enterprises production company, Tommy Dorsey ran the show: "He was a general who saw the whole picture. You knew why he was the leader of the band! That's what he was presenting, and that's what was appealing to the public. Dorsey created a concept and the content for the show. Nobody was going to tell Tommy Dorsey what to do. He executed it all to the best of his ability and got the best people he could hire. He was a man with star power."

Leonard Stern stressed, "Bullets Durgom was the catalyst—he was the link between Gleason and Tommy Dorsey. He had worked closely with Tommy years before. He probably was the one who renewed the interest in Tommy Dorsey—or kept it current. Bullets also had a reverence and a respect for Jackie's talent."

But on TV, Stern pointed out, the Dorseys never learned to capitalize on their obvious personal differences as the Smothers Brothers later did. Tommy and Jimmy considered themselves musicians; the Smothers Brothers were fundamentally comedians who happened to be musicians. Comedy had played a rather insignificant role in either one of the Dorseys' presentations. Now that they were seen on national television, to bring a comedic approach to *their* very real personal differences would never have occurred to them and would have been completely out of character.

There were big highs—and lows—yet to come.

Tommy's profound respect for Count Basie's band was shown in the New Year's Eve 1955 *Stage Show,* on which Basie and Joe Williams were guests. On the show, Basie debuted his soon-to-become-classic rendition of "Every Day." Earlier, Tommy had made several excursions to Birdland to witness this amazing jazz machine in performance. When longtime Dorsey fans would approach Tommy and say, "You have the greatest band in the country," he would invariably say, "No, Basie has the best band in the country." And just as he had done years before with the Jimmie Lunceford band, Tommy ordered his musicians to go to Birdland to see exactly what Basie was doing. Barzie was there to check on who attended and who didn't.

Trombonist Bill Hughes, who is now celebrating his fiftieth year with the Basie band and recently took over its leadership, remembered one Birdland engagement in which Dorsey sat in with the trombone section every other night: "There was an Ernie Wilkins arrangement of 'Moonlight in Vermont,' which featured Henry Coker, one of our trombonists, that Basie liked to play. Tommy heard it and decided he, too, wanted to play it. Basie featured him on that particular number probably five or six times. Tommy had that fantastic ability to pick up that horn and play high notes without any difficulty. He could create a beautiful sound when he needed it and a raucous sound when he needed to do that. He always had an instinct for playing at the right tempos. He had so many King trombones of his own that he wound up donating trombones to our entire section." Dorsey also had the entire Basie band as his guests at the Café Rouge.

In January 1956 the Dorsey band moved around the corner from Birdland to play weekends at Roseland, before returning to play at the Statler through late June, while continuing on *Stage Show*. That particular Statler engagement meant a great deal to Billy VerPlanck, who joined the band there: "Tommy invited me down there for supper. The leader's going to hire me—a third trombone player. He [Dorsey] stood over me, and I swear to Christ he seemed to me like he was eight feet tall. He says to me, 'What I want from you is one hundred and ten percent!' I didn't know what the hell to say. This is the greatest gig in the world. I've just been doing six hundred miles a day with [Charlie] Spivak, and I'm now playing the Statler with this marvelous band." It was during his tenure with Dorsey that VerPlanck met band singer Marlene Paula, who substituted for Lynn Roberts and later became his wife, Marlene VerPlanck.

VerPlanck's trumpeter friend, Joe Cabot, who worked for Dorsey, James, Goodman, and Krupa, among others, described the elation of joining a great band: "I remember coming up out of the pit at the Paramount in 1947 with Gene Krupa. All of the sections of the band, one after the other, played the drums preceding Gene's drum solo on 'Drum Boogie.' That was one of the biggest thrills I ever had. I felt I was part of something. That's why you did it. . . . When you were with big bands in those days, you lived in an iron lung on that bus, but you were part of a family. It was that way with Dorsey." Cabot added, however, that Dorsey's orientation to his men was always "I am the boss!"

The February 1956 issue of *DownBeat* reported with considerable fanfare that Tino Barzie had negotiated a million-dollar contract with the Statler

Hotel for the Dorsey band, partly on the strength of its television exposure. Under the terms of the contract, the band would play at the hotel six months a year for the next five years, commencing with an engagement that would extend from September 21 until March of the following year. The brothers were guaranteed seven thousand a week and also a substantial percentage of the cover charges.

This deal seemed a godsend. It would help preserve Jimmy's declining health by keeping the band off the road half of the year. In addition, it would result in the band's being more in demand on the road. Just how soon the road would end for Tommy, no one could have guessed.

When Sarah Vaughan was brought back for a second appearance on the January 18, 1956, *Stage Show*, her manager, George Treadwell, insisted that she precede the other guest star. The other guest, whom Treadwell dismissed as an untalented "hillbilly singer," was a twenty-one-year-old former Tupelo, Mississippi, truck driver turned singer named Elvis Presley, who had been heavily influenced by African-American blues singers in the Mississippi Delta area where he grew up. Arthur "Bigboy" Crudup, among others, had exerted a profound influence on his singing. The late record producer Sam Phillips, a swing fan who believed Tommy Dorsey had started it all in the late 1930s with "Boogie Woogie," had already produced several records of the young singer that had sold rather well on his Sun Records label in Memphis.

Tino Barzie remembered:

In those years, black entertainers weren't given the chance to appear on the major TV shows. We had presented Louis Armstrong, Duke Ellington, Count Basie, Lionel Hampton, and Dorothy Dandridge for what our budget afforded. And by having booked all those people to come on our show, our ratings in the South weren't doing well. We scheduled a production meeting about how we could improve our ratings. We had Perry Como as our competition in the winter of 1956. I started looking around for new acts—like some country-and-western people. Somebody [Steve Yates, a country music agent] turned me on to an act handled by [Colonel] Tom Parker. I asked, "What's his name?" "It's Elvis Presley." I said, "Elvis? What kind of name is that?"

I tracked Presley down in New Orleans [where he was headlining *The Louisiana Hayride*] and spoke to Tom Parker. I told him we'd like to use Elvis on several shows. He was thrilled to death. I booked Elvis for the following Saturday. I bought him for four shows for a total of five thousand dollars—for Elvis Presley!

Harry Kalcheim of the William Morris Agency negotiated the contract, which also called for an option for two other appearances, which was later picked up. Elvis's fee was then raised to fifteen hundred a show. He wound up performing on *Stage Show* a total of six times.

Tommy and Tess Dorsey met Elvis at Presley's rehearsal at Nola Studios, where Presley showed a great respect toward Dorsey. When Jackie Gleason announced at the first rehearsal for the show, "I don't like this guy," Barzie recalled Tommy said, "I like his kisser [his face]. Don't worry about him." Most of the band agreed with Gleason's opinion.

Pat Chartrand commented, "During our rehearsal with him, some guys fell off the bandstand laughing at Elvis. It was so shocking to all of us, we couldn't believe it." John Frosk added, "We didn't like him because he looked dirty, and he needed a haircut. We thought he never bathed." But at the end of the rehearsal, Louis Bellson recalled, Tommy said, "You see that guy Elvis Presley—he's going to be one of the biggest names in show business in a short time." Once again, Dorsey recognized talent when he saw it.

"Special guest" Bill Randall, the New York disk jockey who had been plugging Presley's upcoming appearance on *Stage Show* on his Saturday-afternoon New York radio show, introduced Elvis. He announced, "We think tonight that he's going to make television history for you. We'd like you to meet him now—Elvis Presley." Presley's national debut on *Stage Show* singing "Shake, Rattle and Roll" and "Flip, Flop and Fly" (two Joe Turner numbers) was like nothing that anyone had ever seen before on national television. It was the raw against the cooked, postwar prosperity versus prewar propriety, an atomic burst of sexual vitality obliterating the palled remnants of Depression-era glamour. The camera crew had even breached television etiquette by daring to photograph Presley below the waist!

Dressed in a black shirt, white tie, dark trousers with a shiny white stripe, and a glitzy tweed jacket, the sloe-eyed Presley had a leering smile, while his body gyrated with unabashed sexuality. A strong country blues sense emanated from the handsome young singer with the long, greasy dyed-black hair, whose forelock drooped over his face, adding to his allure.

Twenty-one years after Benny Goodman's breakthrough, and thirteen years after Frank Sinatra's spectacular rise to stardom, the country's next major pop music icon was about to be born. RCA Victor had already signed this new phenomenon. Ironically, he was about to replace Tommy Dorsey as the biggest-selling artist in the history of the company.

Barzie recalled the avalanche of hate mail from outraged viewers: "There were letters like, 'How could you two fine gentlemen, Tommy and Jimmy Dorsey, present somebody like this? We've respected you and enjoyed you.' The funniest part was our ratings went up, and they went up again the second week."

Mike Dann observed that "Elvis was not at ease in front of an audience unless he was singing. Dorsey brought out the best in him because he gave Elvis a quality that many people never realized Elvis had. At the same time, he legitimized Elvis. . . . There was a lot of betting going on that it wouldn't last, it wouldn't work. But Dorsey knew where talent was going. Elvis was so exciting. . . . I think the key point here is that people don't realize that this was the jumping-off place for Presley."

Kinescopes of these performances of almost five decades ago still represent incredible television. The contrast between the tradition the Dorseys represented and the uninhibited Presley was absolutely astonishing, to say the least. The impact of Presley's performance brought down the curtain on the era of romantic popular music and, through the power of television, marked the launching of a brand new musical trend.

Elvis Presley *was* rock 'n' roll, which was suddenly embraced by the emerging generation as its own music. Its sound shattered the complacency of the 1950s and broke the ground for the antiestablishment culture coming in the following decades. The combination of saxophones and brass no longer carried the melody; guitars took their place, underlined by an incessant pounding drumbeat. And with its visual impact, television would suddenly cause the look of a musical artist to become almost as important as the content of his or her music.

Despite the lack of respect Dorsey's musicians had shown for Elvis's appearance and his music, the Dorsey musicians couldn't help but admire the humility of the young singer. After the show, Barzie invited Elvis to come over to Roseland to see the Dorsey band play for dancing. Barzie remembered, "When he got there, he said to me, 'This is really the big time!'" The twenty-one-year-old on his second visit to New York—he had previously been turned down by *Arthur Godfrey's Talent Scouts* show—had no idea that that particular Roseland building was about to be torn down, or to realize that by 1956 venues for dance bands were hardly big time!

Elvis was the only guest star on his second *Stage Show* appearance, on February 4. He sang "Tutti Frutti" and "Baby, Let's Play House." On his third appearance, the following Saturday, he shared the billing with Ella Fitzgerald and comedian Jackie Miles, and he sang "Heartbreak Hotel" (with the Dorsey band wailing behind him) and "Blue Suede Shoes." On the former tune, the Dorsey Brothers Orchestra contributed an arrhythmic arrangement that didn't gel with Elvis's interpretation. Charlie Shavers's trumpet solo left the singer with a sickly smile on his lips.

For his fourth appearance, on the February 18 *Stage Show*, Elvis drew an even larger audience because the Gleason show had switched time slots with *Stage Show* in order to combat the popularity of *The Perry Como Show*. (Coincidentally, Presley had been first offered to the Como show but had been turned down.)

The significance of his newly found popularity was reflected in Elvis's next-to-last appearance on March 17. Tommy introduced him by saying, "His entertaining and provocative style has kicked up a storm all around the country. Here is the one and only Elvis Presley!" Elvis broke into "Blue Suede Shoes," followed by "Heartbreak Hotel," his first RCA single record, which already had gone to number one in the country.

His arsenal of bumps and grinds again alternately shocked, terrified, and delighted the television audience. In those years, this same audience had taken to heart the homilies and reassurances—and, yes, the mediocrity—represented by performers like Arthur Godfrey, who perhaps might be described as a kind of homespun country uncle. Elvis Presley represented the complete antithesis of all of that. He had nothing to learn from Tommy Dorsey musically.

Today it's commonly believed that Ed Sullivan, who featured Elvis *after* he'd guest-starred on the shows of Milton Berle and Steve Allen, actually introduced Presley. The deplorable lack of interest and knowledge so prevalent in today's culture of all kinds of history enters into this morsel of misinformation. The fact that it was the Dorseys who did so, and because they were by now weekly visitors to American homes, plus their successful touring schedule, gave them even more importance in the media.

Besides the *Look* spread, there were other major stories in the premiere issue of *Playboy; American Weekly* (the major Sunday Hearst newspaper supplement); and *Saturday*, the magazine of the *New York World-Telegram and Sun*. A several-page feature story in a long-gone magazine called *TV Fan* celebrated Tommy Dorsey, the family man, with pictures of him with Janie and their two children, Suzy and Steve, in their Greenwich home. (The story appeared forced.)

Countless musicians in Great Britain who had heard him play were impressed and inspired by Dorsey during the 1950s. The highly respected trombonist Don Lusher was one of the principal soloists of the Ted Heath Orchestra, the most popular English band. Lusher remembered being especially excited about going down to the Statler to see the Dorsey band immediately after the Heath band arrived in New York for its first American tour in the spring of 1956:

> It was better than I had anticipated from having heard him on records. I thought . . . he would be the big-time bandleader who wandered out to the microphone, say, six times in the whole evening and play very quietly and nicely. . . . No. We saw him four nights on the trot, and he played the whole time—sometimes extremely loud with the band, at other times just whispers. We had heard all sorts of things, that he was a fiery man, unpleasant in some ways. I think that was because he believed very strongly in certain principles. . . . He had a first-class band always and had first-class money and conditions to offer.
>
> When it comes to playing "I'm Getting Sentimental over You," he made it sound so easy—I find personally it's not an easy tune to play. That is, if you try and play it like Tommy Dorsey, not taking any liberties with the phrasing . . . you try it in a nice sort of tempo, like Dorsey, bearing his sound and his phrasing in mind—I do not find that easy; I don't think I ever will.

For others, Dorsey's music has a more cautionary effect. For them the result of his calculatedness is a kind of musical inauthenticity. Dick Nash has played the role of Tommy Dorsey on numerous records emanating from Hollywood for more than forty years—or from Sinatra's *I Remember Tommy* album to Steve Tyrell's "I'll Be Seeing You," a track from a recent CD. While agreeing with much of Lusher's evaluation of Dorsey's technique, Nash felt his jazz playing was "kind of stilted. It was preplanned. It wasn't free."

His analysis of Dorsey's breathing technique is reminiscent of Buddy Morrow's: "I didn't [particularly] like his phrasing because he would pick out a place to breathe in a safe spot so that he could carry on and not have to stop up high and reattack up high. [He did that] for safety's sake. That's why he was so clean and consistent. Learning to play the trumpet first made him want to get through phrases safely and gently. But in the meantime, when he did breathe down below, he could really get a big breath and come back in the lower register. Then he would phrase on up and sing it out and build it up to what he wanted to do and then come back down again. And he would go eight bars." Nash concluded with the same remark Jo Stafford had made: "He had tremendous breath capacity. He was a big man who had a big rib cage."

If Dorsey's endorsement of Presley was sincere, in his mind there was still no question as to who the greatest singer was. That spring Frank Sinatra's album *Songs for Swingin' Lovers*, arranged by Nelson Riddle, was being heavily programmed on radio. The album combined the influence on Riddle of Sy Oliver's writing, the discipline of Tommy Dorsey in the orchestra's crisp musicianship, and the Dorsey-inspired singing style of Frank Sinatra.

Tino Barzie recalled, "Every night, when we would get in the car, the first thing Tommy did was to play with the radio. He wanted to hear somebody playing that album. He used to say, 'That son of a bitch is the greatest singer ever! He knows exactly where to go and what to do. The little bastard used to look at me and watch what I was doing when I was playing and he'd ask me, 'How do you hold notes so long? How do you hold that phrase so long?'"

According to Lee Castle, "Tommy used to say, 'I have to give Frank credit. He's got good taste. He won't let anybody push him around.' So I said to him, 'I wonder where he got that from?' Tommy started laughing."

At about the same time, Sinatra realized that his most recent completed film, a western called *Johnny Concho,* in which he played the title role and also produced, was a certified turkey. Forever a brilliant marketer, Sinatra realized he needed a significant event to bring attention to the world premiere of *Johnny Concho*—anything to disguise how bad the movie really was. He came up with the idea of reactivating the stage shows at the Paramount by headlining with Tommy and Jimmy Dorsey for a week.

Hank Sanicola, who had made the transition from song plugger to becoming Sinatra's personal manager and also served as his bodyguard, called Tino Barzie to translate this idea into a reality. Tommy, unwilling to let his grudge against Sinatra interfere with a significant business opportunity, okayed the deal with one stipulation: "I conduct the orchestra. It's *my* orchestra." He insisted that he had to be onstage with his band during Sinatra's performance. Sinatra agreed to Tommy's terms. It was also agreed that Nelson Riddle would come to New York just before the August 15 gig began in order to rehearse his arrangements for Sinatra with the Dorsey band.

Having to deal with Frank Sinatra again gave Dorsey considerable apprehension. He loathed the situation that confronted him with the upcoming engagement at the Paramount, the place where he had first featured Sinatra as *his* band singer during the winter of 1940. As shown by recent troubling incidents, it appeared that a growing depression was overtaking Tommy's long-held belief that he was invincible and could handle any situation put in front of him.

Just before the rehearsals were to begin, as Janie New recalled, "Tommy hit his [car] horn as he drove up out front, and I went to a window and looked down. There were Tommy and two gentlemen, one of whom was Nelson Riddle. The other was Dave Rose. Tommy, of course, was friends with both of them. He said, 'Hi, E-flat.' That was his nickname for me. I'm told that on a trombone it's a very light note and very hard to reach. I think that was my first meeting with Nelson. I know it was also the first time I had met Dave Rose."

Nelson Riddle said the reason he agreed to spend the weekend with Tommy and Janie was "I had never seen him other than as an employer. I wanted to see what he was like just as a fella."

The next morning Jane awakened, looked out the window, and saw a solitary figure walking down the road next to the lake on the Dorseys' property. She quickly dressed and joined Nelson, who was sitting on a white birch log tossing pebbles into the lake.

"I joined him and asked him what he was doing up so early," she recalled. "'Well, the quiet got to me,' he replied. We looked up at Tommy's bedroom, and he said to me, 'Janie, do you have any idea how much that man taught me?' I told him that I had a pretty good idea. He said, remembering the days with the Dorsey band, 'He taught me everything I know. Every note I write I learned from that man upstairs.' Nelson added, 'People rave over my arranging today, and I just think to myself, God bless Tommy Dorsey. If it hadn't been for him, I never could have done it.'"

When Tommy said to Nelson, the next night, "I really like the things you've been doing with Frank," Nelson essentially repeated what he had told Janie: "I'll tell you the truth: Much of the skill and ability to do these things came from my time with you." In a rare candid moment, Dorsey had let his guard down to show his vulnerability. He began to cry. Nelson rushed over to embrace him and added, "That's true, you're the one. You're the one who steered me."

In his depressed state, Dorsey confessed, "Nelson, I don't want Frank to come to rehearsal and give me orders or cast any aspersions on me or embarrass me in front of my boys. I couldn't stand that." Nelson said, "He won't do that. Don't worry, Tommy, he won't."

"I got up and went over to Tommy and put my arm around him," New remembered. "I said, 'Tommy, you know he's not going to do anything like that. He wouldn't dare.'"

On Monday, in New York, Nelson and Tommy listened to several of Sinatra's records and went over the scores that Nelson had brought along. Nelson realized that some of his arrangements for Sinatra were out of tempo and therefore more complicated than Dorsey was used to. He found it odd showing Tommy how his arrangements should be played."

Tommy's melancholia continued to surface. He said to Riddle, "Look at this: You're writing for him [Sinatra]. You worked for me. [Now] he's the big star. He worked for me [starting at] $125 a week. Here I am still playing one-nighters with a band."

At the rehearsal, before Sinatra arrived, Dorsey told the band, "Do whatever he says, but just remember, everything he knows he learned from me." Bill Miller, Sinatra's longtime pianist, remembers the intricate system of communications designed to keep Tommy from ever losing face: "I remember that Frank and Tommy got along fine. The only thing was, if Frank wanted to change something in an arrangement or to delete eight bars and go to the rhythm section, or something like that, I had to be the one to go to Tommy and talk to him about it. Frank would never go directly to Tommy. I was the secretary. I presented things in such a way that Tommy was always very gracious."

Sinatra gave Tommy equal billing, and Jimmy got 50 percent of Tommy's billing. All shows during the first two days at the Paramount were complete sellouts.

Jazz educator and publicist Arnold Jay Smith attended several Sinatra-Dorsey performances "with a bunch of guys," moving down from the back of the balcony to the front with each show, just as the bobbysoxers had done years before. Smith recalled:

The Dorsey band rose from the pit of the Paramount to start the stage show. After Tommy's theme song, the band played "Song of India." Lynn Roberts sang "I've Got the World on a String." We booed her. After a while she got the message and said, "Yeah, I know it's Frank's song, but I'm going to sing it anyway." After that, Joey Bishop came out. He was a relatively unknown comic at the time.

Sinatra came onstage without any introduction. Whether they knew what to do—some young girls ran on the stage and started to tear his clothes off. They took his handkerchief, they took his tie after they ripped it from his neck, and he let them. The guards were very amicable. They didn't chase the kids from the stage. Sinatra and Tommy did "Marie" together. Sinatra was in his milieu; it was what he loved to do. It was a long show. Sinatra kidded about *Johnny Concho,* saying, "I wish they didn't have to show this picture over again. I'd come out and do another show for you if they'd let me." Everybody screamed so loud you'd think the balcony was going to come down.

After the second day, Sinatra came down with a severe cold and couldn't finish out the week. Jackie Gleason, Red Skelton, Ed Sullivan, and Walter Winchell were called on to take over Sinatra's star spot.

All summer long, the country was in a constant state of excitement over Elvis Presley. He was on television, was constantly talked about—sometimes with derision—in the press, and was about to debut in movies with a starring role in *Love Me Tender*. And now the Dorseys suffered unforeseen indifference to their music, as did so many other pop music veterans.

At the Steel Pier in Atlantic City a zealous teenage fan of Tommy's, the future stockbroker Jim Duke, came to see the band perform at this important dance-band venue, where it had played countless times over the years. Duke recalled, "The band played with little verve—understandable, I suppose, given the size and demeanor of the crowd. As the Dorsey brothers stood near the edge of the bandstand, some guy, obviously three sheets to the wind, kept asking Tommy, 'Do you remember Bix?' Needless to say, he was ignored. I also well remember the four-bar trumpet chases between Charlie Shavers and another trumpeter [probably John Frosk], dueling with their horns partially pointed toward each other on 'Well, Git It!' and the entire trumpet section playing the Bunny Berigan solo on 'Marie.'"

What had thrilled young audiences over the years was beginning to register as dated, especially in view of the new music predominating on radio and television. Young people now wanted to hear *their* music played by musicians of their own age group.

In the fall of 1956, America's prosperity was of decided help in the reelection campaign of Dwight Eisenhower in his race against Adlai Stevenson. Adults who had first seen the Dorsey brothers leading their own band during the dismal economic times of the 1930s enjoyed spending their newfound wealth on trips to New York, which often included coming down to the Statler to relive their past if only for a night. They sometimes brought their sons and daughters to introduce them to the Dorseys' music. One night Tommy treated the audience to four-year-old Steve Dorsey singing "Standin' on the Corner" (written by his old friend Frank Loesser, from his newly opened Broadway musical *The Most Happy Fella*) with the band.

Tommy was still full of get-rich schemes while buying and selling stocks based on tips from his wealthy friends and newspaper articles and books he read on the stock market. One of his schemes involved investing in a company that manufactured buttons used by prominent clothiers. Another was E-Z Pop, which made popcorn quickly and easily. A third one was a company that made chocolate, strawberry, lemon, and other flavors of straws. He also briefly considered buying some other music-publishing companies, but never actually did so. He still had hopes of starting his own record company.

Though he was no longer an MCA client, Dorsey maintained a friendly relationship with Larry Barnett. Barnett recalls his impression of Dorsey at that time: "I think he began to hate the music business. He wanted to be a successful businessman. I also think he would have liked to be a producer of motion pictures. He liked talking about finances and making money. I suggested that he buy bonds and tax-free bonds that were very cheap and you wouldn't pay taxes on, but he wouldn't go for that. He wanted to be the smart guy, and he wanted to outsmart everybody else."

His feelings about perhaps getting into a new kind of business were symptomatic of the uncertainty that was so much a part of him that final summer. He knew he couldn't really give up the band. "The Brother" and Mom depended on it to keep financially solvent. And then there was his own family to support and the house in Greenwich to pay for.

Dorsey's home life was in shambles. From the beginning, Tommy's relationship with Janie had been contentious and less than honest. By some accounts it had also been violent. An associate of Harry James's manager, Pee Wee Monte, who requested anonymity, remembered accompanying Monte to the Casino Gardens one night in 1948 for an early-evening meeting with Tommy. They walked in to witness Tommy slapping New, whom he had married only months before, and then saw him drag her across the dance floor by her hair and throw her out on the boardwalk. When asked about the truth of this incident, New at first hesitated and then firmly asserted, with an obviously troubled look on her face, "If he had laid a hand on me, the marriage would have been over then and there!"

Yet Smitty Carbone described in detail an afternoon she spent a few years later in Las Vegas when she and Vince were in the back seat of Tommy's car, with Tommy and Janie up front, driving down Las Vegas Boulevard near what was then the Desert Inn:

> We were all drinking. Tommy said something to Janie, which made her very angry. [In those days] women carried purses that were made of metal. Janie's was mother-of-pearl. She had removed her makeup and filled it with silver dollars. When Tommy made this remark, she hit him on the head with her purse. God that must have hurt! Tommy quickly opened the car door and pushed her out of the car. She fell on her butt.
>
> Vinnie screamed, "Tommy, Tommy! Remember who you are—you're Tommy Dorsey! If this gets in the paper, oh my god!" Tommy stopped the car, got out, picked up Janie, cuddled her in his arms, put her in the front seat, and then said, "Give me that damn purse!"

Dorsey, of course, had been a serial philanderer for a matter of years, but he kept a macho double standard. He would fly home unexpectedly in private planes, attempting to find Janie with other men. Finally, he hired a private detective, who photographed her with singer Johnny Johnston having sex. Dorsey proudly showed the pictures to members of the band.

Finally, New filed a divorce action against Dorsey on October 24, 1956, at Fairfield County Superior Court in Bridgeport, Connecticut, on grounds of extreme cruelty. Temporary alimony was set. In a preliminary hearing, the judge suggested that pending the granting of a divorce, the two of them should live in their own locked bedrooms, perhaps an unusual arrangement for a couple about to divorce. They lived in separate wings of their home, which was called "Ho Hum Hollow"—a misnomer for sure!

Tommy's old friend George T. Simon saw a lot of Tommy that summer and fall. Simon noticed, "The decline of the band business bothered him. He always seemed to be fighting with something or somebody. He was not a content man at this time. The thought of divorce and losing his two children put a toll on him."

As an example, when bassist Billy Cronk gave his notice, Tommy chased him down the street in New York; sometime after John Frosk had left the band, Tommy threw furniture against the wall in his Paramount Theater dressing room, threatening to have Frosk (a Canadian) deported!

Stage Show ran through the summer on CBS. After Labor Day, the band returned to the Statler. The September 22 program marked the official end of the show, when the Gleason show returned to its full-hour variety format. In that same month, the Dorseys participated in a fiftieth anniversary recording for Paul Whiteman, which reunited various members of his orchestra. It was the Dorsey brothers' last recording together.

The retired MGM film producer Doug Laurence, who had begun a friendship with Dorsey as a teenager, and who had hired him twice to play for him at the Home Show in Los Angeles, spent several hours one mid-autumn night with Dorsey and Tino Barzie at Hamburger Heaven in New York. He recalled Dorsey's mood: "It was the first time in my entire life I had ever seen Tommy suffering. He was a fallen hero. God, was he down. He discussed his upcoming divorce and how he was going to hide his assets. He brought with him [Janie's] bills from Saks Fifth Avenue—they amounted to a thousand dollars—and enormous telephone bills. According to him, she was a bitch. And not only that, but she was the first woman in the world, I think, who ever told him that he was too old for her."

When Tommy celebrated his fifty-first birthday on November 19 at the Statler with Tess and Jimmy, he could look back on decades of triumphs. He had kept the band going all those years through the inevitable ups and downs of the music business. It was his refuge, his creation. It gave him a tremendous feeling of accomplishment because *his* musicianship and leadership had made it successful. Nothing else in his life gave him the sense of control he craved above everything else. Yet he couldn't control the country's changing musical taste. He couldn't stop time. And he couldn't bend his wife's will to his own.

He wasn't in the best of health, either. Several weeks before, in a checkup at Johns Hopkins Hospital, the beginning of an ulcer was discovered. One of his doctors suggested to Dorsey that he should drink some wine before dinner.

Six days after his birthday, on the Saturday of Thanksgiving weekend, November 24, the band did its customary fifteen-minute radio show on CBS live from the Statler. After finishing the gig to end the week, Tommy drove to a favorite Italian restaurant in the Bronx with Lee Castle, where he had arranged to meet Vince and Smitty Carbone, who had attended the band's performance that night. Smitty Carbone remembers Dorsey's eating rigatoni and saying, "We're [he and Janie] getting along better. Sometimes she likes to eat Italian food that I bring home." At 5:30 A.M. Dorsey and the Carbones left the restaurant and drove to their respective homes.

The next afternoon, according to New, "Tommy puttered around the garden and played with the children." At 3 P.M. Carbone called Dorsey as prearranged. They had a brief conversation, and Dorsey promised to call him that evening.

That night, Dorsey and Janie, plus her mother, Ruth Hightower, dined on veal scaloppini and steak, which Tommy had brought home the night before. They enjoyed the hearty meal, and Tommy had two glasses of wine with his dinner. (New said that his drinking had previously caused problems between them.)

Sometime after 8:30 P.M., Dorsey went to his room in the northwest corner of the house, saying he wanted to watch television and planned to sleep late the next morning. At about 9 P.M., Dorsey called Carbone, who later stated that Dorsey sounded incoherent. He thought he was drunk. It could have been the combination of wine and the sleeping pills that Dorsey often ingested.

Concerned, the agent then called New at her private number in the house and asked her to check on Tommy to see if he was all right. New put the receiver on a table, knocked on Dorsey's bedroom door, and was told by Tommy that he was busy talking to Carbone on the telephone. After New relayed this information to Carbone, he hung up.

Shortly thereafter, New called Dorsey on his line. Dorsey told her he was about to go to sleep. At 11:30 P.M. she called Carbone and informed him that she had tried the door of her husband's bedroom and found it locked. She said she could hear his television set playing and could also hear him snoring.

Carbone, who lately had been using the office in the basement of Dorsey's home to book the band, arrived for work Monday morning at 10 A.M. He was told by New that Tommy was still sleeping. When Dorsey hadn't appeared by 2 P.M., New tried the door to his bedroom but found it was still locked.

Tino Barzie had spent the early part of Thanksgiving with Jimmy and Tess Dorsey at Tess's apartment and then drove up to Pittsfield, Massachusetts, to spend the rest of the day with his family before returning to New York. When Carbone telephoned Barzie that afternoon to inform him he could see Dorsey lying on his bed, presumably through the keyhole, Barzie told him to break in and see what was going on. Barzie immediately took a train up to Greenwich.

Carbone placed a ladder against the outside of the house, climbed up to the second floor, and was able to open the unlocked window in Dorsey's dressing room and climb in. There was Dorsey lying on his back, with his right knee bent, covered with blankets up to his chest. Underneath he was fully clothed in a black sports shirt, gray slacks, and black socks. There was vomit on both sides of his face, mouth, and nose, and on both sides of the pillow on which his head rested. There were no signs of life. Carbone immediately called the Greenwich hospital and then the Greenwich police department.

There were four Greenwich police officers who investigated the death, including Chief of Police David W. Robbins. Patrolman Joseph Trefny discovered a note written in pencil that read, "Janie, You and mother have been such Golddiggers that you dug underneath my love for you. I love you Janie. God Bless you 'cause your [sic] so miserable." Though Tommy Dorsey's final note sounded suicidal, none of his inner circle believes that despite his recent depression, he had any intention of taking his life.

After the discovery of the body and the arrival of the police, New was extremely distraught and on the verge of collapse. Dr. John Bolton was called, and on his arrival, he attended to her.

A gold pillbox with the initials *TD* inscribed on it was discovered. It had a slide drawer with two compartments, which contained both neutral and greenish-colored pills. The body was removed to the Greenwich hospital morgue.

On Barzie's arrival at the Dorsey home, New became angry upon encountering him. The policemen requested that he and Carbone leave the premises. They went downstairs to the office. One of the policemen talked with them about showing the note to New. Barzie and Carbone begged him not to show it to her. A copy was made of the note in order to present it to her later.

Upon viewing the body, the medical examiner, C. Stanley Knapp, determined that Dorsey's death was caused by asphyxia due to the inhalation of food particles into his lungs. He had become sick to his stomach while he slept and was choked by food that lodged in his windpipe while vomiting. The retired trumpeter Chris Griffin said, "Isn't that ironic, the guy with the greatest breath control died from choking." It was officially designated that Dorsey had died somewhere between 2 and 4 A.M. that morning. Four days later, Knapp's conclusion was amended to state that the death was caused by Dorsey's being anesthetized by barbiturates when he choked to death.

When finally shown the explosive note, New asked the policeman, "I wonder who he means by 'mother'? He called my mother Ruth. He never called her mother." When questioned further, she also said that everything had been fine between her and Dorsey on their last night together. She also stated that she had been hopeful that their problems could be resolved.

When Barzie went to the police station, he was reprimanded by Chief of Police Robbins for giving a statement to the press from a bogus note *he* had written under Dorsey's name that read, "Dear Janie, Thank you very much for the dinner. It was wonderful, and be sure to thank your Mom. I am leaving early in the morning. Kiss Susan for me before she leaves for school." It was signed "T." Barzie said he had fabricated the note "to relieve the pressure on Mrs. Dorsey."

One important fact went unreported: The day after Tommy Dorsey died, November 27, 1956, divorce proceedings between him and New had been scheduled to open at Fairfield County Superior Court; but of course that never took place.

Because of his previous divorces, it was impossible for Tommy to be interred in Shenandoah. New wanted the burial to be near Greenwich, but Jackie Gleason took over and had Barzie make plans for Tommy to be buried at the Kensico Cemetery in Valhalla, New York, not far from White Plains.

Dorsey's death was given major coverage in newspapers throughout America. The *New York Daily News*, then the nation's largest newspaper in circulation, emblazoned, "Tommy Dorsey Found Dead in Locked Room" in large type across its front page. The next day, the story's writer, George Trow, speculated, in typical tabloid fashion, that Dorsey "may have died because no one heard him fighting for his life."

Upon hearing the news of Tommy's death, many friends of hers and Tommy's hurried over to Tess Dorsey's apartment. Tess revealed that Tommy had talked to her on Sunday night complaining of not feeling well. Tess's nurse companion, Jeanie Horn, said that upon hearing the news Tess had been given sedatives but didn't fall asleep until 1:30 in the morning.

Jimmy rushed over to her apartment after learning of Tommy's death and spent most of the day with his mother and the others. He said to Cork O'Keefe, who was also a visitor, "I don't think I'll last out the year." Upon his return to his suite at the Statler, he refused to take any telephone calls. Lee Castle led the band that night. He said to the audience, "Jimmy will be back in a day or two, and we'll keep going." Tommy's trombone rested on an empty chair in front of the band.

That afternoon Jess Rand was on the Columbia Pictures lot in Holly-wood. He decided to drop in to see Frank Sinatra on the *Pal Joey* set. He ran into Hank Sanicola, who told him Tommy Dorsey had died. "When Frank heard the news, he told George Sidney [the director] he couldn't work anymore that day and went home," Sanicola related.

John Frosk was backstage warming up before playing a concert with the Benny Goodman band in Seattle. He heard the news of Dorsey's passing on the radio and immediately knocked on Goodman's dressing-room door. Benny was sitting down, playing scales, when Frosk informed him of Dor-sey's death. Benny's response was "Is that so?" In characteristic Goodman fashion, he continued practicing.

Doc Severinsen remembered, "The day that I heard Tommy died—boy, that had a horrible effect on me. I was in New York, where I was a studio musician, and I was doing okay. I had been thinking: I want to go back with Tommy's band. But when I heard the news, I felt like, 'Oh, man. I'll never see him again. I'll never get to play with him again.' I had the feeling of 'Look where I am now.' A lot of it was attributable to having worked with him. It was such a loss. God, he was a giant!"

Sy Oliver's response was "They say no one is irreplaceable, but I'd like to see someone replace Tommy."

Although it had been several years since Candy Toxton, now married to Mel Torme, had been involved with Tommy, his death had a dramatic effect on her: "When I was pregnant, I opened the newspaper one day and saw the story, 'Tommy Dorsey Dies.' I went into spasms and blacked out. I lost my baby that day. I knew that it resulted from reading about Tommy's death."

A viewing of the body was held at the Frank Campbell Funeral Home at Madison Avenue and Eighty-first Street in New York. Dolly Sinatra, who had enjoyed knowing Tommy when her son sang with the band, came over from Weehawken to pay her respects. But Frank chose not to fly in for the service, which took place at Campbell's on Thursday, November 29.

The funeral, a nonsectarian service, was attended by over three hundred people. The upstairs gallery, where the eulogy was piped in, was completely filled, as was the downstairs. Hundreds more stood outside on the sidewalk. The coffin was covered with purple orchids and golden chrysanthemums. On it was a note: "For my dearest friend—Jackie Gleason." Above the coffin was a huge wreath of flowers circling a brass trombone that had been sent by Louis Armstrong, who was on the road.

Besides Gleason, other personalities attending included Guy Lombardo, Tex Beneke, Paul Whiteman, Joe Venuti, Eddie Condon, Dick Haymes, Martha Raye, and Russ Morgan. Pat Hooker and Lieutenant J. G. Tom Dorsey III of the navy air corps, who got emergency leave to come from Hawaii, were there, but not Susan or Steve Dorsey, whom their mother deemed too young to attend.

The organist played "I'm Getting Sentimental over You" over and over as the mourners filed in. Billy Cronk, Lee Castle, and Joe Cabot sat in a row filled with Dorsey musicians. Cronk brought momentary humor to the proceedings when he became so incensed at the wrong chord changes being played in Dorsey's theme song by the organist that he leaned forward and said to Lee Castle, "If the Old Man [Dorsey] doesn't climb out of that box and kick the shit out of that guy, then I know he's really dead."

Janie New arrived with her mother. Her anguished cries were heard at several points during the eulogy given by BMI executive George Marlo, who had previously run Dorsey's publishing company. Marlo concluded his ten-minute talk with the remark, "At this moment, I feel Tom is in the number-one chair of the brass section of Gabriel's celestial music. In departing, Tom, you are leaving a pair of shoes difficult to fill."

A contingent of twenty-three limousines proceeded to the cemetery in Valhalla. There were two large tombstones, one horizontal with "Dorsey" inscribed on it, and the other, in a vertical position perpendicular to it, with the following inscription: "Thomas F. Dorsey, Jr. 1905–1956," and below that "Tommy" and then, "November 19, 1905" and "November 26, 1956," and then the first four bars of "I'm Getting Sentimental over You." Below the score was an engraved bell of a trombone with the inscription "The Sentimental Gentleman of Swing." Gleason paid for Dorsey's funeral service and his elaborate tombstone.

Art Carney's brother had died the same week. Gleason gave him the following Saturday, December 1, off from *The Honeymooners* but then decided to forgo his regular show. He wanted to mount a tribute to Tommy. With the assistance of Barzie, George T. Simon, Jack Philbin, and others, a memorial program was put together which was televised in Gleason's time slot.

Frank Sinatra begged off from appearing, saying, "I didn't like him. It would be inappropriate for me to appear on a memorial show." Buddy Rich took Sinatra's refusal as a signal for him not to appear either. (Bill Miller feels that perhaps the real reason for Sinatra's refusal was that *he* wanted to produce the tribute.)

Gleason narrated the show with a combination of sincerity and schmaltz. The show opened with a rousing "Royal Garden Blues" played by former Dorsey alumni Max Kaminsky and Pee Wee Erwin (trumpets), Bobby Byrne and Russ Morgan (trombones), Joe Dixon (clarinet), Bud Freeman and Boomie Richman (tenor saxophones), Joe Venuti (violin), Carmen Mastren and Eddie Condon (guitars), Sandy Block (bass), Howard Smith (piano), and Moe Purtill (drums). From Hollywood, where portions of the show also originated, Axel Stordahl conducted the Dorsey band and Matt Dennis played piano on his "Will You Still Be Mine?" which Connie Haines reprised. In New York, Dick Haymes, with Lee Castle conducting the band, sang "Daybreak." Again in Hollywood, Jo Stafford, with her husband, Paul Weston, conducting, sang "Little Man with a Candy Cigar" and "Embraceable You." Bob Crosby did "Dinah," with instrumental assistance from Red Nichols, Charlie Barnet, Joe Bushkin, and others. Vic Damone, taking Sinatra's place, sang "I'll Never Smile Again" and then dueted with Connie Haines on "Oh, Look at Me Now," along with additional choruses by Bob Crosby and Jo Stafford back in New York. Jimmy Dorsey, looking completely devastated, went through the motions as he conducted a medley of his brother's hits, which included Charlie Shavers being featured on "Well, Git It!" That was followed by a short trombone solo on "Once in a While." Stuart Foster sang "This Love of Mine." Tommy's last male singer, Tommy Mercer, did "There Are Such Things." Sy Oliver sang "On the Sunny Side of the Street" and sang a duet with Lynn Roberts on "Yes, Indeed." After all that, the band played "Song of India," "I'll Never Smile Again," "Boogie Woogie," and then "Marie," with Jack Leonard on the vocal and Jimmy contributed a dazzling alto solo. Vinnie Forrest beautifully played all of Tommy's trombone solos standing behind a curtain in silhouette.

Paul Whiteman gave a brief, heartfelt salute to Tommy, and Jimmy thanked Gleason for making the tribute possible. Due to the problems inherent in live television, when the show ran long, Gleason was preempted from saying his closing lines: "I wish I could say—the way announcers used to do, 'Join us tomorrow night for more music by Tommy Dorsey and His Orchestra,' but I can't—because there are no tomorrows left for us with Tommy. . . . Good night everybody."

9

Epilogue

THE DAY after Tommy's death, Jimmy Dorsey said to columnist Earl Wilson, "What am I going to do now that Brother's gone? It's pretty late in life to start all over again." This comment said it all: He was lost without "The Brother" who ran the band and took care of everything.

Professionally, Jimmy made a fresh start, if not a completely new one. Tino Barzie continued managing the band and helped make the decisions so that the band could continue. Jimmy changed the billing for the band to "Jimmy Dorsey and the Fabulous Dorsey Orchestra." Its theme song reverted to Jimmy's "Contrasts." A reworking of Tommy's theme deleted his famous trombone solo and started with the second reed interlude. During Christmas and New Year's weeks, Jimmy led the band on NBC radio's *Bandstand*, hosted by Bert Parks, and on a CBS remote broadcast.

The band finished the Statler engagement on January 3, 1957. Flea Campbell and Lynn Roberts left at the end of the engagement as Roberts was pregnant with their first child. In the closing weeks of 1956, Campbell watched Jimmy's spirit deteriorating: "I'll tell you. He took Tommy's death harder than anybody. He went right downhill." Lee Castle said, "He cried every night after that. He said, 'Brother took a powder on me. He left me alone.'"

Jimmy's lung condition worsened. He was informed that he would have to have his left lung removed. The operation took place at Doctor's Hospital in New York. The press was told that the growth was not malignant; Jimmy believed that the cancer was removed, but it wasn't. Following the surgery, Jimmy rested until January 21, the start of the winter tour.

A few weeks before he died, Tommy had convinced Larry Barnett that MCA should sign Jimmy. "I think Tommy was too embarrassed to say that *he* wanted to come back as well," Barnett believes. He met with Jimmy in the hospital, where Jimmy told him that he was broke and needed twenty-five thousand dollars before agreeing to sign a five-year contract. Barnett gave him the money as a loan against future commissions.

The huge commissions then being paid to the agency by actors like Jimmy Stewart, Cary Grant, Doris Day, Clark Gable, Marlon Brando, Tony Curtis, Gregory Peck, and Montgomery Cliff and playwrights like Arthur Miller and Tennessee Williams had long since dwarfed the kind of money brought in by bandleader clients such as Guy Lombardo, Harry James, Charlie Barnet, Sammy Kaye, and Wayne King, much less the money paid by Tommy Dorsey, Benny Goodman, and others in their heyday.

There was more in the deal for MCA than the fact that Jimmy was carrying on the Dorsey legacy. On its release, Jimmy's single record of "So Rare" (a tune which he had first played back in 1937) for Fraternity Records, a small Cincinnati-based record company, received a tremendous response from the nation's disk jockeys. The arrangement written by Howard Gibeling was completely rewritten by Neal Hefti, emphasizing the prevailing musical mood of the country with a strong rock 'n' roll beat. Jimmy's wailing solo was very much in the style of Earl Bostic, "Sam the Man" Taylor, and other "honkers" of the time.

For Jimmy, tasting the sweetness of this success didn't come easily. When Harry Carlson of Fraternity Records initially approached Jimmy about recording the song, Jimmy, in his usual self-effacing manner, said, "I just don't want you to get hurt. Why fool around with a has-been?" Tommy initially had had no objection to Jimmy's making some money by recording with the band.

The Dorsey band had recorded "So Rare" on November 11, two weeks before Tommy's death; it wasn't released until late January, but Tommy had heard an advance copy of it. He was furious: "The Brother" was selling out to the musical taste of the kids! He screamed at Jimmy, "How could you bastardize the Dorsey sound! I ought to hang you. I'll buy up every copy of it and burn it."

When Jimmy returned to the road after his cancer surgery, the absence of Tommy's powerful presence and financial support made it unbearable for him. Now he had to be a bandleader once again. Having Tino Barzie with him was helpful, but he missed Tommy terribly. As Tess Dorsey saw it, "My Jimmy never got over my Tommy."

On February 27, 1957, two days before Jimmy's fifty-third birthday, the band played all of Jimmy's hits at a concert in San Antonio, which I attended. For most of the numbers, the response from the small weekday crowd at the General Jonathan Wainwright Memorial Auditorium that night was lukewarm at best. Jimmy remarked more than once during the concert about how rock 'n' roll had shoved the big band out of the musical picture. By his gaunt physical appearance, and particularly by the rasping sound of his voice, it was obvious that he was a very sick man. Despite that, he seemed pleased, yet bewildered, by the fact that he had a potential hit record in "So Rare." The audience's response to "So Rare" was much more enthusiastic than that of the Dorsey hits of yesteryear that were played that night.

This was to be Jimmy's final road tour. His seriously weakening condition, compounded by his drinking, was evident in subsequent dates in the Southwest and the Midwest. At the Orpheum Theater in Minneapolis, the scene of many previous triumphs for Jimmy Dorsey, he was booed by the audience when he stumbled during his saxophone solos. Neither the press nor the general public was aware of his illness.

When the band returned to the Big Apple to open at Roseland on March 19, recalled John Frosk, who rejoined the band after receiving a telegram from Jimmy in Hong Kong while with Benny Goodman: "Everybody in the music business was there. The reason was they knew Jimmy was sick, and they didn't know how long he would last. He would sit on a high stool and play. One night after intermission, we started without Jimmy. Tino came up and asked, 'Where's Jimmy?' Somebody said, 'He went back to the hotel.' Tino ran as fast as he could to the Warwick Hotel. Supposedly, when he opened the door to Jimmy's room, he found Jimmy ready to climb out the window. After the engagement was over, I went with Jimmy to the Bal Harbor Hotel in Miami Beach, where he could rest and recuperate."

Cork O'Keefe flew to Miami to visit his old client. Appalled at Jimmy's appearance, he had him flown to New York, where he again checked into Doctor's Hospital. He never left. He died of lung cancer on June 12, 1957.

A requiem mass was held three days later at St. Patrick's Cathedral on Fifth Avenue with about a thousand mourners in attendance. The love he had engendered over the years while Tommy overpowered him in popularity was evident in the large turnout.

Jimmy's body was brought to Shenandoah for burial next to his father in Annunciation Church Cemetery. In comparison to what Tommy's passing had received seven months earlier, the press coverage of Jimmy's death was minor. The memorial show Jackie Gleason hosted was heard on CBS radio.

Jimmy's friends remember him as warm, simple, and unassuming. He was never meant to enjoy the lasting success of The Brother. Softness, quietness, and gentleness were qualities that were the antithesis of a successful band-leader. He simply didn't have the flair, much less the drive, dedication, and leadership qualities, that Tommy possessed. He always knew that.

"So Rare," the last hit by either brother, was truly rock 'n' roll, the music that his late brother vowed had ruined the band business. At the funeral, Guy Lombardo predicted that the success of "So Rare" (which eventually reached number three on the Billboard Pop Chart, remained on the chart for thirty-eight weeks and became a gold record) "will bring back the band business." It was wishful thinking.

The combined number of hit records amassed by the Dorsey brothers remains astounding to this day: a total of 286 top-forty Billboard Pop Chart hits. In addition, at the time of their deaths, they had sold 110 million records. These staggering totals came at a time long before mass media marketing was even thought about. On September 11, 1966, the U.S. Postal Service would commemorate the importance of the Dorseys as part of a four-stamp block honoring important bandleaders.

The loss of her two beloved sons in such quick succession was naturally a staggering blow to Tess. She drew on her staunch Catholic faith and stoically withstood her terrible loss. Weeks later, she observed, "The strong one died first."

Tess moved to Mar-Lin, Pennsylvania, outside Pottsville and lived her final years with Connie and Bill Motko in their home. She died at the age of ninety-three on June 22, 1968. To the end she remained extremely proud of her sons' contribution to the country's music and how much happiness it had brought to so many people.

Tommy died leaving no will and reportedly left only about $15,000—the result of many years of *Livin' in a Great Big Way*. In view of the divorce proceedings that had been scheduled, Pat Hooker and Tom Dorsey III opposed New's being designated as the administrator of Tommy's estate. They agreed to it only when New set up a bond of $200,000 to cover legal costs.

New, with two small children to support, was compelled to sell the heavily mortgaged Greenwich home for $90,000 and moved her family to an apartment. Her financial problems were complicated further by the fact that Tommy had left $26,000 to Pat Dane in the form of an insurance policy after she informed him that she had been injured in a boating accident, which prevented her from working. He had responded by insuring himself in her name. Three years later, New sued and won a judgment for $6,347 against Dane to cover taxes on this insurance policy paid by Tommy's estate.

There would be other lawsuits. A year later, Tino Barzie sued Tommy's estate and collected over $22,000 on an unpaid loan dating back to when he had managed the band. In desperation, New put Tommy's lucrative publishing companies up for sale. She also sold to Columbia Records the tapes that Tommy had stockpiled over the last few years. Fortunately for her, the album *Tommy and Jimmy Dorsey in Hi-Fi* sold well; it would reach a peak of #8 on the Billboard Pop Chart in 1958.

Tex Beneke had started the "ghost band" trend when he took over the leadership of remnants of The Glenn Miller Army Air Force Band in March 1946 with a Capitol Theater gig. In June 1956, in collaboration with the Miller estate, agent Willard Alexander, who had launched the Swing Era in 1935 with Benny Goodman, resurrected the band, designating drummer Ray McKinley to lead a new Glenn Miller Orchestra. Alexander vigorously objected to the term *ghost band*, insisting, "There are no ghosts in any of this. All we're trying to do is keep up with the demand for a certain kind of music that has persisted for several decades."

Since Janie New continued to need money to support her family and because she legally owned the rights to Tommy's library of arrangements, she was naturally very interested when Alexander approached her about creating a Tommy Dorsey band. In 1957, trombonist Warren Covington became its leader. The cha-cha was the dance craze of the time, and the new Dorsey band's record, "Tea for Two Cha Cha," reached number seven on the Billboard Pop Chart in September 1958 and remained on the chart for fourteen weeks. The *Tea for Two Cha Cha* album that followed owed much of its success to the hit single.

After a few years, Covington left to form his own band. In spite of the often combative relationship between New and Tino Barzie, in late 1961 Barzie convinced New that he could successfully create a Tommy Dorsey orchestra under the direction of ex-Dorseyite tenor saxophonist Sam Donahue. For its debut date in Santa Monica, Barzie put together a nostalgia-oriented package, which featured the Dorsey band, along with guest stars Ziggy Elman, Bill Raymond, Helen Forrest (who had starred as a band singer with Shaw, James, and Goodman, but not with Dorsey), and a new Pied Pipers.

Ghost bands continued to tour extensively with varying success. The cost of keeping a band on the road became prohibitive. Well-paying engagements in the lounges of the gambling casinos in Las Vegas and Lake Tahoe helped keep them alive.

Larry O'Brien joined Sam Donahue's refurbished Tommy Dorsey Orchestra in January 1962, to play the original Dorsey solos. When he asked Donahue, "Do you want me to play Tommy or me?" Donahue said, "Split the difference."

In the summer of 1963, Barzie induced Frank Sinatra, Jr., to assume the male band singer's chair once held by his father. Sinatra, Sr., figured there was no better finishing school for a young singer than the Tommy Dorsey band, singing many of the songs he had originally made famous. Frank, Jr., gave a certain cachet to this Tommy Dorsey Orchestra, but soon bookings for dance bands became even harder to come by.

America was suddenly enamored of the frug and the watusi, dances where the partners don't even touch; the fox trot and the jitterbug were yesterday; and discotheques were the new places to dance, not ballrooms. But then four lads from Liverpool, England, changed music and the world when The Beatles made their American debut in February 1964 on the *Ed Sullivan Show*.

For several years in the late 1960s there was no Tommy Dorsey Orchestra per se. Instead, Frank Sinatra, Jr., fronted a septet led by Sam Donahue with Larry O'Brien playing some Dorsey material. When this combination lost its luster, it disbanded. O'Brien moved to Las Vegas and later became the leader of the Glenn Miller Orchestra, a job he has held for more than twenty years.

Janie New continued to express her very definite ideas about how the Tommy Dorsey band should function. This led to frequent hassles with her various bandleaders and agents.

In late 1966 leading into 1967, Urbie Green took over the leadership of the next Tommy Dorsey Orchestra for an extended engagement at the Riverboat in the basement of the Empire State Building. Green, one of the most revered of the more modern trombonists, and New didn't get along, however, which resulted in his resigning the leadership. For seven years thereafter there was no Tommy Dorsey Orchestra.

Bill Watrous, a trombonist whose remarkable technique has gained him a sterling reputation as both a musician and a teacher, was recommended to New by Willard Alexander during the late 1970s to take over the leadership of the Dorsey band. New wanted him to audition and ordered Watrous to record Tommy's theme with piano and bass accompaniment.

As Watrous recalled, "I recorded the last eight bars. Willard then told me that Janie wanted to interview me. I went to the Plaza Hotel, where she was staying with her daughter. She asked me why I didn't play all of the tune. I said, 'At these prices, the eight bars is all you get. If you want to go and pay for a recording for me to go and do this, I'd be absolutely delighted, but I have no intention of doing that. You don't need the whole nine yards to be able to tell whether I can handle the job.'"

New asked Watrous what he thought of Dorsey's music, which he termed "one of the greatest. The band is wonderful." When Watrous referred to Dorsey as a "razzmatazz player, he wasn't a jazz player," New called his statement elitist. She ended the meeting by saying, "I'm not really very impressed with what I'm hearing." Watrous didn't get the job.

With New's approval, in April 1974, Murray McEachern, who had created a solid reputation for years as a trombonist with Paul Whiteman, Glen Gray, Benny Goodman, and Billy May before becoming a first-call studio musician, inaugurated a new Dorsey band. (As an alto saxophonist he had played the Johnny Hodges parts with Duke Ellington's band the year before.) After two years on the road with the Dorsey band, McEachern suffered a debilitating stroke; he passed away several years later.

After another hiatus Buddy Morrow, who coincidentally had led the Glenn Miller band for a short time, took over the leadership of the Tommy Dorsey Orchestra in 1979 and continues to the present. Coming back from cancer surgery on his tongue in 2001, at eighty-six years old, Morrow is back playing many of Tommy's famous solos, although some of them he has handed off to Steve Duncan, sixty years his junior.

As for New, she devoted the rest of her life to perpetuating the importance of Dorsey's music, sometimes at the expense of her children and friends. She married again, but it didn't work out. Tommy Dorsey was, after all, a difficult act to follow.

In 1952, Bill Finegan, along with his sidekick, fellow arranger Eddie Sauter, formed the Sauter-Finegan Orchestra. Fundamentally a concert orchestra, launched by RCA Victor, the band never quite found an audience. It disbanded in 1957. In the intervening years, the modest arranger and composer wrote commercials for television, taught jazz studies at the University of Bridgeport (Connecticut), and wrote occasional charts for various jazz artists such as his forthcoming string project for cornetist Warren Vache.

Jamie Finegan, Bill Finegan's son, now working as a music teacher and freelance musician, became a member of the Dorsey band's trumpet section for nine months in 1986 at the age of twenty-four. This was immediately after studying music at the University of Bridgeport and the Berklee College of Music in Boston.

Finegan remembered the long jumps through the Midwest and Canada on the band bus *Night Train* (named after Buddy Morrow's big hit record of the 1950s): "Your chops got so ferocious from the endurance built up from playing every single night. There was a vibe on the bus after a good night on the road that everyone in the band felt. It was a phenomenal time in my life."

Finegan, however, saw the limitations of being a member of a touring big band: "It teaches you what you don't want to do more than what you want to do. You're playing the same tunes every night. You have no responsibility other than to be coherent and play what's on the printed page in front of you for two or four hours a night. I didn't enjoy being a mechanic. It was an anthropological experience."

Playing many of his father's charts gave Jamie a new appreciation for his father's vaunted musical abilities: "I realized why he was so respected—the way his parts played. He took a lot of care in voicing them so that each person's part was lyrical. . . . His scores were challenging, but rewarding if you could play them. He really cared about doing it right. Musicians realize that."

Finegan noted the fact that the Dorsey band had a reputation as a "drinking man's band," in contrast to the Miller band, which had achieved a reputation for being more straightlaced. "I guess it had something to do with the [freewheeling] kinds of musicians that Tommy chose as against those Glenn used to hire. It's probably still true today," said Finegan.

The future of young jazz musicians today is both limitless and, at the same time, highly uncertain. With better training they are better prepared musically, but conditions simply aren't the same. Stardom is also no longer around the corner for bright young big-band musicians as it once was, chiefly because the band business is at a complete standstill.

Musicians who worked with Doc Severinsen in his twenty-five years as leader of the *Tonight Show* band, when Johnny Carson was the host, say that he ran the band with the same demand for perfection that was so much a trademark of Dorsey's. Severinsen still practices every day and, at seventy-eight, remains a first-rate trumpet player years after most of his contemporaries have long since lost their lip. He says the mental image of Tommy's embouchure can still help him correct his own.

Now the pops conductor of symphonies in Denver, Milwaukee, Minneapolis, and Phoenix, Doc features former Dorsey vocalist Lynn Roberts on several dates a year. He proudly related, "When we do a big-band concert and play the Tommy Dorsey things, she and I know exactly what we're doing. It's like it was yesterday. Dorsey left a real imprint on you."

Along with Buddy Morrow, other octogenarian Dorsey alumni who are still active include Buddy DeFranco and Louis Bellson. After leading the Glenn Miller Orchestra from 1966 to 1974, DeFranco, eighty-three, invested his money wisely. He now divides his time between homes in Panama City, Florida, and Whitefish, Montana. He continues his decades-old regimen of practicing at least three hours daily, which has helped him maintain his stature as one of the three essential jazz clarinetists of all time. He is still in demand for jazz festivals, recordings, and occasional jazz club appearances like the Iridium in New York. Summing up his three stints with Dorsey, he says, "If you could put up with him, and he could put up with you, you could learn a lot from him."

Bellson, at eighty-one, makes selective appearances in both Europe and the United States at jazz clinics, festivals, and night clubs, and also as a spokesperson for Remo Drums. Clint Eastwood, long a devoted jazz fan, threw a party at his Carmel Highlands ranch on Bellson's eightieth birthday. Bellson absolutely electrified the audience that night with his still powerful playing.

Ex-Dorseyites Jo Stafford and Paul Weston, who married in 1952, purchased their masters from Columbia and Capitol after seeing the abrupt change in popular music that took place. Both of them had enjoyed flourishing careers. As a pop singer Stafford had a cascade of hit records that lasted close to two decades, such as "Long Ago and Far Away," "I'll Be Seeing You," "I Love You," "Make Love to Me" (her biggest seller), "You Belong to Me," "Shrimp Boats," "Jambalaya," and many others.

It was the close collaboration between Stafford and Weston as singer and arranger that made "You Belong to Me" a pop music masterpiece. Weston's romantic albums were among the first commercially successful "mood" albums. His *Crescent City Suite* album provided a symphonic jazz portrait of New Orleans.

In addition to rereleasing their earlier records on their Corinthian Label, Stafford and Weston came up with the innovative and hilarious duo of "Jonathan and Darlene Edwards," whose records were completely out of character with their own highly craftsmanlike work. Their spoofing approach consisted of playing the wrong key changes on piano (Weston-Jonathan) and the worst corny out-of-tune singing imaginable (Stafford-Darlene). Their brilliant satire *Jonathan and Darlene Edwards in Paris* won a 1960 Grammy for best comedy album, and four others followed.

Weston died in September 1996. Stafford today spends considerable time with her children, Tim, a guitarist and record producer, and Amy, a singer, and her three grandchildren. She remains a voracious reader, especially of World War II material—a period very close to her heart since during that time the popularity of her records caused her to be called "GI Jo." In 1990 she came out of retirement for one night to sing "I'll Never Smile Again," backed by the Hi-Los, when Frank Sinatra was presented with the Ella Award by the Society of Singers at the Beverly Hilton. She reveres Dorsey today as much as she ever did. "He was special," she says.

Other Dorsey veterans came to sadder, or more clouded ends. In stark contrast to the disciplined musical lives exemplified by Morrow, DeFranco, Bellson, Stafford, and Weston, there was the tragic end of Ziggy Elman. The boisterous trumpeter maintained his allegiance to Dorsey throughout the late 1940s, after his own band failed, by filling in whenever Dorsey needed him.

As a studio musician, however, Elman didn't last long. Paul Weston, who featured him on several albums, once explained to me, "The life of a studio musician is very different from that of a traveling musician who plays two or four hours a night. Ziggy couldn't handle studio calls for two sessions a day, and his drinking got the best of him." Before too long his famous iron lip was gone. After the fiasco of being fired from the movie *The Benny Goodman Story*, when he was unable to re-create his immortal "And the Angels Sing" solo, his reputation took a steep decline. Soon he was unable to function as a live performer as well; Ziggy Elman died at the age of fifty-four on June 26, 1968, at a time when he was barely surviving, with only periodic teaching jobs in Los Angeles.

And then there was the fate of the most celebrated Dorsey alumni, the two who matched Dorsey in volatility: Buddy Rich and Frank Sinatra. After his final departure from Dorsey in 1955, the peripatetic Rich appeared with various musical organizations and led small groups on records and in nightclubs. But most of these endeavors were essentially directionless, and they may have helped contribute to his suffering a massive coronary in late 1959. He was slow to recover his strength, but it had absolutely no effect on his unique personality.

In 1962 he joined Harry James for the most rewarding sideman experience he ever encountered. James paid him well, gave him featured billing, and allowed him to wear his own clothes onstage. Rich got along well with

James. The lure of leading his own band once again proved to be too strong, however, and in the summer of 1966 he left and debuted his new big band at The Chez in Hollywood to tremendous acclaim.

The release of a "live" album on United Artists Records from the Chez the following year was a hit during the height of Beatlemania. Always quick to adopt the latest pop fads, Rich turned "mod" in his dress to go along with his complementary idea of building a new library of contemporary tunes for his band, such as his dynamic instrumental version of Lennon and McCartney's "Norwegian Wood," arranged by Bill Holman. This approach grabbed the attention of members of the rock 'n' roll generation, as did his sarcasm, cockiness, and complete irreverence.

Johnny Carson took notice of Rich's newfound appeal—and his dazzling drum solos—all of which made for great television. He often sat in with Doc Severinsen's band, whose regular drummer was Dorsey alumnus Ed Shaughnessy. Carson wound up featuring Rich fifty-nine times as a guest on the *Tonight Show,* over a period of about fifteen years. With this kind of exposure, "Kong" (as Mel Torme dubbed him) thought he had it made. He believed that his popularity would never end and refused to play any dance dates offered his band. (He was a jazz musician at heart.) Eventually, his record sales cooled off, and so did the demand for his band.

But Rich's arrogance didn't cool off. The famous tape that consisted of Buddy telling off his band that circulated during the 1980s throughout the jazz business represents an onslaught of unabashed terror. ("I'm up there workin' my balls off tryin' to do somebody a favor and you motherfuckers are suckin' all over this joint. . . . I'm accustomed to working with number one musicians. I'm NOT accustomed to working with half-assed kids who think they wrote the fuckin' music business. You got a way to go!") In the ferocity of this personal attack on his musicians, damning their ineptness, the voice may have been Buddy Rich's, but the sentiment and feeling were pure Tommy Dorsey.

In March 1987, at the age of sixty-nine, Rich checked into the UCLA Medical Center for treatment of brain cancer. As part of a normal procedure, he was asked by the nurse if he was allergic to anything. "Yeah, country-and-western," was Rich's rejoinder. He was released from the hospital to stay with his sister for the last week of his life. His wife, Marie, and his daughter, Cathy, were with him at the end on April 2, 1987. Frank Sinatra, who abhorred attending funerals, gave the eulogy at the funeral, where old friends and a few employers, like Artie Shaw, paid their final respects.

Many disliked Buddy Rich's cocky manner; no one could fail to appreciate his extraordinary talent. There has never been a big-band drummer like him. We shall never again witness his equal.

Unlike Rich, Frank Sinatra resisted the onslaught of rock 'n' roll. During the 1950s, his most artistically fulfilling decade, he recorded some twenty-seven top-ten albums. At the end of the decade he made clear his complete hatred of the new music: "Rock 'n' roll smells phony and false. It is sung, played and written for the most part by cretinous goons. . . . [It] is the most brutal, ugly, desperate, vicious form of expression it has been my misfortune to hear."

By the dawn of the 1960s he had established himself as *the* consummate musical artist in popular music. His newly found popularity owed much to the sense of cool that emanated from his image as the prototype of the swinging bachelor that was reflected in his music. This well-crafted image was actually based on his close friend, composer Jimmy Van Heusen.

In 1961, for the third album on his newly established Reprise label, Sinatra brought Sy Oliver to Los Angeles to arrange and conduct a tribute to Tommy Dorsey, *I Remember Tommy*. His veteran pianist Bill Miller remembered that on the album's first recording session there were only a few strings (three violins, one viola, and one cello): "Frank said to me, 'What the hell is this?' I had presumed that Sy should have known we'd at least use eight violins, two violas, and two cellos—at least twelve strings. On the next date he added strings, but they were all just duplicating the same parts we [already] had. It was merely increasing the volume, which didn't make sense, but Frank just let it go."

I Remember Tommy had a decided charm. It was obvious that it was a project Sinatra really believed in, and having Sy Oliver involved gave it validation. While a few of the circa 1940 and 1941 arrangements Sy had written for him when he sang with Dorsey were reprised, "Imagination" and "The One I Love Belongs to Somebody Else" were newly conceived at a much brisker tempo than the originals. Oliver wrote for the 1961 Sinatra, not the band singer of twenty years earlier. "The One I Love" proved to be a delightful romping duet for Sinatra and Oliver and, at the same time, revealed the profound respect they had long held for one another.

Oliver told George T. Simon, who appropriately wrote the liner notes for the Sinatra album, "Tommy [Dorsey] was like ripe olives. You either liked him a great deal or not at all. In many ways, Frank was just as definite a personality. . . . They're two of the few people who hired me who didn't tell me what to do."

After his successful years at Decca Records, in the 1950s Sy moved on to produce records and head A&R at several other labels. He led small bands for engagements at the Rainbow Grill in New York during the 1970s and 1980s as well as repertory big bands in concert at Carnegie Hall to play the ageless arrangements he had written for Jimmie Lunceford and Tommy Dorsey. He passed away in New York on May 28, 1988, at the age of seventy-seven. His extensive musical library was donated to the New York Public Library of the Performing Arts in 1995 by his now-deceased widow, Lillian.

In the aftermath of his post-1953 success, Frank Sinatra insisted on exerting complete control over every aspect of his career. This meant making his own decisions on every creative situation from his recordings, to his choice of film roles and director, to the media. In time his constant need for maintaining control had adverse repercussions on his career choices.

Almost every album from the mid-1950s until the early 1960s seemed to include the word *swingin'* in its title. And over a period of several years his movies (especially his "Rat Pack" films) became similar and therefore tiresome and self-indulgent. By the mid-1960s his creative juices were not what they once were; he could no longer deliver on the first or second take as he had been doing for years. He refused to concede that fact, however, and no one would dare tell him.

The British invasion and then the emergence of a new group of American rock 'n' roll stars brought Sinatra's recording career almost to a standstill. His best work in serious dramas like *The Man with the Golden Arm* and *The Manchurian Candidate*, were behind him. The appeal of his once highly praised annual television specials fell victim to the changing tastes of a society swept up in a new youth culture.

Following that trend, his third marriage was in 1966, to twenty-one-year-old actress Mia Farrow. It lasted a year and a half. Farrow had a flower child's sensibilities—yoga, zen, and ESP. Maharishis and martinis simply didn't mix.

Over the next two decades, Sinatra crisscrossed the country while also touring Europe, Australia, Brazil, Japan, Egypt, and southern Africa, finding a new appreciation in concert audiences. His 1940s theme song had been "Put Your Dreams Away." His now middle-aged following relived their dreams of yesteryear through his appearances. The many years of "ring-a-ding" living, however, had taken their toll. As publicist for Woody Herman, George Shearing, and the Basie band, all of whom worked with Sinatra, I saw firsthand how his voice began to lose its tenderness, its range, and its resonance. His peerless sense of time remained, and by increasingly relying on his patented hand gestures and body language, he still could effectively put over his songs.

His thinness had once contributed to his electricity and sex appeal, but his paunch, toupee, and jowls told the story of advancing late middle age. That didn't seem to matter to his fervent fan base, however.

The influence of Tommy Dorsey was always there in his singing. His ballads became more emotional and even more autobiographical as the years went by. In the early 1970s, he began giving credit to the songwriters and the arrangers, something that heretofore he hadn't even considered. This was a practice he adopted from Tommy Dorsey, which had been a nightly ritual during his years with the band.

The antecedent for Reprise Records, the company Sinatra founded in 1961, with its artists owning their own masters and leasing them to the company, was an idea first conceived by Dorsey. Sinatra called his production company Essex Productions, the same name as one of Dorsey's publishing companies. And like Dorsey, he even delighted in showing off his own elaborate electric train set. He proudly displayed it to millions on one of his last television specials. It took up an entire bungalow of his Rancho Mirage estate.

Vince Falcone, who played piano and conducted for Sinatra during the 1970s and 1980s, reflected on the perfectionism he and Dorsey shared. "Frank saw Dorsey dismiss musicians off the stage without reason or explanation. If you didn't do what Frank wanted you to do, he didn't come up to you and say, 'This is the way I want it. . . . ' His favorite expression was 'Where are you working next week?' I've seen him angry with musicians, but I never saw him show disrespect for a musician. I also remember him saying, whenever something would come up, he would say, 'This is how Tommy would do it.'"

Sinatra expressed completely different feelings about Dorsey over the years. At a June 15, 1979, concert at the Universal Amphitheater, after warmly introducing Harry James, he mentioned that Harry had let him out of his contract, then added, "And then there was Tommy Dorsey. When I wanted to get out of my contract with him years later, it cost me seven million dollars [sic]." He stamped his foot on the stage and glaring downward continued, "You hear me, Tommy? You hear me? I'm talkin' to you," as if Dorsey were smoldering in hell for the wrongs he'd committed against him. Is there any wonder that one day in the 1950s Dorsey said of Sinatra, "He's the most fascinating man in the world, but don't stick your hand in the cage."

An older Sinatra struck a different note about his mentor one night in the summer of 1991 at the bar in the Hotel De Paris in Monaco. Drummer Greg Field had just started touring with Sinatra. He was a perfect choice for the job. His first important professional association had been with the Tommy Dorsey Orchestra Under the Direction of Murray McEachern. Fields and bassist Chuck Berghoffer sat down to drink with their boss. Berghoffer asked Sinatra, "Who were your influences, especially for time?" As Field recalled, Frank started to talk about Tommy Dorsey. "It was a surprise to hear somebody of Frank Sinatra's stature talking with such reverence about anybody else. . . . When he was talking about Tommy Dorsey he was obviously talking about somebody who had a huge musical influence on him, but it went beyond music. That's what we [both] felt from that conversation. Frank really loved him." Sinatra went on to relate to Field and Berghoffer his frequently told stories about how he discovered that Dorsey could play such long fluid lines on ballads without seeming to take a breath. Field noted, "The way Frank built those lines on ballads, it sounded like a trombone line, and the way you would phrase it."

By the mid-1970s Sinatra's music was out of step with contemporary American sensibilities. He tried singing such ill-advised songs as "Bad, Bad Leroy Brown" and those of Rod McKuen. He was trying desperately to be "with it," but instead he wound up sounding anything but hip. The sophisticated audience that had long adored him lost interest.

Jo Stafford, his former musical compatriot, summed up his plight by stating succinctly, "You don't understand. He has to have this!" as she rigorously clapped her hands, indicating the engulfing warmth of adulation that could only be supplied by a live audience.

Frank Sinatra, Jr., began conducting the orchestra for his father in 1988. Vince Carbone became his personal manager. Carbone remarked that despite the elder Sinatra's increasing forgetfulness in his last years of touring, "he never stopped telling those stories about life on the road with Dorsey." Battling dementia, Frank Sinatra left the concert stage at the end of 1994. He died at Caesars-Sinai Medical Center in Los Angeles on May 14, 1998.

Indeed, Frank Sinatra and Tommy Dorsey were two of a kind—volatile, demanding, yet charming and engaging. Their dueling egos would never allow them to ever form a lasting bond of friendship, but musically they were close brethren. The artistry in American popular music gained substantially through their collaboration.

In 1956, Pat Dane had a small part in Humphrey Bogart's last movie, *The Harder They Fall*. Eventually she moved back to her native Florida. Her last years were spent living in the town of Bluntstown, forty miles from Panama City, working as a librarian. She died in 1995.

Janie New Dorsey passed away on August 24, 2003, in Miami; she arranged for herself to be buried next to her "beloved Tommy" in Valhalla, New York. Tommy's oldest child, Pat Hooker, died in Williamsburg, Virginia, nine days later. Tommy's three other children survive. Tom Dorsey III, seventy-four, long retired from IBM, resides in Greenwood Village, Colorado, with his wife, Barbara. As Janie's heirs, Steve Dorsey, fifty-two, and Susan Dorsey, fifty-six, now own the Tommy Dorsey Orchestra.

The volume of concert dates, cruise ship bookings, and private dance dates for the Dorsey band declined after the September 11 attack. Until then, the band had been on the road for close to forty weeks a year.

Flea Campbell continues to tour with the band, playing second trumpet and the jazz solos. He also serves as its road manager. Asked to describe today's audience, Campbell says, "It's mostly senior citizens—people who think they remember Tommy Dorsey, but they probably don't. Let's face it, they're going to be gone soon. At one time I was optimistic, but I'm not really anymore. There's no recording, no television appearances, no new bands. The only place to hear this music is when we do our concerts. Every time we play a concert there's a standing ovation at the end. There's nothing to take its place, so when it's gone and when the audience is gone, what's left?"

Tommy Dorsey's recording catalog remains a steady seller for BMG/Bluebird. The boxed set of Sinatra-Dorsey recordings that was released in 1994 sold exceedingly well. In 2004 *Young Blue Eyes*, consisting of air checks, was also successful. In the fall of 2005, there will be a release of a Sony/BMG three-CD set as well as a single Sinatra-Dorsey CD released to commemorate Tommy Dorsey's one hundredth birthday.

On the death of baseball great Ted Williams in 2002, after watching several days of television news coverage Bill Finegan came to a sudden realization: "I was seeing Ted Williams, but I was really hearing Tommy Dorsey. The straight-from-the-shoulder way that Ted always approached things was exactly like Tommy—his opinions on just about every topic, the authority with which he spoke, and even his speaking voice had much the gruffness that Tommy had. It was an amazing experience to see Ted but hear Tommy."

Interviewing John Frosk, Joe Cabot, and Billy VerPlanck together in the fall of 2003, forty-seven years after they last worked for Tommy Dorsey (at the time of his death), it was readily apparent to these musicians that Dorsey's presence was still very much a part of their lives. Frosk said, "Tommy had class. I admired him a lot." When asked if Dorsey was the model for any bandleader he ever worked for, Cabot answered, "Not even close." VerPlanck offered, "I worked for a lot of bandleaders. I met Tommy Dorsey, and he was everything that I imagined him to be."

In his own view, Tino Barzie said, "I have no idea whether or not it would succeed today if Tommy Dorsey came back. . . . But from the way he performed that music, that music would have stayed around a long time with Tommy leading the way. I'll always remember him saying before the start of a set, 'Time to play big league ball.' From the minute he started the theme song 'til we finished that night, everything was business. I don't think Tommy would have ever given up—never!"

Barzie completed his speculation by saying, "Holy Christ, if he ever did come back, I'd be happy to work for him again—for nothing. I loved him. There was just nobody like him."

Notes

Chapter 1: Music, Music, Music

2   **many of the mine owners:** John O'Hara, *Appointment in Samarra.* (New York: Harcourt, 1934), p. 49.

3   **Thomas Francis Dorsey, Jr., came next:** More than a decade ago, it was reported that Tommy was actually born on November 26. This date was noted on his baptism record. There has never been any explanation concerning this discrepancy, and its validity has often been questioned. *Parade Magazine*, March 1954.

   During the coal strike of 1902: Robert Wyatt and John Henry Johnson, *The Gershwin Reader* (Oxford and New York: Oxford University Press, 2004), p. 30.

4   **George Gershwin was paying:** Richard English, "The Battling Dorsey Brothers," *Saturday Evening Post*, February 2, 1946, p. 19.

   He often found himself coaching: *Parade Magazine*, March 1954.

   people with thin lips: Ibid.

   Dad bought us some instruments: Mort Goode, "Break Off, Make Off, Take Off," liner notes to *The Complete Tommy Dorsey*, Volume 1 (RCA Victor Records), 1980.

5   **but very badly:** Herb Sanford, *Tommy and Jimmy: The Dorsey Years* (New Rochelle, N.Y.: Da Capo paperback edition, Arlington House, 1972).

   Jimmy duplicated the triple tonguing: Robert L. Stockdale, *Tommy Dorsey on the Side* (Metuchen, N.J., and London: Institute of Jazz Studies, Rutgers University and the Scarecrow Press, 1995).

6   **The Father:** Lewis W. Gillenson, editor in chief, *The Esquire Jazz Book* (New York: Thomas Y. Crowell, 1947).

   hoping to stem this rivalry: Mort Goode, op. cit.

7   *I leaned more to brass:* Richard English, op. cit.
     they had to do it in their own way: Ibid.

8   *I didn't have nobody:* Ibid.
     she learned to play the E-flat ballet horn: Herb Sanford, op. cit.
     Mary's interest in music: Parade Magazine, op. cit.
     Five dollars was a lot of money: Richard English, op. cit.

9   *and get it he did: Panther Valley Gazette,* July 2002, reproduced from the
     Shenandoah Herald, Labor Day weekend, 1945.

12   *They're getting too fast:* Richard English, op. cit.
     We learned a lot of tricks: Curt Williams, series of articles on big bands,
     Valley Gazette, March 1996.
     The band's repertoire consisted: Eddie Condon's Treasury of Jazz, edited by
     Eddie Condon and Richard Gehman (New York: Dial Press, 1956), p. 291.

13   *it was time the dancers went home:* Robert L. Stockdale, op. cit.
     The kid brother played: Cleo Lucas, "From Coaldust to Stardust," un-
     published manuscript, p. 29.
     exposure in important locations: Geoffrey Wolff, *The Art of Burning
     Bridges: A Life of John O'Hara* (New York: Knopf, 2003), p. 72.

14   *The Sirens Are Coming:* Amy Lee, "Tommy Fell Asleep on the Job,"
     Metronome, 1940, p. 1.
     the first band to travel by car: Geoffrey Wolff, op. cit., p. 72.
     The Sirens' solid dance beat: Herb Sanford, op. cit., p. 18.
     The Sirens contract was: Amy Lee, op. cit., p. 1.

15   *the stepping stone to Madison Square Garden:* Herb Sanford, op. cit.,
     p. 18.
     employ the Dorseys: Amy Lee, op. cit., p. 1.
     he became an important organizer: The Biographical Encyclopedia of Jazz
     (Oxford and New York: Oxford University Press, 1999), p. 260.
     Louis Armstrong was the first: Whitney Balliett, *Collected Works: A
     Journal of Jazz, 1954–2000* (New York: St. Martin's Press, 2000), p. 615.

16   *already unmistakable:* Ibid., p. 34.
     Bix had seen Louis Armstrong: Orrin Keepnews and Bill Grauer, *A Pic-
     torial History of Jazz* (New York: Crown, 1955), p. 16.
     He almost smiled: Russ Tarby, "The Sweet Man," *Syracuse New Times,*
     April, 22, 1998.
     weren't blown—they were hit: Jazz, The First Century, edited by John
     Edward Hasse (New York: William Morrow, 2000), p. 32.

17   *The jazz flavor of the Goldkette band:* Geoffrey C. Ward and Ken Burns,
     Jazz: A History of America's Great Music (New York: Knopf, 2000), p. 141.
     in his driving arrangements: Herb Sanford, op. cit., p. 24.
     [it] swung like mad: Geoffrey C. Ward and Ken Burns, op. cit., p. 141.

Chapter 2: Bites of the "Apple"

19   ***Praise Allah:*** "Big Apple" was written by Lee David and John Redmond and was published by EMI Mills Music, 1937.

    considerable work for musicians: Richard Sudhalter, *Lost Chords* (New York: Oxford University Press, 1999), p. 307.

20   ***The corny stocks [arrangements]:*** Mezz Mezzrow and Bernard Wolfe, *Not Really the Blues* (New York: Random House, 1946), p. 80.

21   ***broke into tears:*** Herb Sanford, *Tommy and Jimmy: The Dorsey Years* (New Rochelle, N.Y.: Arlington House, 1972), p. 28.

22   ***the gin he had bought:*** Robert L. Stockdale, *Tommy Dorsey on the Side* (Metuchen, N.J., and London: Institute of Jazz Studies, Rutgers University and the Scarecrow Press, 1995), p. 4.

23   ***March 15, 1925:*** Richard Sudhalter, liner notes to *Best of the Big Bands* (Columbia Records), 1997.

    Jimmy, more musically advanced: Robert L. Stockdale, op. cit., p. 16.

    No one cared about straight playing: Stanley Dance, *World of Earl Hines* (New York: Scribners, 1977), p. 48.

25   ***Tommy accepted the offer:*** Gary Giddins, *A Pocketful of Dreams* (Boston, New York, and London: Little, Brown, 2001), p. 143.

    something new or different: Brian Casey and Stan Britt, *The Illustrated Encyclopedia of Jazz* (New York: Harmony Books, 1978), p. 159.

26   ***Don Redman, one of the true:*** William Ruhlmann, "Living in a Great Big Way in Swingtime," *Goldmine*, June 10, 1994, p. 18.

    W. C. Handy, composer of: Howard J. Waters, Jr., *Jack Teagarden's Music* (Stanhope, N.J.: Walter C. Allen, 1960), p. 14.

28   ***Whiteman used Tommy:*** Brian Casey and Stan Britt, op. cit., p. 159.

    Tommy would often regale: Eddie Condon, *We Called It Music* (New York: Henry Holt, 1947), pp. 149–150.

29   ***we all turned up again:*** Richard Sudhalter, *Lost Chords* (New York: Oxford University Press, 1999), p. 364.

    The close friendship: Robert L. Stockdale, op. cit., p. 35.

30   ***awestruck by Teagarden's talent:*** Sam Lanin, unpublished manuscript, p. 194.

    musical taste and lip control stemmed:. Robert L. Stockdale, op. cit., p. 139.

    Mole often worked: Mort Goode, liner notes to *A Time for Change: The Complete Tommy Dorsey* (RCA Victor Records), 1981.

31   ***all he could talk about was:*** Stanley Dance, *The World of Earl Hines* (New York: Scribners, 1977), pp. 90–91.

    he went into the 'woodshed': Ibid., p. 33.

some 140 million records: Bill Crow, *Jazz Anecdotes* (New York: Oxford University Press, 1990), p. 283.

33   *It sounded as if:* Robert L. Stockdale, op. cit.

34   *Tommy was drunk:* Ibid.

movie attendance had doubled: Stan Cornyn with Paul Scanlon, *Exploding* (New York: Harper Entertainment, 2002), p. 6.

35   *the abrupt closing of Great Day:* Robert L. Stockdale, op. cit., p. 139.

$750 a week: William Ruhlmann, op. cit., p. 18.

36   *Tommy Dorsey sent me:* Herb Sanford, op. cit., p. 35.

he owed them too much money: "Two Rounds of the Battling Dorseys," in *Reading* Jazz, edited by Robert Gottlieb (New York: Pantheon Books, 1996), p. 503.

A bulletin board on the wall: Robert DuPuis, *Bunny Berigan: Illusive Legend of Jazz* (Baton Rouge, London: Louisiana State University Press, 1993), p. 33.

37   *imparting a buzzing, rasping quality:* "Kazoo (Bazooka, Blue-Blower)," in *The New Grove Dictionary of Jazz*, Volume 1, edited by Barry Kernfeld (Oxford: Oxford University Press, 1988).

stored in the refrigerator: Robert DuPuis, op. cit., p. 33.

38   *Tommy made it a habit:* Charles Edward Smith, "Pee Wee Russell," in *The Jazz Makers*, edited by Nat Shapiro and Nat Hentoff (New York, Toronto: Rinehart, 1957), p. 112.

39   *trying to keep peace:* "Two Rounds of the Battling Dorseys," in *Reading Jazz*, edited by Robert Gottlieb (New York: Pantheon Books, 1996), p. 503.

Tommy got into an argument: Ibid., p. 502.

recorded with some twenty-two: William Ruhlmann, op. cit., p. 18.

featured Tommy on trumpet: Ibid.

arranged the record deal: Richard Sudhalter, liner notes to *Best of the Big Bands—Dorsey Brothers* (Sony Music's Columbia Legacy), 1992.

40   *"Melancholy Baby" found:* Richard Sudhalter, *Lost Chords*, op. cit., p. 368.

"Ooh, That Kiss": Ibid.

These marked the first: William Ruhlmann, op. cit., p. 18.

the DBO was billed as the Travelers: Robert L. Stockdale, op. cit., p. 195.

41   *lost the show:* Amy Lee, "Dorsey Brothers Name Didn't Mean a Thing!" *Metronome*, 1940.

42   *musicians who understood:* Richard Sudhalter, *Lost Chords*, op. cit., p. 371.

43   *Connee also recorded on her own:* Ibid., pp. 371–372.

two months later: Robert L. Stockdale, op. cit., p. 234.

a resounding and enduring hit: William Ruhlmann, op. cit., p. 18.

44   *305 banks had failed:* Robert L. Stockdale, op. cit., p. 256.

Chapter 3: "I'll Never Say 'Never Again' Again"

46   **to add to O'Keefe's representation:** George T. Simon, *The Big Bands* (New York: Macmillan, 1967), p. 47.

he was a member of the bands: Leonard Feather and Ira Gitler, *Encyclopedia of Jazz* (New York: Oxford University Press, 1999), p. 464.

47   **Glenn made an economic decision:** George T. Simon, *Glenn Miller and His Orchestra* (New York: Thomas Y. Crowell, 1974).

Tommy stood out in front: Herb Sanford, *Tommy and Jimmy: The Dorsey Years* (New Rochelle, N.Y.: Da Capo Press paperback edition, Arlington House, 1972), p. 44.

The Dorseys had often played for Bing: Ibid., p. 118.

We were trying to hit: Albert McCarthy, *Big Band Jazz* (New York: Exeter Books, 1974), p. 194.

the celebrated prince of Wales: Leonard Feather and Ira Gitler, *Encyclopedia of Jazz* (New York: Oxford University Press, 1999), p. 188.

49   **Ann Sothern (Harriet Lake):** Robert L. Stockdale, *Tommy Dorsey on the Side* (Metuchen, N.J., and London: Institute of Jazz Studies, Rutgers University Press, 1955), p. 351.

50   **Tommy yelled right back:** George T. Simon, *Glenn Miller* (New York: Thomas Y. Crowell, 1974), pp. 64–65.

Simon praised Glenn Miller's: George T. Simon, *The Big Bands*, op. cit., pp. 142, 144.

51   **doesn't mean anything:** Robert L. Stockdale, op. cit., p. 346.

Never heard of them: Ibid., p. 347.

Sands Point Bath Club: Leonard Feather and Ira Gitler, op. cit., p. 144.

52   **prevail on radio:** Joseph Loredo, liner notes to *The Essential Dorsey Brothers, 1928–1935* (Collectors Choice Music, CCM098-2).

53   **Glenn Miller's arranging touch:** Robert L. Stockdale, op. cit., p. 361.

the notorious Huey Long: Albert McCarthy, *Big Band Jazz* (New York: Exeter Books, 1974), p. 194.

54   **the performance proceeded flawlessly:** Robert L. Stockdale, op. cit., p. 361.

introducing the Dorsey Brothers: Herb Sanford, op. cit., p. 46.

Ray McKinley created: Ibid., p. 353.

55   **Lester Lanin's band:** William Ruhlmann, "Livin' in a Great Big Way in Swingtime," *Goldmine Magazine*, June 10, 1994, p. 19.

56   **arguments between the Dorseys:** John Tumpack, "Woodland Hills Resident: Roc Hillman Witness to Dorsey Brothers Breakup," *LA Jazz Scene*, May 2002, p. 22.

soon we'd have an arrangement: George T. Simon, *Glenn Miller*, op. cit., p. 65.

59   *five on the Billboard Chart:* William Ruhlmann, op. cit., p. 19.
      Eberly had continued working: George T. Simon, *The Big Bands*, op. cit., p. 145.

60   *five hours sleep a night:* Ibid.
      a wet bar: *The Evening Herald of Shenandoah, Ashland, Mahanoy City,* August 6, 1983.

61   *confided to friends:* Ibid.
      shoes were smudged: Herb Sanford, op. cit., p. 47.
      "Chasing Shadows": William Ruhlmann, op. cit., p. 19.

62.   *a matter of time:* John Tumpak, op. cit., p. 22.
      the tempo stinks: Herb Sanford, op. cit., pp. 47–48.

63   *His debut with the band:* George T. Simon, *The Big Bands*, op. cit., p. 149.
      the brothers' split: Ibid., p. 366.

64   *sit and listen:* Mort Goode, "Break Off, Make Off, Take Off," liner notes to *The Complete Tommy Dorsey*, Volume 1 (RCA Victor Records), 1980.
      "Top Hat, White Tie and Tails": Herb Sanford, op. cit., p. 367.
      jam with them: Ibid.
      For you I'll do it: Ibid., p. 49.

65   *are heard laughing:* Robert L. Stockdale, op. cit., p. 368.
      appearing as guest stars: Ibid.
      you're the boss: Herb Sanford, op. cit., pp. 49–50.

Chapter 4: "I'm Getting Sentimental over You"

68   *the right road:* Mort Goode, "Break Off, Make Off, Take Off," liner notes to *The Complete Tommy Dorsey*, Volume 1 (RCA Victor Records), 1980.

69   *a musician's band:* Ibid.

71   *RCA bailed him out:* Ibid.
      the label insisted: William Ruhlmann, "Livin' in a Great Big Way in Swingtime," *Goldmine*, June 10, 1994, pg. 20.
      young arranger, Paul Weston: George T. Simon, *The Big Bands*, (New York: Macmillan, 1967), p. 160.

72   *was superhuman:* *New York Times*, Sunday, April 17, 2005, pg. A ZM1.
      people back to work: Peter J. Levinson, *Trumpet Blues: The Life of Harry James* (Oxford University Press, 1999), p. 34.

73   *African-American bandleaders:* Ibid.
      The Lindy was: Ibid.
      the King of Swing: Ibid., pp. 34–35.

75   *arguing over the tempo:* Mort Goode, op. cit.

76   **the most significant records:** John Tumpak, "Jack Leonard—Big Band
     Crooner and Hollywood Businessman," *LA Jazz Scene*, August 2000, p. 23.

77   **Tommy could only afford:** Mort Goode, "A Time for Change," liner
     notes to *The Complete Tommy Dorsey* (RCA Victor Records), 1981.
     Bose showed up drunk: Ibid.

78   **Bose was stranded:** Ibid.
     no trace of animosity: Max Kaminsky with V. C. Hughes, *My Life in Jazz*
     (Evanston, Ill., New York, and London: Harper & Row, 1963), p. 81.
     he could interpret it: Ibid., p. 204.

79   **he adds to the overall performance:** Burt Korall, *Drummin' Men* (New
     York: Scharmir Books, 1990).
     Davey's energy force: Ibid., p. 208.

80   **Then he'd invite Ziggy [Elman]:** Ross Firestone, *Swing, Swing, Swing*
     (New York and London: W. W. Norton, 1993), p. 230.

82   **personally helped his men:** Ibid., p. 83.
     had sandwiches sent: Ibid., p. 58.
     The musicians had to travel: Herb Sanford, *Tommy and Jimmy: The
     Dorsey Years* (New Rochelle, N.Y.: Da Capo Press paperback edition, Ar-
     lington House, 1972), p. 60.

83   **quickly borrowed the services:** Ibid.
     favorably impressed: Ibid.

84   **a popular expression:** Ibid., p. 61.

85   **split the billing with some hillbilly:** Arthur Marx, *Red Skelton: An Unau-
     thorized Biography* (New York: Dutton, 1979), p. 64.
     The thirty-minute-long Tommy Dorsey Show: Herb Sanford, op. cit.,
     p. 61.
     $250,000 a year: Lewis A. Erenberg, *Swingin' the Dream* (Chicago: Uni-
     versity of Chicago Press, 1998), p. 164.

87   **Axel Stordahl and Dick Jones wrote:** Ibid.
     Paul and Axel became close friends: Ibid.

88   **as well as the mood:** John Chilton and Richard M. Sudhalter, *Bunny
     Berigan* (Alexandria, Va.: Time-Life Records, 1982), p. 41.
     On the bill in Philadelphia: Herb Sanford, op. cit., p. 63.

89   **added a little bit:** Mort Goode, liner notes to *The Sound Takes Shape: This
     Is Tommy Dorsey*.
     "lifted" from black musicians: Ibid.
     sold 1 million copies: Ibid.
     rebuffed by Doc Wheeler: Robert DuPuis, *Bunny Berigan: Elusive Legend
     of Jazz* (Baton Rouge and London: Louisiana State University Press,
     1993), p. 138.

91   *in attendance once again:* Herb Sanford, op. cit., p. 70.

matching neckties and socks: Mort Goode, liner notes to A *Time for Change: The Complete Tommy Dorsey* (RCA Victor Records), 1981.

92   *he stayed neat:* Ibid.

93   *grossed $600,000:* William Ruhlmann, op. cit., p. 22.

94   *quite emotional:* George T. Simon, op. cit., pp. 164–165.

95   *Chester was signed to Bluebird:* Ibid., p. 147.

96   *Dorsey didn't speak to Hagen:* Earle Hagen, *Memoir of a Famous Composer Nobody Ever Heard Of* (Philadelphia: Xlibris Corporation, 2000), p. 29.

come on the bandstand stoned: Ibid.

97   *trained himself to lose:* Max Kaminsky with V. C. Hughes, op. cit., pp. 98–99.

98   *We pretended that the applause:* Herb Sanford, op. cit., p. 111.

take back the award: Ibid., p. 116.

101   *got a favorable reception:* Ibid., p. 134.

102   *put myself in a similar position:* Bernie Woods, *When the Music Stopped: The Big Band Era Remembered* (New York: Barricade Books, 1994), p. 51.

cost became prohibitive: Ibid., p. 143.

103   *like Jack and Charlie do:* John E. Usalis, "The Fabulous Dorseys," *Evening Herald of Shenandoah*, September 10, 1991, p. 1.

it was Tchaikovsky's theme: William Ruhlmann, op. cit., p. 24.

105   *two-beat style based on swing effects:* Leonard Feather and Ira Gitler, *The Biographical Encyclopedia of Jazz* (New York: Oxford University Press, 1999), p. 505.

Sweet bands made money: William Ruhlmann, op. cit., p. 25.

a basic lack of sincerity: Ross Firestone, op. cit., p. 229.

106   *make it sound like Lunceford:* Herb Sanford, op. cit., p. 164.

109   *$750 a week:* "Rich + Torme = Wild Repartee," *DownBeat*, February 9, 1978, p. 15.

I thought that was important: Ibid., p. 43.

110   *DeWitt went on to sing:* William Ruhlmann, op. cit., p. 25.

take him away: Peter J. Levinson, *Trumpet Blues: The Life of Harry James* (New York: Oxford University Press, 1999), p. 78.

The note was written: Ibid., p. 79.

111   *Tommy asked him to sing "Marie":* Kitty Kelley, *His Way: The Unauthorized Biography of Frank Sinatra* (New York: Bantam, 1986), p. 51.

If we don't do any better: Peter J. Levinson, op. cit., p. 78.

Jo Stafford received a collect call: John Tumpak, "Jo Stafford, An American Musical Icon," *LA Jazz Scene*, October 2002, p. 15.

Chaper 5: "I'll Never Smile Again"

114 **$110,000,000 that year:** Lewis A. Ernberg, *Swingin' the Dream* (Chicago: University of Chicago Press, 1998), p. 166.

That's the only difference: Peter J. Levinson, "Frankie," *Palm Springs Life*, February 2002, p. 68.

115 **becoming roommates:** Mel Torme, *Traps: The Drum Wonder: The Life of Buddy Rich* (New York: Oxford University Press, 1991), p. 54.

116 **All that matters to him:** Kitty Kelley, *His Way: The Unauthorized Biography of Frank Sinatra* (New York: Bantam, 1986), p. 56.

118 **he became his hero:** Ibid.

the vengeance aimed: Peter J. Levinson, op. cit., p. 77.

120 **circumvent the loyalty:** Arnold Shaw, *Sinatra: Twentieth Century Romantic* (New York: Holt, Rinehart, Winston, 1968), p. 25.

had also managed the Berigan orchestra: Robert DuPuis, *Bunny Berigan: Ellusive Legend of Jazz* (Baton Rouge and London: Louisiana State University Press, 1993).

121 **Bunny Berigan has made:** Ibid., p. 223.

122 **in the back seat:** Mel Torme, op. cit., p. 56.

Dorsey put together a replacement: Ibid., p. 224.

The two songs were released: William Ruhlmann, "Livin' in a Great Big Way in Swingtime," *Goldmine*, June 10, 1994, p. 26.

123 **the orchestra was barely utilized:** Joe H. Klu, "Man Here Plays Fine Piano," *Mississippi Rag*, October 2001, p. 4.

you belong to my people: Remembrance from Frank Sinatra, Jr., contained on his Angel CD *As I Remember It* (7243 36681 20).

125 **more than thirty-one hundred:** William Ruhlmann, op. cit., p. 22.

126 **Apollo Theater in Harlem:** Robert DuPuis, op. cit., p. 225.

127 **had a bandstand built:** Bernie Woods, *When the Music Stopped: The Big Band Era Remembered* (New York: Barricade Books, 1994), p. 51.

costing him $7,300: Leonard Lyons, "The Lyons Den" column, *New York Post*, November 28, 1956.

130 **I can live without a singer:** Ibid., pp. 63–64.

smashed in with a shovel: Mel Torme, op. cit., p. 67.

131 **"And the Angels Sing":** David French, "King of the Sidemen," *Mississippi Rag*, May 2003.

132 **The respect Ziggy engendered:** Ibid.

134 **the mammoth new dance palace:** Dennis McDougal, *The Last Mogul: Lew Wasserman, MCA, and the Hidden History of Hollywood* (New York: Crown, 1998), p. 14.

135   *The Dorsey band was hot:* Ibid., p. 94.

136   *Rich took his cymbals away:* Mel Torme, op. cit., p. 65.

140   *the band had traveled over a million miles:* 1942 MGM biography questionnaire form of Tommy Dorsey.

143   *He sings pretty fair:* John Usalis, "The Fabulous Dorseys," *Evening Herald of Shenandoah*, September 7, 1991, p. 6.
       Thank you very much: Ibid.
       Tips on Pop Singing: William Ruhlmann, "Vocal Refrain by Frank Sinatra," liner notes to *Tommy Dorsey–Frank Sinatra: The Song Is You* (RCA Victor boxed set), 1994.

148   *Dorsey returned the check:* "Kicks Plague Tommy Dorsey," *DownBeat*, May 1, 1941.

149   *attack on Pearl Harbor:* Ibid., p. 71.

150   *Tommy broke it up:* Kitty Kelley, op. cit., p. 153.

151   *The answer was affirmative:* Albert J. Lonstein, *Compilation/Comments* (New York: Revised Publications, 1983), p. 23.
       The Songs, recorded in Hollywood: Kitty Kelley, op. cit., p. 146.
       Frank had become a star: Ibid.

152   *This increased the size:* Gunter Schuller, *The Swing Era* (New York, Oxford University Press, 1989), p. 690.
       The strings made the orchestra: Mel Torme, op. cit., p. 72.

153   *the fight was over:* Dave Dexter, Jr., "Tommy Socks Jimmy," *DownBeat*, July 1942, p. 48.
       Jimmy wore sunglasses: William Ruhlmann, "Livin' in a Great Big Way in Swingtime," op. cit., p. 28.
       only six musicians were left: Mel Torme, op. cit., p. 73.

154   *The song was never recorded:* *Billboard*, September 5, 1942, p. 19.

156   *at a salary of $650 a month:* Kitty Kelley, op. cit., p. 12.
       That was arranged by Manie Sachs: Arnold Shaw, op. cit. pp. 39–40.

157   *a sanitized version of Porter's original:* Liner notes to *Tommy and Jimmy Dorsey: Swingin' in Hollywood* (Rhino Records R2 75283), 1998.
       In 1942, one major hit: Lewis A. Ehrenberg, op. cit., p. 1965.

Chapter 6: "Opus #1"

160   *recorded specifically for the armed forces:* William Ruhlmann, "Living in a Great Big Way in Swingtime," *Goldmine*, June 10, 1994.
       the shortage of the shellac: "MGM Execs Come Out of Dream," *DownBeat*, March 15, 1942, p. 13.
       Tommy re-signed with RCA Victor: Charles Emge, "Movie Dough Eyes Big Wax Profits, New Firm in Offing," *DownBeat*, February 25, 1942, p. 12.

The recording ban didn't affect Dorsey: Mel Torme, *Traps: The Drum Wonder—The Life of Buddy Rich* (New York: Oxford University Press, 1991), p. 76.

161 **based on the actions of Willie Moretti:** Kitty Kelley, *His Way: The Unauthorized Biography of Frank Sinatra* (Toronto, London, Sydney, Auckland, New York: Bantam, 1986), p. 63.

162 **He wanted success:** Peter J. Levinson, *September in the Rain: The Life of Nelson Riddle* (New York: Billboard Books, an imprint of Watson-Guptill, 2001), p. 115.

164 **he should have accepted twenty thousand:** Kitty Kelley, op. cit., p. 63.

166 **on a circular platform behind her:** William Ruhlmann, op. cit., p. 29.
Rich was so upset: Mel Torme, op. cit., p. 78.
renewed the on-again–off-again problems: Ibid., p. 79.
hide Rich's papers: Ibid.

169 **he was not an ideal father:** Wilford Kale, "Dorsey's Daughter Stays Sentimental over His Music," *Richmond Times-Dispatch*, December 17, 1957, p. 7.

170 **a cameo role as well:** Ibid.

171 **the actress retied the halter:** Mel Torme, *It Wasn't All Velvet: An Autobiography* (New York: Zebra Books, Kensington Publishing, 1990), pp. 111–112.

172 **she was wearing dark glasses:** Fabrice Zammarche and Sylvie Mas, *A Life in the Golden Age of Jazz: A Biography of Buddy DeFranco* (Seattle, Wash.: Parkside, 2003), p. 50.

174 **Tommy fired the veteran baritone:** "Dorsey Dorsey!" *Metronome*, February 1944.

176 **a noticeable difference in style:** Peter J. Levinson, op. cit., p. 49.
blood-and-guts-type arrangements: Ibid., pp. 49–50.
I had enough time: Nelson Riddle, *Arranged by Nelson Riddle* (Miami: Warner Bros. Books, 1985), p. 166.

177 **From December 1944 until June 1945:** Keith Keller, *Oh, Jess! A Jazz Life* (New York: Mayan Music, 1989), p. 116.

178 **They tell you:** *Look* magazine, April 4, 1944, p. 47.

179 **it was a definite and unique quality:** Charles Fountain, *Another Man's Poison: The Life and Writing of Columnist George Frazier* (Chester, Conn.: Globe Pequot Press, 1984), p. 3.
Tommy Dorsey's very presence: Ibid., p. 82.

182 **She said she had been threatened:** "Society Girl in Hall Fight," *Los Angeles Examiner*, August 7, 1944, Part 2, pp. 1–3.

183 **had acted in self-defense:** "Courtroom Scene at Dorsey Trial," *New York Journal American*, November 28, 1944.

Fifteen Weary Marines in San Diego: "Dorsey Lawyer Battles Giesler on Who Had Knife," *Los Angeles Herald*, December 1, 1944.

he was unable to specify: Carl Greenberg, "Actor's Testimony on His Cuts Hit by Defense Quiz," *Los Angeles Examiner*, December 1, 1944.

184   *ordered the trial to proceed:* "State Case on Dorsey Completed," *Los Angeles Herald*, December 5, 1944.

   the various discrepancies: Ibid.

   I was never worried: "Judge Freed Dorseys," *Los Angeles Herald Express*, December 7, 1944.

185   *canceled after his indictment:* "TD's Indictment Cancels Movie and Air Offers," *DownBeat*, October 1, 1944.

186   *were the theme songs of choice:* Peter J. Levinson, op. cit., p. 54.

   his former solo opportunities: Fabrice Zammarche and Sylvie Mas, op. cit., p. 60.

187   *Bop musicians for the most part rejected:* "Bop (Bebop, Rebop)" in *The New Grove Dictionary of Jazz*, Volume 1, edited by Barry Kernfeld (New York: Grove Dictionary of Music, 1988), p. 137.

   Gillespie began working with Parker: Leonard Feather and Ira Gitler, with the assistance of Swing Journal, *The Biographical Encyclopedia of Jazz* (Tokyo: Oxford University Press, 1999), p. 514.

188   *Melody seemed to be beside the point:* George Wein with Nat Chinen, *Myself Among Others: My Life in Music* (Cambridge, Mass.: Da Capo Press, 2003).

   If you want to play that way: Bill Crow, *Jazz Anecdotes* (New York, Oxford: Oxford University Press, 1990), pp. 129–130.

190   *DeFranco is broke:* Fabrice Zammarche and Sylvie Mas, op. cit., pp. 60–61.

   they had mutual respect: Ibid., p. 62.

191   *You never knew one minute from the next:* Ibid., pp. 55–58.

192   *Sinatra and Riddle would begin collaborating:* Leonard Feather and Ira Gitler with the assistance of Swing Journal, op. cit., p. 113.

193   *a black trumpeter in the band:* William Ruhlmann, op. cit., p. 52.

   Tommy had signed a deal: "Dorsey Dorsey!" *Metronome*, February 1944.

197   *Dorsey immediately went after Rich:* Peter J. Levinson, op. cit., p. 46.

   We had been flown from LA: "Nelson Riddle Talking," *Crescendo International*, August 1967, p. 10.

   There are three rotten bums: Whitney Balliett, *Super Drummer: A Profile of Buddy Rich* (New York: Bobbs-Merrill, 1968).

198   *This was really surprising:* Fabrice Zammarche and Sylvie Mas, op. cit., p. 66.

203 ***There were numerous other factors:*** Peter J. Levinson, *Trumpet Blues: The Life of Harry James* (New York: Oxford University Press, 1999), p. 162.

Today's younger generation: Ibid.

205 ***between January and June 1946:*** William Ruhlmann, op. cit., p. 30.

Chapter 7: The Rules of the Road

209 ***The famed Dorsey feud:*** Thomas F. Brady, "Bank of America Sues on 2 Movies," *New York Times*, March 15, 1950.

the Bank of America sued: Ibid.

211. ***the pizza operation was a failure:*** Ibid.

214 ***featuring Gordon Polk singing:*** Arnold Shaw, *Let's Dance: Popular Music in the 1930s*, edited by Bill Willard (New York: Oxford University Press, 1998), p. 88.

was uninspiring: William Ruhlmann, "Livin' in a Great Big Way in Swingtime," *Goldmine*, June 10, 1994, p. 31.

215 ***Dorsey then went one giant step:*** Fabrice Zammarche and Sylvie Mas, *A Life in the Golden Age of Jazz: A Biography of Buddy DeFranco* (Seattle, Wash.: Parkside, 2003), pp. 63–64.

Bellson came up with the idea: Ibid.

a trifle more bearable: Ibid., p. 64.

220 ***really sensible and humble:*** Ibid., p. 54.

224 ***Pat Dane even sent:*** Fred Dickenson, "The Sentimental Gentleman's Georgia Bride," *American Weekly*, insert in *New York Journal American*, June 20, 1948, p. 15.

This is the last marriage: *Time* magazine file report from Bill Howland, April 6, 1948.

227 ***Dorsey recorded Finegan's instrumental:*** William Ruhlmann, op. cit.

The melody had been: Loren Schoenberg, liner notes to *Tommy Dorsey and His Orchestra: The Post-War Years* (RCA Victor Records) 1993.

228 ***making statements [about bop]:*** Ralph J. Gleason, "TD Told to Open Ears to Bop," *DownBeat*, September 23, 1949.

231 ***the real sonority:*** Ibid.

237 ***helped swell these figures:*** William Ruhlmann, op. cit., p. 31.

238 ***Jack Leonard and Dick Haymes guested:*** Ibid.

on the road for MCA: David W. Stowe, *Swing Changes . . . Big Band Jazz in New Deal America* (Cambridge, Mass., and London: Harvard University Press, 1944), p. 105.

239   **signed by Tommy Dorsey:** Ralph Gleason, *The Swing Era 1932–1942,
Swinging Is a Way of Life* (New York: Time-Life Records, 1970), p. 42.

250   **Why do you judge me:** "View from the Other Side," *Jazziz*, January 2004,
p. 17.

Chapter 8: The Final Reunion

255   **the decade led to McCarthyism:** James Harvey, *Movie Love in the '50s*
(New York: Knopf, 2001).

258   **"Melancholy Serenade":** Ibid., p. 118.

262   **the Dorseys' reunion:** Robert L. Stockdale, *Jimmy Dorsey: A Study in
Contrasts* (Lanham, Md.: Scarecrow Press, 1999), p. 520.
a subterranean engineer: "Art Carney, 1918–2003," *Los Angeles Times*,
Section A–1, November 12, 2003.

263   **Tommy and the band also recorded:** Robert L. Stockdale, op. cit.,
pp. 521–522.
Dorsey Brothers Encore: James Bacon, *How Sweet It Is: The Jackie Gleason Story* (New York: St. Martin's Press, 1985), p. 522.
You're here, aren't you?: Chip Deffaa, *Swing Legacy* (Metuchen, N.J.,
and London: Scarecrow Press and Institute of Jazz Studies, Rutgers University, 1989), p. 146.

266   **six radio remote broadcasts:** Robert L. Stockdale, op. cit., p. 523.
brought Gleason to the attention: James Bacon, op. cit., p. 204.

267   **broadcasting from the Statler:** Ibid., p. 531.
"My Friend, the Ghost": William Ruhlmann, "Livin' in a Great Big
Way in Swingtime," *Goldmine*, June 10, 1994, p. 53.

269   **Both versions flopped:** Ibid., pp. 53–54.

270   **Gleason supervised:** Robert L. Stockdale, op. cit., p. 535.

275   **We've both calmed down:** Doug Meriweather, *Mister, I Am the Band:
Buddy Rich—His Life and Travels* (North Bellmore, N.Y.: National Drum
Association, 1998), p. 50.
another reconciliation: Ibid., p. 51.

276   **Jack and Tommy recapitulated:** Ibid., pp. 51–52.

277   **film biography of Parker:** Robert L. Stockdale, op. cit. p. 547.

282   **The Whiteman show featured:** Ibid., p. 549.

287   **guaranteed seven thousand a week:** Ibid., p. 559.
untalented hillbilly singer: Peter Guralnick, *Last Train to Memphis: The
Rise of Elvis Presley* (Boston: Little, Brown, 1994), p. 244.
exerted a profound influence: Nat Hentoff, *American Music Is* (Cambridge, Mass.: Da Capo Books, 2004), p. 15.
"Boogie Woogie": Ibid., p. 240.

288   *negotiated the contract:* Ibid., p. 241.

　　　showed a great respect: Ibid., p. 242.

　　　remnants of Depression-era glamour: Frank Rose, *William Morris and the Hidden Agency: History of Show Business* (New York: Harper Business, 1995), p. 204.

　　　Dressed in a black shirt: Peter Guralnick, op. cit., p. 245.

290   *He sang "Tutti Frutti":* Ibid., p. 249.

　　　Charlie Shavers's trumpet solo: Ibid., p. 251.

292   *He had tremendous breath capacity:* Les Tomkins, interviewer, "Trombone Talk with Dick Nash and Don Lusher," courtesy of the International Trombone Association, 1974.

　　　Tommy started laughing: Chip Deffaa, op. cit., p. 154.

294   *He found it odd:* Ibid., pp. 133–134.

　　　still playing one-nighters: Ibid.

297   *The decline of the band business:* George T. Simon, *The Big Bands* (New York: Macmillan, 1967), p. 175.

299   *Dorsey went to his room:* "Tommy Dorsey Chokes to Death on Food While Asleep in Home," *New York Times*, November 27, 1956.

　　　he hung up: Greenwich Police Department Follow-Up Report concerning sudden death of Thomas F. Dorsey, Jr., Serial No. B–24803.

　　　she could hear his television: Ibid.

300   *called the Greenwich hospital:* Ibid.

　　　A copy was made: Ibid.

　　　Knapp's conclusion was amended: "Dorsey Drugged When He Choked," *New York Times*, December 3, 1956.

301   *Tommy's trombone rested:* "The Band Played On," *Newsweek*, December 10, 1956, p. 11.

302   *For my dearest friend:* Ibid.

303   *too young to attend:* "Hundreds Mourn at Dorsey Rites," *New York Times*.

　　　shoes difficult to fill: "The Band Played On," op. cit.

　　　twenty-three limousines: Ibid.

304   *Good night everybody:* George T. Simon, op. cit. p. 177.

Chapter 9: Epilogue

305   *Jimmy led the band:* Robert L. Stockdale, *Jimmy Dorsey, A Study in Contrasts* (Lanham, Md.: Scarecrow Press, 1999), p. 585.

307   *Jimmy remarked more than once:* Peter J. Levinson, "The Big Band Scene," *Taro Leaf*, November 1957.

　　　on March 19: Robert L. Stockdale, op. cit., p. 587.

　　　Appalled at Jimmy's appearance: Ibid.

308   ***Guy Lombardo predicted:*** Ibid., p. 589.

the U.S. Postal Service: Ibid.

New set up a bond: "Dorsey Estate Fights Settles In," *New York Daily News*, January 1, 1957.

the heavily mortgaged Greenwich home: "GE Man Buys Home of Tommy Dorsey," *New York World Telegram and Sun*, November 1, 1957.

New sued and won: "Dorsey Ex Says $26,000 Dwindles," Associated Press, November 13, 1956.

309   ***There are no ghosts:*** Richard Severo, "Cotton Pickers Go Back to Big Band Roots," July 6, 1974.

313   ***If you could put up with him:*** Peter J. Levinson, *September in the Rain: The Life of Nelson Riddle* (New York: Billboard Books, 2001).

315   ***You got a way to go:*** Bill Milkowski, "The Buddy Rich Tapes," *Jazz Times*, March 2002, pp. 17–18.

318   ***He's the most fascinating man:*** Kitty Kelley, *His Way: The Unauthorized Biography of Frank Sinatra* (New York: Bantam, 1986), p. 64.

Index